DATE DUE

IS
CURLY
JEWISH?

IS
CURLY
JEWISH?

A POLITICAL SELF-PORTRAIT
ILLUMINATING THREE TURBULENT DECADES
OF SOCIAL REVOLT 1935–1965

Paul Jacobs

ATHENEUM

NEW YORK

1965

To my beloved Ruth,
who makes everything possible

IS
CURLY
JEWISH?

A FEW YEARS ago I was asked what business I'd been in during the depression. "Trying to overthrow the government by force and violence," I answered, "but business was lousy."

That business is one of the justifications for this book: I was part of the radical community which flourished from the depression until the end of World War II. Usually the importance of the radicals' role in that period is exaggerated, especially by ex-radicals; ironically, it is only as ex-radicals that they exercise any influence. Nevertheless, I am convinced it is impossible to understand important aspects of the world today—the cold war, the civil rights movement, and the new student generation, for example—without an understanding of the radical community to which I belonged.

Thus, even though my part in the activities of that radical community was minor and sometimes uninformed, a knowledge of the forces that shaped my development may help make comprehensible the world as it was then and as it is now.

But this book is not a history of the thirties, worthwhile though that might be. And it is not really an autobiography, either: such a book would interest only a few people. Instead, I have tried to describe how the period from the thirties to the middle sixties looks from a special radical view and to discover whether that view is related to how I feel about being a Jew.

Curly is me, of course, although he exists only in my imagination, where he is seventeen years old and six foot one, with lots of wavy hair—unlike me, in my middle forties, five foot six and bald.

By choice, the cast of characters in this book is incomplete: it includes only people (and not all of them, either) whose relationships with me have been primarily political and religious. And in some cases, where I do not wish to discuss the radical past of those who have not done so, publicly, themselves, I have used fictitious names, and only first names at that. But all these people exist; my unwillingness to reveal their real identity is one reflection of a tragic and shameful part of our recent history.

I DIDN'T become a radical because my early childhood was unpleasant or because I suffered from anti-Semitism. My parents were nonintellectual middle-class German Jews who had emigrated to the United States in the years before World War I and spoke English with only a faint accent. Both of them came from the mercantile rather than the scholarly tradition, and when I was born in 1918 my father was prospering in the import-and-export business. The standards held up for us to emulate were always those of the rich and prominent German-Jewish families of New York, who were envied models for my parents. We never quite made it, though, and so instead of going to private schools I went to nice middle-class public schools and played with nice middle-class boys—and girls, too, whenever I could cajole them into empty lots or back yards.

We lived in an apartment house on a quiet tree-lined street in the upper Bronx, just off the Grand Concourse. Most of the houses on the block were one-family homes, two or three stories high with stoops in front and yards in back. For a few years, until it burned down, I went to a wooden school located right across the street from our house. One block away there was a church and down the street an Orthodox synagogue, which we didn't attend; for my parents were Reform Jews who belonged to a brick temple on the Concourse.

The small world in which I grew up was a fairly happy one. It's true that once I fell down a flight of steps leading to the alley alongside our house, cutting a deep gash in my forehead, and I remember screaming in fright as my mother pressed a wet washcloth hard against the cut to stop the flow of blood. (Even today I never use one.) And of course I fought with my older brother, Clifford, in our room: silent, bitter fights, in which by unspoken agreement neither of us would cry out lest our parents hear the noise and punish both of us. When we did get punished, we were whipped half-heartedly with a small version of a cat-o'nine-tails, a few strands of leather attached to a short handle.

But we were never beaten cruelly, nor was there ever any serious discord between my parents. Sometimes they argued, and then I would run from the room, but my father adored my mother and rarely called her anything but "Schatzie." Sometimes they grew angry at my brother and me if we wouldn't eat our hot milk soup with the hard green peas in it or willingly go with them to visit the relative with a Mongoloid daughter whose thick, furry tongue hung so frighteningly out of her mouth. They had a very strong sense of family, which they tried to impose on my brother and me but which neither of us seemed to share, even as little boys.

Although sometimes I believed that my parents loved my brother more than me, and once ran away to show them how sorry they would be if I was dead, I still knew they loved me. And if my father was often stern with me, my mother was almost always gentle.

We had a car, too, even when I was still a very little boy, and it was a source of constant delight; for nearly every Sunday we went for drives out into Westchester to visit friends of my parents, or across the river on a ferryboat to New Jersey to see my uncles and aunts.

During the summers my parents, my brother, and I drove to middle-class hotels in Massachusetts, upstate New York, or the Catskill Mountains, and some years we had small summer cottages at places like Rye Beach or Throggs Neck.

The most joyful discovery of my early childhood was the public library, with its whole top floor full of children's books. I became a voracious reader, taking out as many books at a time as the rules allowed, reading them as quickly as I could, then returning for another batch. I discovered the joys of the city at the same time: the firehouse just a block or two away, where I stood gaping at the engines for hours on end; the empty lots where my friends and I roasted potatoes over forbidden fires; Van Cortlandt Park with hundreds of acres for us to roam, pretending to be explorers; and, best of all, the street games we played until it was so dark we had to go home.

We played ringelevio, our local version of prisoners' base, for hours at a time. The street was a field for stickball, a game played by baseball rules but substituting a broomstick handle for the bat and using a rubber softball. The diamond was narrow and long, with sewer covers for home plate and second base, while first and third bases were marked out with chalk. The street was also a rink for the ferocious games of hockey we played on roller skates. When there were only two or three of us, we played stoop ball, in which a rubber ball was bounced off the steps of a house, after which the bouncer ran for a base. We developed all kinds of complicated games with marbles, and we played variations on mumblety-peg with dull pocket knives. We played in the school yard, too, fooling around with basketball and softball after classes were over for the day, and as we got older we took bike rides and roller-skating expeditions. Saturday afternoons were reserved for the movies, where for ten cents we sat for hours in the dark, watching the lighted fantasies on the screen.

Elementary school was always easy for me, and my traumas there resulted from my unrequited love for a teacher, Miss Kelly, and from getting caught showing another boy a crude little drawing of a naked pregnant woman looking into a mirror and saying to herself, "What a little screw will do!" Though I wasn't at all sure just what the caption under the picture meant, I nevertheless refused to tell the principal who had given me the cartoon—to have done that would have been a violation of the code against squealing.

Not squealing was a mark of grit, a quality esteemed very highly in my group of friends, especially by my closest friend, Bob, who always stood next to me in line at school because we were exactly the same height. From that chance physical similarity developed a very close personal relationship.

And every Sunday except during the summer I walked to a Sunday School in a nice polite middle-class temple, where we didn't learn Hebrew or much of anything else that made any impression except about sex, which wasn't on the formal curriculum. The girl who sat next to me for two years gave me private lessons in that as we sat in the last row of the classroom, our busy exploring hands hidden from the teacher's view.

I remember one other thing about Sunday School: the Happy Days Club, a great gimmick to raise money for the temple. If you or someone in your family had had a happy day during the week, you got up on the platform in the temple vestry during the assembly period; when your turn came, you stepped forward to tell what the day had been—maybe a very good report card, a new baby in the family, your mother's birthday—and made a contribution (of an unspecified amount) to the temple.

Now, all this was very boring to hear week after week until I realized that I could tap my father for a contribution every Sunday and then split it with the temple fifty fifty. I didn't keep my half of the money all for myself, but instead impressed my fellow students by distributing free candy bars and peanuts.

When I was thirteen I became a "bar mitzvah boy." In a Reform temple at your bar mitzvah, which took place on a Saturday morning, you sat up on the pulpit with the rabbi in front of your family and your own friends. At the appropriate time during the service you read a section from the Torah in painfully memorized and badly mispronounced Hebrew. This was followed by a short speech in painfully memorized and stiltingly elocuted English. All bar mitzvah speeches in my youth began with "Dear Parents, Relatives and Friends," continued with proper obeisance to the magnificent religious education you had received at the hands of the rabbi (who, incidentally, always wrote the speeches), and ended with a stirring peroration wherein you described how you would now take your place in the ranks of the Jewish people. After the rabbi had placed his hands on your head and mumbled, as in my case, a few platitudinous phrases as a blessing, the ceremony was concluded with the rabbi preaching, in rolling organ tones about the spiritual content of "Joodeyism." Then you took your place among the Jewish people by being the guest of honor at a reception hosted by your parents at which all your relatives and friends presented you with gifts of ten-dollar gold pieces and fountain pens.

So I grew up, nominally Jewish on Sundays and on the Jewish holidays, like Rosh Hashanah and Yom Kippur, when we stayed away from public schools. My being Jewish didn't make much of an impression on me or my friends. I don't know how many of my childhood friends were Christians, since we lived in a neighborhood where there were many non-Jewish families. At grade school, too, I must have known many children who were not Jewish and while I was in the first grades, I would drop my eyes to steal furtive glances at the Christian boys when they stood at the urinal next to me, for then I was still curious about how a foreskin looked. But the really acute sense of difference between Christian kids and myself focused on the Catholic boys and girls who attended parochial school. I was very much aware of them, partially because they were associated with the nuns who taught in the parochial school and who frightened me with their black habits, their faces all squinched together under them as if they had no ears or hair. There was a flourishing folklore about nuns among non-Catholic children: "Hold your buttons when you pass one or they'll fall off" was one such bit of wisdom, and so we fearfully clutched the buttons on our clothes. We were equally convinced, of course, that if you stepped on an ant it would rain the next day, and the fact that the buttons didn't fall off our clothes or that the rain did not come had no effect on our beliefs.

There were no Christmas-Chanukah festivals when I went to grammar school, and even in our home Christmas was a more important holiday than Chanukah. It's only in recent years that Chanukah has been endowed by some Jews with significance by being transformed into a Jewish Christmas so that their children won't feel discriminated against when it's time to pass out the gifts. But when we were kids my brother and I always hung up Christmas stockings, although we didn't have a tree. Every year we were given lots of Christmas presents, too: an erector set, a chemistry outfit, books, sleds, clothes, and all the other things that make Christmas the nice greedy holiday it is for children. At Easter time we got chocolate eggs, and it didn't seem to disturb my parents that the eggs were a Christian symbol. Indeed, the atmosphere in our house was as much German as it was Jewish, since we were Reform Jews. I said my nightly prayers in German, my parents didn't observe the kosher dietary laws, and my mother didn't light candles on Friday night (on the contrary, it was more likely that she and my father would play bridge with their friends on Fridays.)

So although we were Jewish, we weren't "Jews," like the men with beards and earlocks or the women with brown wigs who embarrassed me when I saw them on the street or on the subway reading Yiddish newspapers. Sometimes during the Passover holiday a Seder was held either at our home or in some relative's house; it was usually arranged with some difficulty because so few in our family were capable of reading the Hebrew service. To us, Hebrew was a language only the rabbis understood. There was Hebrew printing in the Reform temple prayer book, on the page opposite the English, but so few prayers were said in it that it was possible to memorize them or mumble a few words. Yiddish was almost as unfamiliar to us, since neither of my parents, nor anyone else we knew well, spoke the language except for the argot that had already become part of New York's own slang.

As a middle-class American Jewish kid, I also knew very little about Yiddish culture. Yiddish was the tongue of unassimilated Eastern European Jews, toward whom my parents had inherited a contemptuous attitude as part of the German-Jewish assimilationist tradition.

The gap between families like mine and the East European Jews was nearly as great as the one separating my parents from their Christian friends. Yiddish was a lower-class language, spoken by people who didn't play bridge or mah-jongg, as my mother did, or read the New York *Sun,* as my father did. Yiddish-speaking Jews didn't call their children Clifford or Paul, but Saul or Isadore or Hyman. In the Gentile world, a "kike" may have been descriptive of any Jew, but to my parents and their friends it was any East European Jew, especially the noisy ones. "Stop acting like a kike" was a frequent admonition to noisy, badly behaved children—or adults as well—who offended the middle-class mores of the German Jews.

At high school, though, I came into contact with a different group of Jewish kids from the ones I had met at home. When I was about twelve and a half I entered an accelerated high school —Townsend Harris—for obnoxiously smart youth. Harris was almost a prep school for the City College of New York, although no one at either place would have recognized it as such. If you passed the difficult qualifying entrance examination, you were graduated in three years and almost guaranteed admission to any college in the United States, although most of the graduates naturally went on to City College, on whose campus Harris was located.

If you were older than thirteen when you first went to Harris and sixteen when you graduated, you were considered almost moronic. The school, which had a great academic reputation, drew its youthful wizards from all of New York City, in contrast to most other high schools, whose student body usually lived in a single geographic area. Before Harris was abolished by Mayor LaGuardia during World War II (because he believed it too expensive to operate in the interests of an "elite" group) it had a long and honorable history of students who became writers, lawyers, teachers, and so on. During my years there and afterward, Harris also turned out boys who became Communists, Socialists, and Trotskyists, like me.

The student body at Harris was very small and mostly Jewish. This fact, which at the time didn't strike me as being odd, coupled with the self-conscious young-genius atmosphere of the school, gave Harris a high degree of intellectual homogeneity. We talked about politics a great deal, both in the classrooms with teachers and, even more, outside among ourselves. This was probably inevitable, considering the times—the depression —and the fact that many of the students came from Yiddish Socialist homes, where politics was constantly discussed.

Politics at Harris was also a compensation for the lack of sports. It was our proud boast that the school had no football team. Even those teams we had, like tennis and baseball, distinguished themselves by never winning. There was one exception: chess. We were very big on chess and usually won all the interschool tournaments. Every noon you could find a few chess games going in the school cafeteria—two boys hunched over a chess board, one usually wearing knickers and the other looking like an owl with big glasses perched on his nose. Around them would be clustered a group of silent kibitzers munching on their sandwiches, while off at the other tables heated arguments went on about the "real meaning" of the Nazi rise to power in Germany.

"Mit Sozialismus" was the way one of my fifteen-year-old classmates at Harris signed his yearbook picture at graduation, and it seemed a perfectly normal salutation to me. Since neither family background nor geography were factors in determining the make-up of the student body, Harris had quite a few poor boys and just as many rich boys mixed in with the bulk of the student body, who came from middle-class homes like mine. At Harris I encountered boys whose voices carried faint echoes of the Yiddish their parents spoke at home. In dealing with them, it took me a long time to overcome the phony pride inculcated in me because of my German-Jewish background—pride which even survived the effects of the 1929 depression on our family.

The objective consequences of the depression weren't nearly as catastrophic in our house as they were in millions of other homes, but they seemed catastrophic to me, especially since I had become such a snob. We weren't at any time during the depression poor enough to go hungry, but our standard of living certainly went down considerably. We had to move to an apartment house owned by a friend of my parents. My father's business suffered so much that, to my shame, my mother worked at home making ties on the dining-room table. And, worst of all, I had to carry my lunch in a paper bag to Townsend Harris instead of buying it in the school cafeteria. Being able to buy lunch was such a desirable symbol of social status that I stole money from my mother's purse in order to do it. Every day I threw the paper bag of sandwiches into one of the trash cans in the subway station or pushed the sack between the banister and the wall of the stairs leading down to the subway station where I took the train to school.

Once I stole money from a relative who came to visit us from Mexico. That time it was to buy a pair of skis because I needed to walk down the street with the skis thrown carelessly on my shoulder. Why skis? I'm not sure, but I think they were identified with that secret image of myself as a rich, tall, young fellow, not necessarily Jewish, who later evolved into Curly. (For a long time I gave up looking in full-length mirrors because otherwise I'd be forced to see that while above the waist there stood a very handsome chap, beautifully dressed—tuck in that scarf a little more . . . ah, now you have it—below the waist I was still wearing knickers. I didn't get my first pair of long pants until my last year in high school.)

The last year of high school, when I was between fourteen and fifteen, was a miserable time, partly because the depression interfered with my living publicly the self I imagined mine, partly because of my terrible conflicts with my parents, and partly because other forces were beginning to churn me up inside, like sex. I was in trouble with my school grades because I was cutting too many classes to attend the burlesque shows on Forty-second Street. I sat in those theaters for hours, trying to nap through the dreadful movies that were shown between performances. With growing impatience I would wait through the dirty skits and the chorus acts that preceded each of the stripper's appearances, when the line of aging and usually ugly chorus girls awkwardly kicked and clomped their way through a series of set routines which always ended with the curtain coming down, to rise a minute later showing the girls standing perfectly still with bared breasts.

This was the prelude to the strip acts, which were the only reason anyone went to burlesque shows. Now that burlesque is considered dead, the sophisticates say they went to the shows to see comedians like Phil Silvers and Milton Berle, who got their start there. Nonsense: no one even knew who the comedians were. We went to the burlesque show to watch the strippers writhing out of their clothes and to squirm in painful frustration as we stared at their naked breasts, trying in vain to get a glimpse beneath the tiny G-strings that we hoped they would just once take off in front of the curtain; invariably they dangled it while standing for the final moment with the curtain draped around them.

Numb from sexual excitement, I would walk out of the dark smelly theater into the bright glaring daylight of Forty-second Street. On the subway home my sense of guilt at having missed another afternoon of classes would grow and be compounded by a sense of frustration so acute that masturbation—my usual method of satisfying my sexual fantasies—was of little use except to ease the physical misery of swollen testicles. And as if all this were not enough, my adolescent misery was complicated still more by the sexual journeys I was then taking with a girl friend.

She was a very athletic girl, encouraged by an equally athletic family; dressed in tight shorts and blouses open at the neck, she practiced tap dancing and soft-shoe routines on a wooden platform in the attic of her house. She was very small, but her legs were strong, with muscular calves and slim ankles. We spent hours together at a variety of physical enterprises which always ended with our holding hands and excitedly stroking each other, although she always stopped my tentative movements up her thighs with a gentle but insistent pressure that kept my hand immobile until unwillingly I began to slide it away.

Her mother was terribly suspicious of us and kept a watchful eye on our activities as often as she could. But even with her mother in the room, we managed, by holding a newspaper or book in front of us, to pretend to read while we both twitched as I caressed her small breasts. To the great relief of her family, my growing interest in radical politics finally separated us. Her lack of interest in politics made me impatient and contemptuous of the athlete. She was an American patriot, as were her parents and her brother, all of whom had been born in the United States. My growing cynicism about the nature of American life brought me into heated arguments with the entire family when I started explaining to them the reality of American life as I was coming to see it at Harris.

The end of our relationship came simultaneously with the graduation of my class from Sunday School. In a moment of either foolishness or laziness, the rabbi had decided to allow the graduates to write their own speeches if they could. And since there were ten of us in the group, he selected the Ten Commandments as appropriate subjects, assigning to each of us one of the dicta. Because I was the star pupil, I was given the most touchy—"Thou shalt not commit adultery." The outcome was catastrophic.

I wrote an attack upon that double standard of Jewish morality which permitted men to sow their oats and women just to sew, ending the speech with a stirring plea that no Jewish girl should come to the marriage bed a virgin. When I presented the proposed speech to the rabbi for his approval his screams of outrage reached a high keening noise far more authentic than the deep rolling tones he normally used in temple. He absolutely forbade me to deliver the speech and I absolutely refused to rewrite it, threatening to boycott the services if he didn't allow me to say what I had written instead of what he now proposed to write for me.

We finally compromised by his reassigning my subject to another boy, not very bright, who could be expected to take a more traditional approach to sex, and giving me "Thou shalt not steal." For this topic, I chose to write and then deliver, in a flaming voice, a bitter attack upon a capitalist system that gave jail sentences to men who stole bread for their families but made heroes of financiers who stole millions for their own gain. And if I wasn't already a member of the Young Communist League at the time I gave the speech, I certainly was close to it.

I discussed politics and religion perpetually with Bob, who was still my best friend. Although we hadn't gone to the same schools or lived in the same neighborhood after a while, we had remained close. We were devoted to each other as boys, as adolescents, and as young revolutionists, and I guess that if he hadn't died in 1941 we might still be friends. Together we first discarded "Joodayism" and, later, capitalism.

It wasn't difficult for me to reject Judaism. Whatever content it had was completely lacking in the pallid diet of pap I was fed every Sunday at temple. And all I learned about being Jewish at home was a set of defensive standards. There were limits, for example, to what Jews could expect from Gentiles, and proper behavior for Jews was based often on the fear that the Gentile world might respond badly to other patterns of action if taken by Jews. All of this knowledge was encompassed in one of the few Yiddish phrases I learned at home: A Jew did not make "rishis."

To "make rishis" was to stir up a fuss of some kind, and it was a cardinal sin, for it supposedly made Jews vulnerable to the potential wrath of the Christian world. This world was conceived of as something like a potentially evil sleeping giant who, if awakened by a loud noise, might, and probably would, turn on the disturber of his peace and do him harm. Even my parents, assimilated as they were to American middle-class patterns and coming from an assimilated German middle-class background, never completely lost their fear of what must have seemed to them a dominant Christian culture. Thus they were caught in not just one but a number of conflicts, two of which created great tensions in the family. One lay in the strain between the German tradition and the American reality about the proper way to rear children, and the other involved the difficulty of retaining some aspects of Jewishness without being conspicuous Jews.

These conflicts were acted out in ugly quarrels between them and me. I discovered very early, for example, that it was possible to fake enough knowledge in Sunday School to win most of the prizes for scholarship; all one had to do was to be able to speak glibly. But in consequence of this discovery I felt contempt for such a sorry excuse for a religious education and resentful that my parents made me give up even one day a week to it.

Everything about Reform Judaism grew more and more repellent to me. In the summer the Saturday services in the temple were canceled, as was Sunday School, as if going to religious services was less important during July and August than at other times of the year. Obviously there was a reason for canceling temple activities; either most of the families were away in summer houses, as was ours, or at the beaches, or the children were away at camp. Nevertheless, since so much of Jewish life centered around the temple, the minimal temple activity all summer was proof to me that being a Jew wasn't nearly as important as my parents had said. What seemed like hypocrisy filled me with contempt for those people, like my parents, who, I believed, perpetuated the deceit by being religious Jews once a year, when they got all dressed up for the High Holiday services.

However, religion was only one of the strains that made life hell between my parents and myself during that period—and it was perhaps the least important. Other conflicts—about sex, money, how late I could stay out at night—sent me into stomach-knotting fits of rage to which my parents responded with their own shouts and threats. The final and most painful rupture between us was caused by my increasing involvement in radicalism: after I had been graduated from Townsend Harris, I simultaneously entered City College and joined the Young Communist League.

CHAPTER TWO

THE PRECISE circumstances under which I joined the Young Communist League are very hazy in my mind—as vague as the names and faces of the other branch members, shadows drifting on the outskirts of my memory. (During the late forties and early fifties, when public confession was considered necessary for the soul and essential for the continued livelihood of ex-Communists, I was always struck by the detail offered by the friendly witnesses before the House Committee on Un-American Activities; they recalled the names of every person with whom they had attended Communist party meetings many years earlier. If my very life depended on it, I could not remember today the names or faces of the people at the first YCL meetings I attended. In fact, I can't even remember where the meetings were held.)

When people ask now why I became a radical then, my answers are somehow always unsatisfactory, at least to me. I assume that my bitter quarrels with my parents and my brother, my father's business difficulties that deprived me of achieving my childish fantasies, and my contempt for the values of the family, especially what I believed to be their hypocritical attitude toward religion, all pushed me into rebellion. But children have always rebelled against their parents and not all of them join the Young Communist League. So I must turn to the times as they were to make myself and my actions understandable.

The depression wasn't something that happened in another country or to other people: it was all around us. The Roosevelt-Hoover campaign wasn't an ordinary election; it was a passionate quarrel between life and death. The shabby men selling apples were on every street corner, and the clusters of flimsy shacks grimly named "Hoovervilles" were not just along the banks of the Hudson River but on every river. And in faraway Europe, Hitler was becoming an ever more menacing and sinister figure and I would scream with impatience at my parents when, like most of their contemporaries, they pooh-poohed him as a clown whom the German people would quickly reject.

Even without the domestic crisis of the 1930s, without the New Deal and the Blue Eagle, without the Emergency Relief Administration and the Works Progress Administration, Hitler forced politics on us and dominated our lives. His name was on everyone's tongue, on every front page, in every newsreel. At Harris we had openly taunted a German professor we suspected of being a Nazi sympathizer and had mocked the Nazi goosestep and the cadenced shouting of "Heil, Sieg Heil!" Then, suddenly, almost overnight, those ludicrous stormtroopers were beating up Jews in the streets. Thus, Hitler became an enemy even in our house as my parents, like many Jews of German descent, began a feverish attempt to help their relatives get out of Germany.

So Hitler was everywhere and forced us to talk continually about politics.

Arguing excitedly about politics, about the depression, about anti-Negro prejudice, about anti-Semitism, and how to fight against German and Italian fascism took up a lot of time at City College, too, where informal student life centered in an area known as The Alcoves, underneath one of the main buildings. There, in huge recesses set around the perimeter of the building, I watched the other students eating their sandwiches from paper bags, studying and playing chess, and, among the politicals, always arguing. Each political group had its own alcove, and an informal understanding existed that no other group would attempt to dispossess it. Very often, though, the "members" of one alcove drifted over to another, either for a discussion if there was any common political bond between them or for a violent argument when the groups were as widely separated as, say, the Stalinists and the Trotskyists.

As far as I was concerned, those alcove discussions were the most important part of life at City College. I knew there were classes, for I had to attend them, and I knew there were other student activities, for the posters advertising the clubs and lectures were everywhere; but for me there was only one world into which I wanted to be taken and accepted: the radical atmosphere which dominated City College in those years.

Most students at CCNY were poor, serious, and smart. It took high grades to get in, and attendance very often required real sacrifice from the student's family. We had no football heroes at CCNY, and the "big men" on campus were those who risked expulsion for publicly protesting and picketing against compulsory ROTC. No cheering band of supporters urged on the CCNY baseball team, for most of the active students were occupied with such tasks as jeering at the Italian Fascist students who were on a tour of the United States and had made the mistake of appearing at CCNY. The campus paper didn't feature many articles about the latest doings on Fraternity Row because there was no Fraternity Row. Even if there had been, the whole paper was so devoted to editorials denouncing the administration, articles telling of antiwar demonstrations, and interviews with leaders of student strikes at other colleges that there was little room for social news.

What I also sought and found as I wandered through the alcoves, listening intently to the talk, was an affirmation of my contempt for and impatience with business and with the making of money, pursuits I identified with my parents. The CCNY radicals regarded businessmen as a very low form of life. Because of the depression, the businessman and business generally had become objects of contempt and hatred. To a CCNY student the business society was not only incapable of preventing unemployment and depression, but actively promoted war and misery. We avidly read *100,000,000 Guinea Pigs,* which exposed the cheating of the American consumer by the avaricious business man, and we made no distinction in our alcove discussions between the corner grocer grubbing out a miserable existence and the wealthy munitions manufacturers—the "merchants of death" whose machinations we considered responsible for World War I.

Books such as *Merchants of Death, 100,000,000 Guinea Pigs,* and, most significant of all, John Strachey's *The Coming Struggle for Power,* had a much sharper influence in pushing me toward radicalism than did any of my teachers at City College. After World War II one of my teachers was charged with having been a Communist, a charge I suspected then might have been true, but all I remember of him as a teacher was that he had red hair, stuttered somewhat, and was a pretty good instructor. He certainly never tried to do any recruiting in class, although years later I heard stories of his occasional violent arguments with Socialist and Trotskyist students.

I have a hunch, too, that for me one of the unconscious pressures toward radicalism was that the movement provided an atmosphere in which I could reject being Jewish without any feeling of guilt. One of the first rituals in the radical movement was the adoption of a party name by which one was to be known in the organization. The origin of the custom was legitimate enough: revolutionists in Europe and Russia always took false names as a device to handicap police persecution. The same technique in American radical organizations may not have been justified by that reason, but it did give us a link, a romantic identification, with the revolutionary heroes of the past. Even granting the legitimate need we felt to change our names in order to escape possible consequences, why was it that so many of the Jewish radicals took as their cover names ones that were conspicuously non-Jewish? No comrade Cohen ever adopted Ginsberg as a party name; instead, he became Green or Smith or Martin, or something equally bland. So, too, when for a short time I became Paul Jackson in the little red membership book, it was because Jackson was a less Jewish name than Jacobs and therefore somehow more American.

Yet many of the comrades I met then came from Yiddish-speaking homes, and their conversations were so strewn with the rich Yiddish phrases they had learned from their parents that I, too, began to absorb them into my vocabulary. But the pronounced Jewish flavor which permeated the New York radical movement had nothing religious about it. Quite the opposite: the entire Yiddish Socialist and radical milieu was militantly atheist or agnostic.

My interest in the YCL was also stimulated when Bob left New York to attend Ohio State University and began writing me about radical activities in which he became involved. In addition, I had made a new friend who lived in the same apartment house as I in upper Manhattan. He, too, was a City College student, and although he was a few years older, we sat for hours in a nearby park talking about the books I was reading—Rolland's *Jean Christophe* and John Reed's *Ten Days That Shook the World.* It was he, I think, who took me to my first YCL meeting.

The YCL episode turned out to be a very short one, for within six months after joining I was expelled. I got kicked out for being a Trotskyite, although at the time I hadn't the foggiest notion of what a Trotskyite was.

The specific circumstance that led up to my expulsion was the break-up by Communists of a Socialist meeting in Madison Square Garden addressed by Norman Thomas. The small-scale riot that disrupted the Thomas meeting was considered a great success by the YCLers, who reported it at one of the meetings I attended, but it left me rather confused, for when my father and I got into our usual violent arguments about politics, he always denounced Thomas as a wild-eyed and even dangerous visionary. My father's business reverses had no effect on his political outlook, and even during the period of his most painful financial embarrassment he continued to vote Republican and to read the New York *Sun.* So I couldn't understand why, if my father, who was such a conservative, hated Thomas, the YCL was attacking him too. Impatiently the leaders of the branch explained the Communists were just beginning to shift from the view that leadership of the socialist parties all over the world were the equivalent of the fascists: a major effort of the Communist movement had been directed toward breaking away the membership of the socialist groups from their leaders in what was called "The United Front from Below."

But I understood very little of all this and continued asking what were obviously very naive questions of my more and more impatient comrades. Finally, at one of the weekly meetings I was told that I had been expelled from the branch for Trotskyist leanings. It was a measure of my ignorance about the hatred the Communists felt toward Trotskyism that I went downtown to the Communist party building on Thirteenth Street and climbed the stairs to the top of the seven- or eight-story building looking vainly on each floor for the headquarters of the Trotskyists.

It was again through Bob at Ohio State that I finally did find the Trotskyist headquarters in New York. At the time I was expelled from the YCL, he had become a member of the Spartacus Youth League, the Trotskyist youth group, and had written me urging me to join the SYL also. He sent me the address of the adult organization, known then as the Communist

League of America, and one night I went to my first meeting at its national headquarters, a loft someplace in the Union Square district of Manhattan.

I walked into a large bare room next to some dingy offices and was greeted by a dark-haired and attractive girl with slightly protruding teeth who turned out to be the stepdaughter of a prominent Trotskyist leader. Bob's name brought me a warm welcome, and she took me around the room introducing me to other people, including her husband, a good-looking young man with a very pleasant voice.

The whole evening was much less grim than the atmosphere of the Young Communist League, where the omnipresent, omniscient, and frightening party line had been so much in evidence as the standard against which all my actions were judged. It was this difference that set apart the SYL from the YCL, for the procedures of the meeting were the same and the discussions just as confusing to me. The same kind of reports were given by the same kind of committees: the chairman of agitation-propaganda (agitprop for short) reported the number of copies of the weekly newspaper sold in door-to-door visits, the number of people who had attended the street-corner meetings held in the city, and the success of the educational classes in the theories of Marxism and Trotskyism; the trade-union chairman discussed the efforts of the members who were young workers to influence the policies of the unions to which they belonged; the head of the student fraction (as these caucuses were called) reported on the ideological struggle being waged at City and Brooklyn Colleges against the Communists; and, finally, the social-committee chairman told of the money-raising parties that were to be held in the next two weeks. After that, someone produced an accordion and we stood to sing revolutionary songs, much the same as those I had been learning in the YCL except that Trotsky's name was substituted for Stalin's. I sang along loudly, faking the words I didn't know and hoping no one could tell the difference.

I discovered other, more important, differences between the Spartacus Youth League and the Young Communist League as I attended more meetings. In the absence of the awesome and frightening party line, the discussions in the SYL seemed more free to me. The arguments between comrades were open, and although some members of the group were clearly more influential than others, political differences were sharply discussed. Somehow, too, the SYL members seemed more friendly, more interested in me as a person, than the YCL group had been, and I did feel more comfortable in this comparatively free atmosphere than I had within the rigid frame of the YCL. In a few weeks, without knowing very much about Trotskyism, I joined the Spartacus Youth League and was assigned to a branch that covered upper Manhattan and the Bronx.

At just about the same time as I began my active apprenticeship in the Trotskyist movement, I quit City College and started another apprenticeship—in the diamond business. Leaving CCNY was no great wrench for me, since I was getting low grades and had no intense desire to stay; perhaps, also, it was a daily reminder that I wasn't the rich young man of my fantasy life. Since my parents believed in business as a career even more than they believed in college, they exerted no pressure on me to stay at CCNY when I told them I wanted to work instead. Their lack of pressure on me might also be explained by their need for the money I would bring in, since in 1934 the family financial problem was acute.

I got into the diamond business through a wealthy cousin who recommended me to friends of his, partners in a firm of diamond merchants called L. & M. Kahn & Co. A week later I received a letter signed by Mr. Alfred Lowenthal, asking me to appear for an interview at the company's Fifth Avenue offices.

I dressed carefully in my best clothes and took the subway to the office in what was then a very elegant building at the corner of Fifth Avenue and Forty-ninth Street. I rode up to the tenth floor, nervously walked down the corridor to the door marked L. & M. Kahn & Co., and went into a little reception room, separated from the rest of the offices by a grilled window and a door that only opened when a buzzing latch was released. I gave my name to a woman who had opened the little window and sat down on a leather bench to wait, with great anxiety, for my interview. In a few minutes Mr. Lowenthal came out and took me inside to his own office, where he talked with me for a long time. He was a man in his late fifties, elegantly dressed, and I was impressed by his white carnation boutonniere. A few days later he called to tell me I had been hired and should report to work.

Being in the diamond business gave me a great chance to live out the fantasy I had of myself as a rich young fellow of "good" background. So, for my first two years as a radical, I opened the offices of L. & M. Kahn & Co. happily every morning at eight thirty. My morning duties included dusting off the delicate scales used to weigh the diamonds, putting cigarettes in the boxes scattered throughout the offices, emptying the standing ashtrays that had smelly water traps in their heavy bases, and generally tidying up the offices for the first appearance of the bosses.

It is incorrect, though, to describe the owners of L. & M. Kahn & Co. as "bosses," for they were anything but bloated, greedy capitalists. Promptly at eight forty-five every morning Mr. Lowenthal, who was one of the two partners in the company, arrived. A distant relative of the Kahn family, he had come to the United States from Germany many years earlier and had originally gone to work in the business as an office boy, just as I had. Over the years he had moved up, finally becoming a partner. On the outside he was a gruff man with a very short temper; on the inside I think he was a kind and good man, anxious to make amends for the hurt his sharp tongue sometimes brought others. He was a dandy, too, always elegantly dressed, his white hair and mustache always carefully groomed. One of my duties as office boy was going to a nearby florist each day to bring him back a fresh white carnation or fat little bunch of blue bachelor buttons, which he then ceremoniously tucked into the buttonhole of his lapel.

Mr. Lowenthal was my ultimate superior, for the administration of the office was his primary function, and it was before his stern eye I quailed if he discovered on his morning tour of inspection that I had neglected to fill the cigarette boxes, empty the ashtrays, or dust the scales properly.

The next to arrive was a young man who was my direct boss and who had graduated from my job a few years before. After he arrived, Mr. Lowenthal, who always waited impatiently for him, went through the daily sacred ceremony of opening the big safe which took up the whole of a small room and contained the firm's diamond stock. The ritual was filled with the twirling of many dials, the turning of many knobs, and wrestling against the great cumbersome safe, which finally gave in, reluctantly allowing itself to be opened. After that, the bookkeeper and office secretary would come in, followed by the company's one salesman. Then, at about nine thirty, the senior partner, Walter Kahn, Sr., a gentleman of great charm who was addressed as Mr. Walter, would arrive with a quiet "Good morning" for everybody. Anywhere from fifteen minutes to an hour later, his son, Walter, Jr., would breeze in, usually with a loud bounce, except when he had a large hangover. Walter Jr. was only a few years older than I was, but he was much, much more sophisticated, and an odd friendship quickly developed between us—one which has lasted happily through all these years.

L. & M. Kahn & Co. represented a very special business tradition in American life—that of the Jews of German descent whose roots dated back to the migration of the 1840s. There were Jews who had come to America before these Germans came—from Spain by way of Holland—but they were few and in some ways remained an almost exotic sect who thought of themselves as Jewish aristocrats. The German Jews of the 1840 migration were a mercantile group who gradually built up a tightly knit intermarried world of wealth, culture, and philanthropic tradition after they settled in New York, San Francisco, and the South. Even before World War I the prosperous German-Jewish world was a society which excluded East European Jews, no matter how wealthy, from its clubs and from its country estates and town houses. It was a world of nights at the concert or the theater and trips to Europe on the *Ile de France* or the *Mauretania;* it was a world into which entry was closed unless you were someone's cousin, at least. (And in my generation and the one just before it, it was also a society which produced some of the damndest radicals this country has ever seen.)

Everybody at Kahn's was nominally Jewish except for the bookkeeper and perhaps the secretaries. But it would have been hard to tell that the Kahns, Mr. Lowenthal, or Herbert Gardner were Jews, for they had none of the outward signs popularly and incorrectly associated with Jews. Most of them spoke the upper-class English associated with the Ivy League colleges they had attended. Few of them ever went to religious services, even in Temple Emanu-El on Fifth Avenue, then as now the elegant cool center of upper-class Reform Judaism in New York. Except in one respect, their lives and their interests had nothing in common with the Jews of the Lower East Side whom I knew from school and the radical movement.

One attribute which linked these quiet upper-class Jews of good manners and good clothes to the noisy Jews of the East

Side and the Bronx was a tradition of philanthropy—a tradition into which I was initiated almost immediately after I began working at Kahn's. Mr. Lowenthal, for example, spent every Saturday morning at Mount Sinai, a Jewish hospital, painstakingly taking difficult medical photos in color on glass plates for doctors, most of whom had come from the Lower East Side or the Bronx. He received no payment for his work, of course, and in addition he paid for all the equipment and developing of the glass plates. Walter Kahn, Sr., regularly attended board meetings of a number of Jewish institutions in the city, and both men contributed regularly to a selected list of Jewish charities.

Soon after I became the office boy at Kahn's, it was intimated that I was expected to help Mr. Lowenthal on Saturday mornings at the hospital. And so each Saturday, no matter where I had been the night before, I met him at the hospital and helped him set up the equipment in a small room off the operating theater and take pictures of the patients. The routine was a fixed one: we arrived at the hospital at about ten and took pictures of patients until about twelve-thirty. Then, in informal payment for my work, I was taken to lunch at a very good French restaurant. From there Mr. Lowenthal and I went to Radio City Music Hall, where we sat in loge seats. Late in the afternoon we would emerge, blinking in the sunlight, and part, he going to the Harmonie Club, the New York bastion of the rich German Jew, for cards with his friends, I to Trotskyist headquarters for political arguments with mine. Once, as a mark of his approval, Mr. Lowenthal gave me a very good camera, obviously in the hope that someday I might take over his role at the hospital. Sadly I must confess that I pawned the camera a few years later in Minneapolis.

Another lesson was drilled into me at Kahn's: there was a sharp distinction, totally unrelated to religion, between businessmen who were gentlemen and those who were not. At Kahn's we dealt only with our counterparts: diamonds were neither purchased from nor sold to firms or individuals who didn't meet the standards of gentlemen. For in the diamond business, where thousands of dollars of goods—as the diamonds were known—were given or sent on approval without any other guarantee than a man's word that the exact goods would be returned or bought, any lack of mutual trust would have been disastrous.

I learned the lesson of the line that separated gentleman from nongentleman when a diamond merchant not then on Kahn's approved list held what was known as a "sight" of a large uncut stone he had purchased. At a "sight," the men in the trade could study the diamond and talk about its possibilities with other merchants while having a drink at a bar set up in the office. I wandered over to the "sight," took a look at the stone, which seemed to me like a large greasy chunk of dull glass, talked with some of the other people there—including a few more office boys who, like me, were cadging food and drinks—and then returned to my own office. There I was confronted by Mr. Lowenthal, who started to question me about the diamond. He asked me about the size and color of the stone, and I described it as best I could, casually mentioning that I'd had a drink and a sandwich. When Mr. Lowenthal heard this, he exploded.

For at least an hour I was lectured angrily about the standards of behavior expected of even such a lowly representative of L. & M. Kahn & Co. as me. He explained in fierce detail that, while it was permissible for me to have gone to look at the diamond, it had been damned improper of me to drink the man's liquor or eat his food, for those were acts one performed only with friends or with strangers who were gentlemen—neither being a category into which this man was allowed. Even today I find myself unconsciously applying Mr. Lowenthal's standards.

In the few years I spent at Kahn's working from eight thirty to five in the afternoon, I lived in a world whose values were dominated by a set of traditions, consciously nurtured in each succeeding generation: the diamond trade is an old and international one, whose guilds date back hundreds of years; whose workers, the cutters and polishers, are among the most highly skilled and paid in the world; and whose customs are fixed, immutable, and religiously observed by all its members.

That world had another dimension, too, for it brought me into direct and sometimes jealous contact with a glamorous atmosphere, where great wealth was assumed and accepted, where people seemed to be properly where they were because their wealth and family background gave them the right to be there. At the surface level, young Walter Kahn was equally at ease arriving hung over at the office in the morning, greeting his father's contemporaries at the theater with a respectful "Sir," or at lunch laughing with his own friends at his current difficulty in conquering some pretty girl.

Everyone seemed to know everyone else in the Kahns' world of the Harmonie Club, and the office conversation was larded with reflections on who had gone to college with whom, what year so and so had been in dancing school, who had married whose relative, and who could be expected to take over the family business.

My own reactions to this world were simultaneously a mixture of contempt for it as a radical and a desire to be more a part of it—a desire rooted in my fantasy of myself. Almost everything about the world which could be glimpsed through the Kahn doorway seemed infinitely better than the atmosphere in which I was living at home. By comparison with the Kahns, my parents seemed gauche and even foreign, although they spoke with only the faintest trace of a German accent. As a businessman, my father had been unsuccessful and had been reduced from taking buying trips to Europe to being a hardware salesman. The German-Jewish middle-class values by which my parents set such great store turned me against them, for part of me contemptuously rejected those values and sneered at my parents for holding them, while another part envied the values but was contemptuous because my parents were unsuccessful in achieving even their own standards. And because young Walter Kahn took me freely into his almost raffish world, filled with girls and parties, I alternated between wanting and rejecting. Occasionally Walter, his close friend Stephen Walter and I would go to lunch, laughing in the elevator at some dirty joke and eating at some good restaurant where I liked the food and atmosphere. But inevitably lunch ended with the three of us arguing violently about politics, for my Marxist orientation came out in the open only a few months after I began working at Kahn's and was the subject of endless discussions, especially after I felt bold enough to read radical literature in the office.

Those two years at Kahn's were painfully split ones. During the day I combined office-boy duties with slowly being taught the mysteries of diamonds, with learning the differences between cuts and qualities and how to pick up a stone deftly with a pair of tweezers so I could study it with a jeweler's loupe screwed into my eye. Under Mr. Lowenthal's careful supervision I learned to take up a pile of small stones—melee, as they were called—and make a tentative separation of them into smaller piles by color and brilliance. Along the way I was taught, too, the meaning of good taste in diamonds (among other things, that gentlemen didn't wear large gaudy diamond rings on their pinky fingers, or on any other fingers either).

Increasingly, though, my interest in a career as a diamond merchant diminished and my involvement in radicalism increased. More and more often I began rushing home after work to shed my Paul Jacobs identity. I'd gobble a hasty quarrelsome meal in the apartment with my parents and brother, leaving as quickly as possible for the branch meeting or the class in Marxism, where I was Paul Jackson. These meetings and classes were usually held in the headquarters of one of the branches, usually a small loft room over a store or in a three-story building with a movie theater on the ground floor, a poolhall and bowling alley on the second floor, and the third floor rented out to small business offices, light-manufacturing plants, social clubs, and organizations like ours.

All of the headquarters looked alike and had the same general atmosphere. On the wall hung large pictures of Marx and Engels, sometimes flanked by photos of Rosa Luxemburg and Karl Liebknecht, the martyrs of the 1918-19 German revolution. But the places of honor on the walls of our headquarters were always reserved for a picture or drawing of Lenin and one of Leon Trotsky. We called Trotsky the Old Man, using the phrase not to refer to his age but to the place he held in our consciousness as the commander of our forces.

The drabness of the rooms (they were always ugly, always painted in the mud-brown color that landlords use to cover up the dirt of an endless procession of tenants who come and go with monotonous regularity) was lightened with posters, first about the German parties fighting the Nazis, later for the Spanish Civil War. Alongside the wall at the back or side of the room a literature table held the pamphlets written by the theoreticians of the movement—Marx, Engels, Lenin, and Trotsky—and these could be looked at and purchased for ten cents or a quarter by neophytes like me. On the table, too, were copies of the organization's newspaper, its monthly magazine, and the mimeographed bulletins put out by the various other branches or committees. And during the internal factional fights, which at that time were beginning to engross the attention of all the Trotskyists, the detailed and to me very bewildering political documents of the contending groups could be picked up from the literature table, to be argued over during the meetings or over cups of coffee as we adjourned to sit in a nearby cafeteria.

Folding chairs were always kept along the walls of the headquarters and brought out for the meetings. Up front at a table the branch chairman conducted the business of the meeting. One corner always contained a hand-operated mimeograph machine and an old typewriter used to cut the stencils for it. And everywhere there were ashtrays, for all of us seemed to smoke so much that by the end of each meeting a blue-gray haze hung over the badly ventilated rooms.

The routine of the meeting was a reasonably fixed one. We would drift into the hall at roughly the time the meeting was scheduled to begin, greeting each other as "comrade," a salutation I used very self-consciously at first until it ultimately became a familiar part of my vocabulary. We stood or sat in little circles, perhaps looking over the new literature or discussing the latest change in someone's political position. Often a comrade would bring a "sympathizer" or "contact" to the meeting to be introduced to the other members. A subtle distinction existed between these two categories, relating to the degree of involvement in the movement. A contact was someone rather new to either the movement or the organization, who had shown some definite sign of interest but was still an unknown quantity. A sympathizer was a person more definitely committed to the group but unwilling or unable, usually for personal reasons, to take the final step of joining and accepting the discipline imposed on members.

Soon after I moved from the stage of being a contact to the status of sympathizer, and then on to actual formal membership, I discovered that being a Trotskyist in New York during the thirties was something akin to having leprosy during the Middle Ages. We were hated and despised by almost every other political group, we were political pariahs, always on the defensive against the vicious onslaughts of the Stalinists, who had taken over control of the world communist movement and its periphery of front organizations. And since the popular front became a successful tactic of the Communist party in 1935, the party influence over liberal organizations grew so great that we Trotskyists ended up as political outcasts.

But in a way, I think, we also gloried in this role, for the isolation forced on us nurtured the attitude that we were the chosen ones, the true martyrs of the Revolution, the only pure inheritors of the Bolshevik tradition established by Lenin and Trotsky during the glorious days of the Russian Revolution.

Our pariah status and defensiveness had another consequence: Trotskyists were the best educated, politically, among the socialist and revolutionary groups. Because we had no long native tradition to sustain us, as did the members of the Socialist party, and no powerful motherland to look to, as the Communists did to the Soviet Union, we were thrown completely back upon our own resources and our intelligences to defend the correctness of our line. This meant that a young Trotskyist like me not only was supposed to study constantly what was happening in the world, but, equally important, was expected to know the complete history of the Russian Revolution in some detail and be able to argue, in a loud voice, about what had happened in China in 1927, in Bulgaria in 1919, in France in 1934, and even sometimes in America.

So out of necessity we became experts, prodigies, the Townsend Harris boys of the revolutionary movement, able to quote the line and page in Lenin or Marx that justified the Trotskyist view of the world.

The implacable enmity generated in those years between the Stalinists and the Trotskyists—an enmity which is difficult for anyone outside the movement to comprehend—pervaded every part of life, the personal and the political, for both groups. As recently as 1963 an ex-Stalinist whose late husband had been a prominent Communist party official came to our house for dinner; over drinks she confessed that, even though she had been out of the party for some years, this was the first time in her life that she had ever been in the home of anyone associated with the Trotskyites. When I asked her somewhat flippantly how she felt about it, she replied seriously, "Nauseous. I know it's wrong, but I can't help it. I'm nauseous." (Her use of the word Trotskyite to characterize me and my use of "Trotskyist" were both hangovers of our different pasts. Generally, we described ourselves as Trotskyists, while the Communists, whom we always called "Stalinists," invariably used "Trotskyite" for us, venomously spitting out the word as if they had suddenly discovered something dirty and horrible-tasting in their mouths.) I'm sure she has overcome her nausea, although she still feels uncomfortable with me; and this is understandable, considering what the

Communists were taught about Trotskyists during the thirties, especially after the now admittedly framed Moscow trials. In those trials the Trotskyists were cast in the role of fascist spies and were always described as "Trotskyite-wreckers." The crimes attributed to them ranged from poisoning childrens' milk to sabotaging factory production, with a little train wrecking thrown in for good measure.

For years Trotskyists were devils incarnate to the Communists, the horrible boogie men out of their childhood. Most Communists believed the lies they were told about the Trotskyists, and they acted on those beliefs with all the fervor they could muster. If they did have any doubts about Troskyist villany, they learned quickly to suppress them, lest their whole life pattern collapse. (The most pathetic of the ex-Communists are those who had to hear Khrushchev say it before they finally conceded, grudgingly, the truth about what the Trotskyists had maintained all along about the Moscow trials. However I have never heard of one of them coming now to an ex-Trotskyist and apologizing in any way for the personal lies and slanders they spread.)

As part of my education as a Trotskyist, I learned to despise the Communists as ignorant, slavish followers of Stalin, people who betrayed the revolutionary tradition over and over again in the interests of Soviet foreign policy. "Our line's been changed again" we sang at all our parties as a popular parody of the Communist positions; the song described in hilarious detail the flipflops made by the American Communists to keep up with the sometimes sudden changes in the policies of the Soviet Union. And I know a girl from a Trotskyist family who as a child was brought up believing that the name of the Soviet dictator wasn't just Stalin but "Stalinthebutcher," always shouted as one word, and a curse word at that.

We had bitter political fights within the Trotskyist group, too, often conducted in pretty abusive terms, but always a sharp distinction was made between such quarrels within the family, so to speak, and those we had with the Stalinists. Learning to make such distinctions was just as important a part of my political education as the lesson I had been taught by Mr. Lowenthal about drinking only with gentlemen. And so, slowly over the months I learned that although the Ohler-Stamm minority faction of the Trotskyists, to which I belonged, denounced the Cannon-Schachtman majority group, and that while later Ohler broke with Stamm and Cannon split with Schachtman, all of them believed the Stalinists to be permanent betrayers of the revolution.

These factional fights were always going on within the Trotskyist organization, often leading to splits and the formation of new groups. The process was a form of political mitosis as each splitting group in turn gave birth to another split, but there was one important difference between body cells and Trotskyist factions; in physical life, division is a process of growth, while among the Trotskyists the over-all number of members remained fixed even as the number of groups proliferated, which meant that each new one was even smaller than its parent. The issues which brought about these solemn splits were extremely complicated even for the politically sophisticated comrades, and so were usually completely incomprehensible to me, a neophyte. I couldn't understand the issues at the time, for I was still learning the difference between a cadre and a center, still unsure of the differences between "democratic centralism" as the Trotskyists used it and as a Stalinist description. I was trying out a wholly new and bewildering vocabulary and at the same time pretending to a degree of political sophistication far above my capacities. But despite my real ignorance of the issues, I represented a vote in my branch, for once a comrade was accepted into membership, the assumption was that he was immediately as capable of making political decisions as any of the old-timers who had been in the movement for years.

My becoming an Ohlerite, as members of the Ohler-Stamm group were called, was less related to the superior revolutionary merits of the group's position than to geography. In the branch of the Spartacus Youth League to which I was assigned because of where I lived, the Ohlerite group was in the minority, and I have never liked majorities. Then again, it may simply have been that the Ohlerites in my branch were nicer to me than were the Cannonites. Anyway, the only sharp recollection I have of this fight, which engrossed the complete attention of the organization for months, is one of Max Schachtman, the witty opposition leader, demolishing Ohler in a memorably succinct speech delivered late one night at a crowded meeting hall in lower Manhattan.

The meeting was held at the climax of the faction fight, when it seemed certain the organization was moving toward a split.

Ohler, an undistinguished-looking man who spoke in an even dull monotone, never raising or lowering his voice, had been talking for more than two hours when finally he wound up with what, for him, was a stirring peroration: "Do you want our party to be nourished on the right breast of opportunism or the left breast of revolutionary Marxism?" he asked, and took his seat on the platform.

As Schachtman stood up to deliver the attack of the majority, he looked around the jammed room and shrewdly estimated the inability of the comrades to absorb any more vocal punishment. "Comrades, to be perfectly frank with you, comrades, I don't really care whether our party is nourished on the right breast of opportunism or the left breast of revolutionary Marxism, just so long, comrades, just so long as it's not nourished on another organ for which God intended a different purpose." A roar of laughter went up from the hall, Max impishly stared at Ohler and then sat down as the meeting broke up. A few weeks later the split did take place and the Ohler-Stamm group organized its own party, the Revolutionary Workers League, proclaimed to be the only true interpreter of Marx, Lenin, and Trotsky.

But despite the continuous splits that divided the Trotskyists —always, the splitters assured each other, on questions of the highest principles—all the groups maintained a loose amorphous common identity. If the Ohlerites gave a party, the Marlenites— all seven of them—came. The leader of the Marlenites was Marlen, of course, who had constructed his party name from the first syllables of Marx and Lenin. I have no idea, any longer, of what esoteric differences separated the Marlen group from the other Trotskyists, but they must have been important ones to him and his immediate family, who made up the bulk of his group.

Yet despite the sharp political differences that separated us from the Communists, we were culturally dependent upon the Communists and their web of peripheral and supporting organizations, for the American Trotskyist movement had no folk-singing groups, no foreign-language associations, no fraternal orders, no hiking clubs, no classes in drama, nor any of the varied other activities which made the "What's Doing" column in the *Daily Worker* so long every day.

The "What's Doing" column was an important part of our daily reading, even though we were Trotskyists. If we wanted to see a movie about the Russian Revolution, we had to go to the

Cameo Theatre on Fourteenth Street, where we would sit in the balcony, cracking sunflower seeds with our teeth, and giggle at the more blatant examples of Stalinist propaganda. Sometimes, as when the screen showed a Russian girl falling asleep to dream of a luminous, fatherly Stalin tossing her baby high in his arms and chucking it under the chin, we would laugh—but always surreptitiously, lest some of the Stalinist faithful in the downstairs section hear us and come up to start a fight. But we thrilled at the heroics in Eisenstein's *Potemkin* and, no matter how often I saw it, the scene in *Chapayev* when the Red Army finally overcomes the White Russians always sent shivers through my body. So, too, when the proletarian heroes, the union members and organizers, rushed out onto the stage in the last scene of the plays presented by the New Theatre League at the old Civic Repertory Theatre, I responded just as viscerally as did any Communist.

Occasionally, if we were really daring, we would go to a social event sponsored by a Young Communist League branch or a Communist party front group. The trick was to find such an event far enough away from our normal area of activity to prevent the likelihood of being recognized as Trotskyists. Then, we would try to make it with the YCL girls, pretending to be potential sympathizers of the group and always hoping that the evening would end up in bed. Of course there was a risk, for if a Trotskyist was recognized at a Communist social event, he was almost certain to be shoved around, and possibly even beaten.

But the party hopping was always pretty dull, for almost always the YCL girls turned out to be nice Jewish girls with thick legs and bad skins. Even worse, most of them had the same ideas of virtue held by nice Jewish girls who weren't in the movement. The only place that offered a reasonable chance of willing Communist girls, or so I was told, was a Communist camp near New York called Nitgedaiget. There, if you were foolhardy enough to risk a week end and could successfully pass yourself off as a party sympathizer, you might end up in someone else's sleeping bag or bunk, discussing the terrible Trotskyists.

In my own SYL branch there was only one unattached and reasonably attractive girl, and I usually tried to sit next to her at meetings, without being too obvious about it. Her name was Betty, she was a few years older than me, I think, and she had nice full breasts. But the only occasion when I came even close to discovering what Betty's body was really like was when a group of us went on an overnight hike to a state park up in Westchester and I managed to arrange it so that my sleeping bag was next to hers. As we sat around the bonfire that night, lustily singing revolutionary songs, I made a few tentative probes, first at holding her hand and then at putting my arm around her shoulders. She responded with enough interest to encourage me into thinking I would press on with further explorations after the group had quieted down and we had got into our sleeping bags. Finally the last song was sung, the last comrade had disappeared into the woods to pee, and, considerably handicapped by the sleeping bag which swaddled me like the sleepers I had worn as a child, I lurched awkwardly closer to Betty.

Then, just as I had managed to jerk my sleeping bag right next to hers—which was hard to do since I was inside it, and damn painful, too, since I had an erection—a spotlight lit up the whole area. Attracted by the noise of our singing, state troopers had arrived in their car and now demanded that we break up the campsite. We tried arguing with them, but in the end, cursing the fascist Cossacks, we had to pack up in the dark, with only flashlights to see by. It took a long time to get all our scattered belongings together, and the cops came back, sweeping us with their damned spotlight to make sure none of us had bedded down again, either in sin or alone. By the time I got myself and Betty packed, my enthusiasm and erection had both disappeared.

Among the younger comrades with whom I associated, there wasn't as much sex activity as there was talk about it—always on a high intellectual level. The American radical movement was a puritanical one, intensely concerned with politics to the exclusion of all distractions. Any manifestation of overinterest in good food or clothes was considered petty bourgeois, and anyone conducting more than one affair at a time was considered promiscuous. I had to be pretty careful of my language, too, for while Walter Kahn, Jr., Stephen Walter, and I used words like "fuck" or "shit" without any feeling of either daring or embarrassment, such language was frowned on in the movement. We did have one comrade, Benny the Ape, whose conversation was filled with "the fucking" this and "the fucking" that, and for whom "cocksucker" was a word of endearment, while "shit" and "piss" were as frequent as "the" and "and," but he was very much the exception.

We were a pretty damn serious lot, with the whole weight of the world on our grim shoulders; a weight we carried humorlessly, except for the bitter satire that was one of our favorite weapons against the Stalinists. In Max Schachtman we had a really virtuoso performer of this art, and listening to him rip apart with savage satire some Stalinist hack capable only of parroting the party line made up in a small way for the usual abuse we took from the Communists. Some humor emerged, too, in the semisocial postmeeting gatherings we held over cups of cafeteria coffee.

Cafeterias were our clubs; we usually patronized those located near the branches or the national headquarters in the Union Square area. It was to the cafeterias that we adjourned in the evenings after meetings, and it was in the cafeterias that we found companionship on Saturdays after groups of us had gathered at the national headquarters to pick up the magazines for next week's house-to-house literature distribution, to use the mimeograph machine, or perhaps just to gossip.

We would meander over to the cafeteria and pull a small oblong ticket with two rows of numbers on it from the gaping mouth of a machine that stood just inside the entrance. Each pull was announced by a bell, whose function has always remained obscure to me. Then we bought our cups of coffee and perhaps, if we were flush, a piece of doughy indigestible pastry called either a prune danish or a cheese danish, depending on the filling. In the very early days of cafeteria sitting, you didn't have to buy anything but could simply sit with a glass of water and then leave, returning the unpunched check to the cashier, who would take it back with a very sour face. And since most of the young comrades were either students or unemployed, and so dependent for money on what they could scrounge from their families, they had very little to spend. Eventually, though, the cafeteria owners got tired of providing free sitting space to indigent young revolutionaries, and signs began to appear on the walls announcing a minimum charge of five cents (the price of a cup of coffee) for every ticket. Later the minimum went up to a dime.

Just as the European cafés and coffee houses had their own special clientele, so did the cafeterias in the Fourteenth Street area, physical location usually determining which group used the place as a social headquarters. We Trotskyists were partial for a long time to a cafeteria just off Fourth Avenue on Fourteenth Street itself, and when it closed we decided to rendezvous at another one near Fifth Avenue. I can still recall the horror on the face of the proprietor the first night we descended on his premises and took over six or seven tables. He looked at us as if to say, "What have I done to deserve this terrible fate?" and we looked back at him, arrogantly, with Benny the Ape saying loudly, "Fuck you, buddy. We like it here and we're going to stay."

It is easy to recollect the radical movement of the thirties through a sentimental haze of warm and happy moments, as if it had been a political idyll in which, charged to a high emotional pitch, we sang revolutionary songs, marched in glorious parades, sat for hours talking about politics, went on week-end hikes, and made love to each other on narrow beds underneath Diego Rivera prints of Mexican workers. Although it is true that we did sing and march and hike and talk and study and try awkwardly to make love, all those experiences were, for me at least, also accompanied by moods of pain and deep depression.

When I was a little boy, I wanted very much to be praised for having arranged my mother's fruit bowl so nicely when her friends came to visit, and I felt very badly when it went unnoticed. I wanted also to be recognized immediately for what I knew I was—different from any other little boy in the whole world. As a member of the Spartacus Youth League, I wanted very much to be praised, too, if not for arranging a fruit bowl, then for making an effective demagogic speech at the street corner meeting; and I also wanted to be recognized as someone uniquely different from anyone else in the crowd around the platform on which I stood, bravely challenging the whole capitalist world.

It may have been that need for approbation and recognition, in a complex combination with strong feelings of social indignation which provided the basis for my willingness to accept the discipline of the radical movement. The political and social phenomena of the era—the depression, Nazism, unemployment, anti-Semitism, Spanish fascism—were all symptoms of an evil and ugly world that Marxism was guaranteed to change; and my own psychic needs helped to push me into carrying out such unfamiliar and usually unpleasant tasks as trying to sell copies

of the Trotskyist newspaper every Sunday morning in apartment
houses where the tenants looked at me with surprise and suspicion before slamming the door in my face. Perhaps some such set
of personal need was present for all my comrades along with
our correct conviction that the world was wrong and we could
help to set it right.

But as a seventeen-year-old fledgling member of the Spartacus
Youth League, I understood very little about the complicated
nature of my increasing commitment to the movement and the
tensions it was producing. Some of those tensions must have
grown out of the conflicts within me, out of my adolescent unwillingness to admit that I was a middle-class boy who had become a radical and not a dashing young rich blade who was turning his back on his class. Even worse, being a radical had added
another dimension to the miserable quarrels between my parents
and me. They were so incapable of understanding me, and I
them, that at home I became an aggressive hostage to a family
life from which I was not yet able to release myself. Physically I
suffered from such painful attacks of giant hives that after these
quarrels I wasn't able to go to work because my feet were too
swollen to put on shoes and my face was huge and puffy. Psychologically they suffered the anguish of seeing their son become a
hostile stranger to them without knowing how to deal with him.

I don't know whether any other SYL members were having
the same kind of traumatic quarrels with their parents, for our
personal lives were generally closed off from each other. Rarely
did we go to each other's homes or meet each other's parents—
the headquarters was the common meeting ground. But as far as
I could judge from appearances, most of the SYL members in
the Bronx or upper Manhattan branches with whom I attended
meetings or sat in cafeterias seemed to come from lower-middle-
class families. They ranged in age from about sixteen to perhaps
twenty, although there was no fixed age at which a youth member joined the adult party organization. That decision was usually made by the adult members who watched over the youth
organization very carefully, selecting for the honor of party
membership those who seemed politically most mature.

A number of SYL members belonged to both groups, for
there was a kind of fluid overlapping of membership, especially
in the Greenwich Village and downtown Manhattan SYL
branches. The comrades who lived in the Village tended to be a

little older. They were the young married set of the movement; if they weren't married legally, at least their liaisons were semipermanent ones. They lived in one-room apartments in which studio beds rested directly on the floor and filled the whole room. Books were kept on shelves made from bricks and planks, and newspapers were stored in orange crates. All the couples were poor, eking out an existence somehow, and when they invited other couples to dinner, the meal usually consisted of spaghetti, meat balls, and cheap red wine. Then, after dinner, we would sit around on the floor or on the bed, listening to records, talking, and sometimes necking.

The more nights I spent arguing about Trotsky and Lenin in the cafeterias; the more papers I pressed into unwilling hands at street-corner meetings; the more such meetings I hesitantly began to address; the more boring classes in Marxism I attended; the more Saturday afternoons I spent at the national headquarters after leaving Mr. Lowenthal; the more nights I spent in Greenwich Village, wandering through the crooked streets looking for the apartment of a comrade who was giving a party or eating twenty-five-cent Chinese dinners at the Dragon Inn before walking over to Sixth Avenue to drink ten-cent beer at George's; and above all, the more seriously I began to take myself as a young revolutionist—the more estranged and isolated I became from my family and the more removed from meeting their standards of being a good Jewish son.

Night after night the painful quarrels with my parents grew worse. "Where have you been?" they would shout bitterly at me when I came home at one or two in the morning, and I would shout back just as bitterly, usually lying rather than admitting I had been at a street-corner or party meeting in Brooklyn or downtown Manhattan. We would berate each other through the closed door of their bedroom until I could hear my mother burst into near-hysterical tears. Then my father would storm out denouncing me, and I would scream back at him until, exhausted, I went to the room I shared with my brother; there he, awakened by the unpleasant noises, would look at me coldly and go back to sleep without talking. Even at the best of times, my brother and I never had much to say to each other in those days, for we were separated by the three-year gap in our ages, by different interests, and by my increasing involvement in the movement.

So life at home was a continual misery, a running sore of

nastiness for all of us during the two years I worked in the diamond business. The misery ended temporarily each morning at the door of Kahn's, for at least there no one considered my being a radical the horrendous crime it was in the eyes of my parents. And no one at Kahn's demanded, as did my parents, that I ought to give up radicalism if for no other reason than that it was bad for the Jews.

And, oddly enough, it was because I worked at Kahn's that now I had a new companion in the movement. Sometime in 1936 I had been sent by Mr. Lowenthal to a wholesale watch dealer in the upper Forties to pick up a watch of his that was being repaired. As I walked into the little reception room, separated, as in all jewelry firms, from the main offices by a partition and a grilled window, I heard someone behind the window whistling the "Internationale," the "Star Spangled Banner" of the radicals. I joined in the chorus, a surprised head popped out from behind the grill, and so I met Jerry.

We exchanged political views over a cup of coffee that afternoon, cautiously at first and then more excitedly as we discovered the unlikely fact that we were both Trotskyists. Jerry had only recently come to New York from New Haven, where his background was astonishingly similar to mine, and he was now working for a relative in much the same way as I was at Kahn's. Soon after this first meeting we shifted from being just political comrades to being friends. I introduced him to Bob when Bob came home from Ohio State, and the three of us were soon inseparable. Together we began eating at the Kvakaz, an East Fourteenth Street restaurant, and drinking tea in the Café Royale on Second Avenue, where Yiddish intellectual life had once centered although by the middle thirties it was already dying away.

Then, in July, 1936, the Spanish fascist generals revolted against the republican government, and that body blow to the labor and radical movement of the world galvanized the three of us into action. Jerry and I decided we had to quit our jobs to begin training as full-time revolutionaries. We started by enrolling in college, the only reasonable explanation we could think of that might satisfy our parents. The choice of the college was an easy one: it was to be the University of Minnesota, and once we'd made that decision, Bob decided to transfer there from Ohio State University.

We picked the University of Minnesota because the Trotskyists were in such strong control of a powerful teamsters' local in Minneapolis that under their influence all the unions in the city went out on a general strike in 1935 to support a strike of one local against the bitterly anti-union employers' council. The Minneapolis general strike was one of the best-organized, best-conducted, and most bitterly fought battles ever conducted by an American union; for a few days the strikers ran virtually the entire city, and for the Trotskyists it became a major event—as close as the organization ever came to demonstrating its possibilities for taking power.

And to us young Trotskyists the men and battles of Minneapolis were legends in their own time. We savored every detail of the battle of Deputy Run, when the strikers chased the police right through downtown Minneapolis; we knew all the intricate logistics of how the strike had been conducted from a headquarters set up in a big garage; in our own minds we were as tough as the striker who had killed a strikebreaker with a baseball bat; and the leaders of the Trotskyists in Minneapolis, the Dunne brothers and Farrell Dobbs, were genuine heroes.

And so I told my parents that I had decided to return to college, ultimately to study medicine, and had picked the University of Minnesota because it was cheap and because it had a good medical school which I would be able to enter more easily if I had done my undergraduate work there. I think all of us— myself, my parents and my brother—were relieved at my leaving, relieved to be released from the daily misery we were all suffering because of me. Besides, by this time I think they must have known I would go with or without their approval.

The difficulties I had in making the break from home were aggravated by the break I was making with L. & M. Kahn & Co. Because I was fearful of the office reaction, I kept delaying telling my employers of my decision. Finally I told Mr. Lowenthal I wanted to talk to him alone. We sat in his office, he in front of his old-fashioned rolltop desk, on which everything was neatly in place, and me alongside, nervously twisting in my chair, afraid to look him full in the face. I told him the same story I had given my parents but, unlike them, he believed me more than they had been prepared to do. The interview was as painful as I had expected it to be. Mr. Lowenthal was shocked about my rejection of a career in the diamond business and perhaps a little hurt, too, that I was turning away from him, my special protector and guide to the business. But despite what would have been a justifiable feeling that I had let them down, the firm presented me with a first-class Pullman ticket to Minneapolis as a farewell gift. And, typically for me at the time, I exchanged it for a coach ticket and kept the difference for use in my new career as a professional revolutionist.

CHAPTER THREE

MINNEAPOLIS was a strange place in those first days—almost like a foreign country. For although I had traveled before, it was always to places where the atmosphere of home and New York had still been very strong. But I walked out of the railroad station in Minneapolis as a stranger, gaping at the low buildings, the big red trolleys that ran across the Mississippi River to St. Paul, and the traffic signals that clanged loudly every time the colors changed.

I hurried directly to the Trotskyist headquarters, where I had arranged to meet Bob and Jerry. The party office was in a converted store located on the shabby periphery of the downtown section; its window displayed Trotskyist and Socialist party literature, Spanish Civil War posters, and copies of the teamsters' newspaper. Hesitating before going in, I peered through a window. Toward the back of the room I could see a man sitting at a desk and a few other people grouped around a table. Finally I went into the store. The room was much cleaner and tidier than any of the headquarters in New York—no crumpled-up newspapers littered the corners, no opened cans of mimeograph ink dripped their black sticky contents onto the tables, and no discarded cigarette butts pebbled the floor.

"I'm a comrade from New York," I said to the man at the desk who had been eyeing me a little suspiciously. "My name is Paul Jacobs and I'm looking for two other comrades from New York who should have gotten here a few days ago. Did they leave a message for me?"

The comrade, who turned out to be the secretary of the

branch, relaxed a little, but not much. "Yes," he answered, "your friends are here. They're down the street eating in the restaurant on the corner."

I left, disappointed at the cool greeting (after all, didn't he know who I was?) and went looking for Bob and Jerry in the restaurant. They were eating at a table, and they at least were glad to see me. Excitedly the three of us began talking about how to begin our new lives as professional revolutionists. As a first step we decided to find a place to live near the university campus, for all of us were really going to be students while we learned about being revolutionists.

We took a bus over to the university and walked around the grassy campus, which seemed huge to me compared to City College's tiny quadrangle. Then we meandered on the quiet, tree-lined streets that surrounded the campus, looking for signs advertising apartments for rent. We knew that if we wanted to avoid the dormitories we had to live in a house that had been approved by the university. At last we found a small furnished apartment in a house owned by an old lady who spoke with a thick Swedish accent. I went back to the station and got my bags while Jerry and Bob returned to headquarters to pick up their belongings.

As soon as we settled into our apartment, we decorated the walls with the pictures of Marx, Lenin, and Trotsky that we had brought with us, and we placed a photo of Trotsky standing with a German shepherd dog in the place of honor on the bookcase we had filled with revolutionary literature.

The apartment had a kitchen and a bathroom as well as a bedroom and living room, but neither its furnishings nor its physical appearance was of any real significance to us; the place was only for sleeping, eating, and arguing about the movement. The party headquarters, not the apartment, was the center of our lives. The day after we moved in, it was to party headquarters we reported for duty.

We must have been quite a headache to the Trotskyist leaders in Minneapolis: suddenly they were confronted with three young Easterners who had presented themselves for revolutionary work without either experience or qualifications. In our minds we were putting ourselves at the disposal of the revolution, to be used as the leadership decided. But obviously their perception of us had far less significance attached to it.

Exulting in our freedom from the restraints of home and
office, we sat around for a few days in the headquarters or in
nearby restaurants, introducing ourselves to the comrades who
came in, discussing with them the growth of fascism in Europe,
the continuing depression in the United States, and the success
of the "People's Front" position taken by the Communist International which had reversed the superrevolutionary "social-
fascist" line that had caused my expulsion from the YCL. Now,
with the slogan "Communism is Twentieth Century American-
ism!" the Communists were busily wooing the religious organizations, trade unions, and liberal groups they had so vigorously
denounced the year before. And as if all this were not enough to
engross our full political attention, fierce fighting was going on in
Spain and bitter internal conflicts were already dividing the Loyalist forces.

Few periods in politics have ever brought forth such emotion-
ally intense responses from Americans as did the three politically jammed years between 1936 and 1939. The only event in
America which comes close to it is the civil rights movement of
the 1960s. When Negro and white youths go to jail singing "We
Shall Overcome," they are having the same kind of highly intense experience we had in the thirties, although, in most cases,
theirs is physically much worse than what we went through. But
in one important respect they are more fortunate than we, for all
their social energy is focused on one question, while we were
plunged into despair or raised with hope by so many events that
we felt as if we were under a massive barrage, as if history were
attacking us.

And for me politics had another confusing dimension, for the
fear of rejection, the misery of discarding an identity and search-
ing for the new one, had to be expressed in the language of politics and to be painfully lived out inside the world of political
events. I wanted to go to Spain, not just because I was involved
politically in the daily anguish of the civil war but also because I
saw myself as a hero. When I was younger and devouring the
ten-cent pulp magazines, I was always a flier, shooting down the
brave German ace who saluted me as he went down in flames,
his white scarf whipping in the wind as I dipped my wings to
honor a gallant foe. In the summer of 1936, in the midst of the
heated political discussions about the Spanish Civil War, I could
see myself at the front, a rifle slung over my shoulder, heroically

shouting "No Paseran! No Paseran!" while fighting so bravely against the fascists that my fame spread all over the socialist world.

Unfortunately, my potential as a military hero went unrecognized in Minneapolis. A week or two after our arrival, we were called to a meeting by the party leadership and informed that not only were we not going to Spain, but we weren't even going to be sent into trade-union work, which at that time held the next-highest prestige inside the organization. Instead Ray Dunne told the three of us that we had been assigned to help build up a Trotskyist youth group at the University of Minnesota campus.

Nothing I had learned at City College prepared me for the University of Minnesota. In the alcoves where I had sat at CCNY, everyone I knew talked about the boys who had jumped up on the platform of the chapel when the Italian Fascist students were speaking and had knocked them into the seats. But at Minnesota the big men on campus were the football players, and all students were expected to attend the games and to root for the team as well, to chant slogans and to sing the university song between halves. At CCNY politics was a common interest for a great number of students, including many who were majoring in physics or literature; at Minnesota politics didn't seem to be the concern even of those who were studying political science.

Soon, though, we discovered that we weren't alone on campus —there were at least a few other students who were politically identifiable as Communists, Socialists, or Trotskyists. As soon as the semester began, the comrades of the Minneapolis branch called a meeting of ten or twelve students who either were members of the Trotskyist youth group or were sympathetic to it. After organizing a branch at the university, we applied to the dean's office for permission to establish a Marxist club, to be used for recruiting new members and sympathizers. The club began holding weekly discussion meetings at which older comrades from the branch in Minneapolis lectured and at which we watched carefully for any signs of possible interest in the sparse audience.

The student group carried on other activities as well. We joined all the student organizations that we thought might provide either potential members or possible fields for militant action. Sometimes we even formed new groups, as for example when we organized a union of students working on National

Youth Administration jobs. The NYA, the youth version of the WPA, provided employment to students who needed part-time work. Drawing on what Mr. Lowenthal had taught me at the hospital, I had applied for and gotten a job as a lab assistant at the university photo lab on the agricultural campus, which was reached by a funny little trolley that ran between the two schools, some miles apart.

I was paid twenty-five cents an hour for such simple lab work as running a print-drying machine, putting rolls of film into developer tanks, mixing fixing solutions, and generally making myself useful. But then I discovered that I was replacing a regular lab assistant whose rate was about forty cents an hour. With the fact that students were being used as cheap labor for a springboard, and with the help of the other comrades, I began organizing a union of NYA students.

At an afternoon meeting with the dean held at our request, six or seven of us piled into his office, behaving as if he were the class enemy and we were the vanguard of the revolution, getting ready to take power. When he asked us what we wanted, I spoke for the group and presented him with our demands in what I thought was Ray Dunne's most Bolshevik style. The dean answered that neither he nor the university administration had any power to increase our monthly pay, since that was set by the government, and that the hourly rates seemed fair to him.

"If we don't get the increases, we'll strike!" I said.

He looked a little puzzled. "You're just students," he answered. "How can you strike? Who will you be striking against? The university? The NYA? The only thing that will happen if you go on strike is that you will lose your jobs."

Disconcerted but still mumbling threats, we filed out of the office and sat in a restaurant to decide on our next step. We had to admit that the dean was right—as students we had very little power to force the university to meet our demands. Then someone had a great idea: why didn't we affiliate our weak union of NYA students to the powerful teamsters' local and go back to the dean with that weight behind us? A couple of us went into Minneapolis, met with Ray Dunne and the party executive committee, and got a somewhat grudging approval of our scheme. A few days later the executive board of the teamsters' local approved our application and we were affiliated to it, although the relationship was a very informal one.

Back we went to the dean for a really nasty meeting, in which he threatened us and we threatened him. Once again he refused to meet any of our demands, and we stormed out of his office. But in a few days we won at least a partial victory, for our hourly rates were increased by the administration.

But I paid a heavy price for the success of this action, which attracted some notoriety at the university. A jealous boy friend of my old girl friend the dancer was attending the university, too. He lived in a dormitory and was a very proper, rich, stuffy young man whom I had always considered a pain in the ass. He had always thought of me as a rival, even long after I had lost interest in her, and he made a point of writing her parents about my activities, telling them to be sure to listen to a March of Time radio program dramatizing a campus meeting at which I had denounced the university administration for some action it had taken.

"Academic freedom is dead in America and its corpse is stinking!" I had shouted to the student crowd from the back end of a truck parked on the campus while reporters took down my words. A week later I proudly listened to a dramatization of my speech, not knowing my father was also listening in New York.

That speech ended the little financial help I had been getting from home. A few days later I received an angry letter from my father denouncing me for having lied to him about what I was going to do at the university. I answered just as angrily, and my relations with my parents became even more painful.

But I kept my misery about my family secret, for it seemed unworthy of a revolutionary. By then the Trotskyists had dissolved into the Socialist party and the Spartacus Youth League members were now members of the Young People's Socialist League. But even though nominally we were in the Socialist party, we still functioned as a Trotskyist caucus. For Bob, Jerry, and myself, the central focus of our lives was on our activities in the Young People's Socialist League branch at the university and in the Trotskyist group in Minneapolis. It was as if every cell in our bodies were infused with a political plasma. When we got up in the morning, we started talking politics, and we didn't stop until we went to sleep. And one night when the three of us got so terribly drunk on gin that we discussed each other's faults, even our aggressions and jealousies came tumbling out disguised as criticisms of each other's failures to meet the political and personal standards of good Bolsheviks.

The following morning we could hardly stand to look at each other, for despite the competition among us, and despite our secret vying for Ray Dunne's approval, the three of us were bound together both by the experiences we were sharing and the long relationship that had existed between Bob and me. We never went through a session like that again, and I think each of us tried hard to forget the cruel things we had said to and about each other. But my own desire for recognition never left me, and I sat through interminable meetings guiltily hoping that when the reports of activities were made, my accomplishments would be mentioned.

I felt I was a political ugly duckling among most of the comrades in Minneapolis, and especially in comparison with Bob and Jerry. They seemed better able to cope with the heavy prose of Marx and Lenin, they seemed more knowledgeable, and their arguments always seemed stronger than mine. The only part of our lives in which I felt more at ease and more competent than Jerry and Bob was outside the movement. I was more sophisticated than they were about food and liquor, I was the best cook among us, and at parties I could always make myself the center of attraction by telling jokes in all kinds of accents.

Most of our social life revolved around the movement. On week ends we went to parties given by couples who were married or living together, and sometimes we threw a party ourselves. Shortly after we arrived, Bob found a steady girl friend, his first real romance with a comrade. Jerry took out a whole series of revolutionary girls while I sneaked off by myself fairly often for dates with a rich girl who lived alone in an apartment in Minneapolis. I don't know how I met her, but I remember that the house had an indoor swimming pool and that after swimming we would lie on the floor of her apartment and make love. But I kept my dates with her secret and would lie to Bob and Jerry about where I'd been, probably because I was ashamed of the attachment I still had to the life I'd touched, enviously, while in the diamond business. Once or twice I did go out with the girl members of the branch, but I found the experience not quite to my taste, for in this area my standards were still of the bourgeoisie. One girl wore men's underwear, and another was wild to have me take away her virginity—a prospect which frightened the hell out of me, since I was still pretty inexperienced.

Life in Minneapolis always remained unreal, never really part of my identity, always something happening outside of me. This was so partly because it was my first sustained period away from home, partly because the physical characteristics of life were so different, and partly because of the tremendous psychological pressure exerted on us by the Minneapolis Trotskyists, who took their radicalism very, very seriously—all of which kept me in a continual state of guilt.

The very texture of life—its sights, sounds, smells, and especially its temperatures—made and kept Minneapolis very different from New York. The winter started earlier than in the East, lasted longer, and seemed fantastically cold. "You won't mind the cold," the local comrades were always telling us, "because it's a dry cold." But by the time the temperature had dropped to twenty below zero, I couldn't make any distinction between dry and wet cold. I just hated the whole goddamned thing, hated being continually bundled up, hated the snow and the ice that stayed on the ground for months instead of turning into slush in a matter of days. Driving a car was almost impossible because it was so difficult to get started, and sliding over the ice always scared me. In the winter the air was so frozen that the insides of my nostrils burned every time I ventured outside, and standing to wait for a bus or a trolley was agony. And once I couldn't help feeling a little spiteful glee when one of the local comrades who was always talking about the "nice, dry cold" got his penis painfully frostbitten because he had been nuts enough to try to pee while waiting for a trolley late one night.

We also ate differently in Minnesota, and it wasn't only because I had less money than when I'd been working at Kahn's. The delicatessens didn't sell spicy hot dogs or pastrami sandwiches. Danish pastries were called "snails," while the malted milks were so thick they had to be eaten with a spoon instead of sipped through a straw. We discovered cheap Swedish restaurants that served lingonberries with everything, and ate Swedish pancakes for dessert. Apartments had no dumbwaiters to carry the garbage down into the cellar or incinerator openings in the hallways into which we could throw papers. The house in which we lived was near the Mississippi River, and the river, lined with trees and grassy banks, seemed much more appropriate to the country than to a big city. The huge lakes, right inside of Minneapolis, were also strange to us, for we knew that cities didn't have lakes—lakes were where you went for summer vacations. But, more than anything else, it was the Minneapolis Trotsky-ists who made me feel somewhat uncomfortable. They really were Bolsheviks, not dilettantes, and we learned very quickly that they were harsh disciplinarians as well. And, like most Midwesterners, radicals or not, they were simultaneously suspicious and contemptuous of New Yorkers. The Minneapolis Trotskyists eyed all New York comrades in the same way as had the fraternity boys who had come to our apartment a few times to look us over as possible prospects. For a little while we had a continuous stream of them, but once they saw the pictures of Marx, Lenin, and Trotsky on the walls and spotted the books and pamphlets, they ducked out hurriedly.

In Minneapolis we learned quickly that it was not easy to prove ourselves good Bolsheviks. The discipline was far stricter than it had been in the more easygoing radical atmosphere of New York, with its nice parties in the Village and the hours spent schmoozing over coffee in the cafeterias. In Minneapolis, if you were assigned to distribute leaflets at a union meeting, you went—for if you failed to show up without a very good excuse, like maybe dying, you had the prospect of facing Ray Dunne's cold eyes and implacable questions. For me, that was like being bawled out by my father all over again. And party meetings in Minneapolis didn't usually end with singing revolutionary songs —that was kid stuff, not for real Bolsheviks.

The signs of this toughness were everywhere. When armed guards were needed to protect Trotsky from the expected (and finally successful) attempts of the Communists to assassinate him, the Minneapolis branch supplied the toughest of the volunteers. When Chicago gangsters had attempted to move in on the Minneapolis local of the teamsters, they had literally been thrown down the steps of the union office and told that they would be killed if they returned. An unsolved murder of a teamster official added credence to the stories that circulated inside the branch about how the leadership in Minneapolis was faced continually with the threat of violent death and beatings.

The toughness of the leaders was combined with a hard, spare, ascetic quality that became a model for all of us. No one drank excessively at the social affairs held in the headquarters, and during the small fraction meetings that were always taking place in the headquarters there was very little kibitzing. The comrades sat around a table taking turns rolling their cigarettes with a little machine, seriously discussing what the fraction should do to build the party's influence in the group to which it was assigned.

The very intensity and grimness of the radical movement in Minneapolis left little room for errors or weakness. After only a few weeks in Minneapolis, I understood very well how it was possible for this group of men to successfully run the teamsters' union and why the Minneapolis general strike had been run like a military operation: Ray Dunne and the people around him were very serious revolutionists.

And one sign of that seriousness was their intense hatred of the Stalinists, an attitude I absorbed very quickly. All of us knew without any doubts that the Communists under Stalin had betrayed the cause of world revolution and therefore had to be "exposed" to the working class for their counterrevolutionary role. But during the thirties exposing the Communists wasn't easy, for not only were they better organized, with better resources and many more members, but even more important, their new, all-inclusive, barbless "Peoples' Front" program made the Communist party out to be a kind of pleasant, bland, "progressive" organization that damn near anyone could join. The "Peoples' Front" line of the Communists gave them the easy access to the community that we openly revolutionary Trotskyists could never achieve. And, even worse, because the Communists controlled or had great influence in a very wide variety of groups, they were able to infect the entire liberal and union movement with their equally bitter anti-Trotskyist propaganda.

In New York City I had seen the Stalinists and the Trotskyists fight it out at street-corner meetings, with shouts and imprecations as their weapons; in Minneapolis we fought physically as well. One day a comrade came limping into the headquarters, beaten by a group of YCLers who had run into him on a trolley car. A week later we caught up with a few of them on a side street and left them bruised and battered in the gutter. During late 1936 and all of 1937 and 1938 the Spanish Civil War and the Moscow purge trials gave us daily doses of Stalinist poison and terror—doses which built up in us such a hatred for the Stalinists that even today at times I am overwhelmed by it.

For American liberals, especially those influenced by the

Communists, the Spanish Civil War was a clear and simple case of the loyalist good guys fighting the fascist bad guys. These people made no attempt to analyze the differences among the political parties that were fighting under the over-all rubric of loyalism, and the bitter internecine political warfare among the Spanish anarchists, Socialists, Trotskyists, and Stalinists was completely unknown to them. For Communist party members the Spanish Civil War was not much more complicated; they were completely convinced that whatever the Soviet Union did was correct, that the Trotskyists and anarchists were allies of the fascists, and that the loyalists could only win through Soviet aid and Communist leadership.

But for us Trotskyists the issues and political alignments in the war were far more complicated. We were convinced that Franco could only be defeated if the war against fascism were turned into a war for socialism, and we also believed—correctly, as it turned out—that the Soviet Union would sacrifice the Spanish loyalists, if necessary, to its own self-interest. Bitterly we knew from reports already beginning to filter back into the United States that the GPU, the Russian secret police, had taken over in Spain and that socialists, anarchists, and Trotskyists were being imprisoned or even shot by the Communists, sometimes right at the front where they were fighting the fascists. And as we devoured the reports coming in from Spain, we read in the anarchist, socialist, and Trotskyist press of how the Russians were using the aid they were sending the loyalists to blackmail the republican government into giving Spanish Communists positions of authority inside the government.

The Moscow trials and the ghastly purges which followed them, wiping out a whole generation of men who had created the Russian Revolution, were an even more traumatic experience for us, for here we Trotskyists were under direct attack. We were forced to defend ourselves against the charges that we were wreckers, saboteurs, and fascists; these charges were echoed by hundreds and thousands of liberals, who swallowed whole this huge monstrous lie of Stalin's and accepted it as the gospel until Khrushchev finally admitted that most of the executed had been innocent of the crimes to which they had even confessed. But that admission didn't happen until 1956, and in 1936 and 1937, at meetings of the National Student League in the Student Union building at the University of Minnesota, we young Trotskyists sat writhing, as one Communist or Communist-influenced speaker after another got up to denounce us as fascists, kin to Hitler, Franco, and Mussolini.

(The vicious atmosphere developed from the slanders spread by the Communists about their political opponents accounts partially, I think, for the shabby role played by some intellectuals in abetting the violent and vulgar anti-Communism of the fifties. It was not until then that these intellectuals for the first time had an opportunity to respond to all the garbage that had been thrown at them for so long. Thus, they joined with the far right, forgetting that their own grievances against the Communists had not been because the Stalinists were radicals, but because they weren't radical enough.)

But despite the fact that we three Easterners shared with our local comrades a common cause against the Stalinists, we were outsiders in Minneapolis; and somewhere below the surface, in some unspoken way, I thought, probably incorrectly, that we were viewed differently because we were all Jews. Some Jewish Trotskyists lived in the Minneapolis area, but in great contrast to New York, they made up a small minority in the organization.

Anti-Semitism became an issue once in Minneapolis, when our campus group arranged a public meeting for a speaker from the Farm Holiday organization in North Dakota, a group which was forcibly preventing farm foreclosures. We were vociferous supporters of the Farm Holiday organization, especially after we discovered that some of its leaders were either members of the Socialist party or sympathetic to it. One of them was in Minnesota on a speaking tour, and we arranged a public meeting on campus for him. The hall was jammed when the lanky, weatherbeaten farmer was introduced, and he held everybody's attention as he described in a flat Great Plains accent how the members of the Farm Holiday group attended foreclosure sales carrying shotguns and pitchforks. When the foreclosure auction began under the watchful eyes of the group, no more than one bid was ever made for the farm and equipment, and that bid was always for one dollar. The sale would then be over and the farm returned to its owner. All of the comrades in the audience were excited and thrilled with this militant speech until we heard the Farm Holiday leader wind up his speech with a denunciation of "those Jew bankers who are trying to steal all the farms in the Dakotas." He went on in some detail about the "Jew" bankers despite our frantic signals to him, which he obviously didn't understand. At the end of the meeting, fortunately only a few minutes later, we rushed up to the platform to berate him for his nonsocialist anti-Semitism, only to be met with his genuine bewilderment. To that farmer, all Jews were bankers out to screw farmers, and he could not understand our horror at what he had said. And despite his identification of all Jews as bankers, he insisted that he was a radical socialist.

Still, the incident had no great significance for me or anyone else with whom I talked about it at the next meeting of the unit. We all decided that the socialist farmer's anti-Semitism was his own aberration, resulting from a rural isolation, in which he had never had any contact with Jewish workers or radicals. And except for that one instance, the "Jewish question" was rarely a matter for discussion, either in our apartment or at the meetings. When we did discuss Zionism, it was as simply another form of bourgeois nationalism, and the events occurring in Palestine were lost to our sight in the bitter news that kept coming from Spain and Germany. On the rare occasions when we did discuss Palestine, we always ended up with a perfunctory call to the Arab and Jewish workers to unite for the overthrow of both Arab and Jewish capitalists.

Early in 1937 our household began breaking up. Jerry, who was pretty skinny, had developed a racking cough and was talking about moving to a warmer climate, while Bob spent all his free time with Hilda, his first and only love. We were terribly broke, too. For a while we had managed to pay the rent on the apartment by dropping classes at the university and getting a refund on our tuition, but soon we exhausted that resource. Finally, when Jerry left for Arizona, Bob and I decided to break up our housekeeping arrangements. Neither of us was going to classes any longer, and, even more pressing, we had taken opposing positions in a new factional fight inside the organization which found me, once again, on the side of the minority.

With the split-up of the apartment, a year began which was so painful and lonely that even now, more than twenty-five years later, I can hardly bear to think about it. I felt completely alone, betrayed by Jerry's defection and Bob's deep amatory involvement. I was homeless, too, drifting around to the apartments of comrades for a few days or a week at a time and sleeping sometimes on chairs at the back of the headquarters. I was so broke and so hungry that I stole empty milk bottles from doorsteps for the deposits, and finally I got so desperate I even rifled the can in the headquarters into which people dropped money to pay for the literature they bought. I was dirty, too, and furtively had to use the public baths in Minneapolis where for a penny or two you were given a small worn bath towel and a thin wafer of gritty soap to take with you into a cold little room that enclosed a gray bathtub. Worst of all, after I took a bath I had to get back into the dirty clothes I had been wearing, for I had no others.

Finally the party leadership assigned me to be the youth organizer in St. Paul, across the river. In a way this was the local equivalent of Siberia, for the adult branch there had only a few members, and the headquarters was a miserable, tiny, and very dark store in the skid-row section. When I first went to St. Paul, I lived in a succession of dreary furnished rooms, from which I was always being locked out for not paying the rent. Then for a month or two I lived with a married couple who were members of the branch and their stone-deaf father, who had been a boiler-maker in the railroad shops. So deafened by his work that he could hear absolutely nothing, he sat all day long in an arm-chair, glowering at me, his suspenders looped over his long-sleeved, highnecked, and very dirty underwear.

The old man, a devout Catholic, never spoke to me except to shout some order about cleaning the house, and I suppose he must have despised me, for I symbolized the corruption of his daughters, both of whom had married Trotskyists and left the Church. Finally the tension between us became so unbearable that I left to move in with another comrade, a Latvian who lived alone in a tiny badly heated two-room house on the outskirts of St. Paul. I had seen this comrade at meetings but had never talked much with him and had no notion of how he lived or what he was like. Although he was working, he was very stingy and didn't share what he had with me. In his mind the bargain he'd made with the organization consisted of supplying me only with a narrow bed in the combination living room and kitchen. An old kitchen range and a small wood-burning stove in his tiny bedroom kept the house slightly warm. Out in back was a filthy privy which, because it was cold, didn't stink, as it certainly would have in the warm weather.

I had bed without board from this comrade all through the

fall and early winter of 1937, and life became more and more of a nightmare as the days went by. My overcoat and a dirty quilt were my blankets, and I slept in my long underwear. In the morning I would struggle out of bed after my landlord had left for work, piss in the sink, and throw a spoonful of coffee into some boiling water. Sometimes, too, I had scrounged enough money the day before to buy a loaf of day-old raisin bread, and I would shovel great chunks of it into my mouth as I gulped the scalded coffee. Sometimes I ate rhubarb, for it grew wild just outside the shack and I could pick it easily. Then, always still hungry, I would drag myself from the house and walk a couple of miles to the headquarters, head down, looking in the gutter in the vain hope that someone would have dropped some money there.

After I had opened the door of the headquarters, I would clean it out if there had been a meeting the night before, sweeping up the cigarette butts and rearranging the chairs. Then the endless days began. Once in a while someone would drop in to look at the literature, and in the late afternoons occasionally one of the members would drop in. But generally I spent my days alone in the headquarters except when I went out to look for jobs which I never found, or when I took the trolley over to the Minneapolis headquarters to report on the work I was supposed to be doing to build up the youth branch in St. Paul. There, in the warmth and bustle of the headquarters, I would lie about my activities, always sensing that no one believed my lies.

The nights were even worse, for then the hunger and the sense of isolation from the whole world was more acute. I always tried to get back to the house late, trying to arrive after my roommate was asleep, but sometimes, when I couldn't face being cooped up with him, I would sleep in the back of the headquarters on four or five wooden chairs pushed together. Only a few weeks after I'd moved in, Ivan had showed me a collection of dirty pictures which he had stacked up in three or four large bureau drawers. It was an incredible array, one that he had been saving for many years the way other misers save string, and many nights he went into his bedroom, carrying along handfuls of his pictures. Then I would hear him groaning as he masturbated, and I would burrow deep under my coat, trying to shut out the sounds that stimulated me, too, into fitful sexual fantasies.

I might not have survived those months in St. Paul without

the help of two sisters who were almost as poor as I and the family of a girl, Paula Meyers, whom I had known at the university. The two sisters, one of whom was crippled, were members of the organization. The healthier one was a waitress and had a miserable job in a St. Paul restaurant, while the crippled girl was unemployed like me, but unlike me was drawing some kind of relief from the city. As often as I could I visited them in their little basement furnished room where we would sit for hours, rolling cigarettes, drinking coffee, eating stale sweet rolls and talking. Both of them were exceedingly ugly, and both of them were exceedingly kind to me. But it was the Meyers family that really saved me from drifting off into some unknown nether world. Paula was a student whom I had gotten to know at the university while she lived with her parents in a solid brick house in St. Paul. Her father was a doctor and her mother was a kind warm woman who never questioned me nor argued with me about my way of life. Paula had a kid sister named Donna, and on nights when her parents went out and she was Donna's baby-sitter, I would go over to keep her company. The Meyers family came from the same tradition of Reform Judaism in which I had been brought up, and on the nights when they asked me to stay to dinner, the atmosphere was a very familiar one. Sometimes, too, when I was very hungry and it was too late at night to wake up the family, I would stand outside the house throwing pebbles at Paula's window until she heard me and opened it. Then she would go downstairs to the refrigerator, make up a few sandwiches, and pass them out to me. Even though I gulped them so quickly that I couldn't taste them, those sandwiches were the best I have ever eaten in my life.

As the days dragged on in gray cold and hunger, I went to the headquarters less and less, did fewer and fewer of the tasks assigned to me, and stayed in bed longer and longer. It was hardly worth the effort to drag myself from under my overcoat, and the hunger pains were less severe in bed. So I stayed in a constant drowsing daze somewhere between sleep and wakefulness but closer to sleep.

After I hadn't shown up at headquarters for some time, two of the comrades came to the house to find out what was wrong. I sent them away without even getting out of bed, and alarmed, they went to Minneapolis to report on my hazy and confused condition. Bob came and took me back to Minneapolis with him, telling me that Ray Dunne wanted to talk to me. That afternoon in the headquarters Dunne informed me that I had to leave Minneapolis, that the party would not be responsible for me any longer.

And so one very cold day, a failure as a Bolshevik, I took the trolley to the outskirts of St. Paul and stood on the highway, stamping my high leather shoes to keep my feet from freezing and fingering the Teamsters Union button I had stuck on the side of my cap in the hope that a truck driver would see it and think I was a member of the union. Finally a car slowed down and stopped for me a few hundred yards away. I ran frantically toward it, my suitcase banging painfully against the side of my leg, afraid the driver might change his mind and drive away without me if I didn't show how eager I was to ride with him, how anxious I was not to keep him waiting an instant longer than necessary, and how grateful I was for his stopping to pick me up.

I got in the warm car and we drove east on the highway, back toward New York.

CHAPTER FOUR

THE RETURN TRIP to New York
turned out to be only a nightmarish extension of the physical
squalor and psychological misery of Minneapolis and St. Paul.

It was bitterly cold on the highway and since I had no money,
I ate very infrequently—only when the driver of the car or truck
that picked me up bought me a meal. Getting a free meal required a careful approach. If the driver stopped at mealtime and
said he wanted to eat, you had to say, "Well, I'll just stay in the
car and wait." Then sometimes he would ask why, and you
could tell him you were broke, which might bring an offer to
feed you. But just as often he didn't ask, and so you waited for
him, getting hungrier and hungrier, watching him eat inside the
diner. And sometimes it was too risky to beg a meal, for the
driver might get suspicious and tell you he had changed his mind
and wasn't going any farther. When that happened, you would
get out of the car and a few minutes later see it flash by, the
driver looking intently ahead at the road, too embarrassed to
turn his head toward where he had left you standing, cursing.

Many other niceties had to be learned about hitching rides. It
was always better if you could get to an intersection where there
was a traffic light, because some of the cars would have to stop
and wouldn't be speeding down the road so fast their drivers
couldn't easily slow down for you. Being at an intersection also
meant that you could ask the drivers to give you a ride while
they were waiting for the light to change, thus giving them a
chance to look you over as a possible risk. When you did this,
you had to be careful to speak in a nice voice, using words that

showed you really weren't a bum but a nice college boy instead.

Another good place to pick up rides was at gas stations or diners, for there, too, you could approach the drivers and try to persuade them to give you a lift. It was usually easier to get a ride from a truck driver than from the driver of a passenger car, but then the trip was much slower and usually damned uncomfortable. But in trying for rides in passenger cars, you had to consider whether you wanted to talk or not, because the drivers were often salesmen who only took you along because they wanted someone to keep them awake or help drive the cars. Truck drivers were usually content to let you fall asleep if you could while the truck was jouncing along, noisily shifting gears up and down.

An informal set of hitchhikers' rules existed in those depression days, observed reasonably well except under extraordinary circumstances. If, for example, you were let out of a car or a truck at an intersection where someone else was already trying to thumb a ride, the protocol required that after exchanging a few noncommittal words you walk down the road, letting him have first chance at the oncoming cars. While you were doing this, you kept hoping that maybe even if a car didn't stop for him it would for you because the driver would see that, although the other fellow was not to be trusted, you were a fine upstanding fellow on your way home to the next town.

Of course none of this mattered if you couldn't get a ride at all, and that trip from Minnesota to New York was the worst I'd ever had for getting picked up. I stood for hours on Midwestern highways, stepping from one foot to the other in an attempt to stay warm, while all the drivers punished me by rushing past without stopping. I tried continually to convince myself that I would get a ride by the time another ten cars had passed, and when that number had gone by and I was still standing, cold and miserable, I'd start counting again up to ten cars, murmuring to myself as a car approached down the highway, "This one will stop, this one will stop," as if the phrase were a magic incantation that would make the car slow down for me if I just kept repeating it. Finally, when darkness made it impossible for any driver to see me standing on the highway and the cold became intolerable, I would start walking down the road, looking for a farmer's barn or for the lights of a town. But whenever I saw headlights coming up behind me, I always stopped hopefully to waggle my thumb.

Early one evening, somewhere on a highway near Chicago, I watched a train roar past on a nearby track. Ever since, that train has been fixed in my memory like a long strip of photos, each separate window a separate snapshot exactly the same size but with different people in it. It is an all-Pullman train, perhaps the Twentieth Century or Broadway Limited, for immediately behind the engine and the mail and baggage cars there is a diner with people sitting at the tables and waiters lurching by in the aisles with their trays precariously balanced on open palms. At one table a couple is lifting glasses in some kind of toast to each other; at the next window a little boy is being fed impatiently by his mother while he turns his head, intently peering out at the dusk; next to that table is one with two fat businessmen cutting into juicy steaks; and so all the way down the car warm people sit and eat comfortably while I stand outside hungry, cold, and envious, especially because I know something of the comfort I see. In the Pullman cars men and women sit and look incuriously out the window as they go by, not even knowing I'm there. Some of them are just waiting a few more minutes before they go up to the diner, others have already finished eating and are now sitting back in their roomettes or compartments belchily digesting their meal, reading or just talking. And as the lounge car shoots by, I see one man lighting up his cigar while the steward is bending down to put drinks on the table next to him. Then the train is gone, leaving only its red lights to continue on for a few minutes, and I am left standing again alone, with no ride, no food, and no place to sleep.

I spent that night of the train huddled sideways underneath my coat on a pile of rags in the corner of a gas station, trying not to smell the acrid odor of the gasoline and not to feel the chill of the concrete below the rags.

In the morning I got a ride on a truck but nothing to eat, and so by noon, when the truck turned off the main highway, I was frantic with hunger. The car that pulled up for me then was driven by a salesman who told me he was in such a great hurry he wasn't going to stop for lunch. When, desperate, I asked him if he had anything to eat in the car, he rooted around in the glove compartment and, of all the insane things to find, produced a jar of *marrons,* sweet preserved chestnuts from France. I opened the jar, gulped them down, and in ten minutes started to vomit them up, forcing the man to stop the car while I heaved. Furiously he threw my bag out of the car onto the highway and drove off without me.

That night I stayed in a cell of the Cleveland jail, sleeping on a wooden bench, kept awake by the sour smell of urine and vomit that permeated the clothes of the drunks in the cells alongside mine. But in the morning the jailer brought me a big bowl of oatmeal, some bread, and a mug of hot coffee. Even more generously, he gave me a dollar to help me on my way.

Once on that terrible trip I was picked up by three wild drunks in a car. The driver was so boozed up on the white moonshine they were drinking from a bottle passing around among them that the car swerved back and forth across the highway. I was frightened and I told them I wanted to get out, but they turned ugly and insisted that I drive if I didn't like the way they were doing it. So I slid over into the driver's seat and began driving slowly and carefully while they continued drinking and trying to get me to take a belt from the bottle. In a few minutes one of them shouted impatiently at me, "You'd better get this car movin'! It's hot and if you don't get humpin', sure as shit, the goddamn cops'll catch up with us! So get movin'!"

Almost instantaneously I slammed on the brakes, sending them toppling back in their seats; frantically I grabbed my bag, wrenched the car door open, and jumped into the brush alongside the highway, leaving them laughing uproariously as they kept weaving down the road.

A few days later I slunk back into New York. My clothes were filthy and a couple of my teeth had been broken off in St. Paul. I was skinnier than I had ever been before; all that was left of the Bolshevik defiance with which I had left home was a remnant of ugly bravado, my only armor against the cold contempt I anticipated from everybody. There were no jobs, of course, for the depression was still on, and I subsisted on what money my mother would give me when my father wasn't around to see. Finally I did get a job in a shower-curtain factory, packing boxes of cheap plastic curtains into large cases. I worked five and a half days a week at this tedious job and got paid about twelve dollars.

But bad as it was around the house, the most painful encounters I had back in New York were with my comrades. For the first few weeks I had to force myself to go to the meetings. Since

I feared above all that the Minneapolis comrades had sent word back to New York that I had been thrown out, I was always anticipating being questioned about my failures. But no one did, and instead I discovered that having been in Minneapolis created something of an aura around me, for to the young New York radicals the class struggle was far more real in the Midwest than it was at their parties in the Village.

For a few months I drifted around New York, on the fringes of everything. Life at home was marginal, and so was life in the movement. During the day I hung around the Socialist party headquarters, one of those vague faces that would always appear at meetings or slide into a chair at the farther end of the cafeteria tables. And rather than stay home at night, I attended whatever social affairs were being given anywhere in the city, traveling long distances on the subway if I had to, just so I might avoid the anger of my father and the anxiety of my mother. I started drinking fairly heavily, too, borrowing money to buy cheap rum and a ghastly blend of whiskey called "Green River," I think.

Mercifully, this period lasted only a few months. It really ended one night when one of A. J. Muste's daughters, whom I knew, found me sitting and swinging drunkenly on a chain that was used to hold back passengers during the rush hours in the Fourteenth Street subway station. She insisted that I go home with her to the cooperative apartment house in the Bronx where the Mustes lived. Muste was a minister who had become involved in radical politics after conducting a strike in Ohio. But he had always remained an outsider in the factional struggles, temperamentally unable to participate in the bitter political quarrels. I spent a few hours talking with A. J., who treated me as gently as he did everyone, trying to find the source of my troubles and then suggesting some answers to them.

By this time, too, the internal pressure was building up again for me to leave home, for it had become nothing more than a bed and a free breakfast surrounded by bitter arguments. But even though bed and board were free, the psychological cost was too high: my very physical presence in the house caused such great tension that all of us were in a state of continual anger and misery. When I discovered that an organizer was needed for the Young People's Socialist League in Rochester, New York, I volunteered for the job and took off, via Greyhound Bus, for upstate New York.

The Socialist party also had a branch in Rochester, headed by a railroad engineer, whom I visited as soon as I arrived. He was an old-time self-educated Socialist radical, in his fifties then, a stocky rugged man who lived on the outskirts of Rochester with his wife and three children. She was a socialist too, although not as intensely involved in the movement as her husband, and she made the best pumpkin pie I have ever eaten.

The engineer had been in the Socialist party for many years before the Trotskyists had joined it. But unlike most of the older Socialists, who fought against the Trotskyist influence, he had become a supporter of our group in the factional fight that started inside the party once we started to Bolshevize the organization. He and I set up a political alliance almost immediately, with the two of us meeting two or three times a week to discuss plans for pushing the Trotskyist line inside the party branch. Later on, when we had become friends as well as allies, we sat and talked for hours in the evenings at his house until it was time for him to start for the railroad yards. Then he would put on his overalls, his heavy shoes, and the peaked cap that marked him as an engineer, and I would ride with him in his old car to the crew-dispatching office where he would sign in before swinging off into the darkness of the tracks, his lunch box in one hand, his gloves in the other. But very often he didn't work at all; he was only a relief engineer and had to wait his turn for a run. On those nights we sat up and talked while his wife made coffee and always served some kind of pie.

From the very beginning Rochester was a much easier place in which to be a revolutionary than Minneapolis had been. First of all, I got a job almost immediately. The aunt of one of the YPSL members attending the University of Rochester, who operated a small apartment hotel in a slightly rundown section of Rochester, needed a combination night clerk and switchboard operator and hired me on her nephew's recommendation. Work started at about eleven thirty at night, when I had to answer the few phone calls that came through on the switchboard, check in the very infrequent new arrivals and give keys to the permanent guests, most of whom were elderly people, safely in their rooms by midnight. At about two A.M. I locked the outside doors and went to sleep on a big sofa in the lobby, waking up at about six, when I had to start calling people to wake them up, take breakfast orders, operate the elevator, and deliver newspapers to the rooms until an elderly bellman came on duty at seven thirty. At eight thirty the aunt swept into the lobby from her apartment on the first floor and I turned over the night's receipts if there were any and told her what had happened during the night. Then I went downstairs to the kitchen for a free breakfast and upstairs to the top floor of the hotel where all the help had tiny rooms.

And I got paid, too, for this snap job, something like ten dollars a week. The hours left me lots of free time for doing my work as YPSL organizer. The only trouble with the job was that Auntie bothered me all the time with complaints from some of the nuttier guests or by telling me that someone had had to knock on the door for a few minutes, late at night, before I awakened and struggled off my sofa to let him in. But our biggest quarrels were because I rented rooms to whores or to couples without baggage. Yet she was always willing to take the money I charged these people, and so, to avoid the arguments, I always told them they had to be out of the hotel by early in the morning. Then I would lie to Auntie, telling her they had brought luggage but had checked out before she got up. The maids knew the truth, of course, but never said anything because I always overcharged the hot-sheet trade a dollar or two and gave the extra money to the girls.

We had two functioning branches of the YPSL in Rochester in addition to the Socialist party organization. One of the branches was for students at the University of Rochester; the other was a citywide organization that met in a headquarters on Joseph Avenue, then the busy main street of the Jewish section of Rochester. (By 1964 Joseph Avenue had become the center of the Negro ghetto which exploded into the riots that shook the city.) During the thirties this Jewish area, which had grown up around the men's-clothing factories in the city, was more like the lower-middle-class atmosphere of the Bronx than the working class tumult of New York City's Lower East Side. But unlike Minneapolis, at least Rochester contained a delicatessen where you could get a juicy hot dog or a real corned-beef sandwich, and there was an "appetizer" store filled with the pungent smell of dill pickles floating in a sea of foamy brine inside the barrels, pickled herrings, smoked whitefish, lox, and Muenster cheese.

It was in that Jewish section of Rochester that I first encountered labor Zionists. The YPSL branch rented space for its weekly meetings from a Jewish socialist youth organization, Hashomer Hatzair. The Hashomer members, who occupied a small house on Joseph Avenue, were all about the same age as the YPSLers and were very close to us politically as well. They hated the Communists almost as much as we did, primarily because the Soviet Union had set up the remote province of Birobidzhan as its own Jewish state, touting its virtues over Palestine. Most of the Hashomer members were preparing themselves to emigrate to Palestine, and ultimately most of them did. They were convinced that the only salvation for the Jews was in their own land, and because they were socialists, they were committed to making Palestine into a socialist country. Since all of them were preparing to live on a kibbutz as farmers and so escape being urban Jews, preparing themselves for emigration meant working on a Hashomer-operated farm in New Jersey.

I sat with them for hours in their headquarters arguing heatedly that Zionism was only another form of petty bourgeois nationalism. But those arguments had none of the rancor and bitterness that were so characteristic of the fight all of us had with the Stalinists. Most of the Hashomer members came from working- or middle-class families and were fairly matter-of-fact about being Jewish. It was always odd for me to hear them speaking in halting Hebrew to each other and ending their meeting by singing "Hatikvah," the Zionist anthem. Sometimes as a result of these discussions a YPSL member would get converted by Hashomer, and once in a while we would win one of their members over to us. One of my personal conversions was a dark black-haired girl whose parents were orthodox Jews. She had a lush body, although she was somehow awkward in her walk and stance. I spotted her first at a Hashomer social and then invited her to a YPSL party, one of those decorous, dull affairs we gave fairly often, at which a few people danced and everybody else just sat and talked politics. After a couple of weeks I began to spend more and more of my free time lying on a couch with her in the living room of her parents' home, necking passionately.

Finding girls was generally a good deal easier in Rochester than it had been in Minneapolis. For some reason the girls in the Rochester YPSL or on the fringes of the socialist movement were much more attractive than the Minneapolis breed had been. In addition, the whole tone of the movement in Rochester was less grim, with the possible exception of the Hashomer Hatzair group. Even the fights with the few Communists you could find in Rochester were tame in comparison with what they had been in New York or Minneapolis.

In Rochester a great contrast existed between the activities of the citywide YPSL branch and the one at the University. Most of the members in the citywide branch were the children of Yiddish socialists who worked in the clothing factories and who were members of the Workmen's Circle, a fraternal lodge of socialists and social democrats. Not many Workmen's Circle members were in the Socialist party, perhaps because the party branch was dominated by such "American" types as the railroad man, who had very little connection with the world of European socialism from which the Yiddish-speaking group derived. Nevertheless these Europeans were proud that their children were in the YPSI and thus directly connected with the movement to which they now had only a looser tie. My status as the YPSL organizer made me an honored guest in their houses where the mommas fed me, the poppas gave me a "glass schnapps" before we ate, and the younger daughters flirted with me.

A more serious atmosphere marked the University YPSL branch, made up of students from the two campuses, one for men and one for women, which at that time were quite widely separated. The students were more intellectual in their approach to politics and shared very little with the other YPSL branch other than a common interest in socialism. The University branch had been started by one of the students and was the only even semiradical activity at the University which seemed, like everything else in Rochester, to be dominated by the paternal spirit of the Eastman Kodak Company.

The primary activity of the University branch was to hold forums at which visiting socialists would speak, followed usually by a dull discussion. Occasionally I succeeded in getting the two branches to conduct some form of joint activity, but generally the student group remained physically and psychologically close to the campus. Perhaps another reason for the separation was the age gap between the two groups. The city branch had in it a fairly large group of high school kids. For them, being in the YPSL was equivalent to my having gone to Sunday School, and they stayed in more as an accommodation to their parents than because of any genuine interest in socialism. They were socialists in the same way that other kids might have been Democrats or Republicans: because that was what their parents were.

It was in Rochester that I first encountered one of the tragic types of the thirties: the well-off man or, in this case, woman who came from an American Protestant background and who became deeply involved in the Communist movement. At first these people could be found on the periphery of some organization set up or taken over by the Communists; from that their commitment grew so intense that finally they could not leave the party without doing the most painful damage to their psyches.

In some ways the girl I knew in Rochester was an archtypical model of the period. I'll call her Ann; her name really doesn't matter, for with a few minor changes in personality she could have been one of many people. She came from an upper-class family with a history of involvement in American politics. I don't remember, if I ever knew originally, why she had come to Rochester, but when I met her she was just hovering on the edge of the radical movement, brought there from her debutante background by a genuine concern for society. Some friend of hers introduced her to me, and we moved very quickly into a relationship complicated at a number of levels.

My first interest in her was focused on her name, on who she was. I wanted very much to recruit her into the YPSL and along with that into the Trotskyist movement, for we *were* interested in people for their names, despite all our protestations to the contrary. In some cases we put up with stupidity, vanity, and a variety of other ugly personal qualities in order to recruit and then keep someone with an authentic American name, especially someone like Ann, whose family name was well known.

I suspect that the desire to have such Americans identified with our movement because of their political value was reinforced by some snobbishness. Having someone rich, famous, or with a rich and famous family background in the organization gave us some status, proved to us that what we were doing wasn't only important to people like ourselves, with undistinguished identities, but had meaning to others, who shared our commitment.

In the case of Ann, another element was at work: recruiting her became associated in my mind with an attempt to wipe out what had happened to me in Minneapolis, to redeem myself from my dismal failures, which I still worried about as a subject for continual discussion among my comrades. Indeed, it was a coup for me to have gotten Ann even interested enough to accompany me to YPSL meetings, where I could put her on display for all to see.

What C. Wright Mills once described as "penis politics" was operating with Ann, too. Although she wasn't beautiful, she was an extremely attractive and striking girl, with a husky voice and a remarkably assured, almost imperious, manner. And, equally important, she was very sophisticated. In the puritanical atmosphere of the YPSL she was, for me, a connection with my fantasy of myself, proving me to be someone like her. All these combined elements gave a kind of charged quality to my relationship with Ann, with a good deal more operating below the surface than showed above it.

Partly, too, I think I liked Ann for her willingness to do things that shocked everyone else. Once she invited me to be her escort to a formal college dance and was unabashed when I arrived to pick her up wearing a proper dinner jacket I had rented but sporting a red tie. We sat drinking in her apartment for a few hours until she decided she wouldn't wear an evening dress to the dance but would instead go in a beautiful and sheer nightgown. And she did, too, wearing only panties and no brassière. We were a sensation at the dance, I must say, since by the time we got there both of us were very drunk and Ann insisted on dropping deep curtsies to all the faculty members and their wives, dipping her shoulders low to the floor so that none of them could avoid seeing her near nudity under the nightgown.

I don't know what might have happened to Ann or to me if I had remained as the YPSL organizer in upstate New York and had succeeded in my efforts to recruit her for the socialist and then the Trotskyist movement. But I didn't stay, and she moved on from Rochester to Europe. A year later I heard through the grapevine that she had fallen in love with a French Stalinist painter and that she was living with him in Paris, a convert to Stalinism. Later I heard that she was back in the United States and had become very active and very prominent in the numerous Communist front groups that sprang up after the Soviet Union was attacked by Germany. At that time she was married to an official in the Roosevelt administration. And I finally saw her again when, on a trip to Washington in the early forties, I went to a meeting at which she spoke.

At the meeting I listened with growing horror as she talked.

She sounded no different than any other Communist hack, giving out the current line. After her speech was over, I went to the platform. Her first reaction on seeing me was to lean forward as if for a kiss, but then she quickly caught herself and withdrew. I assumed she suddenly remembered what I was and was seeing me as a Trotskyist rather than as a person. She nevertheless invited me to a formal dinner party that night at her apartment, where she and her husband were going to entertain some high officials in the New Deal together with some important Russian visitors. I declined with thanks and left, marveling at how the war and the identification of American Communists with the Russians had given the Stalinists such remarkable access to and status with some fairly important figures in Washington political circles.

After the war was over and I had been discharged from the army and was back in active political life, I kept finding traces of Ann. She had divorced her husband, who a few years later was accused of having been a member of a Communist group within the New Deal administration. Then she married again, this time someone much like herself—a man named Charles, from the same kind of family background as hers, a man who also had been attracted to the Communists during the thirties. During the war he had served with great bravery in espionage agencies. Immediately after the war, Charles went to work for one of the largest Communist front groups. It was during this period that I first knew him and fought bitterly against him inside an organization to which we both belonged. After he married Ann, I saw both of them only once, on a street corner in New York City. When I spotted them and called out, they rushed across the street and almost ran in the opposite direction from me.

Later, after Stalin's death and the awful revelations that followed it, I heard that Charles had broken with the party, but only a few months later he died. Since then I have never heard a single word about Ann, who dropped completely out of sight. Sometimes I wonder what has happened to her, whether her experiences in the Communist movement embittered her, as they did so many others. Or perhaps she looks back nostalgically on those exciting days in Paris, Washington, and New York when being a Communist was so much a part of being either in the political mainstream or in a swift current that flowed into the mainstream; when one knew with certainty who were the friends and who the enemies.

At the time I was trying to recruit Ann in Rochester I was also traveling to Syracuse to set up a branch of the YPSL at the University there. It was in Syracuse that I met Teddy Bardacke, the younger brother of a friend, Greg Bardacke, whom I knew in the radical movement in New York. Greg, who was more than six feet tall and very handsome, was in a left-wing group of the Socialist party.

When Greg heard that I was going to Syracuse to start a YPSL branch, he told me to see his brother, who was a graduate student at the University, and to tell him that I was to stay with him. And so I went to Teddy's apartment near the University and rang the bell. The door opened and there stood Teddy.

"Who are you?" he asked. When I told him I was a friend of Greg's, he reached down, picked me up, and hugged me. Teddy was delighted when I explained I had come to Syracuse for the YPSL and that I hoped he could put me up for a while. We went into the apartment, where he lived with two or three other students. One of them, Teddy's closest friend, whose nickname was Eemy, was going to medical school; another was a physics major, and the third was in the social sciences. It was clear that Teddy and Eemy were the leaders and carried the others along with them into the escapades that gave the apartment a wild, joyful quality.

Life with Teddy was out in the open, exposed either in joy or misery, but exposed all the time. When Teddy was happy, the happiness burst out of him in shouts of glee, in boisterous buffeting, in huge strides across the room to hug you, in mock boxing matches (Teddy had been on the boxing team at Syracuse, where boxing was taken as seriously as chess at Harris). When he was miserable, he cried openly, he shrank up into himself, his peanut face completely woebegone, unhappiness surrounding him with a palpable aura.

Just as Walter Kahn had opened one kind of door for me, Teddy opened another. He came into my life when I was ready to find out that I didn't have to be ashamed of my needs nor suppress them. Teddy's view of the world assumed that you grabbed at life's ass as it went by and gave it a damn good feel, enjoying every instant of its wiggling response. It was okay, I discovered, to make love even to girls who weren't in the movement, as I'd done; it was okay, as Teddy had done, to screw the professor's wife if that was what she wanted; it was okay to laugh at the solemnity of the radicals, to have your girl write your term paper, to put a phony "SAFE" sticker on the broken-down jalopy we all drove that had no brakes and no horn, okay to get free hospital care by lying to the admissions office about how much money you had, to ignore the "Visiting Hours from 2 to 3 Only" sign when you got in the hospital, to talk about sex openly and freely, to be openly Jewish or Negro or whatever else you happened to be, and to use, freely, language that was considered obscene or profane by most of society.

Girls and sex were very important parts of life in that Syracuse apartment. And after I had been there only a few weeks, spending most of my time making YPSL contacts, Teddy and Eemy were so worried because I didn't seem to have a girl that they fixed me up with a date.

The girl was a friend of theirs, a nice jolly girl who, they assured me in advance, had the biggest boobies of any girl on the campus and loved fucking. Just to make sure that everything would work out all right, the boys cooked dinner in advance for us, so that she and I could eat in the apartment and then retire to the living room where we would neck for a while before going to bed. The only trouble with the evening was that, as it worked out, Teddy and Eemy insisted on staying in the apartment after they cooked dinner. As a result, after Rachel and I had finished eating and adjourned to the living room, one of them would peer into the room about every fifteen minutes to check on my progress. Fortunately Rachel had a sense of humor and quickly joined the game, making all the proper noises as we jiggled together on the couch. As it turned out later, the boys were right about her, both in their description of her physically and of her taste for lovemaking.

It was hard to be serious in Syracuse, even about such a serious business as building a YPSL branch on the campus. Teddy was perfectly willing to help me in that task, although he was being wooed at the time by the local organizer for the Young Communist League. But being helped by Teddy was no great advantage, as the YCL organizer discovered, too, when he asked Teddy to let him go through all my papers some day while I was out of the apartment. Teddy agreed readily and then could hardly wait for me to come back so that we could put together a phony set of papers for the YCLer to be examining when I would burst into the room to catch him in the act.

That's just what we did, too. And after the initial confrontation the YCLer and I sprang apart to opposite corners of the room, then advanced toward each other warily while Teddy and Eemy sat laughing uproariously, egging us on, hoping we would end up in a fight. But all we did was fight verbally as I threw a quotation from Lenin's April Theses at him and he counterpunched with a charge from the Moscow trials. I retaliated with a heavy blow from Marx and he came back at me with a phrase from Stalin. But then I started making up quotations to prove the Trotskyist case and he grew frantic, hopping around from one foot to the other, while Teddy rolled on the floor, laughing.

Only once did politics come between Teddy and me, and then it was because of a girl. Teddy had been dating a Communist girl from New York who was so rich she could afford to come up to Syracuse for week ends whenever Teddy wanted her. Her name was Sarah, and even though she was rich, she wore no make-up and dressed in the ugly radical style of the period, including heavy lisle stockings as a boycott of Japan because of that country's attack upon China. When Sarah spent the week end with Teddy, none of the rest of us got any sleep; whenever she had an orgasm, which seemed to be a continuous process starting from the moment she took off her clothes, she shrieked and screamed so loudly that the whole apartment reverberated. All of us in the living room could accurately chart the minute-by-minute progress of the lovemaking by Sarah's noises. Even if Teddy hadn't told us so in some detail, it was very obvious to all of us—and, indeed, to the whole neighborhood—that Sarah either liked or hated fucking very, very much.

But as much as she liked it and liked doing it with Teddy, she couldn't stand me or the notion that I, the Trotskyist enemy, was living with her week-end lover. She consequently put the screws to him, demanding as the price of her continued trips that I leave. Reluctantly Teddy came to me and explained the situation, assuring me that he wasn't going to throw me out completely but would make arrangements for me to get another room in the same house. But what he neglected to tell me was that in exchange for this room, which was in the cellar, I was expected to stoke the old wheezy furnace three or four times a day and a couple of times at night.

This arrangement didn't last very long because I started making Teddy do the stoking while I was at meetings and because he began feeling ashamed of himself. Finally he told Sarah that he wouldn't keep me out of the apartment any longer, and true to her word, she took off, leaving him minus his crazy bed companion. I moved back in, and the Sarah episode finally ended when one night while Teddy was moping about his loss, Eemy and I went into the next room and started acting out, complete with noises, the lovemaking of Sarah and Teddy, with me playing Sarah's role and Eemy pretending to be Teddy. At the very peak of the act, while I was loudly screaming out one of Sarah's climaxes, Teddy burst into the room and jumped on both of us, pummeling us unmercifully, banging our heads against the wall while the two of us laughed so hard we couldn't defend ourselves against his fury. Very rarely did we ever talk about Sarah again, perhaps also because by this time Teddy had met a new girl, Frany, and the two of them were spending all their free time together, in and out of bed.

Every once in a while the subject of Jews came up in our conversation but not very often, though all of us were Jewish. Because one of the boys came from a Yiddish-speaking home I learned some more of those felicitous Yiddish phrases which tell everything except in translation, where they say nothing. But even if we were all Jewish and our conversations were always filled with Yiddish phrases, the matter of being Jewish wasn't very prominent in our minds. It never occurred to any of us, for example, that Teddy and Frany shouldn't get married just because Frany wasn't Jewish. In some vague sort of way we just assumed that such a question was of little if any significance.

The hectic but happy life in Syracuse came to an end when my mother called me from New York to tell me that my father was very sick, perhaps even dying. She pleaded with me to come home to help him in his work. He was a salesman again, selling wicker bathroom hampers and toilet seats covered with plastic to retail stores. Reluctantly I left Rochester and Syracuse and once again set off for New York, still a revolutionist, but this time in a far less troubled mood than when I had returned from Minneapolis.

CHAPTER FIVE

S UBSTITUTING for my father as a salesman of toilet seats was a far more difficult task for me, I soon discovered, than trying to build a revolutionary organization. And going back to New York again turned out to be almost as disastrous an experience as it had been the first time. My father had become very ill, too sick even to call on hardware and variety stores. The company—or "firm," as it was always called—with which he was associated had its plant in Long Island City. He was told that I might take over his accounts while he was ill even though I had no experience and was much younger than any of the firm's other salesmen. In my father's mind the arrangement was to be a temporary one, since he was convinced he would soon be well and back at work. Perhaps, too, he also hoped that I might like the work so much that I would want to keep on and so fulfill his dream that some day we would all be in business together.

But I hated every moment, every hour, every day of the business life, and instead of trying to understand some of my father's problems, how painful it must have been for him to be dependent on me, I showed my resentment openly, and our relationship grew even worse than it had been before. Partly I hated the role in which I had now been cast, hated walking into hardware stores out in Brooklyn or Queens, hated waiting for the owner to finish helping a customer before he turned to see what I was selling, hated having to listen to stupid jokes, hated the interminable discussions about which toilet-seat models sold best, hated having to sell myself in order to sell the hampers, and above all hated being dependent upon these people I so despised.

It really didn't matter what business my father was in—toilet seats or diamonds—nor what position I held with the "firm," for I felt a basic general resentment at having to give up doing the all-important work of revolutionary politics for the unimportant work of making money. It seemed so clear to me, so obvious, that the world was coming apart and that a war was inevitable that I grew impatient with anyone unwilling to view the future as we radicals did in terms of a catastrophe which demanded every effort if it was to be averted.

And so once again, during the spring and early summer of 1938, I led a dual life. I was living at home, and in the mornings I would go into my father's room to discuss with him which of his customers I should see that day. He had long lists of all the stores in the city which were in his sales territory, and we would go over the names while he instructed me on what to say and what kind of merchandise to show each store owner. Then we would discuss how many new accounts I might be able to open after I had finished calling on the old ones. All of this took about an hour while I grew increasingly impatient until I could leave the house to walk to the garage where my father kept his car and start driving on his rounds.

All day long I went from store to store, trying to persuade dubious hardware men of the merits of the sample hampers and toilet seats that I took into the stores with me. Some of the owners were friends or old customers of my father, and I got orders from them far more easily than from those who didn't know him. After having made a sale, I would write up the orders, leave a copy for the customer, and trundle the samples outside to the car. If after a few hours I hadn't made any sales or only small ones, I'd get so discouraged that I'd spend the rest of the day in some neighborhood movie before driving back home.

Then another session with my father would begin as I showed him the order book and tried to explain the reasons for my failures at not having sold more merchandise.

"You're lazy!" he would shout at me. "You don't give a damn about my business! You can shout on street corners but you can't talk in a store. You act as if you're ashamed of being a salesman, as if being a salesman was something wrong!"

And, guiltily, I would shout back until my mother would rush in and try to calm down my father while I got out of the room and the apartment as quickly as I could, back to my real life in the movement.

By this time I had become an extremely effective soapboxer and spent at least two or three evenings a week speaking at street corners all over the city. On the other nights I went to meetings—Socialist party meetings, YPSL meetings, and meetings of another radical group I had joined secretly, the League for a Revolutiontary Workers Party, commonly shortened to the LRWP. The group was also called the Fieldites, after its founder, B. J. Field, who lived with his wife, Esther, in a Lower East Side apartment whose walls were lined with more books and records than I had ever seen before in a private home.

The Fieldites had been one of the first splinter groups in the Trotskyist movement. The original dispute that had caused the split was never clear to me, but by the time I joined it the organization had built up a whole body of complicated political positions separating it from both the official Trotskyists and any of the other splinter groups.

My initial contact with the Field group came through Jerry, who had joined the LRWP after leaving Minneapolis. I have no notion any longer about what impelled me to become a member, but it was decided that my membership should be kept secret so I could work on behalf of the Fieldites inside the larger Trotskyist group, which in turn was still inside the Socialist party trying to take it over. My jumbled state of political affiliations was not unique, for others inside the official Trotskyist organization also secretly belonged to splinter groups. Such things considered, it's hardly any wonder that confusion was the lot of the government agents who operated as spies inside these groups under the mistaken impression that they represented some kind of threat to the body politic. (I once had an opportunity to scan a report filed by such an agent about an organization to which I belonged, and I have never read such looney nonsense in my life. The only relation between the report on the organization and the reality of its operations was that the name of the group was spelled correctly. Otherwise the report was absolute fantasy, a magnificent example of the storyteller's art.)

The LRWP was very small, numbering no more than fifteen or twenty in New York and an equal number in its Canadian section headquartered in Toronto. It nevertheless published half a dozen pamphlets every year and a badly printed newspaper every two or three months and used up reams of mimeograph paper every week for documents that explained in precise detail the LRWP position on every political or economic question of major significance. No radical or revolutionary organization was considered or considered itself to be "serious" unless it had a "press." It was through the "press"—which may have been only a broken-down, hand-cranked mimeograph machine—that the group's positions were put forth and other organizations attacked for their failures in Marxist analysis.

"Comrade, have you read the LRWP's attack on the theory of the Soviet Union being a degenerated workers' state?" might have been the opening remark in a conversation among a group of radicals meeting either socially or at a meeting. This gambit would then be followed by a heated argument which, like the initial stages of a chess game, followed a fixed pattern that could be reasonably anticipated.

And whenever one of the inevitable faction fights broke out inside the loose constellation of Trotskyist organizations, all the other groups followed the struggle. The group members would buttonhole each other whenever and wherever they met, pulling sheaves of mimeographed papers from their pockets, saying, "Comrade, have you read our faction's position on the role to be played by the revolutionary cadre in the development of a labor party in America?"

Then a furious discussion would start as the protagonists locked in a bitter ideological argument from which familiar phrases and whole sentences would momentarily rise in the air, only to fall unheard and dead onto the dirty floor of the headquarters, for if these discussions had one thing in common, it was that nobody listened to anyone else's position.

In such political fights the tiny LRWP had one big advantage: our pamphlets were laboriously printed by a few members who had learned linotyping and printing as part of their training for work in the movement.

The LRWP had a curious collection of members. In addition to Field, who earned his living as a consulting economist to Wall Street brokerage firms, there were three or four graduate students from Columbia plus a motley crew of other exotic types. An electrician who worked for Consolidated Edison was the only real worker in the group. The Canadian section was headed by a brilliant young man who had started his career as a concert violinist only to switch to politics. He was an incredible linguist, the first person I ever met who could learn difficult languages in only a few months. Often I used to sit in open-mouthed wonder listening to him carry on conversations in three or four languages simultaneously. The Canadian group also included a fur merchant from Montreal and three or four members who came from St. Agathe, a Jewish suburb of Montreal.

All of us, together with the other radical groups, shared a sense of impending disaster. We could not escape a feeling of catastrophe. The civil war in Spain was dragging on through a series of interminable battles which the fascists were winning, while inside the loyalist forces the Communists were gaining more and more control. At the headquarters somber comrades told each other new stories of the murders of European socialists, anarchists, and Trotskyists by Communist agents in Spain. George Orwell's critical analyses of the war were appearing in the non-Communist left press, corroborating all our dismal beliefs about the war. In Germany, Hitler was smashing every sign of possible opposition with armed gangs of storm troopers. The depression still dragged on in the United States, generating the feeling among us that none of us would ever find jobs.

But at home, among my parents and their friends, this grim world had no reality except as Hitler's rise to power brought German Jewish refugees to America. Hardly a week went by without some member of the family getting another letter from Germany asking for help to get out, begging for the magical affidavit required by the United States government as the first step for immigration. Such an affidavit obligated an American citizen to accept financial responsibility for the refugee. And after a few years the letters came so often that an almost routine kind of family discussion would begin immediately after the request arrived. Primary responsibility for signing the affidavit was assigned whenever possible to those members of the family with the most direct blood links to the would-be immigrants: parents, children, or brothers and sisters. After that a diminishing chain of responsibility was set up, reaching down to third or fourth cousins. Long painful arguments took place as the phone rang with the word of a new relative who wanted to get out and the family tried to decide who would sign the affidavits. As the number of refugees grew, the decisions about who was to give the affidavit became more difficult and angry, for soon all the members of the family who were willing to do so found themselves accepting responsibility for bringing over more and more distant relatives. And a few rich relatives in our family refused to help anyone, in spite of being wealthy enough in some cases to bring out whole families. The curses heaped upon their heads should have been enough to make them wither and die, but somehow they seemed to survive and even grow richer. Indeed, the issue of the affidavits sometimes split families and old relationships ended as the bitter quarrels broke out over who was to sign the papers.

But to my absolute fury, my parents and their immediate circle seemed incapable of making any connection between what was happening to the Jews in Europe and the larger world of politics. It was as if they believed Hitler's existence to be just a temporary bad dream which would go away when the night was over. When they sat in each other's living rooms, talking about what was happening, they kept reassuring each other that German anti-Semitism was only a passing phase, one that would soon disappear. "After all, the family has lived in Germany for many, many years," someone would say, "and they were always good Germans. None of them were in politics, they always minded their own business and they fought in World War I. Everybody knows that the German Jews were good Germans, so it's impossible for this Hitler to last. Something will happen to him."

But nothing did, and even after the refugees arrived in New York, they too seemed unable to make the connection between what had happened to them and politics. They were only able to talk about how they suffered from the loss of their *Geschäft,* their business. As I sat listening to them complaining about their fate in the living rooms of the apartments on the Upper West Side of New York, which had become a refugee enclave, I heard them sometimes direct their anger against the Socialist and Communist parties, as if they had been responsible for Hitler's rise to power. Then it would take all of my mother's frantic warning looks to keep me quiet, to prevent me from bursting out in rage at them for being what they were—stolid, middle-class, nonpolitical, and fearful German Jews who had convinced themselves that in their prosperous Germany nothing bad could ever happen to them.

Such reactions to Hitler were far more characteristic of the middle-class Jews than they were of either the Jewish working class, with its union and radical orientation, or the Jewish upper class, with its more intellectual view of the world. But my family contained no workers of any kind, not a single plumber, electrician, tailor, or garment worker, and even those few members of it who plied a trade, like one uncle by marriage who was a butcher, were entrepreneurial proprietors, not employees. Their values were middle-class ones, and their view of the world was controlled by those values plus a slightly uneasy identification of themselves as somehow being Jewish.

The very reverse operated for me. Hitler's treatment of the Jews was fairly low on the list of political reasons I had for hating the Nazis. To me, it was more important that he had smashed the Social-Democrats and the trade unions, as well as the Communists. In general, the question of what was happening to Jews as such did not have much interest for me. Not even the fierce battles between Jews and Arabs in Palestine during 1938 and 1939 had any greater significance to me because Jews were involved. The articles written about the Arab-Jewish conflict in the radical press tended to view the struggle as one between rival imperialist groups, usually concluding with a stirring call for both the Jewish and Arab workers to join hands in a common fight against British imperialism and its lackeys among both the Arab and Jewish bourgeoisie.

Hitler's treatment of the Jews in Germany also had little or no effect upon my conception of myself as being Jewish. It didn't cause me to identify myself any differently than I had earlier with being Jewish, it didn't stimulate me to any greater interest in Jewish matters, and I didn't take any more sympathetic a view about Zionism than before. Perhaps to have become in any way more Jewish would have been too threatening to the view I had of myself as the non-Jewish Jew. And despite the savage brutality of the Nazis, many Jewish radicals I knew believed the Nazi persecution of the Jews to be in no significant way different from what was happening to Socialists, Communists, trade-union leaders, and anyone else who opposed Hitler.

Most Jewish radicals were caught in a terrible dilemma in our view of how the Nazis should be smashed: as Marxists, we were convinced that German fascism was only another, although much more brutal, form of German capitalism. Therefore only the revolutionary working class could defeat the fascists, and any fight waged against the Germans by another capitalist country was only another form of imperialist conflict. Thus we assumed that the war we were predicting in Europe would be an imperialist one, which we had to oppose. Therefore we put out of our minds the particular horror to which the German Jews were being subjected, trying not to let the fact that we too were Jews influence our judgment about what we believed to be the only way Nazism could be defeated.

But during the spring of 1938 it was difficult enough for me to merely survive in the day-to-day schizophrenic existence of mornings and afternoons spent selling hampers and toilet seats and evenings devoted almost exclusively to speeches, secret meetings with the LRWP leaders, open meetings of the Socialist party and YPSL branches, and secret meetings of the Trotskyist caucus inside the Socialist party. There was little time to worry about being Jewish. My father was also growing more and more ill, until he had to be hospitalized.

By then the daily arguments between us had stopped, for he was no longer capable of doing more than suck in each individual breath as if it were going to be his last. My mother, my brother, and I began spending more and more time in the hospital, sitting at his bedside, while he grew gaunter and more incoherent every day. Soon it became obvious to Cliff and myself that he was going to die. Every morning when we got to the hospital, there seemed to be another tube stuck into him: first up his nose, taped back to his forehead; then to his arm, connected to a large bottle hung from a bedside stand; and finally two tubes snaked under the blanket, to drip a yellow-greenish fluid into containers set on the floor.

Suddenly one day, while my mother was out of the room for a moment, he reared up, let out a terrible gargle, and fell back on the bed. Cliff shouted for the nurse, but we both knew it was over and that he was dead. Seconds later the nurse and a doctor rushed into the room, and while she immediately stuck a needle into him, the doctor began massaging his heart. But in a few minutes they both stopped what they were doing, the nurse pulled a sheet over his body, and the doctor wrote on the chart, "Ceased," looking at his watch to note the exact time the "ceasing" had taken place.

Outside the room my mother was trying frantically to get back in. The doctor walked into the corridor to tell her that her husband was dead. She screamed and pushed into the room, where she fell on her knees next to the dead body, crying hysterically for her "Schatzie." Cliff and I stood by awkwardly, not knowing what to do and finally putting our arms around her, all three of us now crying together.

So the bitter quarrel between my father and myself ended. We had never had much to say to each other, for the gap that normally exists between parents and children, between two generations, had been widened even more for us by his having been born in Germany and we in the United States and by my commitment to a political theory about which he knew nothing and could not learn to understand. And when my father died, my mother started to die, too, for her life in the preceding years had been centered primarily on him and his needs.

It was understood that my life as a salesman was now ended. My father's business associates asked if I wanted to take over his sales territory but were relieved when I declined what was to me only an onerous and ugly burden. I was free to return again to being a full-time Bolshevik, only haunted now and then by the reproaches I saw in my mother's eyes as she would suddenly begin to cry bitterly over what she had lost. And though she never said it, I was always conscious that she believed I was in some measure responsible for my father' death, that the mean and nasty scenes between us had contributed to his dying so young. Perhaps she was right, too.

We buried my father with all the ugly ceremonies considered essential to a proper American middle-class funeral. It was my first direct experience with that unctuous breed of undertakers whose professional glib sympathy turns on and off in direct relationship to the size of the bill they can persuade the family to run up. In my father's case, the hypocrisy was worse than usual, for the funeral director was a member of the same fraternal group to which he had belonged. When Cliff and I resisted the undertaker's attempts to sell us an incredibly costly coffin, he started whining at us that "we weren't showing the proper respect for our father" and that he, as a friend of our father, "was ashamed of us." Then he tried to talk Mother into spending far more money than she could afford from what Dad had left her. But we prevailed; all through the ceremony in the funeral chapel in midtown Manhattan he glared at me and I glared back.

It took some weeks to straighten out all my father's affairs, and by then my mother was talking about moving from New

York to California, in the hope that a racking cough, from which she had suffered for many years, would disappear. My brother was to go with her, but I refused, insisting that I wanted to stay in New York. While she was making her slow preparations for this uprooting move, I returned to full-time radical politics.

The summer of 1938 was a time of feverish political activity in the movement. Every night I spoke at a different corner in the city. We didn't use soapboxes, of course, but roughly constructed stands or even occasionally the rumble seat of a Model A roadster that belonged to a comrade, Fred Goldwater, one of the few people earning enough to afford a car. Fred, a member of the well-known Goldwater clan in New York, had gone to private schools after his mother died when he was an infant, and lived with his father, a pharmacist. One of Fred's uncles was the New York Hospital Commissioner for whom the Welfare Island hospital is named; another uncle was the law partner of the Democratic boss of Manhattan, and an aunt was a well-known figure in social work and philanthropy. Fred was a very moody fellow, quick to flare up in anger and impatient with what he thought slowness or stupidity. He would grow particularly furious when anyone started to talk about the Jewish question and was more virulent in denouncing the Zionist movement than anyone I ever knew in the radical movement. (Only recently Fred and I talked about this period in our lives as we sat drinking coffee in the kitchen of his little house in Jerusalem, where he now lives with his Israeli wife and two children.)

Getting a street-corner meeting started was not just a matter of going up to any corner and putting up a stand, for the logistics were rather complicated. First the local branch holding the meeting decided on the neighborhood, depending upon what audience it was trying to reach that night. Meetings were never held on places like Fifth Avenue but were concentrated in either working-class or lower-middle-class sections. Then we had to take into consideration how much automobile traffic passed the corner and whether there might be subway noise over which the speakers might have to shout. We had to know how strong the Communists were in the neighborhood, for we were almost certain to be heckled by them and even knocked from the stand if they could get away with it. This meant that some comrades had to be assigned as guards. Sometimes it was possible for us to venture into areas where the Communists were strong by setting up a temporary alliance with another political group which was also an enemy of the Stalinists. In those cases, we either held a joint meeting or, if our political differences made that impossible, we took turns supplying guards for each other on alternate nights.

We had to worry also about being heckled or beaten up by the local fascists, primarily the Irish Catholic followers of Father Charles Coughlin, the Detroit priest who tried to create a semi-fascist movement in the United States until he was silenced by the Church hierarchy. Sometimes, too, if the meeting was held in the Yorkville area of Manhattan, we were confronted by members of the German-American Bund, the American supporters of the Nazis. When they showed up we knew there was going to be a battle.

But these fights never lasted for more than a few punches; before we could hold a meeting, we had to inform the local police precinct of our plans, and a policeman was always on the scene to break up any disorder and stop the meeting if the crowd got too unruly or the speeches went on late enough to disturb the people sleeping in the area.

To make sure the corner which we had picked was available, one or two of the comrades were assigned to go there in the late afternoon or early evening and either put up a stand or block off the corner. There wasn't as much automobile traffic then as now in New York, and the streets weren't as jammed with cars looking for a parking place, so that it was almost always possible to stake out the corner we wanted in advance. As it grew dark the comrades assigned to the meeting as speakers, guards, or literature sellers started arriving at the corner, standing around the stand talking, in a little knot about the latest news from Spain or gossiping about some of the other comrades.

The first speaker who climbed up on the platform always acted as the chairman for the night and took five or ten minutes to announce the opening of the meeting, the organization's name, and its socialist principles. While that was going on, the rest of the comrades all stood in a semicircle in front of the platform, like shills at a shooting gallery, trying to attract customers. The next speaker, usually a novice, or perhaps a girl whose voice wasn't too strong, would follow the chairman. By then a crowd would slowly begin to gather, until after about twenty minutes or half an hour the first comrade would finish talking and the chairman would climb back up again to introduce the second speaker. The same procedure was followed, except that this speaker was usually better than the first and better able to hold the crowd. By this time, if the meeting was at all successful, a fairly good-sized number of listeners had collected, perhaps drawn by the shouts of the hecklers or swollen by a delegation from one of the opposing groups, waiting for an opportunity to break up the meeting. Very often people stopped to listen for a while, then drifted away either to be replaced by new ones or sometimes to come back later after having taken a walk, had a soda, or stopped at a delicatessen for a corned-beef sandwich.

Finally the chairman would introduce the main speaker, who would then harangue the crowd, which sometimes grew to a few hundred people, for anywhere from forty minutes to an hour. Between speeches the comrades selling literature and newspapers would move through the audience, keeping a wary eye on the hecklers and noting who either brought something or showed more than a passing interest in the speaker's utterances. An attempt was made to engage these listeners in conversation because the real pay-off for these meetings was in the number of new contacts for membership that could be made.

After the final speech, if the meeting hadn't been broken up by a fight or dispersed by the police officer, the chairman would answer questions about the organization's position. Then the meeting would end, usually with all the comrades adjourning to a cafeteria to discuss the successes and failures of the night.

Some attempt was made by the New York headquarters to coordinate all the street-corner meetings and to assign speakers to those branches which didn't have enough good ones of their own or wanted a special orator. As soon as it was discovered that I had a deep resonant voice and a good command over the crowd from the platform, I began getting assignments to speak all over the city. Night after night I traveled all over Brooklyn, Manhattan, or the Bronx. I grew so skillful at being the main speaker that soon I could go on for a long time without even stopping for a sip of water, always maintaining control of the crowd, even when the heckling grew very severe. One night in August I was assigned to speak at a meeting in the Bronx, on a corner where a few neighborhoods merged, including one section where the Coughlin movement had a lot of strength. While I was making my speech, I spotted a pretty redheaded girl in the crowd looking up at me. I looked her over during the speech, wondering if I could make a date with her.

The meeting finally ended, and when I jumped off the platform the girl was still there, even more attractive than she'd looked from the platform. She'd come to the corner with another girl who looked somewhat like her, whom I discovered to be her sister. But I got no place with the redhead, who refused either to give me her name or to tell me more about herself than that she already knew what the YPSLers were and had some contact with them at City College evening session, which she was attending. In a few minutes she left, and, disappointed, I turned to help the comrades dismantle the platform before we walked to a cafeteria.

On the same night of the following week I was back at the same corner. By the time I got up on the platform, the crowd was big, unruly, and beginning to move restlessly. I waited for a few moments and then began speaking, starting in low but very quickly projecting my voice up to a bellow. Taking off from the fact that my birthday fell in August, I began by shouting, "I've made it to twenty, but I don't know whether I'll live to see my twenty-first birthday, because by this time next year it is almost certain that the world will be at war and that the American government will have dragged us into that imperialist war!"

It was just then that, simultaneously, a woman in the crowd suddenly burst out singing "The Star-Spangled Banner" in a loud, quavery voice and some shouting Coughlinite toughs began moving up to the front of the platform while the YPSLers guarding the platform braced themselves tensely for an attack. I stopped talking for a moment to look around for the cop who had been at the fringe of the crowd a moment before, hoping he would see what was going on and move in to break up what looked as if it were going to be one hell of a fight. I couldn't spot the cop, but as I launched once again into a fierce attack on the American warmongers, I heard his voice, shouting, "All right, break it up, break it up!" Just then, while everything was moving —the crowd, the toughs, the "Star-Spangled Banner" lady, the cop, the YPSLers, my voice, me—I noticed the redheaded girl in the crowd angrily shouting at a heckler to keep quiet. I started talking with her the instant the meeting was over, which wasn't long afterward, since the audience got so unruly the cop insisted that we finish up.

This time the girl told me that her name was Ruth Rosenfield and introduced me to a young man whose arm she was holding. I suggested that, since it was my birthday, we should celebrate it with a drink. While we were walking to a bar, I managed somehow to convey a message to Ruth that she should get rid of the boy friend, which she did in a suprisingly easy fashion after he had bought the drinks.

I walked her home that night while she told me about herself and her family. The girl who had come to the meeting the week before was her twin sister. She had an older brother, who worked in the wholesale fruit market, and her mother, a widow for many years, had supported herself and the three children by operating a little dress shop in her Bronx apartment. Ruth had worked, too, since she graduated from high school and went to CCNY, where she was president of the Anti-War Club, an organization dominated by the YPSLers. I found her exciting on every count—she was bright, laughed at my jokes, had the kind of legs I liked, looked as if she had a great figure under her clothes, seemed sexually uninhibited, and, as an extra added bonus, had the right kind of politics. Before I left her that night, we made a date for the following Saturday. On that date, after we ate on Fourteenth Street, we went back to my mother's empty apartment, where all the first impressions I'd had about her were verified. A week or so later we decided to get married.

Naturally I wasn't working and had no prospects for a job, and since Ruth was about to quit the job she had, getting married wasn't going to be easy. Ruth and I knew that her mother and mine would both oppose our marriage and for the same reasons—that no one living as I was had the right to be married. And finally, I also had to discuss the marriage with my comrades in the LRWP, for by this time I was preparing to quit the Socialist party and act as an open organizer for the Field group. And since there were no funds in the organization to pay me, we planned to go on relief, as a number of other members had already done. But when, at Field's house one night, I told the comrades about my plans to marry, their immediate reaction was, "You don't have to get married to get on relief. You can just live together and do it. We've got plenty of envelopes you can use to prove you've been a resident."

The postmarked envelopes to which the comrades referred were very precious, for they were used over and over to help get comrades and friends on the relief rolls. The postmarks on them were used to establish the year's previous residence in New York City that was a requirement for drawing relief benefits. If a comrade or friend wanted to go on relief but couldn't meet the residence requirement, the name on the face of the envelope was erased with ink eradicator and the comrade's name written in. Then, after the envelope was used to satisfy the relief investigator that the person applying for relief had gotten mail in New York more than a year earlier, the envelope was returned to the LRWP's tiny shabby headquarters, to be carefully preserved for the next time it was needed.

But satisfying the legal requirement of residence wasn't the only obstacle faced by us revolutionists in our efforts to get a little subsidy from the capitalist world. Many of the people in the relief bureau were Communists, and they made sure that no Trotskyist or Trotskyist sympathizer ever drew the benefit if they could stop it. Fortunately for us, we too had a few people working in the relief bureaus, and either we were warned whom to watch out for or we tried to apply at offices where there were no Communists who might identify us.

By this time a fairly sizable body of lore had accumulated about how to beat the capitalist world and survive in the depression. We all knew how to jump the gas and electric meters, so that our utility bills were always very low, and we all knew that the jumps had to be taken off a few days before the meter reader's monthly visit, both because the jumps were illegal and because if no gas or electricity at all had been used, the meter reader would have been suspicious and perhaps come back unexpectedly.

We knew, too, all the tricks needed in the unemployment offices as well as the relief bureaus, for while we tried hard to get on relief, we tried just as hard to avoid having to take any of the very few badly paid jobs that might be around. Since you couldn't be forced to work at jobs other than the ones for which you had been trained, we always registered for unemployment in some obscure classification for which no opening would ever come up. This meant that we had to have letters from nonexistent companies for which we had done our nonexistent work; after we printed some company letterheads on the small press of the LRWP, we could write whatever letters were necessary to prove the previous employment histories, always making sure to point out that the company was no longer in existence. Fred Goldwater, who was working at some kind of engineering job in this period, was always a good name to sign to those phony letters.

Naturally we'd learned how to eat cheaply, and in the summertime, when we were out on the hot city streets, we were adept at making free lemonades at the Horn and Hardart Automats by taking iced-tea glasses, filling them with water, adding sugar, and then squeezing the lemons that were stuck on the rims. But the Automat wasn't a very good place to sit because smoking was prohibited. And of course we ate in all the cheap foreign restaurants—Kavkaz on Fourteenth Street, where good Russian food was served in an outside garden, the Dragon Inn in the Village, the Jewish restaurants on Second Avenue, where you could fill up on delicious onion rolls, rye bread, and challah.

None of us were very troubled by the lies we told or the illegal acts we carried out, whether it was jumping meters or using phony envelopes to get on relief, for all of us were convinced that we were in a war with the capitalist class; a war in which they had so many more weapons than we that we were only getting a little bit back of what was rightfully ours anyway. The only thing that bothered us was getting caught, as happened once to a comrade who was on relief but hadn't jumped his gas meter and so began to run up a pretty high bill. He finally figured out that the only way he could pay the bill was to bring the meter dials right around to where they'd been some months earlier, and to accomplish that purpose he began burning gas twenty-four hours a day. He read by gaslight, slept by gaslight, and made love by gaslight. Night and day all the burners on the stove were lit and the oven was on. The room was always incredibly hot from a couple of gas heaters that were never turned off. For months he managed to keep the gas company's meter reader out of the apartment until one day when the relief investigator came on a check-up visit and the meter reader sneaked into the apartment behind him. When the gas-company man shined his flashlight on the meter and checked the amounts consumed against the previous reading, he nearly fainted from shock. Hastily he ran from the apartment back to the nearby gas-company office and got a couple of supervisors to corroborate his readings. They entered the comrade's apartment just in time to find him stupidly trying to take the whole meter off the wall. It was then that he was arrested. I've forgotten how we got him off, but one of our sympathizers, who was a lawyer, pleaded for him and had him released from the charges. Then, in what we thought was a very spiteful gesture, the company cut off his gas completely.

Ruth and I, therefore, weren't deterred in our plans by either parental objections or the fact that we had neither jobs nor money. But before we could decide just when we were to be married, I got sent off by the LRWP to Louisville, Kentucky, to make contact with a small Trotskyist group that had indicated an interest in joining our organization. I asked Ruth if she'd like to see me off on the trip. When she agreed, I took her with me in the subway to the Holland Tunnel. There, on the street, while she stood amazed, I bade her good-bye and hitched a ride through the tunnel under the Hudson River into New Jersey. It took me four or five days to get to Louisville, riding freight trains and hitchhiking, because although I had a little money that Field had given me, it wasn't nearly enough for fare.

I never did accomplish my mission in Louisville, for I came down with influenza only a few days after my arrival. The Louisville comrades put me up in someone's furnished room and took turns nursing me until I was well enough to get out of bed. Then we wired Field for money to get me back to New York by bus, and when the money arrived, they saw me off. Unfortunately, I had been sent only enough money for the fare, and for the day and night the trip took, I ate practically nothing. When the bus finally arrived in New York, I fell out of it, literally into Ruth's arms as she stood there waiting for me.

It took me a couple of weeks to recover, and by then we had decided to be married on New Year's Day of 1939. A good deal of the earlier tension between my mother and myself dissipated itself during this period, for she had begun to make some adjustment to my plans. I even began trying to explain socialism to her, but with little real success. One day, though, we were able to talk fairly openly about sex in a discussion triggered by her finding a diaphragm in my jacket pocket.

The diaphragm, which I had forgotten was there, had been given me by a girl, a comrade, whom it didn't fit. In those days such birth-control devices were a good deal more expensive than they are today, and you just didn't throw away a perfectly good one merely because it was the wrong size. The girl had passed it on to me, thinking it might turn out to fit Ruth, and I had put it in my pocket, expecting to give it to Ruth so she could have it checked.

When my mother handed the little round case to me asking, "What is this?" I answered, "It's for birth control," and showed her the diaphragm inside. She had never seen anything like it before, since she knew of only one kind of birth-control device, a condom, used by the man. When she saw the diaphragm's diameter, her eyes widened in horror. She looked at me, absolutely aghast that she had produced a monster who needed such a wide sheath. Hastily I explained to her that the diaphragm wasn't used by the man but by the woman. Visibly relieved, she then wanted to know how it worked, and I told her all about the fitting process. Finally, though, the discussion broke down when she inquired why I was carrying it around with me if it was for Ruth's use and I started laughing at what sounded, even to me, to be an insane explanation of why the diaphragm was in my pocket. We never did finish my mother's sex education.

My mother found only one tiny ray of light in my forthcoming marriage: not only was Ruth Jewish, but she came from a family that on her father's side had come to the United States from Portugal, via Germany, two or three generations before. It was clear, too, that Mother liked Ruth and, unlike most mothers, felt that Ruth was too good for me. Over and over she tried to dissuade me from taking such a nice Jewish girl into the miserable, precarious existence I was living. But we were determined, and finally my mother reluctantly accompanied me to City Hall to sign the application for a wedding license. (It was something of a blow to me that, because I wasn't twenty-one, I couldn't be married without my mother's consent, even though I hadn't lived at home for five years and thought of myself as a mature revolutionist.)

Then we were faced with a crisis. Both my mother and Ruth's were determined that we should be married by a rabbi, while we were equally adamant that we weren't going to be. But after a few sessions of parental tears and crying, we finally gave in and agreed to have a Jewish wedding. Since Ruth's mother said she would make the arrangements, we left it all to her. The night before the wedding we went to a series of New Year's Eve parties, and both of us got very, very drunk and only went to bed after dawn.

Ruth was still slightly tipsy when we arrived at the address we had been given for the wedding, an apartment house near where Ruth's mother lived in the Bronx. The rabbi, who had been suggested to Ruth's mother by a friend of hers, lived in the basement, we discovered. When we arrived he was in the process of chasing out of the room a bunch of kids who attended a Hebrew School he taught there. He seemed very confused by our wedding party, which consisted of two tearful mothers; Ruth's brother, who had a wild temper and was so disgusted by the shabby surroundings that he kept shouting, "Let's get the hell out of here and go down to City Hall"; my brother, who was to act as best man but who had also gotten drunk the night before and came wandering down into the basement very confused; Ruth's sister, who was cursing the whole business in a continuous undertone; Fred Goldwater, who was going to drive us to a furnished room we had taken on West Seventieth Street; Ruth, who had the hiccups; and me, now amused by the whole breakdown of the apparatus.

Finally the rabbi stumbled through the ceremony after having made a false start and reading from some other ceremony for a few minutes first. I broke a glass underfoot in true orthodox fashion; he mumbled Hebrew words at us that none of us understood; Ruth and I got the giggles when in the middle of the Hebrew we suddenly heard our names and addresses given in English; and so we were married.

CHAPTER SIX

A FEW DAYS after our marriage we applied for relief. But the moment the investigator sent by the relief bureau walked into the room, I knew we were in for trouble—she was a Stalinist who recognized me. As I expected, our application was turned down on the grounds that both my mother and Ruth's were in a position to give us financial support.

After this rejection, we decided to leave New York, for it was obvious that life in the same city with our mothers was going to be so difficult as to make everybody miserable. We met with the Fields and other members of the LRWP executive committee, and it was decided that we should go to Chicago, where I was assigned to organize a branch of the organization. Chicago was selected because we had a few sympathizers there and because a tiny Trotskyist splinter group, headed by a woman, also had its headquarters there.

The woman, whom I had known in New York, had split from her brother after he had split, in turn, from the Ohlerites, a group he'd helped to found and of which I'd been a member when it split from the official Trotskyists. The Chicago group had three or four members there and two or three in New York; naturally enough, its national headquarters was in Chicago.

I hitchhiked to Chicago, and Ruth joined me a few days later, having driven with a salesman her mother knew and bringing with her our meager belongings. We found a cheap little apartment on the South Side, near the University, in a house where we shared the bathroom with a great many cockroaches and half a dozen cheerful Filipinos. The landlord was a bookie who liked us very much, even taking us occasionally to the gambling joints out in Cicero, where we watched him lose the money he made from the suckers who bet with him.

From the moment we arrived in Chicago we were painfully poor. I had no income from the organization and couldn't find a job, and the only job Ruth could get was a temporary one on a WPA project at a very small salary. We ate lots of cornmeal, given to us by friends who got it from the relief bureau, and smelts, tiny fishes that sold for nine cents a pound. Eggs were cheap then, too, and we ate a lot of them plus stews made from the cheapest cuts of lamb or beef, as well as spaghetti with meat balls made from the least expensive hamburger. Occasionally we'd supplement these meager meals with some delicacy that I stole from the A&P shelves.

We were so poor that we even used other people's discarded streetcar transfers to get around Chicago. Our entertainment was an occasional cheap movie or, far more frequently, playing Chinese checkers with two friends who were almost as poor as we. Together the four of us would scrape up fifty cents, which would buy two quarts of pretty good beer, and spend the evening drinking the beer and talking endlessly about politics.

It was politics all the time, especially since a war in Europe seemed to be almost certain. In a curious way we were almost a little glad that the dire prophecies we had made were about to be fulfilled. But we were also deeply distressed by the clear signs that the fascists were winning in Spain. The only occasions on which we didn't talk politics were when we went to visit Ruth's aunt who lived in Elgin, just outside of Chicago, or on a few Friday nights when we went to other relatives of hers who were pretty rich and lived in a fancy apartment on the North Side.

Both of us found this Friday night crew of relatives about as revolting a group as we'd ever encountered. The whole family life centered around the unmarried son, a man in his forties, who was a professional gambler. He was vulgar and grossly fat; everyone in the family called him "Sonny," deferring obsequiously to him as he sat at the head of the table noisily sucking in his food. Behind him stood a man who never opened his mouth but whom we assumed was dear "Sonny's" bodyguard. These weekly family dinners, traditionally held on Friday nights in Jewish families, were attended by Sonny's two unmarried sisters, his mother, a brother-in-law whom Sonny had set up in dental practice after he'd married another sister, the sister and their son, a spoiled kid of about nine or ten whom Sonny regularly took with him to nightclubs and gambling joints.

Only the food, which was very good and served in great quantities, enticed us to the apartment, but after a few visits not even that was enough to make us put up with conversation that never dealt with any subject except the amount of money Sonny was making. After we cut out the visits, Sonny's chauffeur would stop by our apartment occasionally, leaving us a shopping bag full of food.

Despite our poverty, we survived, discovering new things about each other. At last I even managed to get a job winding armatures with a company that bought old or broken electric generators and rebuilt them. I got fired, though, when I got into a row with a foreman. By this time six months had gone by, and I was also getting very discouraged about the possibilities of setting up the LRWP branch or of completing the merger with the other group.

None of our handful of Chicago sympathizers seemed inclined to take the final step and join the organization, despite the long hours I spent with each of them trying to persuade them to take their place in the revolutionary march toward socialism. My interminable negotiations with the other group were not bringing us any closer to merger than we had been when I first arrived in Chicago. Week after week we exchanged documents and held endless discussions to search for mutually agreeable political positions on such matters as whether the Soviet Union was a degenerated workers' state or a bureaucratic one, or whether Trotsky's theory of a permanent revolution applied in colonial Africa, or whether a revolutionary situation had excused France during 1934, and on theories of democratic centralism in party structure.

Ruth had gotten a better job at a furniture company through an employment agency whose ad had specified that the company —a Jewish one, incidentally—only hired single Christian girls. Ruth told the agency that her name was Field, that she was a single girl living with her mother, and that she was an Episcopalian. In exchange for the lies, she'd been hired and had been working there for a month or two. But we hadn't made all the payments on the fee the agency had charged Ruth for the job, nor did we worry about it.

Then, on a warm Sunday morning, I opened the door of our tiny two-room apartment in response to a knock. I had no clothes on and I didn't bother asking who was knocking because I assumed it was Nat, a comrade who had stopped to visit us on his way to California. I had gotten him a room for the night in the same house in which we lived and told him to come for breakfast with us when he got up in the morning.

But when I opened the door, it wasn't Nat. A strange woman stood there, clutching a Bible in her hand. Hastily I shut the door as she gasped.

"What do you want?" I asked then.

"Is Ruth Field there?" she answered.

"Just a minute," I said, rushing back into the bedroom where Ruth was still sleeping.

"Ruthie, Ruthie, wake up. I think the woman from the employment agency is here. She probably wants her damn money."

Ruth got up, went to the door and asked, "Who is it?"

"You'd better open the door, Miss Field," came the answer. "It's for your own good."

"I'm not going to open up unless I know who it is."

"Then I'll just wait out here until you do."

I pulled Ruth back into the bedroom and told her to go out the back door into the apartment of the next-door neighbor, a Filipino family with whom we'd gotten friendly. Then I quickly put on a pair of pants, shoes without socks, and a shirt and rushed down the back stairs to come around to the front entrance. I walked slowly up the steps to our apartment on the first floor, whistling loudly. On the landing the woman stood, still knocking on the door and telling Ruth Field to come out. Looking at her as if I'd never seen her before, I asked if there was anything I could do. She turned around and stared at me, amazed, certain that only a few minutes before she had seen just such a one as me standing naked inside the apartment.

"I'm looking for a Miss Ruth Field," she said finally.

"Nobody here by that name. I live here by myself. See?" I said, opening the apartment with my key and throwing the door wide so she could look inside at the now empty two rooms. Without a word she turned on her heel and ran down the stairs. I got Ruth and woke up Nat, and we sat laughing about the woman's seeming panic. But the three of us were also convinced that Ruth would be fired from her secretarial job the following day, as soon as the lady from the employment office could get on the phone and tell the owner of the furniture company that Ruth wasn't single and living with her mother, that her name wasn't Field, and that maybe she was Jewish after all.

Just as it didn't worry us to tell lies about our past places of residence in order to get on relief, we weren't disturbed by lying about religion in order to get a job. The existence of anti-Semitism in employment was just another example to us of why capitalism had to be overthrown and replaced by a socialist society in which such prejudice was impossible. Filing a complaint with an organization such as the Anti-Defamation League was outside the context of the radical movement, and no antidiscrimination laws or commissions existed then. We just lied, as Ruth had done, and hoped to get away with it. And in her case it was easier to lie because she didn't fit the stereotype of what a Jewish girl was supposed to look like.

But now that it seemed as if Ruth would lose her job because of the lady from the employment agency, we decided to leave Chicago and return to New York, especially since the tiny group I was negotiating with for a merger had just split again, this time because the two members in New York accused the three in Chicago of being bureaucratic. I wrote our comrades in New York, explaining what had happened, and I received permission to come back.

The week we left, the signing of the Nazi-Soviet mutual-aid pact was suddenly announced. Absolute chaos hit the whole radical movement. The Trotskyists and the socialists excitedly rushed around to contact every Communist and Communist sympathizer, pointing out that the sudden shift in the Russian position, plus the immediate approval given it by the American Communist party, was a complete verification of every attack that had been made upon the Soviet Union as the real betrayer of the workers. The capitalist press, too, leaped upon the pact with glee, and the newspapers were filled with stories of how the Communist party officials in New York at first refused to believe the news and then, when it had been verified, began lamely to justify the Russian position.

The Stalin-Hitler pact, as it soon became known, was the first real crisis of the Communists in America, and with it the party took a real blow. It lost a great many members overnight, espe-

cially those liberals who had been attracted to the Communists
by the party's noisy anti-Nazi protestations and by the aura of
heroic antifascism with which the party had managed to sur-
round itself. Overnight, too, Communist-front organizations had
to be converted from militant antifascism to much more neutral
positions. The large and very popular American League Against
War and Fascism changed its name to the American League for
Peace and Democracy; trade-union leaders like Harry Bridges
on the West Coast and Ben Gold of the furriers in New York
switched overnight from support of the Roosevelt administration to bitter denunciations of F. D. R. as a warmonger intent on
plunging the United States into a conflict in which American
workers had no interest.

But incredible as it seemed to the rest of the radical movement, the Communists were able to survive even the Nazi-Soviet
pact. They were able, even, to hold on to many of the Jews.
What they had left now were the really tough party people plus
those who were so involved psychically with the idea of being
Communists that they had to rationalize away all their doubts
about what had happened.

I knew a psychically involved Communist in Chicago. He was
a scientist, and we argued bitterly every time we met at the home
of his girl friend. Typically for that group, his idea of the Communist movement had been formed by what the party *professed*
to be during the People's Front period from 1935 to 1939—a
bulwark against fascism anywhere in the world, whose members
were dedicated to the fight against prejudice and for a decent
world. And to these people the Soviet Union, with its continuous
denunciation of the fascist countries plus the aid it had given to
the Spanish loyalists, appeared as one of the few bright hopeful
forces in an ugly and grim world.

It is no wonder, then, that prior to the Stalin-Hitler pact this
scientist found it so hard to understand my bitter tirades against
the Communists. By the time I met him, he was so involved in
the party that he never saw me as anything but a Trotskyist. He
could no longer admit to anyone, especially to himself, that the
party was wrong.

The tragedy of this scientist's life is that of the country as a
whole. America refused later to understand or to admit that the
Communist party had been attractive enough to make attachment to the Communist cause an understandable consequence of

any feelings that the society was sick, which it sure as hell was. This scientist and others like him were wrong because they did not subject their political beliefs to the same hard intellectual processes they used to test their scientific theories. Subsequently they suffered for having been Communists even though being a Communist to them meant being concerned with the good of society rather than just with their own narrow professions. But I am embarrassed to make judgments on them, for as I look back on my own political actions, I realized that my *not* being a Communist was a good deal more accidental than I like to admit and that I didn't study my set of political beliefs much more carefully than they did. I was just luckier in becoming an anti-Stalinist early in life rather than late.

Our return in defeat from Chicago to New York was the usual routinely dismal one for me, although it wasn't so grim for Ruth. We hitchhiked back together this time, with pretty good luck, too, for the trip only took two days and nights. Ruth's presence had helped considerably in getting rides for she stood out on the highway seemingly alone until a car stopped. Then I piled into the car before the surprised driver had any chance to object. But the little fun we had on the trip turned out to be the last of its kind for a long time to come, for when we got back to New York everything turned sour for us.

We were so broke that we had to move in with Ruth's mother for a month or so while both of us looked futilely for work. Finally Ruth found a job as a secretary again, and we took an apartment in the Village sharing it with Jerry, who was on relief, and with Fred Goldwater, who by this time had established a close relationship with Ruth's twin sister. We had no furniture except beds in the apartment, but unlike the place in Syracuse that I'd shared with Teddy, there wasn't much fun at 49 Jane Street. I had signed the lease for the apartment, and nominally it was ours, but in fact it wasn't. People were in and out of the apartment all the time, and Ruth was starting to object strenuously to the mess she thought everybody seemed to leave for her to clean up, as well as the lack of privacy.

Our lives were also complicated by the fact that the LRWP was beginning to come apart. We had become a very incestuous group, whose personal and political lives were so intertwined that sharp differences over political questions led very often to breaks or bad strains in personal relationships. Some of us were growing dissatisfied with Field's leadership, and when signs of restlessness appeared during the ever more sparsely attended weekly meetings we held in our dingy headquarters, we had to face not only Field's disagreement but his wife's personal attacks. Soon people who had been old friends stopped seeing each other and set up new relationships with comrades who had been more distant in the past.

One of the group's big problems was that we had nothing to do except to have political fights with other groups or among ourselves. Our "mass" activities at the time consisted mainly of either starting or participating in sitdown demonstrations in the relief bureaus of lower Manhattan. All of us would crowd into one relief bureau, pretending that we didn't know each other. Then one of the comrades would make a demand for additional rent or food money, a demand that was almost always denied. The denial was the signal for the beginning of the demonstration, which went on with shouting of slogans until the cops came and hauled us out of the office. But once the momentary excitement of the demonstration and arrests was over, it was hard for us to believe we had really advanced the cause of revolutionary socialism by persuading a few bewildered people to shout and mill around inside the offices of the relief bureau.

When we were dispossessed from the apartment for failure to pay the rent, Ruth and I moved once more, this time to the Lower East Side, where we shared an apartment with another married couple in the organization. We lived on the top floor of a tenement house, and the rooms were laid out so that from one of the windows we could see our own front door. It was a good thing we could, for it gave us a chance to see whether the person who had pushed our bell looked like one of the many bill collectors chasing after everybody in the apartment. If it was a bill collector, we simply didn't answer the bell, and if one of us came up the stairs while the collector was on the stoop, he did not attempt to get into the apartment.

But the strain of being the only one working and living with so many other people kept getting worse for Ruth, and we began having bitter quarrels. I remonstrated with her about her failure to measure up to the standards of proper Bolshevik behavior, and she met my faultfinding with a stony glare, followed by an outburst of hot-tempered shouting.

Then the war in Europe broke out, and some of our comrades

from Canada started sneaking across the border illegally, fearful that the Canadian police would jail them for the group's loudly proclaimed past opposition to the war. Three of them showed up one day at our apartment; naturally we had to put them up. One, who had been deported from the United States a few years earlier, gave us considerable concern about his presence, which had to be kept secret. Now eight people were living in the small apartment, a condition not designed to lengthen tempers. Even worse, the Canadians were damned temperamental. One of them got on everybody's nerves because he was obsessed with his approaching baldness and spent a lot of money on hair restorers which he massaged into his scalp by the hour. He also did exercises for his flat feet, so that any conversation with him had to be conducted while he was rising on his toes and dropping back on his heels, simultaneously rubbing ointment into his thinning hair.

Of course the Canadians had to spend most of their time inside the apartment, for we were convinced that they would all be arrested if they walked the streets. And while we were trying to work out a plan for a better place in which to hide them, another one arrived. Perhaps arrived is the wrong word, for he literally fell on the floor when we opened the door for him. He was writhing in pain and clasping his abdomen. We were so convinced that he was dying, perhaps from a ruptured appendix, that we telephoned immediately for an ambulance from Bellevue, the free city hospital located not far from where we lived. A few minutes later, we heard two sirens, and looking out the window, we saw a police car accompanying the ambulance swinging in alongside the curb in front of the house.

Panicked, we pushed the other Canadians into the front room just as the ambulance interne and one of the policemen came into the apartment. It took the doctor only a minute to find out that Oscar was very sick, and he turned to the police officer standing alongside him and said, "Holler out the window for your partner and the driver to come up with a stretcher."

The cop started to walk through the apartment into the front room overlooking the street where we had pushed the illegal immigrants. We all stood petrified as he moved until one girl almost leaped in front of the closed door.

"You can't go in here," she said very determinedly.

"Why not, lady?" asked the cop.

"Because my baby just fell asleep and it took me three hours to get her asleep and so I'm not going to let you wake her up."

The policeman looked a little dubious but decided not to get mixed up with an angry New York momma. Instead he walked out into the hallway, where a few curious neighbors had gathered to see what the excitement was all about, and went into one of their apartments to relay the doctor's message. The instant Oscar was down in the ambulance and the police were gone, we decided to move the Canadians to a little deserted summer house we knew about on a New Jersey lake.

That decision made, Ruth told me that either the two of us moved out of the apartment or she would move alone. So, with some doubts, some feeling that I was failing in my duty to the movement, we rented a tiny apartment of our own in a converted brownstone house on Seventieth Street just off Central Park West. We were alone for the first time since leaving Chicago.

After that I got a job running the linen-supply department for the Standard Brands Pavilion Restaurant at the World's Fair, and we began slowly to shave off the burden of debts and worries that had plagued us since we'd gotten married. The quarrel between us about my commitment to the movement eased too, for now that we were living alone, the main source of Ruth's irritation was gone. But we weren't quite alone, for occasionally comrades would borrow our apartment for lovemaking; some nights we had to stand on the street outside, waiting for the light in the front room to be turned off as a signal that they were leaving. Sometimes, too, the difference in our attitude toward the movement came to the surface, as it did when the Canadians decided to return home. Since they had entered the country illegally, we had to get them back the same way, and I was asked to drive them secretly across the border. Ruth objected strenuously, but I carried out my Bolshevik duty and set off one rainy night with the three Canadians in Fred Goldwater's dilapidated convertible.

We drove all night and crossed the border at Buffalo the next day after washing and shaving at the house of a local sympathizer. We had equipped the comrades with enough phony letters and credentials to pass at least a casual inspection, and fortunately, that's all we got from both the American and the Canadian officers. I then drove the comrades to Toronto and turned around immediately. I had to cross back again into the United States at a different station than the one through which we'd entered, for I was fearful that the American border patrol might just remember my having gone across with the others. I also didn't know whether any record had been made of the entry of four men into Canada.

I had no trouble in getting back at a small station in the middle of New York State, and twelve hours later I was home in New York, relieved that we had gotten rid of the Canadians. But Ruth was angry and stayed angry for quite a while, not just because of the risks involved with the police, but because I had made the long drive to Canada and back without getting any rest.

As usual I was jobless again, for the World's Fair had closed. A few weeks later I was hired as an assistant news editor of a magazine called *Super Market Merchandising,* a trade journal for the operators of supermarkets, just then starting to become a big business.

But it was just as hard for me to work up any enthusiasm about writing stories on how best to stack oranges for sales at point of contact as it had been for me to sell toilet seats. Even worse, since I couldn't take the magazine seriously, I learned very little about how to write for it. The end of my potential career in supermarket merchandising came when in one afternoon I told the managing editor of the magazine, who happened to be a relative of the boss, that a layout she had done was lousy and then, bored with writing descriptions of new carts for ladies to push through the aisles, sailed a very fancy paper airplane out my office window. Unfortunately, instead of catching an updraft in the building shaft as it always had before, it made a few weak turns and fluttered into the boss's room, landing gently on his desk.

Jobless again, and this time clearly because of my own fault, I had so little sense of future that I was distraught. I made a joke of what had happened at the magazine whenever I talked with friends or comrades, but even while I was poking fun I was damned unhappy about not working again. Right at this time, too, Ruth and I had another personal crisis, for a girl I had known in Rochester showed up at our apartment babbling a wild story of having been thrown out of a moving car by her lover, who, she said, had tried to kill her. In addition, she was pregnant although unmarried.

I got her a room down the street from us and furnished it with our few wedding gifts after she had pleaded with me to help her out when her mother, who thought she was married, came to visit her. Her mother did come and left a few days later; by then the girl had decided to get an abortion. So one morning I took her to a doctor's apartment on Gramercy Park South, where the operation was performed. In the afternoon someone else brought her back to the little furnished room and helped get her into bed. I told her that if she needed help she was to pull down the window shade, and sure enough the next morning I looked out and saw the shade down. I rushed down the street over to the house and hurried into her room. She was moaning heavily and the bed sheets were covered with blood. Frightened, I threw off the sheets and saw that she was hemorrhaging badly.

"I'm going to call the doctor," I said. "Try not to move."

She only moaned in answer as I tore down the steps and back to our apartment. There I called the abortionist, who sent a nurse. For the next week a couple of us took turns tending Sylvia and following all the instructions the nurse had given me about packing her and keeping her clean so that infection would not set in. In about two weeks she was well enough to get up, and one day she simply disappeared without paying her room rent, so that the landlord confiscated our wedding gifts. We never did get them back, either, for we never had enough dough to pay off the landlord.

Badly discouraged by all these personal and political failures, I called my old friend Walter Kahn, and a few nights later the two of us went to dinner. We drove to a restaurant in Westchester, where I stuffed myself on paté de fois gras with drinks and rare steaks with more drinks. We talked about the days at Kahn's and he told me all the news of the firm and of his friends. Later that night, after I got home drunk, I passed out before even getting to bed, woke up on the floor, and just made it to the bathroom before vomiting huge gobs of undigested goose liver and steak all over the toilet.

The melancholy of unemployment continued to get worse, for I no longer even had any political activity to keep me occupied. I had resigned from the Fieldites, together with about half the other comrades, leaving only a handful of the faithful in the organization. And in another month or so the whole organization disappeared into political limbo. But despite the break in my organizational connection to the Trotskyist movement, the awful news of Trotsky's assassination on August 20, 1940, came as an unbelievable shock, an idea that could not be accepted, something the nervous system refused to absorb. Hastily I rushed to the Trotskyist headquarters to join with a group of bitter and somber comrades whose internal differences were submerged temporarily in our grief at the murder of the Old Man.

And not one of us doubted who had ordered the assassination. Later that night a comrade who had fought against Franco in Spain was sitting in a Fourteenth Street cafeteria reading the more complete news stories which gave all the ghastly details of how the assassin had worked his way into the confidence of the Trotsky household and then smashed a pickaxe into Trotsky's skull. A Stalinist who knew the Trotskyist slightly sat down at the cafeteria table with him, and remarked, "Well, we finally got that bastard." Without a word the Trotskyist picked up the heavy sugar bowl with his right hand, grabbed the back of the Stalinist's head with his left, and smashed the bowl into the Stalinist's face. As the blood started streaming from the stunned Communist's broken nose and cheekbones, the Trotskyist walked quietly out of the restaurant.

No one who was ever connected seriously with the Trotskyist movement has ever forgotten that pickaxe blow. Then and now it was for us the culmination of Stalinist brutality and treachery, the horrible confirmation of everything we had come to believe about the degeneration of the Bolshevik spirit of the Russian Revolution. Revulsion was the universal reaction to the murder in every segment of the radical movement except among the Communists, who greeted the news with open glee. We had all anticipated that it might happen and had tried for years to prevent it. We knew that hundreds of thousands of innocent people had been murdered by Stalin in the name of a holy war against Trotsky; we were convinced that Stalin was responsible for the death of Trotsky's son in a French hospital; we had seen how Sequierios, the Mexican Communist painter, had led a machine-gun raid on Trotsky's home months earlier in an unsuccessful attempt to assassinate him; and we knew that the Communists had planted agents in our own organizations, sometimes in high places.

But in the prewar days the fierce combat in which we were engaged with the Communists was fought out, on our side at least, without recourse to what we called the "capitalist police." We had our own ways of trying to deal with Stalinist agents, about whom all kinds of ugly tales circulated in Trotskyist circles. And we did not go running to those we thought of as the class enemy for help in fighting the Communists, including even those Communists who we were convinced were acting as Soviet agents inside the United States government.

The Old Man's assassination brought a heavy pall of depression over the whole Trotskyist movement; a depression that lasted for many months even among those people, like myself, who had cut their organizational ties. Then, just as I was falling into a very deep personal depression as well because of my continued unemployment, I heard through the radical grapevine that the International Ladies Garment Workers Union was hiring organizers.

The union was starting a new campaign against garment manufacturers who fled New York and opened shops in tiny farm towns all over the East. Some of these runaway factories were owned by gangsters, the leeches who had been brought into the industry first by the employers to fight the union and then by the union, which out of necessity had also hired hoodlums to beat off the attacks being made on it. Now the gangsters, especially those associated with Murder, Inc., had taken over whole plants.

I went down to the ILGWU headquarters and had a very short interview with Louis Stulberg, the official who was heading up the new drive.

"Are you still a Trotskyite?" he asked me.

"No, I don't belong to any organization now."

"Okay, we may be hiring some organizers in a few weeks. Leave your address with my secretary, and if I can find a place for you, I'll let you know."

Convinced I was being let down softly, I left my address, never believing I would be hired. Two weeks went by and no word came from the union. I called Stulberg once or twice, but his secretary always said he was out of town. Then, one morning, I went downstairs to the little table in the hallway where the mail was placed and saw an envelope with the union's name on it. For a long few minutes I was afraid to open it and face a letter telling me that Stulberg was sorry but there was no job open for me. Finally, though, I tore the envelope apart and found that I could start work the following week.

CHAPTER SEVEN

O NE MORNING in 1941, just a few days before I left on my first organizing assignment for the ILGWU, I walked down the outside steps of our apartment in New York and saw two men coming up. As we passed, they looked at me and I looked at them, sensing somehow, perhaps from their gray suits and gray hats and gray faces that they were FBI men. At the top of the steps they turned to look at me again as I stood staring up at them from the sidewalk. Then they walked down the steps as I waited for them.

"Are you looking for me?" I asked.

"Are you Paul Jacobs?"

"Yes, I am."

"We're from the Federal Bureau of Investigation and we'd like to talk with you. Could we go upstairs to your apartment?"

Inside the apartment they showed me their credentials and very politely began questioning me about my activities with the Trotskyists in Minneapolis. It was obvious that they already knew many details of where I had lived and what I had done. They told me also that they knew I had left the Trotskyists and was not even in the LRWP any longer. Within a few minutes they got around to asking me very politely if I would consider being a government witness in the Smith Act trial of the Minneapolis Trotskyists scheduled to begin a few months later. A number of the Minneapolis group had been arrested on charges of advocating sedition in the first court test of the Smith Act, which had been passed in 1940.

Equally polite, I declined their offer. They then suggested, without ever saying so specifically, that perhaps it might be advisable for me to cooperate with the government lest at some point in the future I, too, might find myself facing some kind of charge. It was all put very delicately, of course, and raised only in terms of what constituted my patriotic duty, considering the fact that I was no longer an active Trotskyist. Still I refused, pointing out to them that if they subpoenaed me I would have to appear, but that any testimony I might give would be of no help to the government's case. Finally they left, asking me to keep them informed of my whereabouts for the next few months.

This encounter with the FBI, the first of a number of such encounters with government agents in the years to come, was a specific reflection of a general political dilemma of the time. I had "broken"—as leaving a radical organization was described —with the particular political positions advocated by the orthodox Trotskyists in Minneapolis, but I was also opposed to their prosecution, not only because I thought it was a violation of civil liberties, but also because I still identified myself loosely with the general Trotskyist viewpoint.

The outbreak of World War II in 1939 and Roosevelt's obvious support of Britain's war effort created a terrible crisis for the non-Communist radical movement in America. We were torn between our hatred of the Nazis and our view that countries such as England and the United States were only capable of fighting an "imperialist" war even against fascism. Pacifists and socialists, who were opposed to the participation of the United States in the war, joined in a loose organizational grouping with reactionary isolationists whose opposition to American aid to Britain was based on their narrow xenophobia.

The only groups which had a clear line to follow were the Communists and their sympathizers. To them the issue of support for the war had one, and only one, dimension: when the Stalin-Hitler Pact was in effect, and the Soviet Union was neutrally on the side of the Nazis, the European war was an imperialist one, not to be supported in any way; the moment Hitler turned on his former allies and attacked the Soviet Union, Britain's war against the Nazis became a holy crusade of the Communist party.

And if the Socialists and Trotskyists ever needed any further reinforcement for their bitter distrust of the Communists, the Minneapolis Smith Act trial reinforced our feelings: the Communists were absolutely ferocious in their demands that patriotism required jailing the Trotskyists, and when they were convicted, the Communists lamented the fact that the sentences were not severe enough.

But for me and others like me, the period was a terribly confused one. We weren't conscientious objectors to war on religious or moral grounds. After the LRWP had been dissolved, I no longer had any organizational affiliation, even though I considered myself generally sympathetic to some of the Trotskyist positions. But most of the Trotskyist groups and other revolutionary Marxists were floundering around during this period on what attitude to take toward the war, and there were sharp differences even among the former members of the miniscule LRWP. A few of our ex-members from Canada, including one of the smugglees, even joined various branches of the Canadian services.

All during the time I worked for the ILGWU, the question of the war troubled me. Soon after I became an organizer, the union decided that its members and staff would purchase Defense Bonds, as they were called then. Shortly afterward I received a letter asking me to sign a form authorizing the union treasurer to make deductions from my paycheck until a week's salary had been accummulated for a Defense Bond to be purchased in my name. I threw the letter away, and a few weeks later I got another one to remind me that I still hadn't signed the form. I threw it away, too. Then I got a phone call telling me to come to New York and see David Dubinsky, the union president. Outside his office I found another organizer also, called in from his assignment in a different area. We were both curious about why we were there together. We found out very quickly when Dubinsky called us in, demanding to know why we hadn't signed the forms, thus preventing a hundred-percent record of staff purchases.

We explained our refusal to Dubinsky, who grew furious, finally shouting at us, "Don't you want to work for this union? Don't you want to work for me?" We took turns answering him, and when my chance came, I said much more bravely than I felt, "Yes, I want to work for the ILGWU and for you, but not under such conditions, not when I can be forced to support something I don't want to support."

He turned away, and I was convinced that my time was up. But instead of firing us, he said, wearily, "All right, get back to work." And no one in the ILGWU ever asked me to buy bonds again.

In the early forties I could not have found a more congenial job than that of ILGWU organizer. The union leaders were still close enough to their own socialist pasts to be untroubled by putting radicals on their staff. (It wasn't until twenty years later that Dubinsky flared up in an angry denunciation of Norman Thomas and others for what he believed to be their unwarranted interference in a dispute between him and those members of his own staff who had organized a union of their own.)

What's more, few other unions were so actively anti-Stalinist as the ILGWU. Of course most of the AFL unions were also bitterly anti-Communist, but their opposition to the Communists was from the right, and anyone who wanted to make changes in the status quo was lumped together with the Communists. The CIO unions at the time were in quite the opposite position: a number of them were staffed by Communists or sympathizers, while in others a bitter underground struggle for control was going on, as in the auto workers' union, where the Reuther brothers were trying to build up enough support to challenge the Communists' position.

But we had no such problems with the ILGWU staff, no worries that one organizer was knifing another for political reasons. Plenty of knifing was going on, all right, but it was based on internal union politics, on personal jealousies and ambitions, rather than on whether the Soviet foreign policy should be supported. And even those of us who were most ambitious personally were motivated by a conviction that what we were doing was important in itself, that it was important to organize shops where wages were pitifully low because the boss got a kickback from the legal minimum wage of thirty-five cents an hour, and that it was important to protect workers from getting fired without cause or because they wouldn't "lend" money to a forelady who never paid it back.

Most of the ILGWU staff was Jewish at that time, with the exception of some Italians in New York and a handful of Protestant officials in the South. The union's staff, its business agents, and many of its member officers reflected the fact that the garment industry centered in New York City was a Jewish trade, in which Jewish immigrant workers had been employed. In the original group of ten organizers of which I had been a part, only one wasn't Jewish. The business agent for whom we worked in Harrisburg was Jewish, too, as was the vice president in charge of the area and nearly everybody else on his staff.

Almost all the organizers who had been hired along with me also had some connection with the radical or socialist movement. One of them, Al Levy, who died recently, with whom I became close friends, had written many of the parody songs of the thirties mocking the Communists, while Alfred Hayes, another staff member hired to write a daily radio serial for the organizing campaign, was the author of the words to the very famous song, "Joe Hill." (Hayes was also a great pool player, and Levy and I spent a lot of our free time in Harrisburg losing to him in a grimy pool hall, while Ruth perched daintily on a chair watching us as, to the accompaniment of our monotonous cursing, he beat us consistently.)

As a consequence of the Jewish and radical or socialist background shared by almost all the organizers, we were unselfconscious with each other. There was no need to hide or disguise what we were: all of us knew the facts about everyone else.

I was happy, too, because I was getting paid for doing what I would have been glad to do for nothing. My weekly salary of forty-five dollars wasn't very big, but it was certainly adequate, and I even had a small expense allowance, plus gasoline money for the car I bought in Harrisburg. Often as I drove around on the Pennsylvania highways, I would think how fortunate I had been to be hired by the ILGWU, for I was able to work at my own pace at a job I really wanted, while everybody else in the whole world was in a shop or a place of business where each day's routine duplicated that of the day before, where the work was always dull and monotonous, and where a boss was always hanging over your shoulder.

In Harrisburg, Ruth and I shared an apartment with Al Levy. Early every morning I would wake him up after a great struggle, since he loved to sleep and objected strenuously to getting up at five on a cold winter morning. But we had to get up that early in order to give out leaflets and copies of an organizing newspaper at the plants we were trying to unionize. Once the distributions were over, we all met for huge breakfasts at a restaurant near the union office. Then the local business agent would discuss the progress of the campaign and make out assignments for that day.

Generally the mornings were free, since all the workers were inside the plants. Starting late in the afternoons, we made house calls, visiting people whose names we'd gotten from our contacts inside the plants. When we stood in their doorways and told them we were from the union, the responses we got ranged from having the door slammed in our faces to being invited in for discussion. We kept making house visits until nine or ten in the evening, when we would all meet once more to exaggerate how well we were doing in the campaign.

In fact, progress was very slow. The workers resisted our organizing efforts, out of fear either that they would be fired or that the plant would close down if the union came in, as had actually happened in Harrisburg a few years earlier. This resistance by workers to union organization was new to me, for in Minneapolis the workers had flocked into the teamsters' union, and while the CIO organizing drive of the thirties had met with great resistance from the employers, it had gotten an enthusiastic response from workers. But in the rural Pennsylvania dress factories the idea of unionization was still new, and the greatest asset of the bosses in their war with the union was the initial suspicion of the workers about the union; suspicion which developed rapidly into active hostility when the employers let out the word through the supervisors and foreladies that they would shut down the plant if the workers voted to have a union contract.

The Pennsylvania organizing campaign ran into even tougher resistance in the small towns around Harrisburg than it did in the city itself. In one such tiny place, Duncannon, to which I had been assigned, the dress factory was the only plant in town providing any employment to the rural area, even though the pay was very low: about fourteen dollars a week if the boss didn't make his workers kick back a few dollars, which happened often enough. In a town like that we first tried to recruit members from among the families of any railroad workers who happened to live there, for they at least knew something about unions. After making those contacts and using the men to put some pressure on their wives, we tried persuading the other women in the plant to sign cards authorizing the union to represent them. Usually it was at this point that the employer would threaten to close the plant and move his equipment to another town.

Shutting down a dress factory was easy. Most of the manufacturing equipment, like sewing machines, was pretty light and could be quickly dissassembled. The machines were then loaded on a truck and the whole factory moved to another town in a rural area, where a new force of women workers was assembled from among the daughters and wives of farm families for whom the money earned in the factory quickly became an important supplement to the meager family income.

Because so much of the union recruiting was done at night, I took a room in a tiny dingy hotel in Duncannon and slept there two or three nights a week rather than making the long drive back to Harrisburg. During the days almost no one in town would talk to me, for it was such a small place that everybody knew what I was doing. A handful of women who worked in the Duncannon factory had husbands who made them join the union, and one lady was actually an enthusiast of the ILGWU. But as the weeks went by, only a discouragingly small number of the others said they would sign the cards we needed before we could get an NLRB election.

The high spot of the campaign in Duncannon came late one afternoon, when I drove out into the hills to make a recruiting call on two women who lived on a farm. One was the wife, the other the daughter of the farmer, and both of them had refused to even discuss the union with any other girls in the plant. The farmer made doubly sure of this by driving them to work every morning, watching them as they went into the plant without talking to anybody outside, and returning in late afternoon in his battered car to wait outside the plant until the shift ended and he could transport them home again.

They lived on a lonely dirt road five miles from Duncannon. I parked the car at the mailbox and walked up the hill to the farm house. When I knocked on the door, it opened to reveal the farmer with a shotgun pointed at me. I was so scared I could hardly answer when he asked me what I wanted.

"I'd like to talk to your wife and daughter," I said.

"What about?"

"About joining the union at the dress factory."

"They got nawthin' for the union and I got nawthin' for the union, neither."

"Well, I'd still like to talk to them," I persisted.

He grunted something I took to be an assent and motioned me outside into the yard. It was only then I saw that the two women were standing next to the water pump, watching the scene. They must have come over from the barn, for they hadn't been there when I arrived. I walked over to them and started explaining all about the union while the farmer stood by, watchful, the shotgun still in his hands. Neither of the two women made any response whatever to what I was saying, and I began to talk faster and faster, by now anxious to end the conversation and get the hell away as quickly as possible.

Suddenly, the farmer broke in. "All right, you talked to them, so now git." He shoved the gun at me, I turned around quickly and started walking down the lane to my car, with him right behind me, the gun pointed at my back. It was one of the longest short walks I ever took, for I was convinced that this farmer was crazy enough to pull the trigger without any warning. When we got to my parked car, he stood grimly by while I climbed inside and drove off, out of his sight. Five minutes later I pulled to the side of the road and stayed there, trembling for a half hour, until I was able to drive again.

The farmer and I ran into each other once more a few days later when I was walking down the street of Duncannon. He came alongside me in his old jalopy, stopped the car, reached down behind the seat, and pulled up a snake! He brandished the snake in my face, and when I jumped away from the car in fright and horror, he laughed insanely. The laugh must have done it for I reached through the car window, grabbed him by the throat and shouted, "You miserable bastard! If you ever shove that snake in my face again, I'll kill you with your own fucking gun! Now get the hell out of here before I kick the shit out of you right now!"

He must have been as scared of me then as I had been of him at the farm, for he dropped the snake, put the car into gear, and tore down the street. I never saw him again, and I heard rumors later that he had been killed when the state police went out to his farm to arrest him on a complaint of rape filed by his own daughter. He refused to surrender and shot it out with the troopers, who killed him.

I had to leave Duncannon unorganized, for the factory owner had used a sickness in his family which took him back to New York as an excuse to shut down the plant. But no matter what I said to the contrary, everyone believed he had closed it because of the union. So I quit Duncannon even more unpopular than when I had arrived; everyone in town held me responsible for the loss of the weekly paychecks.

Organizing runaway shops, especially those owned by gangsters, was a potentially grim operation. Our crew had assigned to it a tough Italian "organizer," whose real function was to handle any of the rough stuff that came up. We called Tony the chairman of the "Education Committee," and he was a very effective educator, about whom all kinds of wild stories circulated. We heard that he specialized in snapping wrists during strikes, and occasionally he boasted that his efficiency at this was so great the snappee never even knew his wrist had been broken until his hand dangled uselessly.

Tony liked to boast that his favorite weapon was a beer-can opener because "it leaves a nice neat stripe down a man's face." For a long time we suspected him of being a phony, but I changed my mind about him when I saw him go after a man in a bar. The guy had made a feeble verbal pass at one of the girl organizers whom Tony thought of as his woman although she tried continually to make him leave her alone. Tony picked up a beer glass, smashed it on the table, and charged at the fellow with the jagged edge of the glass, shouting, "I'm going to change your goddamned face!"

A couple of us grabbed him and hung on while, cursing and screaming, he tried frantically to pull out of our arms. The man scuttled off into the night, and we hustled Tony out of the bar and back to his hotel room, the girl crying hysterically all the time. It felt as if I were watching a gangster movie while simultaneously being in it, a feeling I never lost whenever I was with Tony.

His terrible temper almost got us into trouble another time, when Al Levy and I took him with us to talk with the manager of one of the shops we were trying to organize. This shop had some kind of tie with one of the mob operations in New York, and we were handling it very gingerly. But the manager had fired a girl who was the leader of the union group inside the plant, and we anticipated a terrible blow to the morale of the few other girls who openly identified with the union unless we succeeded in getting the firing rescinded.

I parked my car on the street in front of the plant, with the girl in the front seat and Tony and Al in the back. It was just before the shift ended, and we wanted the other girls to see that the union actually did do something for its members, although we knew that all we could do was try to persuade the manager to take the girl back. While we were sitting in the car waiting for him to come out, he spotted us from the plant window and in a panic called the police, who sent a squad car with two men. Because Al and I didn't want the cops around when we talked with the manager, I told Tony to get rid of them.

Tony got out of our car and walked back to where the police had parked, directly behind us. He responded instinctively to the two cops as he had been trained to do in dealing with New York City policemen: he took a ten-dollar bill out of his wallet, folded it into a tiny square, put the square inside a book of matches, and held out the matches to the cops.

"Have a match," said Tony.

"We don't smoke," answered one of the policemen.

"Take the matches," responded Tony, growing a little angry.

"I told you we don't smoke. We don't need any matches."

"Take the matches! Take the matches!" he started to shout, assuming that the cops wanted more money and growing furious at the idea that small-town policemen required bigger bribes than those in New York.

The cops started to get out of the car, convinced for their part that they were dealing with a looney. It wasn't until then that Al and I, who had been doubled up laughing as we watched them argue, started out of our car, sobered instantly by the potential of trouble between Tony and the two policemen. Fortunately Tony finally realized that ignorance, not cupidity, was at the root of his troubles with the police; he opened the book of matches to show the ten-dollar bill, complaining, "What's the matter with you guys? Don't you know how to do it, anyway?"

It turned out they did know how to "do it." They drove away just as the plant manager came out of the building expecting to find them in the street. When he saw only Tony, Al, who had lumbered out of the car, and me, he blanched and backed up to the wall.

"No rough stuff," he pleaded. "The boys said there wouldn't be no rough stuff. The boys said there was a deal and there wouldn't be no rough stuff."

I reassured him that he was right, that no rough stuff was going to be used, and sent Tony back to the car. Then Al and I tried to persuade him to take the girl back to work and he promised to talk it over with "the boys" in New York. We didn't really care whether he did, because we had already decided to hire the girl to help us in making house calls, and we had made our point by showing the workers in the shop that we were ready to protect the members against such acts by the bosses.

Tony's presence was very useful, too, when very late one night Al and I drove down to York on a tip that a runaway dress factory was getting ready to move again in anticipation of our coming down to organize it. We got to the location at about midnight, and sure enough, the factory was all lit up. Outside the door to the plant a couple of men were hauling sewing machines into a parked truck. I peered into a window of the factory and saw a small chubby man whom I assumed to be the owner supervising the unscrewing of a pressing machine from the floor. We waited around for an hour or so until the boss finally came out on the small loading dock of the factory building. I got out of the car and called over to him, "Cohen, I want to talk to you."

He turned to squint into the darkness and then walked slowly to where I was standing.

"Who are you and what do you want?" he asked.

"I'm from the ILGWU, and what we want is for you not to move the shop again. We're tired of chasing you, so stay here. We'll fight it out here in York."

"Who's going to stop me from moving this shop?" he blustered. "You're going to stop me? If I want to move, I'll move, and nobody's going to stop me."

I turned around to where my car was parked. "Tony," I called, "Al, come here for a minute."

The two of them climbed out of the car, the light from the street lamp making them look twice as big as they really were. They walked slowly over to us.

"Cohen says he's going to move the shop even though I told him not to do it."

Tony gently took hold of Cohen's lapels and pulled him slightly forward. "Look, Mr. Cohen," he said very quietly. "Don't move the shop. You do like we say. If you move the shop, I'm going to come after you and then I'm going to take out your eyes and eat them for grapes."

Cohen turned absolutely white. In a frightened whisper, he

said, "So okay, I won't move the shop."

He didn't but we never got around to organizing him anyway. Actually, the Harrisburg campaign was a very quiet one, especially by comparison with the kind of violence that had occurred in the organizing work done by the union years before, when the gangsters had been brought in by the bosses to fight off the union. We got an idea of what this had been like when a union vice-president who had come out from New York to discuss the progress of the Harrisburg campaign started reminiscing with a group of us as we sat in the union office about the character of the violence that prevailed in those earlier organizing campaigns.

"Look at the inside of my mouth," he said, pulling down his lower lip to show us that the whole interior of his mouth had been stitched.

"That happened when I got run down by a car, deliberately, during a strike in Brooklyn. I was out on the street, watching the pickets, when these gangsters come tearing down and hit me with the car. Everybody ran away, they were so scared, and I had to crawl to a drugstore on the corner. When I got inside, the druggist took one look at me and fainted, I was bleeding so bad. Then they took me to the hospital and sewed me up. I didn't get out of the hospital for months."

"Did you know who the gangsters were?" someone asked him.

"Yeah, I recognized them, but after we found them, no one else would have."

"What do you mean by that?"

"I mean that after we caught those bastards, we took them up to an empty loft, put them on the floor, and walked over them for a while. Then we gave them back to their friends. They learned their lesson that time."

But by 1941 organizing for the ILGWU, even organizing gangster shops, wasn't as grim a business as it had been in the earlier days. The fights that did take place broke out spontaneously from picket-line quarrels or when somebody took a crack at an organizer giving out leaflets. And the campaign in Pennsylvania was lightened for Al and me at least by our somewhat bizarre sense of humor. Once we bought two dozen white mice, tied ribbons around their necks, and set them loose under the door of a shop. No work got done in that plant for a week or more until the mice had disappeared, and even then production was very slow.

On another occasion Al and I hired a stilt walker from a county fair to parade up and down the street outside a second-floor dress factory. The plant windows were open and the workers could see only the stilt walker's head and shoulders while he paraded back and forth urging them to join the union. It took a minute or two for someone inside to grasp the fact that they were being spoken to by a man walking back and forth as if he were on the sidewalk while they were actually on the second floor. Then came the screams and so much tumult the plant had to shut down.

Six or seven months after the campaign in Pennsylvania had begun, it ended, almost a complete failure. We'd organized only a few shops, although we had succeeded in getting wages raised all over the area—employers were so frightened of the union they increased rates to keep the workers satisfied. When the organizing drive was called off, a few of us, including Al and myself, were kept on the staff. I was sent alone to investigate the possibilities of organizing a textile-dyeing and dress factory in a small upstate New York town. The plant was owned by a man who operated a much bigger nonunion shop in Chicago. A few weeks after I arrived, Ruth joined me and we started the routine of making house visits to all the workers in the plant.

This campaign was much more successful than the one in Pennsylvania. Since the town was a railroad junction and had a big railroad shop, many of the factory workers had husbands or brothers who were union men. But before we had a chance to request union recognition from the employer, he decided to lock out the plant, and we decided to call a strike against him.

On the first morning of the strike, a few pickets were already standing in front of the plant when I drove up at six, and within the next fifteen minutes fifty more walked down the street to the factory entrance. I was very worried, for it was the first time that most of these people had ever been involved in a strike.

To my great relief, by seven o'clock, when the morning shift usually went to work, a couple of hundred pickets were slowly parading on the sidewalk, making a long narrow ellipse that closed off both of the plant entrances. The weather was warm, and most of the men were in shirt sleeves, the girls in slacks.

Across the street, under the watchful eyes of the police, only a dozen unhappy nonstrikers huddled, trying to summon up enough courage to go through the picket line. I moved quickly around the outside of the line, pulling the men I had assigned as picket captains over next to the plant wall, where we were hidden from the police by the strikers.

"Look," I said very hurriedly, "in a few minutes those goddamned scabs across the street are going to try breaking through the line. The cops'll bring them across the street and then tell you to open up and let them through. Do what the cops say, but only open up the line on the street side to let the scabs through. Then close it up again as fast as you can, and while the scabs are in the middle, beat the shit out of them. Tell the guys not to hit any of the women if they can, but let the girls do that. Tell the girls the first thing they should do is kick off the scabs' shoes and then work them over. One more thing—as soon as you see the scabs start across the street, start shouting at them as loud as you can. The noise'll scare them and confuse the cops for a little while anyway."

The picket captains went back into the line and I could see them moving along with it, passing on my instructions to the strikers. Suddenly the scabs broke out from their cluster and started walking rapidly across the street, two cops alongside. Instantly, as if they had trained themselves in this maneuver for years, the picket captains started shouting, "Don't Go to Work in a Jewshop! Don't Go to Work in a Jewshop!" The whole line started repeating the same rhythmic chant, and seconds later the sidewalk erupted into a tangled, screaming mass as the strikers opened their line for the scabs on the street side and then closed ranks tightly. The pickets hurled themselves onto the strike breakers, kicking them, flailing at them, and screaming, "Stay out of the Jewshop, you bastards! Keep out of the Jewshop!" while the frantic cops tried to get through the tangled crowd to pull the strikers away from the scabs.

And I was nearly as frantic as the police, running from one part of the fight to the other, trying to take a good crack at some of the scabs and shouting at the top of my lungs, "Shut up about the Jewshop! Shut up!"

But either I wasn't heard or my shout was misinterpreted, for the pickets kept on hollering their slogan, and the uneven fight continued for another few minutes. A couple of police cars sirened up at last, and enough cops piled out to break up the small riot by simply charging into the crowd and tearing the strikers away from the scabs. None of the strikebreakers were seriously hurt, but all of them were battered badly enough to keep them from trying to get in the plant again that day. The police were furious and warned me that they'd arrest everybody if another fight took place, but it was a great triumph for us, and later that morning, when we met in the strike headquarters I'd rented near the plant, the union members gabbled excitedly with each other about what each of them had done during the fight.

I called the meeting to order from a little raised platform at one end of the hall, and gradually they quieted down.

"You did great," I congratulated them. "You showed those scabs that you had enough guts to keep them out today and that you'll keep them out tomorrow and the next day and every day until we win this strike. There was only one thing wrong this morning and that was when you started shouting, 'Don't go to work in a Jewshop.' "

They looked at me, puzzled, as I explained to them that just because their employer happened, in this case, to be Jewish was no reason for them to call the plant a "Jewshop." I told them I was offended by that because I was Jewish.

Simple disbelief was their reaction to that. Then I pointed out that Ruth, whom they all knew and liked, was Jewish too. Once more, disbelief, and I heard someone in the audience mutter, "How can she be a Hebe? She's got red hair."

Almost in desperation I told them that Dubinsky, the president of the union which was running the strike, was also a Jew. To this, one of the strikers said openly, "We never heard of Jews in unions. There ain't no such thing. But if you don't want us to talk about Jewshops, we won't."

It was Minneapolis all over again, only this time union members whom it had taken months for me to recruit were doing what the president of the Farm Holiday group had done the night he'd denounced the "Jew bankers" at the Socialist meeting. And, just as all of us in Minneapolis had been completely dumbfounded by what we'd heard from the radical farm leader, so too was I surprised by the attitude of these workers, with whom I'd spent months organizing an ILGWU local, slowly overcoming their fears of getting fired for joining the union.

With their limited perspective, it was perhaps understandable that they'd "never heard of Jews in unions." There weren't many, if any, Jewish coal miners, steel workers, or railroad engineers, and except in some large cities like New York, where many Jewish house painters and plumbers worked, the building-trades union had very few Jews, either. Most of the Jewish workers in America at that time were in the needle trades and so lived in New York, Chicago, Rochester, and Los Angeles, where the garment industry was still concentrated.

A few days after the strike started and showed all the signs of dragging on for a long time, the plant owner came in from Chicago. I was told he was in town as soon as he arrived, and the next day, while walking on the main street, I saw a stranger, obviously the employer, coming toward me. He was accompanied by the plant bookkeeper and the plant manager, with whom I'd talked a number of times. I saw the manager whisper to the owner, who stared curiously at me as we approached each other.

As we came abreast of each other and I nodded to the manager, the owner said to me, "You're the union organizer, aren't you?"

"That's right."

"You're Jewish, too, aren't you?"

"Yes," I answered. "Why do you ask?"

"Listen," he said. "Why do you want to make rishis and stir up these goyim about the Jews? What do you care about these dumb goyim, anyway?"

Instantly a dam of rage burst inside me. Barely in control of myself, I managed sanctimoniously and stupidly to blurt out at him, "Look, you miserable son-of-a-bitch, it's guys like you who make anti-Semitism, not people like me."

I saw him again a few days later, when a group of pickets stopped a truck from going through the factory gate. While I was standing out in the street with the truck driver, telling him what the strike was all about and suggesting he drive back to his loading depot in the next town, a dozen strikebreakers rushed out of the plant and started to open the truck doors. No police were around that afternoon, and a hell of a row broke out, with the driver and me fighting off the scabs until the pickets charged in from the other side of the truck. In a couple of minutes all the scabs had been clobbered badly enough to make them run inside the plant. Then, while I was talking again with the driver, who by this time was also mad, someone suddenly rushed out of the plant and walloped me behind the ear.

I spun around, and before I could see that it was the elderly plant bookkeeper, I slammed him so hard that I knocked him clear across the sidewalk and against the factory wall. His glasses fell off, his false teeth flew out of his mouth, and then he started crying, fumbling around for his glasses with one hand, feeling his jaw with the other, while the tears ran down into his now slack mouth.

Rushing over to him, I picked him up and started shouting at him. "Goddammit, stay inside the plant! What the hell are you doing out here, anyway? You don't belong here. Get inside and stay inside before you get killed!"

It was right then that the owner ran out, shouting that he'd have me arrested and put in jail for hitting an old man. Insane with rage, the two of us stood screaming at each other until a police car drove up and the cops separated us.

The next night I got into another fight when I got caught coming out of the plant at three in the morning after having dumped a huge knapsack filled with strong powdered soap into the plant water tower. An old Irish Revolutionary Army man, who worked in the railroad yards, had told me the soap would clog up the tubes of the plant's steam boilers and force a shutdown in production. There I was, creeping out the plant gate, having climbed, scared out of my mind, up a rusty ladder to the platform that held the water tank. Suddenly a big drunken strikebreaker came lurching out of the night toward me.

"What the hell are you doing?" he shouted. "Get the hell out of here, you little Jew bastard, before I knock you right on your ass." It would be nice if I could say it was then that I bravely hit him, but the truth is that I was so frightened I started to run. Then I spotted some of the union pickets, whose leader I was supposed to be, standing and watching me. So I had no choice but to stop and turn to face the drunk who lunged at me, took a tremendous roundhouse swing at my head, and missed. I tripped him as his body went off balance, and he fell into the gutter. He got up and rushed at me again, and I kneed him hard in the groin. He went down on one knee, and I kicked his balls. That did it for him and for me too, for while he lay there screaming in pain and clutching himself, I hunched over, vomiting all over myself.

A few months later we finally won that strike, but only after

Ruth had been beaten up by four husky women strikebreakers who caught her walking alone in a railway underpass near the plant. The beating set off a wave of fury among the railroad workers in the town, all strong union men, led by the old Irish revolutionary who had tipped me off about soap chips. They demanded that the Mayor take some action, and he in turn told the owner to settle the strike or move the plant. The next day, we sat down in City Hall, under the Mayor's eyes, to negotiate a settlement.

But in all the months I had worked as an ILGWU organizer, that strike was the first time I'd had to face the issue of union members seeming to be anti-Semitic.

In 1942 my brother, who was living with my mother in Los Angeles, received notice that he was to be drafted. My own draft status was also 1A, and I knew that I, too, would be getting my notice sometime in the next six or eight months. So, once the strike was settled, I took a leave from the ILGWU and we went to Los Angeles. There we took over from my brother, who went into the army very soon after we arrived.

We lived in Los Angeles with my mother for nearly six months while I worked in a defense plant and Ruth for a brokerage company. All the time we were there, I was still unresolved about my attitude toward the war; my irresolution was shared by a whole group of former Trotskyists then living in San Pedro. Most of them were working in the shipyards or in the Merchant Marine, and they all lived close to each other, in one beach area, an enclave of displaced New Yorkers.

For years the American left had been predicting the war's outbreak in precisely the kind of doomsday tones I had used the night I spotted Ruth from the soapbox. Armageddon was coming, we had warned repeatedly, and now we were proved correct. We had been convinced that World War II would be an imperialist one, necessarily to be opposed by socialists and radicals. Indeed, we had often traced the failure of the socialist movement in the post-World War I period to the support it gave to both sides in that war.

But even though in World War II no one I remember ever equated the Americans and the British with the Nazis, a nagging doubt still remained about what we, as revolutionary Marxists, should do, with an additional element of self-interest sometimes added to confuse the question still further. Ultimately we had to make a decision—should we or should we not support the Allies against the Nazis and Italian Fascists? Should we volunteer, be drafted, or refuse service on political grounds and go to jail, as did the conscientious objectors?

I didn't get much help in answering these questions from my ex-comrades when Ruth and I drove down on week ends to San Pedro for a visit with them and I asked for advice about what to do. Some of the comrades managed to avoid making any decision by simply going into the kind of war work that kept them out of the armed services. I knew of one group back in New York that had opened up a factory producing military equipment and managed to wangle deferments for a great many ex-radicals who would otherwise have been drafted. But no such device was open to me in Los Angeles, and my industrial skills were far too limited and primitive to get me a deferment on grounds that I could not be spared from war work.

After thinking about it for quite a while, I decided that as long as I had to go, I'd try to become an officer so that I wouldn't have such a hard life. Once again I was trying to live out that fantasy of myself which I'd constructed while just a kid. Incidentally, volunteering to go as an officer wasn't viewed with much favor in revolutionary Marxist political circles, for the theory was that if you had to go in, you should try to be in a place where you could influence the masses. Thus those comrades who tried to become officers had to offer pretty wild rationalizations for their actions. In one case, when a comrade who volunteered as an officer was being twitted for what he'd done by a group of his friends, he responded in dead earnest with, "Comrades, you don't understand that now the situation is different. The workers now *have* the guns!"

But I didn't have to worry about making any rationalizations about becoming an officer, for no one would have me. So, like millions of others, I was drafted, and in May, 1943, I was sworn into the Army Air Force.

The war years were very curious ones. I was never sent overseas, partly, I suspect, because of my known Trotskyist background. And physically I didn't suffer except once when I was a private and got in a fight with a sergeant who called me a "Jew bastard." The fight started when I was on a detail washing down the top floor of the barracks and some of the water I was using slopped down the steps to the ground floor, where the noncoms slept. From the bottom of the steps the sergeant screamed up at me, "Watch what you're doing, you Jew bastard," to which I naturally responded, "Go fuck yourself" and threw the bucket at him, water and all. Fortunately, the bucket missed his head, but the water drenched him. He ran up the steps, roaring in fury, and I leaped down them. We rammed together midway in a flailing knot, rolling over each other all the way down the steps; I ended up on the bottom getting my head slammed up and down on the floor. By the time the fight broke up, I had gotten some damned hard lumps from him.

The only other situation in which my being Jewish came up was when I entered the army and was asked my religion so that it could be stamped on my dogtags. I said I had no religion and then found out that this made me fair game for all the chaplains. After being bombarded for a week by suggestions that I attend Catholic, Protestant, Hebrew, and I even think Christian Science services, I gave up and had my dogtags stamped with the initial "H" for Hebrew, thus at least removing myself from the anxious ministry of the other groups.

Occasionally, too, I would wander into a canteen operated by one of the national Jewish organizations, but I could never stay very long: they seemed to be all run on the assumption that Jewish delicatessen was enough by itself to make these places attractive. But my estrangement from Jewish middle-class values was so complete that I was an alien among the small-town businessmen's daughters who self-consciously and heavy-handedly played their hostess roles as they circulated among the GIs.

The war didn't mean an end, either, to the continuing battle still going on between the Communists and the rest of the radicals. My first military encounter with this old and bitter quarrel occurred a few days after I was drafted, during an orientation lecture about the objectives of the war, given by the Information and Education Division of the Armed Services. We sat on the ground at the training center in Fresno while a young lieutenant explained the nature of the conflict to us. And as I listened to him discuss our ally, the Soviet Union, I heard the same old crap: Russia was an economic democracy, different from ours but fundamentally just as democratic; the Russians were the most consistent and heroic antifascists, and on and on and on. During the discussion period afterward, I began to argue with the lieutenant, pointing out the history of the Stalin-Hitler Pact and the injustices of the Moscow Trials, but it turned out to be a very short argument: he simply ordered me to shut up and sit down.

That kind of argument went on all during the war, except that in some cases it didn't stop at just words. I heard that in the OSS, for example, any time a Stalinist and a Trotskyist or socialist went out on an assignment together, often only one came back. Within the European partisan and underground movements the bitter struggles between the Communists and the anti-Stalinist radicals often resulted in killings that were reminiscent of what had occurred behind the Spanish loyalist lines. And later on, in the military-government operations in Japan and Germany, there were bitter political battles in which the non-Communist left supporters were at a disadvantage, for the official United States policy was one of support for our Russian allies.

In the United States the Communists denounced all strikes, and their old hero, John L. Lewis, became a fascist and a fifth columnist when he shut down the coal mines. They were the greatest advocates of speed-up, and to them the unions had only one function—to increase production. The Communists even opposed any really conscientious efforts to fight discrimination inside the armed forces. Thus, when Al Levy, my fellow-organizer from the ILGWU, was court-martialed and convicted for protesting the bad treatment given Negro soldiers, the Communists denounced him publicly for obstructing the war effort. Fortunately for Al, the ILGWU started putting pressure on the army, and a newspaper publicity campaign in New York focused enough public attention on the case to get him released from the guardhouse after he'd served three months of his sentence.

I came close to running into the same problem myself in 1945, when a counterintelligence corps man paid me a visit to warn me that I had been reported for spreading wild rumors and hostile stories about the Soviet Union. We talked about the possibility that I might have to face a court-martial for my alleged offense and I told him that I would welcome it. Fortunately, though, the war in Europe ended just then, and evidently it was decided to drop the matter. A long time later I discovered that the reports on my alleged anti-Soviet activities had been turned in by a Communist who was stationed at the base and with whom I'd had many bitter arguments.

That soldier hadn't been concerned very much about reporting me to the CIC, for in his mind I was just as much an enemy as the worst Nazi. But I was in a very different position regarding him: even though I considered him an enemy of the workers and of socialism, I wasn't a strong supporter of the American government either, and so I could not "turn him in" to what I still believed were the institutions of capitalist repression.

Yet I don't want to suggest that the whole war was taken up with this bitter struggle between the radicals and their Communist enemies; it wasn't. Neither were very many people actually involved in those political battles. In fact, damn few men and women in the country knew anything about the existence of the conflict or would have cared if they had known. Yet even though perhaps only a few thousand individuals were involved, the stakes were high and the consequences were often serious ones, especially in the immediate postwar years.

But for soldiers like me, there were plenty of other things to do in the army besides fight the Communists. First of all, there was all the ordinary business of day-to-day living; of trying to get passes for town; of worrying about where we were going to be shipped to and when; of figuring how soon you should get promoted from a private; of barracks inspections and bitching about lousy meals in the mess hall; of picking up girls and trying to get laid, something which practically never happened in spite of all the stories all the GIs told of their success when they got back to the barracks.

The only way in which my life differed from that of millions of other soldiers was that I was better off than most. After only a year of being shipped from one place to another, I ended up in the permanent cadre at an air base just outside Fort Wayne, Indiana. There I worked on the post newspaper, eventually becoming its editor. I even lived off the base in an apartment with Ruth, and nights I worked on the daily morning newspaper. Because my own post paper was the pride of the commanding officer—it always won a prize in an annual competition—I was protected and got away with actions that might otherwise have landed me in the guardhouse fairly regularly.

We had a Negro photographer on the army paper who, unlike Negroes I'd known in the movement, cared nothing about politics. Sherman Scott was a corporal, and he was probably the only Negro assigned permanently to an otherwise all-white newspaper staff, for the air force, like all the other armed services at that time, was still a disgracefully segregated institution. The one company of Negro soldiers we had on our base worked in the officers' mess and did all the other dirty housekeeping jobs. The men lived in separate barracks and ate in their own mess hall, and they had very little contact with any white soldiers except with the musicians and a few others like myself.

Scotty had come to the paper as a photographer before I joined the staff, and his position was a very anomalous one. Officially he didn't exist in the table of organization; in fact, however, he was the best-known person on the paper and on the whole base. Scotty was very good-looking, slim with a deep brown color, a small mustache, and snapping black eyes. He wore tailored gabardine uniforms in complete defiance of all the regulations and flamboyantly drove a car bigger than that owned by anybody on the base, including any of the officers. It was a huge, long Chrysler nicknamed "The Green Hornet," and every week end Scotty and some of his buddies would take off in the "Hornet" for Chicago.

Scotty's only interests were money, sex, and clothes, in that order. He and a few other Negro noncoms had separate rooms in their barracks, furnished better than any army quarters I ever saw. Scotty's walls were adorned with photos of officers' wives and female civilian employees on the base: photos he had taken himself. And remarkable as this collection was, it was nothing compared to the one he kept in his foot locker, for there, hidden in a mass of personal junk, was an additional group of photos that Scott had taken of these same girls and women, many of them nude.

Scotty didn't seem to be handicapped by having to carry around a great burden of racial prejudices. His mother had married a white widower after Scotty's own father had died, and he had been brought up in a huge family of white stepbrothers and stepsisters, his own Negro brothers and sisters, plus four mulatto kids, the product of the union between his mother and white stepfather. Scotty really didn't understand how white people could be deeply prejudiced against Negroes, since he wasn't capable of such prejudice against whites. He went everywhere assuming, initially at least, that he had a right to be there, and was always a little surprised when he encountered any difficulties.

Once I asked him to take a picture at a USO club in downtown Fort Wayne, and he came back an hour or so later with a long face, complaining that he'd been refused admission to the club by a white soldier posted there. Furious, I grabbed a jeep and roared into town, Scotty bouncing in the seat next to me. I pulled up in front of the USO, charged out, and started to chew out the soldier. He was a private, and a scared one at that, who told me he'd been given orders to keep any Negroes out of the club. When I demanded to know who had given the order, he pointed to one of the civilians working in the USO office. Just then the officer in charge of the special services at the base arrived, and I made a formal complaint to him; as a result the civilian was told not to keep anybody out of the USO, and especially not Scotty.

I went back to the jeep and waited for Scotty to take his pictures inside the USO. In a few minutes he came out, and as we drove away he turned to me with a big grin, saying, "You know, buddy, I could have taken care of this whole thing myself with just one call to that captain."

"Goddammit, then, why didn't you? Why'd you come back to the base and ask me to come downtown to straighten it out?"

"Well," he answered, "I knew you'd get a kick out of making a fuss, and I didn't want to spoil your fun."

The war in Europe ended, and preparations were made for the war-crimes trials in Germany, but I was not very much interested in them. My feelings of political ambivalence about the war were still fairly strong, although they had been shaken by the ghastly photos of the concentration-camp victims. But I couldn't help reflecting bitterly on how neither the United States nor Britain had done very much to help either the Jews or the political victims of the Nazis until after Hitler marched into Poland.

After the dropping of the atomic bombs and the surrender of the Japanese, I was transferred to an airbase just outside Indianapolis to await discharge. I arrived at my new station late one night and walked into the orderly room of the squadron to which I'd been assigned. A short, dark-haired sergeant was sitting at the desk, and I asked him in which barracks I could get a bed.

"I'm sorry, sergeant," he answered, "there just aren't any beds free tonight. Maybe you should go back to town and return in the morning."

"No, sergeant," I said, "I'm not going to do that. I'm too tired. There must be a bunk someplace where I can sack out for the night."

"Well, why don't you sleep in mine, then? I'm on charge-of-quarters duty anyway, so I'll be here all night."

"Thanks very much," I said. "That's very nice of you. I don't suppose you happen to have anything to read here, do you? I'm a little restless."

"There's some comic books over on the desk."

"No, I don't think I want any of those. Have you got anything else?"

He looked at me a little dubiously, and then reached into the drawer of his desk and pulled out a book, saying, "I don't suppose you'd be interested in this."

I looked at the book, saw that it was one I'd already read, and answered, "That'd be fine but I've read it."

We chatted for an hour or so, and when he told me his name was Adam Yarmolinsky, I asked him if he was related to Avram Yarmolinsky, a famous Hebraic scholar. Adam told me that Avram was his father and that his mother was Babette Deutsch. She was a well-known poetess whom I knew of through her sponsorship of a committee that had held a hearing to investigate whether or not there was any truth in the charges made by the Stalinists against Trotsky during the Moscow trials. After the hearing, at which Trotsky testified, the committee, headed by John Dewey, had issued a report clearing Trotsky. In the six weeks Adam and I were together awaiting discharge, we became friends and talked of our future plans. He was planning to go to Yale Law School as soon as possible after he was discharged.

An important decision about my own future was facing me at this time. Al Levy, who had managed to get a transfer to the army discharge center in the Chicago area, came to visit us in Fort Wayne most of his week ends, and together we decided not to go back to our old organizing jobs with the ILGWU. Instead, we were determined to start a weekly labor newspaper of our own in Fort Wayne. It was to be a paper without advertising, to be supported by block subscriptions from unions and mailed directly by us to the union members. Today, when I think about my decision not to go back to the ILGWU, I jokingly ascribe it to combat fatigue, but I don't really know why returning to the union no longer interested me, especially since the two men for whom I'd worked directly had always been decent and kind to me.

I nevertheless postponed writing David Gingold, the vice-president for whom I'd last worked, to tell him of my decision not to go back. Then I got a letter from him, saying he'd heard I was getting out of the army and asking when I would return to work since he was holding my old job open. Filled with shame for not having informed him, I went to see him while I was in New York trying to raise money for the paper and explained that I wasn't returning.

Our weekly labor newspaper, named *The Counsellor,* turned out to be a great flop, even though we managed to get letters of approval for it from both William Green, A.F of L. president, and Philip Murray, CIO chief.

The principal backer of *The Counsellor* was Georgia Lloyd, the daughter of a pacifist and socialist who had been known in World War I as the "Millionaire Pacificist." Georgia herself was active in many of the good causes in the Chicago area. Nevertheless, we hadn't managed to raise enough money to pay ourselves anything, so both Al and I had to work at other jobs during the day and put the paper out at night. I worked in a lumber yard and then on a construction gang with Al. We were printing *The Counsellor* in Indianapolis, and once a week we had to go there by bus, put the paper together, and bring the copies back with us.

One reason *The Counsellor* failed was that it was too far out for the relatively unsophisticated union members in the Fort Wayne area: sometimes we ran headlines up the side of the page, and sometimes we turned the type upside down to make a point. We wrote columns that were filled with obscure gags no one outside of New York and Chicago understood, and we used lots of girlie pictures that offended some of our readers. We also managed to antagonize the business interests in town by exposing some scandalous operations in the local housing authority. Finally, we'd also cut ourselves off almost immediately from the biggest union in town, the United Electrical Workers, by running an editorial denouncing Stalin and Hitler. Since the union was at the time heavily influenced by the Communists, we lost any possibility of getting it to subscribe for the locals in the area.

In only a few months, it was clear that we weren't going to make it, and *The Counsellor* folded, with very few people in

Fort Wayne even aware enough of its existence to mourn the loss.

Then my brother called from Los Angeles to tell me that my mother was dying. She'd been very sick for quite a while and had been hospitalized while I was still in the army, but she had improved enough to go home again. Like me, Cliff had just gotten out of the army and was working at some crumby job which paid him very little. Both of us were broke, and by now the little money left by my father was all eaten up by hospital and doctors' bills. I went out to Los Angeles immediately. While I was there I got a brief letter from Georgia Lloyd. She wrote that she'd been told my mother was dying of cancer, and since she knew how expensive such sicknesses were, she was sending a check to help us out. In the envelope was a check for, I think, fifteen hundred dollars, and never before or since have I felt so overwhelmed by such a spontaneous act of generosity. Mother's cancerous agony ended a few weeks later, but before she died she said to me in one of her few lucid, noncomatose moments, "You know, Paul, you're a good son when you're three thousand miles away from me, and you knew this before I did."

Now Cliff and I once again went through the barbarity of the funeral business, but this time it was even worse than when my father died. We had to buy a coffin in Los Angeles and then ship my mother's body to New York, for she had asked us to bury her in the family plot next to my father. We found an undertaker in Los Angeles who showed us all his expensive caskets while we kept asking to see the cheapest models. In disgust, he left us and called in an assistant, who took us into a room where, hidden in a closet, they kept a cheap wooden casket with the screwheads showing. We bought that one and then had to pay for a shipping case to enclose the casket in the plane. We then paid the plane fare for the body, and I flew with it to New York, where Ruth joined me from Fort Wayne for the funeral services. Cliff stayed in Los Angeles, since we didn't have enough money for two fares and I had to return East anyway.

In New York I got in touch with the same ghoul who had buried my father, since I figured he was as good as any other undertaker. He picked up mother's body at the airport, and in an hour or so he called me at an aunt's where I was staying to tell me that we would have to buy another coffin.

"What's the matter with the one we have?" I asked.

"It's too big," he said. "The graves in New York are smaller than the ones in California. You'll have to get another coffin before we can inter your mother."

Mother's long illness had prepared me for her death, and I was prepared to fight back at the undertaker. In some way he had come to symbolize for me all the corruption of the capitalist society and the organized religions which went along without resistance to such unbelievable gouging of people in their weakest moments. And fight we did, Ruth and I, even though we knew we were going to lose. I had to buy another coffin, and once again I bought the cheapest I could get over all the protests of the undertaker, who was practically in tears that I was burying my mother in such a cheap casket.

Then I started hitting back at him, with Ruth at my side, as we sat in the discreet office of the funeral parlor with the Jewish menorah in the windows.

"How much of a trade-in allowance are you going to give me for the coffin we bought in Los Angeles?" I asked.

"A trade-in?" he shouted, his unctuous manner completely lost. "You can't get a trade-in for a used coffin! It's against the law to use a coffin more than once."

"Okay. Then just give us the coffin. It's ours, we paid for it and we want it."

He was nearly hysterical with rage by this time, jumping up and down on the seat of his chair.

"What are you going to do with a used coffin? You're crazy!"

"It's none of your business what we do with it. I'll use it for a bed or a phone booth. Just give it to me."

He finally calmed down enough to stop spluttering, and we worked out a deal for an allowance on the coffin. Then I began with the shipping case, which had cost forty dollars and which I knew he'd just use to send a casket someplace else, probably charging forty dollars again. We went through the same hysterical routine. By this time I was beginning to enjoy myself, and once again I got an allowance for the case. Then I refused to hire more than one limousine for the funeral service, and we left.

He came back fighting the next day when, just before the service started, he waved me into his office, presented me with a bill, and insisted that I pay it immediately or the funeral service wouldn't start. Fortunately Ruth's mother had enough money in her checking account and I paid the bill, insisting that he give me a detailed and itemized receipt. Then, when we went into the chapel where the service was being held, I saw that he had carefully arranged the flowers around the coffin so everybody could see that it was one of the cheapest.

But we had the last small victory, for just as we were leaving the cemetery after the ceremony, I noticed some of his assistants throwing the artificial grass used to cover the gravesite into the now empty hearse. Quickly, I looked at the bill, for I recollected having seen an item listing a payment for the grass and, sure enough, there it was. I called over to the undertaker, "Take the grass out of the hearse and put it in with me. I paid for it and I want it."

For a moment I thought the man was going to have an apoplectic fit right there in the cemetery. I waited until he seemed to have gained control of himself again. "Of course," I said, "if you want to make a deal with me, I'll be willing to pay you a rental fee for the use of the grass while we were here in the cemetery. But it's not going to be what you charged me on the bill. For that kind of money, I'll keep the grass and use it for a putting green."

We made another deal right on the spot, and he returned a few dollars to me in cash. I've never seen the man again and I have no notion of whether he's still alive, but I'll bet he remembered that funeral for a long time.

Ruth and I returned to Fort Wayne, where she still had her job as secretary to the director of the small Jewish Community Council. But we had decided to leave Indiana, and I started looking for jobs in New York and Washington, writing letters to everybody I knew in the unions. In a few weeks I heard that the editor of a union newspaper was being promoted and that I had been recommended as his replacement. I went to New York for an interview and almost had the job but blew it when I got into an argument about race relations with the man I was supposed to succeed. He told me that, because of its southern membership, the union paper tried not to print pictures of white and Negro workers together in any social situation. I got angry and told him to take his job and shove it. Back to Fort Wayne I went, still unemployed, and when I got home to our apartment and told Ruth what I'd done, she said only, "I don't blame you. That's what I would have done, too."

For a few more weeks the job hunt went on without success

and I was falling back into the same dismal mood I'd been in before I'd been hired by the ILGWU. Then, the miracle happened again: I got a letter from a girl who worked for the CIO during the war telling me that the American Jewish Committee, which now employed her as an assistant director of its labor operations, needed another person in that department. She suggested I come to New York for an interview she would set up with her boss.

So I went back for an interview, somewhat dubious about working for a Jewish organization. But after talking with the director, a former A.F. of L. official, the job became more attractive to me. A few weeks later I got a letter telling me I was hired, we said good-bye to all our friends in Fort Wayne, and we came back to New York, where I began a new career as a professional Jew.

CHAPTER EIGHT

H E Y, Paul, I've been meaning to ask you something for a long time," the butcher in Nyack, New York, said to me as Ruth and I stood in front of his display case. "What do you do for a living?"

"I'm in the race-relations field," I answered.

"No kidding?" He looked around to see if his wife, who acted as the cashier, could hear him. "Do me a favor, any time you get a tip on a good horse, give me a ring."

Astounded, I agreed and never did explain to him that working in the field of race relations had very little to do with horses. Still, it was a fair assumption on his part, for in 1947 the notion of "race relations" as an occupation was still fairly new.

What does the American Jewish Committee do? And what about all those other Jewish organizations—the Anti-Defamation League, the American Jewish Congress, the American Council for Judaism, the Jewish Labor Committee, and the American Zionist Council—what do they do?

A fanciful way of describing the work of these groups is that some guy walks into the toilet of a ginmill on Third Avenue, New York, and while he's standing at the urinal, he notices that someone has written "Screw the Jews" on the toilet wall. He goes outside and immediately calls up the Anti-Defamation League of the B'nai B'rith and the other organizations. An ADL man rushes down to the bar, carefully dusts the wall with fingerprint powder, photographs the prints, and goes back to the ADL office to check them against the two million prints of known anti-Semites. Thereupon the ADL publishes a photo of the slogan in its bulletin, proving that anti-Semitism is on the increase in the United States and therefore everybody should join the B'nai B'rith.

When the man from the American Jewish Committee arrives at the bar, he purses his lips, studies the slogan from all angles, and leaves quietly. Shortly thereafter, the Committee announces that it is making a large grant to a social-science research center at Columbia University to do a survey of anti-Semitic wall writing since the burial of Pompeii. At the same time its own staff writes a pamphlet proving that a Jew invented the martini. This pamphlet is then exhaustively pretested and tested for its effect by the AJC's research department. After all the bugs in the pamphlet are taken out and all possible "boomerang" effects eliminated, it is distributed by all the liquor dealers in the country, to be put in bars where drinkers can pick it up to read while they are getting stoned. The AJC also announces that at its next annual meeting a distinguished medical authority will address the members on "Alcoholism and Anti-Semitism: A Clinical View," to be followed by a workshop discussion.

The American Jewish Congress representative shows up at the bar, and while he is inside the toilet looking at the writing, two dozen pickets from the organization are already marching up and down outside, carrying signs that say "Tear Down the Wall!" and "We Demand Action by the UN!" Back at the Congress' national office the legal staff is busily preparing a brief, to be taken to the Supreme Court the next morning requesting the Court to issue an order forbidding the sale of liquor in the United States to anyone making an anti-Semitic remark.

In the meantime the Jewish Labor Committee is arranging a whole series of week-end institutes for members of the bartenders' union. At these institutes speakers will discuss the history of the AFL–CIO, pointing out that Samuel Gompers, its founder and first president, was Jewish and that Arthur Goldberg, United States Representative to the United Nations, began his notable career as a CIO attorney. In the weeks that follow, every state AFL–CIO convention will pass a resolution, sponsored by the JLC, calling on union members not to pee in anti-Semitic urinals.

The American Council for Judaism calls a press conference in a fancy New York hotel where its spokesman, flanked by two Arabs representing the American Friends of the Middle East, makes a statesmanlike statement which has already been delivered to the United States Secretary of State. In the statement the

Council denies that anyone could have written "Screw the Jews" on the toilet wall because in America there is no such thing as a Jew, but only Americans of Jewish descent, and a pretty vague descent at that. The Council therefore calls upon the Secretary of State, the President, and all the Govenors in the country to condemn strongly the efforts of Israel and the Zionists to identify Israel with American Jews.

Finally the American Zionist Council steps into the picture. Its operation is the simplest and easiest to understand. It simply borrows the photo of the slogan taken by the ADL and reprints it in the AZC bulletin under the caption: "If you [not us, of course] emigrate to Israel, you can write 'Screw the Christians' on the toilet walls there."

Actually, of course, all these organizations are very serious about their activities, and much of what they do is very worthwhile. But I hadn't understood the details of these operations when I went to work for the American Jewish Committee, even though I had known of the Committee's existence while I was still a kid at L. & M. Kahn & Co. In those days the Committee had been a small but very influential organization with chapters scattered all over the country. Its work was performed quietly, without publicity, and generally behind the scenes, defending the rights of Jews. The Committee's constituency was predominantly made up of the kind of wealthy influential Jews of German descent who were members of the Harmonie Club in New York or who came from distinguished German-Jewish families in the South and West. The Committee was never vulgar in its approach, nor had it ever sought much support among the growing East European Jewish middle- and lower-class groups. When the Committee decided on a policy, one of its leaders discussed the matter with the appropriate government officials. And the organization's fund raising was done quietly among the leading Jewish families of America rather than by mass appeal.

But the war had changed the character of the Committee, and by the time I joined its staff, it was on its way to developing a new concept of its operations, including carrying on work within unions. It was also finding it necessary to compete for the support of a wider group of people whose allegiance was being given to more middle-class institutions, such as the Anti-Defamation League or the more militant American Jewish Congress. In contrast to the Committee, which believed Jewish interests could be defended effectively without creating a public furor, the Congress was vociferous and aggressive wherever it felt Jewish interests to be at stake.

The doubts I'd had about working for a Jewish organization were quickly resolved once I started functioning on the AJC staff. It turned out not to be very Jewish except in the formal sense, and I discovered that being a "professional Jew" made no difference whatever in how I lived except that we had more days off than other people, for in addition to such regular holidays as Christmas, New Year's, and Thanksgiving, we didn't have to work on the Jewish holidays, either. The AJC staff even included a few Orthodox Jews who ate only kosher food and stopped working early on Friday afternoon so that they could get home to the Bronx or Brooklyn before sundown. But there were few of them, and you could hardly tell they were gone. I soon lost the slight embarrassment I felt about suddenly becoming Jewish, for although I was an employee of the American Jewish Committee, I was no more Jewish in the religious or moral sense than I would have been had I been working for some Protestant organization operating in the same general field.

Starting from its original premise that the quiet elimination of anti-Semitism was the best way to quietly defend the interests of American Jews, the Committee had moved into the broader areas of community and race relations, fields that grew very rapidly in the postwar period. Organizationally the Committee staff was divided up into a number of divisions; a high degree of coordinated effort was always being talked about, even if it was never achieved.

The labor division, operating under the name "National Labor Service," for which I had been hired was one of the smaller operations. Its whole staff consisted of David Sigman, its director, who had been regional AFL representative from Wisconsin; Hilda Siff, the girl who had gotten me the job; me; and a couple of secretaries. Similar divisions, staffed by people with backgrounds in their assigned fields, worked with business groups, fraternal lodges, veterans' organizations, women's clubs, and community groups. All of us had the responsibility of trying to get these organizations to integrate into their programs all kinds of materials and plans about race relations in general and, more cautiously, about Jews specifically.

A general merger of interests had taken place at the American

Jewish Committee between the organization's "lay leaders," as its voluntary supporters—the community figures who were its constituency—were described, and the organization's full-time paid staff, its professionals. At this time the primary community base of the AJC was still among the old German-Jewish assimilationist families, non-Zionist in their views, without any deep roots in Jewish religious tradition. Quite a few staffers—enough to have some influence on policy—had been recruited from radical or socialist backgrounds similar to mine. They were also non-Zionist and nonreligious, though for a different set of reasons.

Thus the emphasis of the Committee at the time was not heavily Jewish, or at least not heavily Jewish in those of its operations which related to the non-Jewish world. If anyone inquired, no attempt was made to disguise or hide the organizational origin of these operations, but neither was the Jewish background pushed into the foreground. My own department, for example, was officially named the National Labor Service of the American Jewish Committee, but only the name "National Labor Service" appeared on its publications, on the theory that an organization without an open Jewish identification could operate more effectively with non-Jewish groups than one, say, like our rival, the Jewish Labor Committee.

For me and many other members of the AJC staff this arrangement was ideal: it provided us with a base from which we could fight prejudice and discrimination without any need to be Jewish. It was the organizational expression of my own ambivalence about being Jewish, my own unclear wish to be something other than what I was. Indeed, most of my own work with the unions dealt with discrimination against Negroes rather than against Jews. I found it difficult to become very concerned about anti-Semitism in unions, since outside of the garment trades, not many Jews belonged to unions and I did not believe anti-Semitism in general to be much of a problem in America. Therefore I used my job at the National Labor Service to concentrate on what I thought was the far more important question in unions—that of anti-Negro prejudice.

As I worked in this field, I began to come into contact with my counterparts, the "professional Negroes" who were on the staffs of national Negro organizations. Their "Negroness" was of about the same level as my "Jewishness"; most of them had no more contact or identification with the mass of poor Negroes than I had with the mass of middle-class Jews. But there was one very important distinction between the "professional Jew" and the "professional Negro": for educated Negroes, working for a "race" organization represented a more important career than a counterpart job did for Jews, since it was one of the few careers open to them. In the Jewish organizations, the "professionals" weren't as important as the wealthy or influential lay leaders who gave the organization its real status. But in the Negro groups, it was professionals such as Walter White, Jr., or Lester Granger who were the key personalities.

My work was all rather intangible, and no specific guidelines could have been drawn up for carrying it out. In the labor division we tried to operate primarily with national and state labor groups, to cover a very wide area. We attended state and national conventions, carrying with us an exhibit of antidiscrimination materials which we set up in the convention lobby. At these conventions we lobbied to get antidiscrimination resolutions passed and pushed for motions urging local unions to distribute the pamphlets and posters we had available. During the summers we attended union-sponsored institutes and schools, where we taught a course in how to fight prejudice and held classes in grievance procedure, public speaking, labor history, and anything else that was needed. We tried to establish friendly relations with as many union officials as we could, so as to have ready access to them; this was especially important in those unions which had some kind of antidiscrimination operation of their own.

We also developed specific materials for unions in cooperation with the staff members whose responsibility it was to produce all the pamphlets, posters, films, and film strips that every division felt was needed for its specific audiences. The labor division even distributed a comic strip to hundreds of union newspapers. Each episode in the strip showed its hero, a brave and handsome union official, fighting the demon of prejudice. The general emphasis of the strip was similar to our over-all line in the labor division—"Discrimination Costs You Money"; this slogan was the title of a pamphlet we turned out on how the bad bosses use discrimination to split the workers among themselves and keep them poor while divided.

Despite its sometimes foolish aspects, the work was interest-

ing and occasionally even rewarding, especially when it meant
teaching at a union institute or school, where there was an opportunity to discuss prejudice with large numbers of union members. We had to confront reality far more often at these summer
schools and institutes than at conventions or meetings of official
antidiscrimination committees, where a whole day could be
spent mouthing pious phrases. At a summer school a discussion
about discrimination with union members was likely to result in
their admitting openly that they thought Negroes were inferior
to whites and that most Jews were businessmen because they
were smarter than Christians.

At one such discussion the instructor, a university professor
who worked during the summers teaching at union institutes,
attempted to answer the union members' ideas about Jewish
businessmen by analyzing how Jews had been forced into
finance through persecution. When he finished, he asked whether
anyone in the class still believed Jews were smarter than Christians. One hand shot up in the back of the room.

"Wouldn't you say that people who teach are smarter than
those who are students?" asked the union member.

Cautiously, the teacher replied, "Well, perhaps not smarter,
but maybe the teachers have had a chance to get a better education."

Unsatisfied, the worker persisted. "But it's the smarter people
who try to get a better education, don't they?"

"Okay," conceded the teacher. "Let's assume that's right.
Let's assume that teachers are smarter than the students. Where
does that take you?"

"That means the instructors like you in this school are
smarter than we are and that's why you're a teacher and we're
auto workers."

"So?"

"So how many of the ten instructors in this school are Jewish?"

The teacher started to run through the staff, realizing with a
sinking feeling that eight of the ten were Jewish.

Weakly he answered, "I guess more than half, anyway."

"That's what I mean," said the auto worker, triumphantly.
"Jews *are* smarter."

If I had been the instructor, I would have told the student that
I knew at least two Jews, Ruth and me, who weren't so smart, at
least when it came to deciding where they were to live. When

we'd come back to New York I had decided—over Ruth's objections, it's true—that we ought not to live in the city, but in the country instead.

We therefore looked for a house to rent in the country. We found one, too, a charming-looking but very uncomfortable and expensive converted barn, high up on a hill on the River Road in Grandview-on-Hudson, a tiny hamlet just south of Nyack. Grandview, like Nyack, was on the west side of the Hudson River, the Jersey side as it is known to New Yorkers, although both towns were in New York state, north of the Jersey border.

Being in the country was very pleasant on summer week ends, but it was a terrible drag all during the winter months and often enough during the rest of the year. Ruth was working as a legal secretary for a law firm on Twenty-third Street, very close to my office. The firm had four partners, all young, two of whom had been classmates of mine at Townsend Harris. So both of us had to commute every day, and the commuting from Grandview to New York was awful, for the only way to get into the city was by a bus that took more than an hour to get from the River Road area where we lived to upper Manhattan, across the George Washington Bridge. There we disembarked and joined the flow of people into the subway station. We then rode on the Seventh Avenue Subway down to Forty-second Street, where we took the shuttle to the east side Subway. After arriving at the Grand Central Station, we got on the local train to Twenty-eighth or Twenty-third Street and, exhausted, walked the few blocks to our offices.

At night, after work, we reversed the procedure and arrived home exhausted again. Even worse, if we stayed late in the city, we had to take the last bus back; this local meandered in and out of all the little towns in the area before it turned onto the River Road. And in the winter, when it was really miserable on the highway, the bus trip often took two hours or even longer if, as sometimes happened, the bus slid off the road into a ditch and had to be pushed out.

But there were compensations for all the discomfort of commuting and the terrible winters. Some of the friends we made while riding on the cold bus were warm and interesting. Like similar places, Nyack was really two communities: one made up of the old-timers who had been born there, and the other made up of the newer residents, many of them painters, writers, or theater people, and it was in this group that we found our friends—people like Edmund and Ann Fuller and Hortense Calisher. Fuller was an editor in New York and Hortense was beginning her career as a writer. We found great pleasure, too, in renewing relationships in New York with ex-comrades, some of whom were still involved in the radical movement, and with old friends like the Kahns, who dated back to my days as an office boy.

We found Scotty again, too, just as ebullient as ever. He had set up a photo studio and modeling agency on One Hundred and Twenty-fifth Street and was living with his wife in a penthouse in one of the most expensive apartment houses in Harlem. By then he had a partner, a plump, round-faced, silky Negro named Buster, who had lots of money that he earned in mysterious ways about which I never asked. I got a good education from Buster, especially when it came to betting on ball games and prize fights.

One night, at a party Scotty was giving, Buster asked me to join him the next day in his box at the Polo Grounds. I answered that much as I'd love to go, I had to be out of town. When he asked where I was going, I told him that I was headed for the South. He looked at me in amazement.

"Christ, man, what the hell you going down South for?"

"I have to give a lecture at a union institute."

"What kind of lecture?"

"About race relations."

"Man, you're crazy to go down South. I never go there. I had a terrible experience once down South."

Now, I thought, it's going to come out, now I'm finally going to find out what makes Buster tick, why he behaves the way he does, now I'll discover how some trauma he suffered as a Negro down South affected the way he has lived since then.

"What happened, Buster?"

"Listen, Paul, I went down South once, to Florida, and I dropped nearly ten grand at a lousy dog track. You'll never catch me down there again."

When we weren't traveling to and from New York, and when it wasn't freezing cold, snowy, or sleety, we had a very pleasant routine in Grandview. Saturday mornings we walked into town, shopped at the Co-op, saw the butcher who wanted tips on the horses, and carried our groceries home on the bus. Our weekend visitors would start arriving after lunch. Bill Worthy, then on the staff of the Workers Defense League, came up very often, for he loved fishing and would sit for hours either out in a borrowed boat or on a wall over the river. Sometimes we had tea or drinks late in the afternoon with the Fullers or some other friends, and in the evenings we'd have a party or just sit outside in the grass admiring the view.

But two things began bugging us during the time we lived in the Nyack area: increasingly I was getting involved once again in a full-time and painful fight with the Communists, and that fight was having unpleasant consequences for us in Nyack.

The great tensions building up in 1947 and 1948 between the United States and the Soviet Union were inevitably reflected inside the American Jewish Committee and in many other Jewish social-service, civil-rights, and community organizations. These internal strains also affected the YWCA, the NAACP, and other such institutions, but they were much worse among the Jewish groups.

One major source of internal tension resided in the United Office and Professional Workers of America, a small CIO union. The union had come into existence in the thirties but hadn't grown much. Its membership was concentrated among the office help working for various other CIO unions, although it did have a small insurance-salesmen division as well. Almost from its start, UOPWA was under the direct supervision of the Communist party faction then inside the CIO. UOPWA's operations expanded during the war, and, like all the other Communist-dominated unions, the UOPWA subordinated the fight for economic benefits to a "Win the War" or an "Open the Second Front" policy. When the war was over, it started to organize the employees of the community and social-work agencies in New York City. No union had made a serious attempt to organize any of these organizations before UOPWA, and since the agencies were all expanding in the postwar period, they were a fertile ground. The union policy became one of militant demands for wage increases and decreases in work hours. Such demands got lots of natural support from the badly paid and overworked employees in the social agencies who were also outside the social security and unemployment insurance benefit system.

The membership of UOPWA in New York therefore grew very quickly immediately after World War II, and the union was successfully negotiating contracts with many of the agencies, especially those whose own top staffs and boards were liberals and therefore unwilling to fight unions. As the union negotiated more and more contracts, its influence grew. Even more important, some of the contracts provided that the union had to be given the opportunity to supply personnel for any new jobs or job replacements before the agencies could do any outside hiring. This meant that some agencies were being steadily staffed by Communists and Communist sympathizers, sent in by the UOPWA office. In one agency, which dealt with refugee immigrants to the United States, Communist party members were putting these new immigrants on the mailing lists of CP fronts a few days after they had arrived in the country.

The UOPWA had a contract at the American Jewish Committee, too, but Communist influence was weaker there than at any other agency in New York. The AJC chapter of UOPWA contained enough socialists, ex-socialists, ex-Trotskyites, and other anti-Stalinist radicals to minimize the Communist influence. These people, like myself, were not only knowledgeable about the CP but were equally as demanding of our employers as the Communists and better at negotiating contracts.

Very quickly Hilda Siff and I moved into the leadership of the AJC chapter of UOPWA. Supported by our own membership, we began to raise hell at the local meetings, made up of all the chapters in the city. And at these meetings we discovered familiar faces from other agencies siding with us in debates and familiar voices voting with us on issues. In a matter of a few months we had found enough radical non-Communists to set up a city-wide caucus of union members from other chapters who shared our feelings about the CP.

But all the time we had to fight on two fronts, for the internal fight against the Communists within the union went on simultaneously with the battle against our own employers. One method that we used to build up our own strength inside the agencies was staffing the organization with people we knew and trusted politically. Every time a new job opened, we rushed around, making phone calls and trying to find out whether some ex-socialist or Trotskyist was available for the job. And when we found them, we recommended they be hired on the assumption that the personnel people would know that political weight should be given to our recommendation.

Filling newly created jobs or vacancies in this way posed no ethical or political dilemmas for me or anyone else in our group, but we did run into a hell of a problem when it came to dealing with Communists who were already working or who applied for vacant jobs at the same time as our people did. In the first case, if a Communist was already working, we concluded that we would have to defend his right to hold the job if the agency tried to fire him, even though he represented organized opposition to our viewpoint. But if a non-Communist radical and a Communist were both applying for the same job, we pushed for our choice, on the assumption that if both of them were equally competent, the non-Communist should be hired. And over a period of months those agencies in which our political orientation dominated began to have a larger and larger group of non-Communist radicals and ex-radicals on their staffs.

In other agencies, Jewish and non-Jewish, an equally perplexing dilemma which confronted liberals was how to attack Communists and still avoid the charge of "redbaiting," considered then to be the absolute worst sin, the nadir of reactionary political methods. Making an accusation of "redbaiting" was one of the favorite devices the Communists used in their battles with their opponents on either the right or the left. The term had come into popular liberal use during the prewar years, when Communists, liberals, socialists, radicals, and union organizers were all indiscriminately lumped together as "Communists" by reactionary employers, government officials, and the mass media. In the liberal lexicon, a "redbaiter" was the slimiest creature in the world and anyone who described a Communist by calling him that, even when it was true and had some significance, dropped automatically into that category.

Simultaneously, the Communists were busily identifying themselves with all the minority groups. No UOPWA meeting was really complete until some member got up to speak and identified himself as, "I'm a Jew and so I know what it means to be discriminated against. And I'm a veteran so I know what it means to fight the Fascists. And that's why I'm against these redbaiters, etc., etc., etc., etc."

Our group's struggle against the Communist leadership of UOPWA was being paralleled inside other CIO unions, too. The Reuther brothers were fighting and beating the Communists in the United Automobile Workers; Jim Carey was fighting them inside the United Electrical Workers, and the echoes of these bitter struggles could be heard inside the national staff organization of the CIO even though Phil Murray was still unwilling to deal with the problem. (It was not until late 1948, when the Communists inside the CIO tried to swing the CIO into supporting Henry Wallace's Progressive Party campaign, that Murray finally decided to weigh in with his tremendous prestige against the Communists.)

Except for the unions, however, and an organization like the American Veterans Committee, the cold war battle lines had not yet been rigidly drawn inside the country. The complete break of the United States with the Soviet Union hadn't taken place, and in March of 1947 American officials went to Moscow to attend a conference designed to halt the growth of bitterness between the East and the West. In the debate over whether or not to abolish the American Communist party, J. Edgar Hoover joined with the American Civil Liberties Union in opposing such a proposal. And even though the country accepted Truman's position of sending aid to Greece and Turkey, the bitter civil war in Greece was hardly understood by anyone in the United States.

In the midst of this rapidly changing world situation, the dilemma of radicals opposed to the Communist party was an agonizing one. We had none of the illusions of the liberal concerning the nature of the Communist party, but we were just as adamantly opposed to the party's suppression by the government as were the Communists themselves. Our position was made even more difficult because it was virtually impossible to explain to the great mass of liberals how we could fight the Communist party inside unions at the same time that we fought against its suppression by the government.

Some of us were also very uneasy about some of our allies, especially the Catholic Church. At the time the Church was moving actively into the trade-union scene in ways we didn't understand very clearly. In the years before the war many of us had admired the devoted Catholic anarchists and socialists who were associated with the Catholic Worker movement of Dorothy Day. We had slept in the houses they ran for the poor in Chicago and on the Bowery, we'd eaten with them, and we'd distributed leaflets and newspapers alongside them at the same public meetings. But in the postwar years we ran into new kinds of Catholic groups engaged in social action. Some were open groups, like the Association of Catholic Trade Unionists, which operated as caucuses inside the unions, but others were more mysterious and seemed to have no membership base.

One day, for example, a phone call came from someone in one of these groups to Carl Rachlin's office, which we were using as the headquarters for the UOPWA caucus. Rachlin's wife and the wives of two of his partners were all members of the caucus—they worked at a Jewish agency where they had become the center of the anti-Communist group inside the union. The man on the phone told Rachlin he wanted to meet with us and discuss future plans for the caucus, and Rachlin set up a meeting for him. He arrived and immediately began telling us that he hoped he'd be permitted to attend a three-day session we were calling in St. Louis, where we were planning to pull together the non-Communists in UOPWA locals from other parts of the country in preparation for a fight against the leadership at a forthcoming national convention.

Surprised and a little perturbed at his intimate knowledge of our plans, I asked him whom he represented. He answered that he carried the proxy vote of several UOPWA locals made up mostly of insurance men in the New England area. I went on to inquire as bluntly as I could who was financing his operations but got no really satisfactory answer from him. A few days later I met with him again, this time in his office, a couple of rooms located in a suite occupied by a law firm. During the course of this meeting he told me to get in touch with him if I ever needed any help in dealing with Catholics or Catholic groups. From some obscure references he made, I gathered that he had some direct connection with the "power house," as the Madison Avenue headquarters of the New York Archdiocese was familiarly known.

I had to use his services only a few weeks later during the UOPWA convention, for right in the midst of our unsuccessful fight a well-known Catholic priest showed up at the convention headquarters, a hotel in Brooklyn, to assist us. At the time the one thing we didn't want was any help from this priest. I made a hasty phone call to the man from the "power house," explaining the situation and asking him to get the priest out of the hotel. The powerhouse must have had a lot of power, too, for within ten minutes the priest was gone.

This kind of uneasy alliance between such diverse groups of anti-Communist radicals, ex-radicals, and Catholics was charac-

teristic of the immediate postwar period. None of the people in
the alliance was happy with the other's presence in it, for although
they were all united in their opposition to the Communist influence, the radicals and ex-radicals were as distrustful of the Catholics' motives as the Catholics were of the others'.

Inside the political world which I inhabited it seemed as if all
our energies were being given over to this struggle for control of
organizations. Everywhere I turned, another battle in this war
was raging. The American Veterans Committee in New York
was literally being torn apart by a struggle between the Communists and their sympathizers and a somewhat strange alliance
of the anti-Communists. And in the midst of all this vicious in-
fighting at conventions, district councils, or branch meetings of
AVC or the NAACP branch in Nyack, were the nonradical and
usually naive liberals, bewildered by the charges, counter-
charges, accusations, and diatribes hurled by one group at the
other.

Physically I was paying one hell of a price for this frantic
activity. There was some kind of local union meeting almost
every night, and since only a few people from our caucus had
been elected to positions within the local, we had to be present
all the time. The AJC chapter also met once a week to discuss
the negotiations between the chapter and the agency, which were
dragging on interminably, taking up still more time. Not even
the week ends were free; often I had to attend UOPWA meetings on Saturdays. In addition, I was going to AVC and NAACP
meetings, which were always bitter. Added to this was my own
work, which took me out of town very often.

Psychologically, too, I was paying a high price for my role. I
was in a continual state of fury at the Communists, relieved only
once in a while by a gag. For example, early in our fight with
the UOPWA leadership, they had assigned a nice-looking,
somewhat plump girl party member to be "pleasant" to me. One
Saturday afternoon, after we had finished a grueling meeting of
the local executive committee, she invited me to her apartment
for a drink. I went along with her, and when we got to her place
I gladly participated in the opening moves in what looked like a
pretty good seduction by her of me. But almost at the point where
I thought she was ready to either undress herself or be undressed,
I had to be the wise guy.

"By the way," I said to her, "I'm sure it doesn't matter to

you, but maybe I ought to tell you anyway. My name really isn't Jacobs, it's Braunstein and actually I'm Trotsky's son."

Rarely in my life, before or since, have I ever heard the kind of language that came from that girl's mouth. I damn near didn't get out of the apartment alive. The next time I walked into an executive committee and sat down next to her, she got so mad that she stood up and stormed from the room, slamming the door so hard it shattered all the glass.

Another time, at a local meeting attended by hundreds of members, I was in the middle of a speech poking fun at the national leadership of the union for its slavish devotion to the Communists when a woman, insane with rage at me, ran up to the microphone where I was standing and spat full in my face. The crowd roared, mostly in approval, and with great effort I restrained myself from chasing her down the aisle and slamming her one. I started to speak again but couldn't be heard over the booing, so I just stood there while on the platform the chairman grinned delightedly down at the scene, making no attempt to quiet the crowd. I tried to speak again and managed to just get out, "I'll make a deal with all of you. You be quiet until I finish speaking and then I'll get my raincoat and run around the room while all of you spit at me." Then the room really exploded, for those people took their politics seriously, and I thought we were surely going to have a riot in the union hall.

Ruth and I paid a price in Nyack, too, for our political views. The word about our activities in New York soon seeped back to Nyack, where a number of Communist party officials lived and where they influenced many liberals. We began to hear rumors on the bus about our being fascists, and very quickly we sensed that at social gatherings we were given the fast brush-off. Some of the more militant party members and sympathizers even called on our landlady to tell her what bad people we were. She, poor lady, was terribly confused, because she knew that we had Negro friends who visited us all the time and lived in the house for long periods. In her mind anyone who had Negro friends had to be a "progressive," a term used to describe people who weren't the kind of redbaiters we were alleged to be.

But we weren't all alone and isolated in Nyack. Edmund Fuller was a great help in defending us within the community. And there were others, too, including Nevin Sayre, the pacificist colleague of A. J. Muste, and an old friend, Walter Blount, who was active in the Nyack branch of the NAACP, which we had joined. There, too, we were having the same kind of political fights, though on a much smaller scale than the ones in New York City.

Impossible as it seems, during all this time, while I was working for the American Jewish Committee and while the efforts of the Jews in Palestine to achieve statehood were being prominently discussed in all the media, I managed to continue to avoid thinking about what it was to be a Jew. I was successfully able to assume that the problem of anti-Semitism encompassed prejudice and discrimination of any kind, but particularly against the Negroes. The American Jewish Committee had been a non-Zionist institution for many years, and a strong fervor for the establishment of a Jewish state was just beginning to make itself felt in the agency; but as yet it wasn't a matter for long and principled argument, since there were few, if any, avid Zionists on the staff.

Our contact with the Fullers and the Sayres in Nyack led Ruth and me into a relationship with the Fellowship of Reconciliation, the pacifist group of which Sayre was the international secretary and A. J. Muste the American secretary. The Fullers and ourselves joined the Sayres and one or two others every week for a discussion of pacificism, nonviolence, and love. It was in those years that Bayard Rustin, George Houser, and, later, James Farmer, were first beginning to explore the uses of nonviolence in race relations. The organization that is now CORE came into existence during this period, too.

I found it hard to accept the religious elements in the FOR view, though I tried hard to open myself to them. Perhaps, the orientation was too Christian for me, although there was a Jewish peace fellowship, too. But in race relations I had come to understand very well how effective tactical nonviolence could be. I participated eagerly in a sit-in at a hotel in Columbus, Ohio, when some Negro delegates to a CIO meeting were refused service in the dining room. Later, in Washington, D. C., Ruth and I were in an early sit-in at the Greyhound Bus Station during a hot summer week end when I was teaching at a FOR-CORE workshop there.

I had been in Washington all week, and when Ruth came down for the week end, we took an air-conditioned room at the new Statler Hotel. On Saturday afternoon, after we'd finished at the school, Bayard, Bill Worthy, Ruth, and I went to the hotel to cool off and have a few drinks. We walked through the lobby, the object of many stares from people who weren't yet used to seeing Negroes in Washington hotel lobbies. And in the middle of the lobby, Rustin and Worthy dropped behind and started talking loudly in a phony dialect, making sure that everybody heard and saw them. Upstairs the four of us dispersed over the room, and I ordered drinks from room service. Bayard stretched out on the bed next to Ruth while Bill and I were sitting in chairs when the waiter arrived with the drinks.

When he walked into the room and saw Bayard on the bed with Ruth, I thought the waiter was going to drop dead. But he managed to put down the drinks and get out of the room with only a furtive glance behind him. Half an hour or so later I ordered another round. In the meantime Worthy had chased Rustin off the bed and was lying there reading the newspaper when the same waiter came back again. This time he saw Rustin sitting in a chair, and his face showed the relief he felt. But it lasted only an instant, for as soon as he put down the drinks, he spotted Worthy now on the bed next to Ruth, and Worthy spotted him, glaring. Deliberately Bill reached over and started to hug Ruth, who hugged him back as the waiter vanished, aged at least ten years by the sight he'd witnessed.

(How innocent, in our seriousness, we were then during the summer of 1947! On the week ends Worthy spent with us in Nyack we talked for hours about nonviolence, for we believed its use would, in not very many years, make the white world understand how irrational and unreasonable race prejudice was. And we teased each other all the time in ways we couldn't do today. Then, when I said something foolish, Worthy used to say, "Stop talking like a dumb nigger"; but today, he's a leader in the Freedom Now movement among Negroes, a movement committed to black nationalism, and I'm sure he could never talk, even privately, to me as once he did. And one night during the Harlem riots of July, 1964, Ruth and I, vacationing in far-off Hawaii, saw Bayard on television pleading with an angry mob to disperse while they were shouting for Mohammed and saying, "Okay, so call me Tom, I still don't want to see women and children killed.")

The winter of 1947-48 was horribly cold and unpleasant in New York. Blizzard followed blizzard, so that the snow and ice never had time enough to melt down to the more familiar dirty slush. The River Road was so icy it reminded me of Minneapolis, and we had to use ski poles to climb the driveway to our house. It took hours to get home, and for weeks we never got back to Nyack until long after it was dark. On a couple of nights when I was out of the city, the snow fell so heavily Ruth never got back at all. We were apart for one whole week end when I'd stayed home on a Friday to work and she'd gone into the city and wasn't able to get back.

The worst part of the winter was the commuting. The bus schedules were completely disrupted by the blizzards, and we spent hours huddled at the stop waiting for the bus to pull up to a lurching halt when the driver saw us. More and more frequently, as the ice and snow on the highway got worse, the bus would slide off the road into a ditch. Then all the passengers would have to get out and push the bus back onto the road.

One morning late in the winter Edmund Fuller and I were side by side, shoving the bus out of the ditch, when I turned to him and said, "You know, this doesn't make any sense to me. I'm paying the bus company a lot of money each month for the privilege of pushing their goddammed bus out of a ditch. Well, the hell with that. I think we'll go back to California. At least it's warm there."

A few months later, after a tearful farewell to our first cat, whom we gave to a neighbor, we drove off in a jeep station wagon back to Los Angeles. We took six weeks to get across the country; Ruth's mother, who came along for the trip, was ensconced high on the back seat, surrounded by our books.

CHAPTER NINE

Bᴇ Y 1948 Los Angeles had mushroomed in the pattern that has become its dominant characteristic today. The bean fields on the outskirts of the city were filled with hastily built tract houses, and these identically ugly divisions were being pushed in every direction to fill long-standing needs for housing. But there was still a shortage of apartments, and we drove the streets for hours before we located a small apartment in a dingy house scheduled for demolition to make room for a freeway. It gave us a few months to look for another place, and we moved in while I began setting up an office of the National Labor Service in Los Angeles and Ruth looked for a job.

A great number of Jewish agencies, including the American Jewish Committee, were then operating in Los Angeles; even when the city was small, it had always had a fair proportion of Jews, especially in the movie industry. But the movie people made up a community of their own, having very little contact with the rest of the city. In earlier years the Jewish community had been dominated for a long time by the older families of German descent who had gone out to California during the nineteenth century and settled in Los Angeles rather than San Francisco. But there was also a fair-sized contingent of Jewish workers, mostly from the garment industry, who had moved to Los Angeles because of the warm climate. Most of them lived in Boyle Heights, the eastern section of the city, clustered around Brooklyn Avenue, where you could find a Workmen's Circle Hall, a Labor Zionist Headquarters, and a good delicatessen. But by 1948 a growing Jewish middle-class group, including many veterans, was also starting to arrive in large numbers.

All of this fast growth, this sudden middle-class influx into the city, meant a great increase in Jewish activities. New synagogues and temples were sprouting up, and a whole new middle-class Jewish enclave, complete with stores, began to grow in the western part of the city, near the intersections of Beverly Boulevard and Fairfax Avenue. The competition among the various Jewish organizations for support from these new arrivals got pretty tough.

The American Jewish Committee chapter in Los Angeles included judges, attorneys, and members of the old families, but not too many people from the movie industry. The group as a whole was conservative. Many of its members were Republicans, and a few of them also held memberships in the American Council for Judaism. And although they were certainly very pleasant and well-mannered people, who lived in elegant Beverly Hills mansions, I didn't find them very congenial intellectually. Somewhat sadly I also discovered that my job for the National Labor Service in Los Angeles required getting much more involved with other Jewish groups than had been necessary in New York. There I had been one person on the staff of a large organization, and my responsibilities were limited to working with non-Jewish groups on the outside. But in Los Angeles I really had to be a professional Jew: for a few months I was the only representative of the American Jewish Committee in the city, and even after another man came to take over the main responsibility of running the chapter, I still had more internal responsibilities within the Jewish community than in New York.

One of the most important places where I had to represent the American Jewish Committee was within the Jewish Community Council, which was simultaneously a loose confederation of all the Jewish groups in the city and the main arena for the competition among them. The Council had a subcommittee, the Community Relations Council, which had a small staff of its own, responsible to the self-perpetuating group of influential individuals who made up the subcommittee. People like me, who worked for the various national organizations, were also members of the CRC in a kind of ex-officio status.

Ostensibly the function of the CRC was to be responsible for Jewish public relations in the city, to represent quietly Jewish positions to the non-Jewish community, and to safeguard the interests of the Jewish community from any anti-Semitic threats. But often the meetings of the CRC became intraorganizational fights as the staffs, each backed by its prominent lay members, battled, sometimes not so politely, over jurisdiction and function. The chairman of the committee, a prominent attorney who represented major movie companies and was a Republican to boot, was the key contact between the Jewish community and the Republican party, as well as being a very powerful influence in the movie industry.

At the first few meetings of the CRC that I attended as an AJC representative, I kept a wary silence, trying to sort out all the players. There were the usual arguments among the staff members of the different agencies over jurisdiction. But the internal relations among the organizations were complicated by two other elements: aggressive Zionist groups were trying to exercise their influence, based on Israel's new status, and my old enemies, the Communists, who were represented directly in the community council by a CP front group, the Jewish People's Fraternal Order, had a few individuals in the CRC who were the same naive "progressive" type I'd encountered back East.

It didn't look as if there was any escape from this problem, especially as the tension grew between the United States and the Soviet Union. So, somewhat wearily, I joined up again in the new war. But this campaign was far more difficult than in New York. Many of the people involved were so unsophisticated politically that it wasn't possible to make the kind of arguments with them that had been so effective in New York. And the issue of Communists operating inside the Los Angeles Jewish community was even more difficult and traumatic to deal with because the case of the Hollywood Ten and the start of the movie industry's blacklisting of real and alleged Communists was beginning to have ugly repercussions.

Some of these repercussions were personal ones, Nyack all over again. When we'd returned to Los Angeles, very few of our old friends were still there, and inevitably, our choice of new ones was limited by the bitter political fights in which I became so quickly involved. At one of the early meetings of the CRC that I attended, for example, I listened in amazement to a member of the group defend stupidly a position taken by the one clearly Communist front group affiliated to the Jewish Community Council. Then I asked for the floor. It was the first time I had spoken at a CRC meeting, and very few people knew me, but by the time I sat down after making a slashing attack on the man who had defended the Communist group, I was already identified in everyone's mind.

And that identification carried much more than purely political connotations. It defined the group in which I might find friends and the group which was going to be made up of enemies, personal as well as political. Some people came up to me after the meeting closed, shook my hand warmly, and told me how delighted they were that another "good American" had come to the Jewish community, while a good many others stalked away from me, glaring bitterly as they did.

Unfortunately the identification was one I would rather have been spared, because, while I was opposed to Communist or Communist-front groups as part of the Jewish Community Council, I was just as bitterly opposed to the kind of anti-Communist activities carried on by the House Un-American Activities Committee and the American Legion. But this kind of a position was only understood by a few people; most of the others thought I was either a vicious redbaiter or some kind of crazy anarchist, depending on their political viewpoint.

Within the next few weeks I got a rapid education in the problems of the Jewish community in Los Angeles. All kinds of currents and crosscurrents eddied back and forth inside the organized structure of the community. Naturally all the agencies were jealous of each other and rivals for support inside the community. Then there were personal antagonisms among the staff members, for some of the ambitious ones were always seeking favor from the powerful community leaders who were in a position to advance their careers. The Zionists fought the non-Zionists for a bigger share of the welfare funds, and the Orthodox rabbis fought among themselves about which group was authorized to give the *kashrut,* the seal of approval needed by the kosher butchers for their operations. And the issue of the Communist role inside the Jewish community was more and more becoming one of the central internal disputes of the community, although it had not yet assumed the importance given to the Arab-Jewish War in Palestine.

As far as I was concerned, though, it had far more importance. The fights between Arabs and Jews that I read about in the papers still seemed to have no direct relevance to my own life: I was detached from them and even somewhat disturbed by what I thought was the aggressive nature of the Jewish position, which looked as if it might bring about another large-scale war. The United Nations decision of November, 1947, in favor of the partition of Palestine, had meant very little to me, and I couldn't understand the emotional fervor with which it was greeted. I'd also often made bitter jokes about the American Zionists who fought the Arabs with full page ads in the New York *Post*. The tone of one such ad, written by Ben Hecht, was a classic example as it described Hecht's joy at the way the Jews were knocking off the Arabs. It seemed to me that if Hecht was so hot to kill Arabs, he ought to have left his nice house in Nyack, not far from where we had lived, and gone to Palestine, where he could have had a chance to use some other weapon besides a typewriter. But except for reading about the Jews in Palestine and getting familiar with the names of their leaders, such as Ben-Gurion or Moshe Sharett, Palestine remained remote and unreal to me, a place that required some support only because it was providing a home for Jewish refugees who had no other place to go.

In Los Angeles, though, there was much less chance to avoid direct contact with those who were working actively on behalf of the Jews in Palestine. I heard rumors that Jews in Los Angeles were involved in smuggling guns into Palestine, and no CRC meeting was complete without an impassioned denunciation of the Arabs by a representative of a Zionist group. These speeches just bored me and when the State of Israel was proclaimed in May, 1948, no thrills of emotion went rippling through my body. The existence of a Jewish "homeland" was a notion that I basically opposed, for it implied that I wasn't at home in America, a concept I couldn't accept either at the conscious political level or in my unconscious, where being Jewish had little importance to whatever I imagined myself to be. And so, while the harsh war between the Jews and Arabs went on until late in the fall of 1948, I was engrossed in other activities, although I did grow very indignant at the murder of Count Bernadotte, the UN mediator in Palestine, by a gang of Jewish terrorists.

My real interests were not in Palestine, I felt.

* * *

In Europe the Berlin blockade and the take-over by the Communists of the East European countries was creating the most exacerbated relations between the United States and the Soviet Union. At home the Chambers-Hiss controversy was just beginning, in the summer of 1948, to rip apart the liberal movement: Alger Hiss was identified by many liberals as embodying the very best qualities that had been found among New Dealers. For these people to conceive of Hiss as being a Communist spy was to destroy utterly their faith in everything they had believed in for many years. Hiss represented the liberal New Deal tradition, the dedicated men who had brought new ideas of government to the country and then gone on to the spirit of wartime cooperation with the Russians that culminated in the founding of the UN in San Francisco.

To those superpatriots for whom the New Deal meant the embodiment of evil and the UN the giving up of American sovereignty to the hated Russians, Hiss's alleged role as a spy was the absolute proof that America was enmeshed in a domestic Communist conspiracy at the very time the Communists were threatening to take over all of Europe and Asia. Many Jews felt terribly threatened by this group, for very often the people who so bitterly denounced the UN, the Communists, and Alger Hiss were the same ones who supported the thinly veiled or open anti-Semitic movements which the Communists and their sympathizers attacked continually to justify their own positions.

People like me, the so-called knowledgeable and sophisticated anti-Stalinists, held neither of these two viewpoints. We weren't shocked to discover that there had been Communists inside the New Deal or that some of them might have been Soviet spies. We didn't know whether Hiss was guilty or not, but the assumption that he might have been was not as inconceivable to us as it was to those naive liberals who didn't really believe that Communists were capable of being spies.

And at just about the time the Hiss-Chambers case was becoming a front-page story all over the United States, the Progressive party campaign of 1948 was splitting the liberals still more. Those liberals who were fundamentally committed to the two-party system and within it to the Democratic party were convinced that Henry Wallace's Progressive party campaign might throw the election to Thomas Dewey. Yet the supporters of the Progressive party included a good many people who had been the most ardent supporters of Roosevelt during the New Deal period. To them Wallace, and not Harry Truman, was the inheritor of the Roosevelt tradition, for Wallace spoke in the Roosevelt rhetoric of a world without war, without want, free from prejudice and hatred, while Truman was proclaiming that the Russians, our wartime allies, were now America's enemy.

Among the most fervent supporters of the Progressive party were those Jews who had become convinced that anti-Semitism had been wiped out in the Soviet Union and that therefore it was a country with which America should have only the friendliest kind of relations. Having identified the Nazi attack upon the Russians with the Nazi persecution of the Jews, they could not comprehend the deterioration of relations between the United States and the Soviet Union.

In California, a state with a long history of social reform movements, the Progressive party could also draw upon a reservoir of supporters from the old EPIC movement that had been headed by Upton Sinclair during the depression and from the many People's Front organizations that had flourished during the late thirties, sparked by the Communists.

This was especially true in southern California, where the anti-Nazi emphasis of the People's Front period had been very attractive, especially to the great number of Jews who worked in creative fields within the movie industry and from among whom the Progressive party drew great support. And in northern California the Progressive party had a great asset in Harry Bridges, who had played a heroic role in leading the San Francisco general strike of 1934. This bitter strike had freed the West Coast longshoremen from the stranglehold of a corrupt union and employers' association and had resulted in bringing about startling changes for the better in wages and working conditions.

Bridges was a folk hero in California, and the continued attempts by the government to deport him only added to his luster. The deportation cases made most liberals very suspicious of anyone who raised the Communist question, for it seemed that the only reason Bridges had been persecuted was because he headed a militant union.

So, too, some avowed Communists were held in high regard by some of the wealthy German Jewish families that had settled in San Francisco during the Gold Rush period and had become tightly integrated into the life of the city. To these people, it was in the tradition of liberalism to meet Communists who were admired because they really did things rather than just talked about them.

Geography, too, had played a part, I discovered, in helping the Communists dominate the tone of the California liberal movement. In those days the only way most people could afford to travel was by train, and so there was very little mobility from the West Coast toward the East. Students, for example, tended to attend the relatively unsophisticated (in the political sense) colleges and universities on the West Coast rather than go to eastern ones, because they were unable to get home from the East during the short vacations. Since these students were therefore never exposed to the kind of tough radical anti-Stalinism they might have encountered at some of the eastern colleges, they carried over into adult life the political attitudes they had absorbed as students and ended up in Wallace's Progressive party.

None of these Progressive party supporters understood at the time that they were still being manipulated, nor was there any reason why they should have. And the kind of attack made upon them and the Progressive party did little to heighten their understanding of the issue, for an ex-radical like me could only speak to them in political language they didn't comprehend, and they grew angry because they didn't know what we were talking about. The fight between the ex-Communists and the Communists was waged around them, over their heads, and the only role they were able to play was that of the victim who gets punished without ever knowing what crime he's committed or even that he's committed one.

Within the Jewish community of Los Angeles the dispute focused on three issues, and inevitably I was soon involved in all of them. The first was the Jewish People's Fraternal Order, which was affiliated to the Community Council, and was facing expulsion from the Council. Next, a few Jewish community centers were allegedly being used by their staffs for spreading party propaganda. Finally, one of the Jewish hospitals supposedly had on its payroll some social workers who were active Communists.

In the case of the hospital, the question for me was: why did it matter if a social worker in a hospital was a Communist? The answer I got was the same one used to justify the movie-industry blacklisting: public relations. Just as the movie people said they couldn't afford to keep Communists on the payroll in the face of a threatened boycott by the American Legion and other patriotic groups, so the argument was raised that, in the case of the hospital, the Jewish community of Los Angeles couldn't afford a Jewish hospital, which was being supported by Community Chest funds, that was cited as a haven for Communists. And when it was learned that the Civil Defense authorities might refuse to authorize the use of the hospital in case of an emergency because it allegedly contained a Communist cell, the CRC used all its influence to keep that story from the press while simultaneously trying to get rid of the social workers involved.

The case of the hospital cell was a delicate one for another reason. I was told in a hushed whisper that an influential contributer to the hospital had been having an affair with one of the Communists and didn't want any fuss made about her. That argument against making a row was one I understood and sympathized with, since it reminded me of Teddy Bardacke and the girl with the loudest orgasm in the world. Actually, the only way in which these few Communist social workers used the hospital for party purposes was to allow some people they knew from the party to stay in the hospital for a couple of days without payment.

The case of the Communist caseworkers was fairly easy to handle. As I remember it, they were called in, reprimanded, and warned that if they continued what they'd been doing they would be fired. Over the next year or two, most of them quit anyway.

But the problems of the community centers and Jewish People's Fraternal Order were far more difficult to handle. All of the community centers in the city were under the nominal direction of a Jewish Centers Association, which had a board of directors drawn from the community and a small staff of its own. Most of the funds used to operate the centers came from the Jewish Welfare Drive, but an additional allotment came from the citywide nonsectarian Community Chest. It was this allotment that, to some of the CRC members, constituted another public relations threat to the Jews: it was rumored that an investigation of the centers was scheduled to be held by the state Un-American Activities Committee. The Centers Association therefore held its own quiet investigation in an attempt to find out whether the programs conducted at the centers were being used to spread

Communist propaganda.

The issue of the Jewish People's Fraternal Order couldn't be kept quiet, though, for that one had to be taken up with the whole Community Council, and the JPFO was not likely to be a willing partner in keeping silent. Therefore some of the powerful community leaders decided to put the JPFO on trial, to say that it was a Communist front, and then have voted it out of the Council.

The organized Jewish community divided roughly into five groups in these bitter disputes. At one extreme were the reactionaries, for whom one word from the American Legion or HUAC was enough to convince them that the Communists were about to take over all the Jewish agencies in the city. At the other end were the real Communists, fighting desperately to retain whatever few positions of influence they held and responding to all the attacks upon them with the cry of redbaiting. In between were those people who consciously identified themselves with one or the other polar group but were not themselves actively part of them; the people who were confused but still linked themselves to one of the positions when they had to take a position; and finally a group made up mostly of Orthodox rabbis and Zionists, who weren't one bit interested in the Communist question. The rabbis' concern was about whether the kosher butchers were really kosher and whether the proper amount of funds were being allocated to the Jewish religious schools, while the Zionists' orientation led them to decide all questions on the basis of what was good or bad for the State of Isreal.

The radical and ex-radical opposition to the Communists was in the thick of the fight. At the staff level there were only a few of us at the time, including my counterpart, Zane Meckler, the director of the Jewish Labor Committee, who had been working with the unions in the area long before I'd arrived and who necessarily viewed me with some disfavor since I was now trying to cut in on his territory. But he was an ex-socialist, and so we were allies within the Jewish community if rivals outside it, in the unions.

People like Zane and myself were the "experts" in anti-Communism, and the knowledge we had of Communist activities was essential to the expulsion of the JPFO or the investigation of the Jewish centers staff. We could go, for example, through all the programs of the centers and pick out those which represented the viewpoints of Communist or Communist-front groups. And we knew the people involved who made speeches or participated in forums and were in Communist groups, for we had encountered them in other places all over the country.

Both Zane and I were uncomfortable in our role as the expert advisors but not enough to stop, because we honestly believed that the Communists were a threat although we never really discussed what it was they were threatening.

I suspect, though, that we also enjoyed watching the Communists getting treated as badly as they had always treated us. For years we'd gotten kicked around by them and now we were in a position to retaliate. It took me, at least, a little while to understand this about myself and to try to guard as much as possible against letting this kind of feelings influence my behavior. I didn't succeed all the time, either, and the fact that the Communists had generally behaved very badly, even evilly, toward any radical opposition didn't justify some of the anti-Communist activities in which I participated.

I was embarrassed especially by some of our other allies, wincing when the American Legion representatives applauded us loudly if we got up at a CRC meeting to make a speech denouncing the way in which the community centers, for example, were being used for the "progressive" causes instead of having a more Jewish content. I was uncomfortable, too, because in truth I cared no more about giving a Jewish content, whatever that meant, to the community-center program than did the supposed Communists I was attacking. I just objected to the specific programs *they* were substituting for Jewish content, since I thought their choices were heavily oriented toward a political line with which I didn't agree.

A number of personal tragedies accompanied all this fighting, sometimes giving it an atmosphere of desperation. One staff man, whom I shall call Charles, the director of an important community agency, got caught in the struggle and was unable to extricate himself. He was a good-looking, gregarious fellow, very popular with the nonprofessional lay leaders, but our little group was pretty suspicious of him; almost always he threw his weight in with what could generally be described as the Communist position. But even though we were convinced he had a political past, he acted as if he had never heard of the groups we mentioned. He always looked blank whenever the name of a

Communist front came up in the conversation and would ask, "What kind of a group is that?" But his past caught up with him in the strangest way: I was walking on the street one afternoon with an old friend, who was still an active Trotskyist, when he spotted this fellow on the sidewalk across from us.

"I'll be damned," he said. "Look over there. You see that guy? I haven't seen him in twenty years. We were in the same Young Communist League unit in the Midwest and I replaced him as the YCL organizer down in the mining areas. After that, he went into party work and I lost track of him. Do you know him?"

"Yes, I know him, too." I explained what the man was doing, and my friend whistled in surprise as I described the innocent manner in which this fellow claimed never to have heard of any party group.

What to do in this instance was the problem, and I'm not sure I solved it properly. It was out of the question for me to disclose the man's past to his boss, the chairman of the agency, who was one of the worst reactionaries in the community. Yet, I wanted Charles to know that I knew who he was; I went to his office the next day and very casually told him that I'd been with someone who claimed to be an old friend of his. When I told Charles my friend's name, he turned a dead white.

"Look," I said, "I don't care that you were in the party, and I don't care that you're trying to cover up the past. I'm not going to blow the whistle on you. But, godammit, quit trying to pull that innocent shit on me, quit pretending you never heard of the Jewish People's Fraternal Order until we started screaming about it. You know damn well who runs the JPFO."

A few weeks later he resigned his job and left community relations for another kind of work. Because he had tried unsuccessfully to hide his past, he was vulnerable from the moment he discovered that it was known. And I suppose he didn't trust me not to unmask him if the fighting got really tough.

There are hundreds, thousands, of Charleses in the United States, victims of their own fears and of the pressures exerted by society against those with a radical past. Not all these men are ex-Communists, either, for I know ex-Trotskyists and ex-members of splinter groups who also acted as if they never were involved in radical politics. What else were they to do except lie when they were confronted with a question about their past which they believed might cost them their jobs if they answered honestly? I know many people who are always worried because of the grave difficulties that would be in store for them if their pasts were uncovered, people who might even wish now they could disclose what they had been but cannot because they've lied too many times in the past. And from a more general viewpoint, the worst aspect of this inability of people to be honest about their past is that it deprives the society of the services of useful men and women. Very few ex-radicals are willing to take a chance and work for a government agency if there is a risk of getting caught up in some hassle in which their pasts are exposed not because the past has relevance to their jobs, but because it makes a good headline for some politician.

But our lives in Los Angeles didn't consist only of fighting Communists inside the Jewish community. We had made more and more friends and began an active social life. Ruth had decided to go to law school, and I was helping her to study at night. We found a new and better place to live. I attended all kinds of union conventions with my portable display of antidiscrimination materials; I taught at union institutes; I traveled up and down the coast to visit the chapters of the American Jewish Committee in Seattle, Portland, and San Francisco; and I even took time out from these activities to negotiate a union contract for the professional fund raisers employed by the Jewish Welfare Federation in Los Angeles.

Those negotiations were very strange ones. The men were all fairly well paid, earning more than I did. Their working conditions were very peculiar, for they didn't work on a fixed schedule of hours every day. It was very difficult to judge how good they were at their jobs. I listened with fascination almost bordering on horror as the fund raisers described their work to me at our meetings. They explained that it didn't really matter whether they were employed by the Federation of Jewish Charities, the City of Hope—a hospital outside Los Angeles—or some non-Jewish community enterprise which was also always raising money: every group used variations on the same techniques, although some were more high-pressured than others.

The basic principle involved was that money, lots of money, had to be raised for all the worthy causes supported by the Jewish community—the hospitals, the community centers, the religious schools, the social-work agencies, the cultural groups, the organizations that defended Jews against anti-Semitism, and, in the years after 1948, for emigration to Israel from Europe and the Arab countries. Once that principle was accepted, it became possible to develop and justify the most important technique in this kind of fund raising—the squeeze. The fund raisers never depended on goodwill or charitable feelings alone as a source for the millions of dollars raised each year. They believed only the squeeze could bring in the large amounts that were needed.

The drive usually started each year at a national conference attended by representatives from all the major cities and major organizations. There the amount of money to be raised from the entire country was determined, and to each city was allocated the amount for which it was responsible, based on the size and character of its Jewish population. There, too, the ratios of distribution were determined for the amounts of money that were to be sent overseas, used for national work, and retained locally in the communities.

After such a meeting the representatives of the Los Angeles board would return home and the local staff of fund raisers, for whom I was negotiating, took over the direction of the work. Some prominent person in the community—perhaps a well-known movie figure, a businessman, a lawyer, or a retired judge —was elected chairman of the drive; a campaign keynote was selected which, in the judgment of the professional fund raisers, would have the greatest appeal.

The real secret of this kind of fund raising, I discovered, was the skillful utilization of large numbers of volunteers. The city was divided geographically by income and by industry. The fund raisers had built up a filing system in which almost the entire Jewish population was listed. Prominent people were approached to take active roles, and they were expected to contribute large sums of money in exchange for the prestige that went with being made chairman of one of the various divisions of the campaign. A leading figure in, say, the liquor business would be called by the chairman of the whole campaign and asked to take over as chairman for the liquor-industry campaign. It would be hard for the liquor dealer to turn the request down, for his social and business standing would drop in the community if the word got out that he wasn't willing to take on his responsibilities.

Once the chairman of the liquor-industry campaign had been selected, all kinds of vice-chairmen were picked; then the fund raising began in earnest. The big liquor dealers were taken out to lunch or dinner one or two at a time, and the need for funds was explained to them. If one of them was active in an organization, someone from that group contacted him and urged him to make a large contribution. At a dinner honoring some important person in the industry, such as the chairman of the state liquor authority, great sums of money would be extracted in pledges from all the guests by the simple expedient of the chairman's reading their names from a card which listed their previous contributions and asking them, as they stood up, how much more they were going to give this year. And there were always a few people at the dinner who had agreed to make sizable contributions but were persuaded to wait until the dinner to announce them, thus encouraging others to vie with them in demonstrating both their financial success and charitable feelings.

This model was used in every industry and with every group, although there were always some natural variations, depending upon the character of the industry and the individuals involved. Certain people, characterized as "special" or "advance" givers, included the wealthiest people in the community, and they were handled individually at a quiet dinner in a home rather than at one of the mass meetings. Even the staffs of the various organizations were expected to make contributions each year, and the amount they pledged was always printed in a booklet, along with the pledges of everybody else in the community. If a pledge wasn't paid by the time the book was printed, the fact of non-payment was noted next to the name, presumably shaming the tardy one into paying and never repeating the process of making a pledge but not fulfilling it.

Working-class or middle-class Jews were handled by neighborhoods, just as in the polio drive. But unlike the polio drive, which concentrated on raising its funds in one night, the Jewish drive was a good deal more persistent, and if the house was dark when the volunteer came, he came back until someone was at home to whom the need for the funds could be explained.

My job of negotiating the contract for the fund raisers was made even more difficult by the peculiar symbiotic relationships that existed between them and their chairmen, the community leaders. They had to be careful with each other, for neither could function without the other. A good fund raiser could make the community leader a success within his own group, and no matter how genuinely devoted to the cause the chairman might be, he was dependent on the fund raiser to make the campaign a successful one.

The fund raisers were the key to the whole operation, these men and women who over the years had developed the art of making the squeeze so precisely that they knew exactly what kind of an appeal to make each year, what kind of pressure to apply, when to apply it, and how much money could be anticipated from the application. They looked at me as if I were an idiot when sometimes I protested to them about their cynicism, about how they exploited the situation in Israel by making it appear that all the children were starving there, about how they used the promise of social prestige as an instrument to get money, and about how they had no hesitation in exposing someone to the most terrible kind of embarrassment at one of their fund-raising "affairs."

"How else do you think we'd get the kind of money we raise? By just asking people politely for it?"

"Well, maybe not," I would answer, "but don't you think that raising money the way you do destroys something in the cause you're working for?"

Astonished, even angry, they would look at me and answer, "Look, it's all very well for you staff people to just take your paycheck each month and be embarrassed at the way we behave, but just don't forget that you wouldn't have an organization to pay you if we didn't raise the money. And do you think a kid in an orphanage in Israel or some refugee in a DP camp in Germany cares one good goddamn where the money that takes care of him comes from or how it's gotten? Grow up!"

Finally, after enough meetings to have negotiated a division of the whole world between the United States and the Soviet Union, we completed the contract negotiations. After that I was approached by the clerical and nonprofessional employees of the Federation to get a contract for them. But by that time I was thinking more and more of getting away from the nonideological professional Jewish atmosphere. It bored me, and I missed the action I'd found as a union organizer.

CHAPTER TEN

Ｉｎ ｔｈｅ ｆａｌｌ of 1948 O. A. Knight,
then the president of the Oil Workers International Union, CIO,
came to Los Angeles to try to rescue a failing strike which the
West Coast locals of the union had called against the major oil
companies. Only one company, General Petroleum Corporation,
whose refinery turned out Mobilgas, was not out on strike; all
the others—Associated, Richfield, Union, and Standard Oil—
had been struck. But, unfortunately for the union, the strike
wasn't very effective. Because they are so highly automated, refineries can operate without a full crew of men, and the companies were able to keep going by using supervisory help, nonunion workers, and union members who returned in increasing
numbers after the start of the strike.

In fact, Knight and others in the union's national leadership
had opposed the calling of the strike but had been overruled by
the California membership, then about 25,000. Faced with what
looked to be a very bad loss for the union, Knight had come to
California to mobilize some community support and perhaps to
organize a consumers' boycott. Someone in the CIO suggested
he get in touch with me, and a meeting was arranged.

We got along very well right from the start. Jack, as he was
called, was a slight, dapper fellow, a former refinery worker who
had worked his way up through the union hierarchy to become
president. He had a miserable job on his hands, too, in the California situation, for the union had only one closed-shop agreement with a major West Coast refinery. At all the others the
union membership constituted only a majority, and not always a

very big majority, of the workers. Just as bad, the leaders in two or three of the California locals were ambitious men, who weren't strong supporters of Knight. It was this group which had succeeded in getting the membership to vote for the strike over the objections of the union officials assigned by the national headquarters to work in the California district.

At the time Knight approached me for some help in organizing community support for the strike, a great amount of violence had occurred, especially at the Union Oil refinery in San Pedro and the Standard Oil operation at Richmond, just north of Oakland. And as if all this weren't enough, Knight was worried because he thought a few of the oil workers' locals were being unduly influenced by some of the Communist-dominated CIO unions.

Because I was on the American Jewish Committee staff, I was able to arrange speaking dates for Knight at a variety of community organizations in Los Angeles, where he presented the union's side of the strike. Naturally he avoided any references to the union's internal stresses, the demoralization of the strikers in the face of continued production, and the whole issue of the role he believed the Communists to be trying to play in the situation. He didn't start to discuss those questions with me for some time, and then only very cautiously, feeling me out as we went along.

Very quickly, though, I was involved, and deeply, in the strike. After a few more agonizing weeks, the strike was finally settled on terms that weren't very good for the union. Actually the locals barely survived the strike and suffered severe losses in membership as well as the cancellation of a closed-shop agreement at the Union Oil Co. Then Knight offered me a job with the union as an international representative, to be stationed in Long Beach at the union's district headquarters. As we talked about what I might do, he made it clear that at first my primary responsibilities would be to set up an internal union education program that might help build up the union strength which had been lost in the strike. Once that had been done, he told me, I'd be expected to do the regular work of a representative: negotiating contracts, processing grievances for locals that wanted help, organizing new plants, and helping to run strikes if they were called. It was obvious, too, that he was also very much interested in what I could do to minimize what he considered undue Communist influence within a few California locals of the union.

The membership and officers of the oil workers' union were predominantly white Protestants, whose politics were fairly conservative. Very few people on the staff had become involved with unions through the radical movement, as I had. I knew that I would be the only Jew on the staff, and one of the very few Jews in the whole union.

But although I wouldn't have admitted it, the lack of Jews certainly was one of the job's attractions for me. Becoming an international representative for the oil workers meant I could get away from being a professional Jew on the staff of the American Jewish Committee. It meant also getting away from the traditional role taken by Jews in unions, for with the exception of the needle trades and social work, which had a great number of Jewish members, Jews in other unions tended to be found mainly in research, legal, educational, or editorial jobs.

Not me, though. I was going to escape in reality from being Jewish, just as I had always tried to escape in my fantasies. I would be just a regular union representative, no different from any other representative. I knew that very few members of the union's staff had come from outside the oil industry, as I had; almost all the staff were men who'd worked in the industry and had been members of a local union before being appointed to the national staff. I was nevertheless convinced—incorrectly, as it turned out—that in time I would be accepted as just another member of the staff, doing the same job as everyone else in the same way as everyone else. And sometimes in my fantasies I would speculate on whether Knight had selected me to be his successor for the presidency of the union. And then, who knows? President of the CIO, maybe? So I resigned from my job at the American Jewish Committee, and early in 1949 I went back to union work.

One requisite of being on the staff of the oil workers' union was that I had to join a local union. The purpose was to make sure that the union's staff wasn't made up of "outsiders" but was drawn from the union membership. This kind of ruling was characteristic of a number of unions but was more strictly observed among the oil workers, who tended on the whole to be even more suspicious of "outsiders" than many other unions. Arrangements were made for me to join a local which held a contract at the General Petroleum refinery near San Pedro and had been the only one in the area not to strike. It was a quiet local, not prone to internal fights nor very militant either. After I was proposed for membership by the district director, even though I didn't work in the refinery, and had been taken by him to an executive-board meeting which dutifully accepted my membership application, I started working out of the union's Long Beach district office, which had jurisdiction over the entire West Coast.

Initially I was assigned to work in the whole state. The nine other representatives remained in one area almost all the time: either in southern California, the central part of the state, or in the area around San Francisco. But since I was assigned to develop programs that would rebuild the membership in all the locals involved in the strike, I was expected to visit every local at least once a month. And although I never discussed it with anyone else but Jack, I was also expected to build some kind of opposition in the two or three locals where there was allegedly some Communist influence.

Doing this wasn't easy, either, for local union officers, who were elected directly by their members, tended to be suspicious of any representative of the international union, who were appointed by the union president. They were especially suspicious of me because I had come from the outside, with no history of membership or activity in this particular union. It was obvious that even the other members of the staff, my fellow representatives, had some doubts about me, for I was just as much a stranger to them as I was to the union members whose local I joined. But I was able to establish friendly relations with a few of them, at least, fairly quickly; for my first assignment on the staff was to defend some thirty-odd strikers whom one of the companies had refused to rehire after the strike was settled. They were accused of having carried out such acts as dumping strikebreakers' cars, resisting arrest, or beating up supervisory personnel. The group included some of the most militant leaders of the local, and it was essential that they be rehired if the morale of the men was not to drop even below what it was when the bad settlement ended the strike.

Every effort to get the strikers' jobs back through negotiation had failed, and finally the best the union could get from the company was an agreement that the cases would be arbitrated. Even in this concession by the company, the odds were stacked against the union. The arbitration was to be carried out by a panel of four outsiders, two appointed by the company and two selected by the union. In order for a striker to be reinstated, he had to get at least one of the company's representatives to vote for him.

I spent my first few weeks as a representative at the company's San Pedro refinery fighting these cases; in this I was assisted by a couple of men who had been active in the local union for many years. Fortunately we won reinstatement for most of the strikers, thanks to one of the two company-appointed arbitrators, who took his impartial role very seriously and voted with our two appointees in many of the cases.

But great as was the victory for the men involved, it earned me some resentment from the other staff members: for an outsider to be assigned to this important job made it appear as if they weren't considered good enough for it. It was obvious to everybody that I was a friend of Knight's, someone he liked to be with after the meetings were over. To make it still worse, local unions that had been serviced by the other representatives began asking for my help in cases that had to be arbitrated. These requests caused some strain for me, too, since rivalry among staff members for the support of local unions is strong. It is always important to union staffers that they negotiate a good contract or win arbitrations, for this is how they demonstrate their effectiveness and prove that they ought to be either reappointed or re-elected instead of having to work at routine daily jobs.

Occasionally, too, in those first months when I tried to be like the other representatives, I would hear a faint whisper about being "Knight's smart Jew," someone who could really argue with employers or present a grievance to an arbitrator. Initially I tried ignoring the whispers; then I began to flaunt my Jewishness in a complicated way that had in it an element of contempt for my critics. I'd say, "I used to be filled with self-hate, like all Jews, until I realized it's true that Jews are smarter than Gentiles, so now I'm filled with self-love." If I was playing poker with the other representatives and lost a hand, I'd crack, "Oh, well, I always knew you bastards were anti-Semitic." Sometimes, too, I would go out of my way to tell jokes with a thick Yiddish accent, thus proving that, although I was Jewish, I was unlike other Jews who never told such jokes except when they were among themselves.

But I still continued my membership on the Community Relations Committee of the Jewish Community Council, although my presence at the meetings had very little to do with the CRC's primary function of protecting the Jews of Los Angeles. My willingness to remain on the CRC was based on a mixture of guilt and a liking for the status it gave me. In addition, after I had left the staff of the American Jewish Committee, I was asked to stay on as a lay member. From the viewpoint of the other members of the CRC, I was kept on the committee only because I was an expert anti-Communist and because I represented a union, thus making the committee more representative, at least in the public eye. I continued to attend CRC meetings as dutifully as I could, considering the amount of traveling I had to do all over the state to visit all the local unions that had been involved in the strike.

I didn't really mind the traveling then, although it was very hard on Ruth to be alone so much of the time. Very often as I drove alongside the Pacific in the afternoon, on my way from Los Angeles to Ventura for a local meeting, I would think of how awful it had been to work in a shop or how I'd disliked having to go even to the American Jewish Committee office every day. Then I would realize how lucky I was to operate at my own pace, without anyone telling me when to come in and when to leave. Even if the long trip ended in a dull union meeting in some small town where the only thing to do after the meeting was drink beer in the American Legion Hall, I was still delighted to be back in union work.

But rebuilding the strength of the local unions to its prestrike level turned out to be a very hard job. The men who had remained out on strike until it was settled were bitter toward those union members who had returned to work while the strike was still on; these had been kicked out of the union for strikebreaking. Before we could get the ex-union members back into the locals, we had first to convince the ones who'd held out that they should be willing to forget what had happened. That wasn't easy, either, especially with the group of activist union members who'd been arrested; "scab" was the kindest word they had for their ex-union members.

I worked out a technique which had some success, but not much. I would go to a regular membership meeting, wait until the normal business had been completed, and then begin my educational session, explaining that since there was no possibility of getting the strikebreakers out of the refineries, they had to accept the idea of taking them back into the union. Otherwise the union would never be strong enough to negotiate properly with the company.

Since that pitch never went down very well, I would follow it up by asking the local members if they'd known someone who'd been a good union member but still had scabbed during the strike. Almost always everybody knew a few people in that category. Then I'd ask if they knew why these former members had scabbed. As they'd start calling out their answers, I'd write them down on a blackboard.

"Pressure from the company," someone would say. "His wife made him do it" was another reason they'd give. "They were scared they'd lose their pension and they're too old to get another job," or, "We didn't teach them enough of what it means to be in a union." By the time I'd finished asking everybody in the hall, the blackboard would be filled with explanations. Then I could start talking about how important it was for us to forget the past and start rebuilding the union.

Generally the technique worked fairly well, but it backfired one night at a meeting of the Long Beach local, the biggest in the state. It was also one of the raunchiest, and a lot of bad feeling had been generated by the scabs. After I finished with my nice forgiving explanation of scab behavior, the vice-president of the local rose from his seat and said, "Okay, you've convinced me that we've got to take the goddamn scabs back into the local, but you can't make me like them. Just the other night, one of them came to my house for the first time since the strike ended, but I wouldn't let the son-of-a-bitch in even though he was one of my best friends before the strike. How come I still hate that son-of-a-bitch even though I know the pressure he went through before he scabbed?"

"I don't know," I answered. "Maybe only a psychologist can tell you that."

"Okay," said the vice-president. "Get us a psychologist for the next meeting."

I went to a friend of mine who was a psychologist for the school system in Los Angeles and asked him if he would come to the next union meeting to answer some questions the members wanted to ask. He agreed, and we drove down to Long

Beach the following week. The meeting hall was packed, and many of the members had brought their wives with them. I introduced my friend to the group and left him alone in the hall while I went into a smaller meeting room in back to discuss proposals for a new contract with a group of men from a much smaller refinery. But I could hear the discussion going on in the next room, and I recognized the voice of the local vice-president when he asked the psychologist the same question he had put to me. Even worse, I heard the answer he got from my friend.

"Well, I've never seen you before," was the reply, "and I know nothing about you. But abstractly I'd say that the reason you feel so strongly about what your friend did was because you maybe wanted to do the same thing yourself but didn't. Maybe you feel so guilty about having even thought of it, you're overcompensating and taking it out in hating your friend."

A dead silence followed. I ran into the hall. No one, literally no one, including me, knew what to do next, knew what to say. Finally the vice-president's wife said, "Maybe that's right. I was getting pretty worried about what was going to happen and I was starting to nag him to go back to work. Maybe he did think about it even if he never said anything to me or anyone else."

The meeting broke up immediately and was never repeated. But I had made a powerful enemy, for the local vice-president held me responsible for having brought to the union hall someone who suggested that he might have scabbed if the strike had continued much longer. He was right, too, to hold me responsible, just as some of the developing antagonism against me had some good basis in the way I was behaving.

Sometimes, for example, I'd be like a snotty juvenile during contract negotiations, not understanding that they were just as much a matter for solemnity to the union members on the negotiating committee as to the company. I would pull gags like pouring a bag of chicken feed on the table after a company official had presented the union committee with a wage offer and then asked me what I thought of it. How funny, I thought; what a character I am indeed—not noticing the strained grins on the faces of the union members.

On another occasion I got into serious trouble during a difficult-set of negotiations with one of the largest oil companies in California. We were meeting with the company officials in the company's elegant board room in its own building in Los Angeles. Every morning, the company committee, headed by a senior vice-president, would file into the room and seat themselves directly opposite us, duplicating our exact order of hierarchy. If I sat at the end of the table, the vice-president sat at the other end, and if I sat in the middle, he sat right across from me. But I refused to sit in one place, moving to a new position each day, and sometimes even during the day, forcing him to keep changing his chair and irritating him more every day.

Finally he blew up over what he thought was a new insult. The men's toilet on our floor was kept locked, and whenever a member of the union committee had to use it, he had to ask one of the company officials for a key. One day just before a lunch recess I borrowed the key and had a dozen copies made. When we resumed negotiations, I waited until the vice-president started telling us how impossible the company found it to meet our wage demand. At that point I interrupted him and threw the dozen keys on the table, saying something like, " 'Well, here's the union's contribution to the company payroll. We'll pay for each committee member's key to the toilet."

That tore it. The vice-president shoved his chair back from the table, said, "I do not intend to tolerate any more insults from you," stood up, and angrily stalked out of the room, followed by his whole committee, leaving me stunned by their departure. And, unfortunately for me, none of the committee members thought the sudden walkout nearly as funny as I did.

The sense of estrangement many of the union members and other representatives felt toward me was heightened by my refusal to socialize with them except for an occasional poker game after district conventions or local union meetings.

Ruth, too, refused to mix with the wives of other representatives and adamantly declined to join the ladies' auxiliary of the local to which I nominally belonged. Another disastrous experience reinforced our decision to remain aloof socially. I was in San Francisco attending a staff meeting when two of the other representatives from southern California approached me about taking them out with me for the evening.

"We figure you know some of the places here in town that the tourists don't usually get to see."

"What kind of places do you mean?" I asked.

"Oh, you know. Different kinds of places. Maybe like those fairy bars we hear about."

That night I took them to the Black Cat, a well-known and usually crowded homosexual bar in the North Beach district. But I felt very uncomfortable in the role they'd assigned me—the guide to exotic experiences. And the instant we walked into the Cat, which was jammed with homosexuals of all kinds, one of the two representatives grew intensely uneasy. He was an older man, very pleasant, who'd worked in one refinery almost his entire life before going on the union staff. Obviously he'd never before been in a room jammed with men openly caressing each other, men dressed in women's clothes, or men who looked as if they were no different than he but obviously were.

After no more than a few minutes he turned to me and said in a thick voice, "I got to get out of here. I can't stand it in here for another minute."

The three of us pushed our way out of the crowded bar into the street. We started walking away from the bar when suddenly he stopped, turned to me and said, "What the hell happened to me in there? I never had anything like that happen before, and I've been in lots of bars."

I reassured him that his reaction was probably normal, although I didn't believe a word of what I was saying. But the last thing I wanted to do was get involved in any discussion with him about why he had reacted so violently at the sight of a room filled with homosexuals.

That experience cured me. From then on I gave up the notion that I could try to act like anything but what I was—a semiprofessional intellectual who was likely always to find his close friends at universities, in the civil-rights movement, among writers, and in any group of people interested in ideas of all kinds.

In the meantime the fight inside the CIO was getting sharper because of the increasing cold-war tension. The Communist-dominated unions were supporting Henry Wallace, who was running for president on the Progressive party ticket. This policy was opposed by Philip Murray and Walter Reuther. Harry Bridges, a strong supporter of Wallace, one of the dominant figures in the national CIO, had been its West Coast director for many years. The state CIO council was split on the Communist issue, and the Los Angeles CIO council was still very much under the control of unions whose leaders were very close to the Communist party, if not actually members.

My role in this internal fight was established the first time I got up to speak at a meeting of the Los Angeles CIO council to which I'd been elected as a delegate from my oilworkers' local. After I finished that initial speech, the knowledgeable people, Communists and anti-Communists alike, knew that in their midst was an old hand at this kind of fight. A few days later I was a member of the executive committee of the caucus fighting to take control of the council away from the Communists. And on the committee with me I found people I recognized from the prewar days in the Trotskyist movement, including one man who had been an Ohlerite in Chicago.

The weekly council meetings were packed with hundreds of delegates from the local unions in the area. A great many of them had no real idea of what the issues were but came either because their votes were needed or, as was true in many cases, because they knew that every council meeting was guaranteed to be at least a vicious wrangle, with each of the two sides denouncing the other and maybe a fist fight. The council meeting was an exciting spectacle, as good as anything that could be seen on TV or in the movies, especially since the Communists and their supporters were fighting desperately to retain their control of the council and the staff jobs that went with control.

The battle in the Los Angeles CIO council was waged by the same kind of curious amalgam of anti-Communists as in New York. Inside our caucus were the followers of Phil Murray, many of them devout, nonintellectual Catholics, for whom Murray's attack upon the Communists was the only signal they needed to join in the fight. There were the ADA Democrats, whose fear and hatred of the Communists had been intensified by their conviction that the Progressive party campaign of 1948 was Communist-inspired. Finally there were the ex-radicals and the radicals without an ideology, whose opposition to the Communists was based on their past enmity toward them.

Thus, when I got up at a local or state CIO council meeting to make a speech denouncing the Communists, I used the same kind of emotional appeals I had made on the soapboxes of New York. Only a few of us were capable of taking on the Communists, and of these few only a small group were bothered, as I was, by what we were doing for a society about which we were doubtful. But we did it anyway, partly out of our old anger at the way in which the Communists had betrayed our ideals, and partly because it was our job to do so. For me the climax came at a crucial meeting of the Los Angeles CIO council. This meeting had been set up by the national CIO to vote on whether or not control of the council was going to continue in the hands of the Communists. Every local union we influenced in the area was lobbied by our caucus to get its delegates to the meeting, which was so sure to be a very large one that it was held in an auditorium instead of at the regular CIO council hall (known, not so affectionately, as the Kremlin).

As the Communists suspected at the time, the meeting was rigged against them from the start. Both sides in the quarrel had signed an agreement that Dick Leonard, a representative of the national CIO from Washington, would act as chairman of the convention. The agreement provided that the two sides each were to name two members of every committee, and Leonard was to appoint the fifth man, who would act as chairman. Leonard had been an outspoken opponent of Walter Reuther in the auto workers' union, and the Communists had some reason to hope he would be neutral in his committee appointments. That hope was wiped out the moment Leonard announced that I had been made chairman of the key committee, which was to establish the rules of the convention. And despite the outraged screams of the Communists, Leonard appointed other people identified with our caucus to chair the credentials committee, which would decide the right of the delegates to vote, and the resolutions committee.

Setting up the rules was simple. We were almost certain, although not positive, that we'd have a majority of the delegates, and we were therefore determined to find out as quickly as possible how the delegates divided. To do this, we wanted to force a vote on the rules. The night before the convention, a meeting of the committee was held in the Kremlin. After the five of us had assembled in the room, I read the proposed rules and asked the two people appointed by the Communist unions whether they wanted to vote for these rules or file a minority report to the convention.

They asked for a discussion of the rules, to which I agreed, pointing out, however, that after the discussion was over, we'd still have to take a vote and the vote was going to be 3 to 2. They left the room for a few minutes to confer with their caucus and came back with a proposal that we modify the rules and get together to run a joint slate in the election to be held at the next day's convention. We three refused both requests, and I pointed out again that we were just wasting time, for no matter what proposal they offered us, we'd refuse it, and the vote would still be 3 to 2. At last they stopped trying to make deals, and we voted 3 to 2 in favor of the rules I had proposed.

The next morning, when I arrived at the auditorium, nearly a thousand delegates were jammed into the seats. Behind them, kept from the floor by a wire screen that extended to the ceiling, were the visitors, including some well-known Communists and dozens of people out to see the show. Microphones had been set up at different locations among the seats. All our floor leaders were on the scene, and from a hasty eye count it looked as if our side had the majority. By the time the chairman rapped the gavel to call the meeting to order, the place was really jumping.

And it kept jumping. When I got up as the chairman of the first committee to report, the booing and applause was so loud that Leonard had to keep banging on the rostrum to quiet the audience. When it finally grew quiet enough for me to read the proposed rules, they brought on another storm of booing and jeering matched by shouts of approval. Then the two others gave their minority reports, suggesting a set of rules which, they announced, had been used by the previous CIO national convention. I spoke against them, a very brief discussion followed, and the vote was called for. The minute the sea of hands went up, we knew we'd won.

From then on we had our way, and the tempo of our attack heightened all the time. Finally Bridges got up on the platform to make an impassioned and emotional appeal for militance rather than kowtowing to the CIO national leaders. When he finished, Leonard recognized me. I spoke from the floor, deliberately picking a microphone next to the large table where Bridges and the delegation from his union were sitting. Almost at the start of my speech, I read from a document which I'd folded over so that it couldn't be identified. It was a speech calling for eternal peace with the employers and attacking those who thought the CIO a revolutionary or radical organization. When I finished, I asked the audience to guess the author of these words. Cries rang out from the Bridges supporters: "Phil Murray! Walter Reuther!" When the crowd quieted down, I opened the document and held it high up in the air so that everyone could

see a large picture of Harry Bridges. And while the place exploded with shouts and screaming, I announced that what I had
read was a speech Bridges had given to a state CIO convention a
few years earlier.

Later that day we took a vote and elected a whole new slate
of officers to replace the ones whom the Communists had controlled and dominated for so many years. And the next day I
went back to negotiating contracts and running educational programs for the oil workers' locals.

But unfortunately not for long. A short time later I got a
phone call from Arthur Goldberg, then general counsel for the
CIO, telling me that I was to be assigned to work on the case
which the CIO executive council had been authorized to bring
against Bridges' union. The charges against Bridges' union and
the other allegedly Communist-dominated unions were being
brought by the president of a very small union, but in fact the
cases were prepared by the CIO staff in Washington with the
help of field workers like myself.

I protested weakly that I did not wish to get involved, not so
much because of my feeling that the ILWU shouldn't have been
thrown out of the CIO, but because I was worried that the other
representatives were getting mad at the small amount of time I
was spending on my union assignment. Whenever I took on an
outside job, one of my colleagues had to fill in for me, and I
think they also resented the fact that I traveled, and did not have
to stay put in California.

I spent the next few weeks in the library of the Hoover Institute at Stanford University, reading through old copies of the
Communist newspapers; then I shifted over to the library of the
University of California, which had a complete file of ILWU
publications. I left for Washington with all the material to help
prepare the case against the ILWU and late in the evening of
May 18, 1950, I was part of an uneasy group sitting in the executive board room of the CIO headquarters on Jackson Place.
Outside, a terrible thunderstorm had subsided, but off in the distance faint uneasy grumbles could still be heard from the sky.
Inside the board room a foreboding sense of tension had been
building up for two days while Bridges defended his union
against the charge that its policies and activities were "consistently directed toward the achievement of the program or the
purposes of the Communist party rather than the objective and

policies set forth in the Constitution of the CIO."

Even though a formal trial was being held to weigh the charges, I assumed the verdict was already known to those who were high CIO officials. The prosecution, led by another CIO official backed up by two members of the CIO staff, one of whom was myself, also knew what the result would be. Bridges was personally handling the union defense supported by a few other officers and a delegation of ILWU members. Almost everybody in the room understood that the decision to expel the union from the CIO had been made months earlier; we were going through the formality of a trial only in order to protect ourselves from any possible court actions Bridges might bring to resist expulsion.

The two days the trial had been going on were marked by a series of ugly incidents. Bridges, a slight, hawk-faced man with a jutting nose and a Cockney Australian accent, was belligerent and bitter about the railroading he and his associates thought, with some justice, the union was getting. Right from the start he had attacked the CIO's right to try his union, the judges who'd been appointed, the charges, and the way in which the trial was being held. And his loud polemics met with the obvious approval of the twenty union members he'd brought with him to witness the trial. They sat together, glowering at us from across the room, the colorful shirts of the Hawaiians among them adding a grotesquely gay note to the grim proceedings.

Of the three judges, all presidents of CIO unions, who sat at a table in the front of the room, only O. A. Knight, my boss, had any real sense of what the trial was all about. As chairman of the trial committee, he was trying to preserve the appearance of impartiality. But despite his protestations of fairness, it was obvious that he too had foreknowledge of the judges' decision.

We had started that morning at nine thirty and had gone straight through the day, taking time out only for lunch and dinner. Most of the time had been spent on the testimony of Everett Kassalow, then working on the research staff of the national CIO. Despite continual protests and bickering from Bridges, Kassalow had presented in dreary detail a long history I had prepared of how the ILWU and Bridges had faithfully followed all the twists and turns in the Communist party line. Mike Quill, president of the Transport Workers Union, had testified the day before, telling in a broad Irish brogue of attending with Bridges

meetings called by the Communist party. Now we were waiting for another witness. After two days of nasty wrangling,
Bridges, edgy with strain, didn't know who the witness was going to be; we hadn't wanted him to know.

The door to the room opened and M. Hedley Stone, a very
short man with a drawn, gray face, walked nervously to the witness chair. Stone was then treasurer of the National Maritime
Union. His sudden appearance came as a great shock to Bridges,
who turned pale. While Stone testified about his membership in
the Communist party, Bridges studied him intently, occasionally
making a loud sucking noise, as if something had caught in his
teeth.

The atmosphere grew more and more painful as Stone continued his testimony, describing how he had attended Communist
party meetings with Bridges. Then Bridges began a grim cross-
examination of Stone, almost immediately asking him, "Did you
ever use any other name but your own?"

The trial transcript gives Stone's reply. "My real name, my
born name, my father's name was Stein, and when I was officially
put into a position to become an organizer for the National Maritime Union, it was Roy Hudson's idea and William L. Standard's
[Hudson and Standard were Communist party officials] to take
my name and change it from Morris Stein to M. Hedley Stone.
Now you knew that all along."

"I never did, and it wasn't the purpose of asking the question."

"No. Now you have me naked."

"I had another purpose in asking the question like that. What
your name was in respect to———"

"You certainly knew it. Everybody else knows it because I
had it published in the *Pilot* [the NMU newspaper] and you
have every copy of the *Pilot*. I published my change of name in
there and let everybody know because afterwards I saw that I
was starting to go off, I was too sincere about it, and starting to
go off where the party was hiding me."

"I have another purpose entirely."

"And I am Jewish."

"That is why I had no intention of asking your name for that
reason but I had another reason."

"I want the record to show that it was legally changed."

Perhaps Stone really assumed that Bridges brought up the

name change to disclose Stone's Jewishness; perhaps Stone merely used the fact that he was asked the question to put Bridges on the defensive. Whichever was true, the fact that Bridges asked the question did put him on the defensive during that initial painful exchange.

But I am convinced that Bridges' raising the question had nothing whatever to do with Stone's being Jewish. Nevertheless, Stein-Stone evidently did feel "naked" when it was revealed that he had changed his name from Morris Stein to M. Hedley Stone.

"Naked." What a word to use, I thought that night, as if the name "Stone" was his clothing, covering his Jewishness from the sight of the world. Suddenly I felt naked, too, watching these two men slash bitterly at each other.

As Bridges continued his cross-examination, the tension between the two grew almost unbearable. At one point in his questioning Bridges asked Stone whether the United States Immigration Service or the Justice Department had ever threatened him with revocation of his citizenship if he refused to testify against Bridges in the government's prosecution of the Australian-born union leader.

Stone answered, "If you want to know, they came to me to ask if I would testify against you and I told them no," adding a moment later, "And they didn't do that once, they did that over a number of years, Harry."

What Bridges didn't know was that Stone had become a witness in the CIO trial very reluctantly. Until the last minute those of us who were involved in the hearing hadn't known whether Stone would appear, and it had taken a phone call from Phil Murray himself to get Stone to Washington. Even then he had resisted coming to the building, and I had spent a painful few hours with him in his hotel room as he wavered between appearing or returning to New York.

All the time I'd been with him in the hotel room, I'd assured him that he would not be asked to testify whether Bridges had been a Communist party member, since the CIO trial was interested only in whether it could be proved that the Communists had been able to control the union for their own purposes. Indeed, I kept explaining to Stone that the CIO trial had been postponed all during 1949 because Bridges was being prosecuted by the government, and the CIO officials wanted to avoid any possibility that testimony from the CIO trial could be used by the government.

But that night at the CIO building it seemed to me that Bridges had lost control of himself. He kept pushing Stone into describing Communist party activities in which Stone claimed Bridges' active participation. Finally Bridges brought up the question which until now had been avoided: "So, if I told you at this time I am not and never have been a member of the party, would you think I was lying?"

Stone turned to Knight. The transcript shows he said, "I don't have to answer what I would think, do I? Do I have to answer what—— I will answer your questions and not on my thoughts."

But Bridges persisted. "Your beliefs. That is what you have been talking about, your beliefs. What would be your belief?"

Still Stone refused to answer. "I would rather not record my beliefs," he said.

"Don't be so backward," nagged Bridges.

"I am not backward. I haven't anybody in back of me to keep pushing me forward."

Still Bridges wouldn't let up. "If I asked you now in view of your testimony as to the meetings that you claim I attended with you for certain reasons and so forth, if I told you now I am not and never have been a member of the party, you would believe I am lying in view of your statement you have made about ducks and other things, is that correct?"

Stone sighed and said, "If you want me to answer this here— and I am testifying to you here and I told you I refused to testify other places——"

Bridges interrupted him again, saying, "Don't be coy."

There was a long moment of silence. Finally Stone took a breath, looked directly at Bridges, and in decisive strong tones said, "I would tell you the answer is 'Yes.' "

The tension in the room snapped. After that answer, the rest of the night and the next day was an anti-climax. And the trial ended, as it had started, with everyone knowing that the decision to expel the union had been made months before. Just before he left the room, Bridges looked at me as if to tell me that he knew very well who in that room was his real enemy.

The fear of Communism which Senator Joe McCarthy exploited so successfully was mushrooming by 1950 and undoubtedly was one of the factors that brought about the expulsion of the ILWU from the CIO. After the end of the war the country had been shaken by the Communist coup in Czechoslovakia and the Berlin crisis. The revelations of Igor Gousenko, the Russian official who had fled the Soviet Embassy in Canada and revealed the existence of a Russian spy ring in operation there, disturbed Americans more. The fear grew worse with the start of the Hiss-Chambers case, and when this was followed in 1949 by the Soviet's first test of their atomic weapons, destroying America's belief that it alone possessed the bomb, apprehension about the Soviet Union grew intense.

In February, 1950, the month in which McCarthy made his first allegation about Communists in the State Department, Klaus Fuchs, one of the top physicists in England, was arrested by the British police for espionage. He confessed that he had given secrets of the atomic bomb to the Russians while he'd been working in Los Alamos as part of a British team. In May, 1950, Harry Gold, an American, admitted to the FBI that he had been Fuchs' contact with the Russians. Gold also confessed that he had turned over to the Russians some sketches and twenty-five pages of notes about the bomb which had been given him in 1945 by David Greenglass, an army sergeant then working at Los Alamos.

Greenglass was arrested in the middle of June, just ten days before the Korean war erupted. And in the middle of July Greenglass' brother-in-law, Julius Rosenberg, was accused of having been a key figure in the espionage ring which had given the Russians the American nuclear secrets. Less than a month later Ethel Rosenberg, his wife, was also arrested, on the same kind of charges, and even Jews like me winced at the way Jews kept turning up in rapid succession as alleged Soviet spies. In the case of the Rosenbergs, their Jewish background couldn't be minimized, for they brought it up continually, even using it as a weapon in their struggle for life, although in fact they had no greater connection with Jewish life than I did. It is conceivable that had they not been Jewish, they might not have received the death penalty from the Jewish judge who presided at their trial. Perhaps he invoked the death penalty from an unconscious feeling of a need to demonstrate that a Jewish judge could be as harsh on Jewish traitors as any other judge.

This harsh judgment raises all sorts of ugly questions. Was it because the Rosenbergs were Jewish that they were tried before a Jewish judge and prosecuted by a Jew? Was it a coincidence that both the Rosenbergs' lawyer and the prosecution used their jury challenges in such a way that no Jews sat on the jury in New York City, with its very large Jewish population? Were those Jewish organizations which worked so hard to demonstrate their support of the death penalty motivated, at least in part, by the fear that the arrest and conviction of the Rosenbergs might have serious anti-Semitic consequences? Finally, why should I, the emancipated Jewish union official, have cringed every time one of the Rosenbergs made a reference to their being Jewish—used being Jewish, so to speak, as a device to explain what they were? The fact that the Rosenbergs were Jewish added a dimension to their case which hadn't been present in the Hiss-Chambers affair.

The whole question of the relationship between Jews and radicalism is a touchy one in America, and discussion of it is usually very muted. Jewish organizations have a natural interest in not reinforcing the anti-Semites who proclaim that all Jews are either Communists or rich bankers, and non-Jewish liberals find it equally hard to discuss the question realistically for fear that they will be helping the anti-Semites. But it is true that although most Jews in the United States were uninterested in the radical movement, American Jews have produced a high percentage of Communists and radicals. Many reasonable explanations account for this fact; but the fact itself must be admitted.

The belief in the innocence of Hiss or the Rosenbergs separated those liberals whose view of the Communists had been naive from the ex-radicals. Because of their own bitter experience with the Communists, the ex-radicals were prepared to believe that some dedicated party members were capable of almost any action in the interests of the party, including spying for the Soviet Union.

It was a fairly easy step for the ex-radical to move from accepting the possibility of Communist guilt to accepting the charge as true even without proof. Ex-radicals had a disposition to believe anything bad about the Communists and even to gloat when another spy turned up, to the increasing discomfiture of the liberals who had defended the Communists during the People's Front and World War II years.

My friend Philip Selznick and I discussed this obsession, in which we participated to some extent, while he was writing a

book on Communist organization for the RAND Corporation,
a research organization that did most of its work for the air
force. Phil, who looked like a college student, taught sociology
at UCLA. On leave to do the RAND study, he had no intention
of remaining there. Phil and I met through a mutual friend in
Chicago who had asked me to seek out Phil in Los Angeles soon
after we'd arrived there. At the time Phil, his wife Gertrude, and
their little girl, Meg, were living in Santa Monica. We all became
close friends, especially after "Red," as Gertrude was nicknamed, and I discovered we both enjoyed cooking.

While Phil was working on his book, a small group of us decided to start a school where we could try to discuss our views of
the Communist problem with Los Angeles liberals. Unfortunately the school was so successful that we had to close it down:
it took up more time than we could give. Every session was
jammed with people who were active liberals in the community,
genuinely concerned about California's future.

Many of these liberals automatically defended anyone accused by McCarthy, including people who actually were Communists. But instead of saying, "Well, even if So-and-So is a
Communist, what significance does that statement have?" they
hotly denied the possibility of the charge. Simultaneously the
more knowledgeable ex-radicals like me found themselves in the
uncomfortable position of having to explain the difference between those who were accused correctly of having been Communists and those accused falsely. In this maelstrom of conflicting
loyalties I discovered that it was extremely difficult to maintain
any kind of independent position: if you attacked Communists
for something they did with which you disagreed, the automatic
liberals charged you with redbaiting and supporting McCarthy;
if you attacked McCarthy and the government's loyalty-security
program, you were accused of being "soft" on Communists at a
time when the cold war demanded total support for the government.

One organization in which I had a particularly difficult time
explaining my position was the Los Angeles branch of the
American Civil Liberties Union. I'd been elected to the board of
directors of the branch soon after I joined the staff of the Oil
Workers Union, and at nearly every board meeting I got into
violent arguments. One of the few people who understood how I
felt, although he often disagreed with me, was Al Wirin, the

ACLU lawyer for southern California. Wirin, who had been involved in many famous and bitter civil-liberties fights, had been a CIO attorney until during the war he testified publicly against the forced evacuation of the Japanese from the West Coast. He was fired from his job because at that time the Communists, who controlled the CIO, followed the Party line, accepted also by most liberals, albeit reluctantly, which was to accede to the evacuation. When I joined the board of the ACLU, Wirin was defending the Communists from the attack being made on their civil liberties by the government. In addition, he was trying to assist some of the people in the movie industry who were being blacklisted because of their real or alleged connections with the Communists.

Blacklisting began in Washington during October, 1947, when the House Un-American Activities Committee held hearings to investigate the alleged infiltration of the movie industry by the Communist party. It was true that the Communists were active in Hollywood, especially during the People's Front period, from 1936 to 1939, and after the Soviet Union had been attacked by Germany in 1941. But the activity was unimportant insofar as the contents of movies was concerned, and this was the issue the Committee claimed to be concerned about in its hearings. All during the thirties and early forties dozens of people —maybe even hundreds and hundreds—in Hollywood had made donations to antifascist organizations without knowing or caring who really controlled them. Thousands of dollars had been raised for loyalist Spain at cocktail parties around Hollywood swimming pools (actually most of them were in Beverly Hills); the names of movie stars who were genuinely concerned about the world adorned the letterheads of all kinds of organizations set up by the party. And a handful of fairly tough Communists in Hollywood did try to run the party operations in what they thought was a hard Bolshevik fashion. But they were unsuccessful, for most of the movie-industry Communists and their sympathizers had been attracted to the party because they thought it was a liberal organization just a little more extreme than most liberal groups.

It was party policy during this "liberal" period, for example, not to allow any propaganda to creep into films, lest the party members lose their favored position. What the party wanted from Hollywood wasn't propaganda but money and prestige.

And they wanted them so much that one party member was severely criticized when he proudly announced at a meeting that he had whistled a few bars of the "Internationale" in a movie scene in which he was shown waiting for an elevator.

Thus from the start the issue of Communist influence on movie content was phony. The Committee was in search of headlines and proclaimed immediately, without any real evidence, that the movies had become propaganda instruments for the Communist party.

Hollywood's first reaction to the Committee in the spring of 1947 was hostile. "Hollywood is weary of being the national whipping boy for Congressional committees," complained the Association of Motion Picture Producers, the official voice of the movie industry. "We are tired of having irresponsible charges made again and again and again and not sustained. If we have committed a crime we want to know it. If not, we should not be badgered by Congressional committees."

Actors, actresses, writers, producers, and directors, all joined with the movie corporations in attacking the Committee. Stars like Judy Garland, Frank Sinatra, and Fredric March denounced the Committee. When the Committee opened its hearings, a group of Hollywood celebrities were in the audience to express their solidarity with the people whom the Committee had attacked or who had been suspended. But the behavior of John Howard Lawson, a Hollywood screen writer and leading Communist, on the witness stand stunned most of the celebrities; although no one had expected Lawson to cooperate with the Committee, none were prepared for the frantic shouting match he carried on with the Committee members.

Their shocked response to the behavior of Lawson was typical of the well-intentioned liberal who was suddenly confronted with people obeying a strange and frightening commitment, people who listened to voices the liberals didn't know existed and didn't want to hear.

The moguls of the industry (I know of no other industry where the title "mogul" fits so aptly as it did in movies) panicked in the face of the Congressional attack, reinforced as it was by the American Legion, which was also trumpeting out the charges that made headlines all over the country. The industry decided it would fire anyone who was a Communist or had participated in Communist activities and wasn't willing to admit these sins publicly and recant what he had done. It didn't matter, either, whether the alleged Communist was a publicly known actor, a writer whom no one knew, or a producer whom everybody hated. All of them and anybody else named as a Communist would be fired.

An actor or writer who was named as having been a Communist had only two choices: he could become an unfriendly witness, pleading the Fifth Amendment and thus losing his job immediately; or he could admit his prior record and, to prove himself worthy to work in the movie industry, give all the names of everybody he knew in the party while explaining to the Committee how he had been duped, hadn't known what he'd been doing, was ashamed of what he had done, and was a loyal American now.

I had gotten my first personal taste of this mess soon after I arrived in Los Angeles, when I was asked to review a statement written by a very prominent actor who had been accused of membership in a whole series of Communist fronts. Since the accusation was true, the actor and his lawyer had written up explanations for his having joined so many groups. He was active in the Jewish community, and it was through one of the Jewish agencies that his lengthy affidavit ended up in my hands. I read through the actor's affidavit and made some suggestions about how it might be beefed up. A day or so later I realized that I'd fallen into a trap and decided to avoid as much as I could any connection with the whole loathsome business. For although these affidavits were ostensibly prepared for approval by the studios, in fact they had to be given a cachet by one of the private individuals in Hollywood who had the informal power to clear people for jobs.

My experience with the affidavit was another good illustration of the dilemma created when people like me, whose opposition to the Communists derived from their radicalism, cooperated in certain kinds of alliances with the anti-Communists of the right. The justification I initially accepted for examining the actor's affidavit was that he was suffering falsely because he'd felt the same concern about society as I had except that he'd been expressing his concern within the Communist front groups. And since I was more knowledgeable than he was, I thought I had a responsibility to help him: if I could advise him on how to get "cleared" by the people who had veto authority over the jobs, I would be doing him a great service, especially if the charges against him were inaccurate ones.

The argument held some merit and was therefore all the more insidious. It was an easy step from reading affidavits critically to preparing them and then going into the clearance business itself —all just for the ostensible purpose of helping people who had been blacklisted to get back to work, just as the men with the informal authority to grant clearances claimed to be doing.

Roy Brewer, then head of the powerful Hollywood local of the International Alliance of Theatrical Stage Employees, was one of these individuals. His anti-Communist credentials were certified by HUAC, for Brewer maintained a close personal relationship with the Committee staff and appeared regularly befor the Committee or before Legion meetings to describe the Communist menace.

Brewer had come to Hollywood originally to take over the IATSE operations from Bioff and Browne, two extortionists who had been blackmailing the studios for years with threats of strikes. Soon after Brewer arrived, he got into a hell of a nonpolitical, purely jurisdictional fight with some of the other unions which were then Communist-influenced, if not controlled. Brewer won this fight when a strike called by the other unions collapsed, and his influence grew greatly after that victory.

In the blacklisting era Brewer's influence in the movie business was nearly unbelievable. He could call up someone in a studio and say, "Listen, So-and-So used to be in the party, but he's out now and he's trying to make a new life for himself. Why don't you give him a break?" And Brewer made such calls very often. But before Brewer would speak to someone in the industry on behalf of So-and-So, he or his lieutenant at the time, Howard Costigan, who came from Washington State, had to be satisfied that So-and-So was genuinely out of the party and wanted to make amends for his past errors. Making amends meant either testifying before HUAC and giving names or making some other public witness to conversion, such as addressing an American Legion meeting on the evils of Communism, speaking at a union convention on the same subject, signing an anti-Communist ad, or somehow making it known that So-and-So was on the side of the angels now.

Brewer didn't get paid for any of this, and I think he was honestly interested as much in trying to help ex-party members get back to work as in keeping those he believed to be still in the party out of jobs. But quite apart from the very important questions of whether the movie industry should have turned over to Brewer the right to make such judgments, thus giving him authority for hirings, there was still another miserable aspect to the whole business: the only standards used in making judgments were based on So-and-So's willingness to spew up the past and publicly confess to his sins.

I watched Brewer at lunch one day trying to explain to Fredric March what he should do to remove any suspicion from himself. Because at that time March had some reason to believe that his career was suffering from rumors that he'd been involved in a number of party fronts, the meeting had been arranged for him with Brewer. The lunch had an insane quality to it. Brewer kept insisting to March that he had to make some public recantation of sins which March refused to acknowledge he had committed. Neither man had any understanding of what the other was talking about. Since March and his wife steadfastly refused to grovel and admit to nonexistent guilt, nothing came of the meeting. Eventually the Marches won a lawsuit against one of the publications which appeared during this period listing the alleged and real Communist affiliations of people in the entertainment industry.

Although I sympathized with some of the people in the movie industry who had made genuine breaks with the party even before being subpoenaed and who had become "friendly" witnesses later on, spilling their guts in public, I never could feel quite comfortable with them. They knew that the only reason they were asked publicly to list names was to provide the Committee with a show. They knew, too, that by giving the names of people with whom in many cases they'd had only the most casual relationship they were forcing them into the same demeaning positions.

I know of one case in which a woman who had been subpoenaed testified fully in an executive session before the Committee staff and one congressman but told them that she would not give any names in the public sessions because she would have to cite her ex-husband, the father of her children, who came to visit the kids frequently. (Very often these executive sessions were rehearsals for the public display, giving the Committee staff an opportunity to know who was going to testify and who wasn't and thus allowing them to plan the order of public appearances in a way designed to get the best publicity effects.) This woman was assured in the executive session that she would be called only toward the close of the hearing and would not be asked any questions that might bring out her ex-husband's role in the party. Instead, she was called early, and when she anxiously asked why, she was told that one of the other friendly witnesses hadn't appeared and she was needed to make that day's newspaper story. She then had to give the names, including that of her ex-husband.

At one hearing I attended, I saw and heard the Committee staff badger for hours a witness who'd been running a minor party operation. When I questioned the Committee investigator about the reason for the Committee counsel's repetitious questioning of the man I was told, "He's the only unfriendly witness we got today, so we have to work him over to make a good showing."

The House Un-American Activities Committee constituted a form of torture in the entertainment industry—a psychological iron maiden which brought out the very worst characteristics of the subpoenaed witnesses. To save themselves, men testified that they had been seduced into the party by their wives; women claimed to have been taken in by husbands; and all of them recited a litany few of them believed: that they were ashamed of their pasts.

The parade of witnesses subpoenaed to appear during those years was endless. These dreadful sessions of groveling or defiance served two functions: "friendly" witnesses could be relied on to give the Committee more names of potential witnesses, and "unfriendly" witnesses could be relied upon to give the Committee more publicity, especially after the "friendly" witnesses started to run out of new names and began repeating themselves. And whenever the Los Angeles newspapers carried a story that the Committee was going to schedule another hearing, ex-Communists in the industry began to worry that they too would receive a visit from the Committee's West Coast resident investigator, William Wheeler. Wheeler, whom I got to know fairly well as a kind of friendly enemy, was an amiable man who knew very little about Communists when he came to the Committee staff from the Secret Service. But he learned fairly quickly and tried to carry out his ugly work without hurting anyone more than necessary.

The harm done by the Committee wouldn't have been possible, though, without the active help of the industry itself, which lived up to its reputation for being solely concerned with making money at no matter what cost to its own. It took only a single phone call from a superpatriot or a single article in the Legion magazine or a single reference in a newsletter such as *Counterattack* or *Aware* to ruin a career. And very often the blacklisted people didn't even know they were being penalized; no one told them unless they were so important that the studios had a stake in keeping them on the job. In such cases arrangements were sometimes made to let the "important" people testify in an executive session, without publicity. And to make the position of the studios even more disgusting, very often blacklisted writers were rehired at much lower fees to write black-market scripts under assumed names.

Fortunately for my own peace of mind, I had found a haven away from the intense political conflicts of Los Angeles, a place where for a small group of people the fights between Communists and anti-Communists had no importance. As often as I could get away from union work and Ruth could take off from her studies, we drove to Big Sur, on the California coast where we spent long week ends with our friends Emil White, Lilik Schatz, and Henry Miller.

Big Sur was the only appropriate place in the whole world for this group. Although I don't usually feel nostalgic about places that I've been—generally where I am now and what I'm doing now is as good or better than where I was in the past—I am nostalgic about the long week ends we spent at the Sur from 1949 to 1953. We had wonderful days and nights, filled with warmth and love and joy with people who have long since left. Miller now lives in Pacific Palisades, the Schatzes have been back in Israel for more than ten years, and Emil White lives there now only part of the time.

The physical strength of the area had a staggering effect upon us, and in the years that followed we never ceased to respond to the mountains that plunged straight down into the sea, ending in huge rock formations over which the high waves broke with great roars. When the sky was blue and clear and the sun hot and bright, you could see for miles out onto the ocean, and even when it was misty or foggy, with the mountains hidden by a curtain of mist, it was still overwhelming.

Big Sur had a wonderful spicy scent, too, a fragrance compounded of the heather that abounded over the hills, the sea salt, and the wildflowers. The narrow two-lane highway that had been cut out of the mountainside for a hundred miles twisted and turned, dipped and soared, so quickly that the driver of the car would hardly have a moment to spare from the road to look at the spectacular views.

Big Sur was wild and rugged, with only a few houses alongside the road and perched high up in the mountains. There was no electricity then, and no telephones once you left the little village. The mailman drove a truck down the highway a few times a week, picking up and delivering mail and carrying food staples.

On our first trip Ruth and I decided to come back as soon as we could. We had been struck by some of the little shacks alongside the highway, especially by one little house, almost hidden by trees, which had a sign, "Books for Sale." The fact that Miller lived in the area was another attraction for me. Although I had only discovered Miller while I was in the army, I had been enormously impressed with the way he'd freed himself from the barriers of language. But I never thought I would meet him.

Still, meet him we did on our very first return to the Sur. We drove on the highway until we found the little shack advertising books. As we got out of the car, we noticed another sign nailed to the fence. It was handmade and proclaimed that paintings were for sale. As we walked to the door of the house, a small energetic man came out and greeted us. We told him we were interested in seeing his paintings and looking at the books he had for sale. He introduced himself as Emil White, speaking with a slight accent, and invited us inside, into a large living room lined with bookshelves. Where there weren't books, paintings hung on the wall, all of them primitives with tiny figures and tiny houses. Emil's library fascinated me, for it was immediately obvious that it belonged to a political person. As I looked the books over carefully and found many familiar names, I assumed that their owner was or had been a radical, and an anti-Stalinist radical at that. After a few minutes of chitchat, I made references which indicated that we probably shared a common political viewpoint.

It turned out that Emil had been born in Vienna, where his name was Weiss; he had been in the European socialist movement and was completely familiar with all the radical groups in America. He told us that he accumulated much of the library while he lived in Chicago, where he'd worked in a book store that we had patronized. He'd come to Big Sur in 1945 with Miller, for whom he acted as secretary. The two of them had lived there ever since—Miller in a house on top of a mountain and White in a shack that had once been used by the prisoners who'd built the Big Sur highway in the thirties.

By this time we were warming up to each other, and White showed us the rest of the house. It had no inside toilet then; the privy, on the hill in back of the house, afforded a fantastic view of the sea. There was a shower out there, too, made from an old oil drum, suspended even further up the hill, where it caught the rays of the sun. White told us he cooked, read, and heated the house by kerosene and asked us to eat with him. We then sat in his tiny kitchen at the first of the many meals Emil cooked for us at Big Sur. I don't remember what we ate, but we must have had a lot of wine to go with it, for to Emil and everybody else in the area, wine was as essential as bread.

When we asked him about a place to stay, he told us about a nearby lodge that had hot sulphur springs out in the open and was run by a friend of his. Later that afternoon we drove a few miles south to the lodge, which was placed on a plateau, a few hundred feet above the sea. After driving down a steep dirt road, we were taken in tow by the gentle homosexual and his friend who operated the lodge. The two of them did the cooking and serving, helped out occasionally by some drifting soul who wandered in and decided to stay. The lodge had very few guests and was run so informally that we made our own beds in the little cabins behind the lodge itself and kept track of how much coffee we drank and what meals we ate so that we could pay our bills accurately.

We spent most of our time on that first visit being introduced to Emil's friends who also lived in ex-prisoners' shacks up and down the highway. All of them were poor, and most of them were artists, like Lilik Schatz, an Israeli, and his wife Louise, an

American girl. They had a shack, built out over a cliff about three miles north of Emil's place. Lilik was a big man with a deep laugh who instantaneously gave everyone a tremendous sense of life. Being with him was like being under a shower of vitality, for everything Lilik did he did in huge gulps.

Lilik especially fascinated me in almost an exotic way. He was the first Israeli I had ever met. I tried without success to place him into the categories of Zionists that I knew from the old days in the movement or from my work in the Jewish community. He wouldn't fit. Obviously he was Jewish, for he told me that his father, an ardent Zionist and also an artist, had been the founder of the Art Institute in Jerusalem, where Lilik had been born and where his mother and sister still lived. Lilik's real name was Bezalel, in honor of the first artist spoken of in the Bible. Hebrew was his native tongue, and although his English had a distinct accent, it was unlike that of the Yiddish-speaking Jews I'd heard. Lilik spoke French, and German also, and superficially at least he gave the impression of being much like other artists I knew who had lived in Paris, as Lilik had done. But every once in a while something special would come through from Lilik—perhaps a word, a phrase, a way of looking at the world—and I would sense that Lilik was really in exile away from Israel.

Louise was a girl from Berkeley whom he'd met while they were both working at a shipyard during the war. She was dark-haired, just as tall as Lilik but quieter. She seemed to wander alongside him, stopping frequently to listen to the voices from the birds, the trees, and the sea. I didn't communicate with her very easily, but Ruth did right from the start and we all sensed that we were going to be friends.

Lilik, like Emil, was very poor and was also part of Miller's life, for he and Miller were doing a book together. It was to be an illustrated version of Miller's *Into the Night Life,* for which Lilik was making silkscreen illustrations. Each copy of the book was to sell for a hundred dollars, and Lilik showed us samples of the prints he'd made. They were marvelous reflections of his personality—strong, warm, filled with large swooping lines, and endowed with great vitality. We sat back fascinated while the words poured out of him to describe working with Miller. Emil sat nearby, occasionally throwing in his version of Lilik's stories.

Very late that afternoon we returned to Emil's shack because he had promised to give Miller a haircut. A moment or two after we entered the house, Miller appeared in the doorway, a slight figure of a man, wearing a cap jauntily on the side of his head. Emil introduced us, and we made uneasy small talk for a few minutes. Most of the conversation was about a scarf I was using for a neckerchief: how attractive it was, where I'd bought it, and how cheap it had been. Then we left Emil to barber Miller.

For the next few years we went back to the Sur whenever we could. Initially the place was a refuge for us, someplace where we could be with people who knew nothing and cared nothing about the concerns of our normal lives, whose lives and interests had very little to do with what occupied us for so much of the time. Emil, who had once been a political person, was now remote from politics, deeply involved in his painting; the Schatzes were content to understand nothing about politics, and Miller was genuinely puzzled by my concern about unions and politics.

Once, much later, I showed him an article from a Russian literary magazine denouncing him and his work as typical products of a decadent capitalism and suggesting that if the revolution came to the United States he would be a prime object for the firing squad. His response was to say mildly, "They don't like me very much, do they?" When I, still obsessed with the Communists, pressed him, "Don't you care that they say they'll shoot you if they take over?" he answered, "I don't want them to shoot me, but I won't kill them to stop it. I'll put my arms around them and kiss them instead." Henry would sit, listening in fascination, as I told stories about strikes and political disputes, but he always ended up by saying, "It's not important. What's important is to create. Why don't you give up all that? You talk so well about what you should write or paint or dance."

Slowly over the months Miller and I became friends. He's a shy man, and I had no wish to intrude myself upon him. But he came to the lodge often to take afternoon baths, and then we would lie in the tubs side by side, talking. Sometimes, too, he spent the evening with us or we would stop at his house if we walked to the top of Partington Ridge. After he and his wife Lepska separated and she took the two children he adored with her, I spent more time with him, occasionally stopping off alone at the Sur on one of my trips for the union. Then the two of us would sit and talk for hours, and he never ceased urging me to write. He would ask, "When are you going to start writing? When are you going to give up all this nonsense?"

And Miller's response to the "Jewish question" was equally simple: to him Jews were some kind of special people, blessed with special kinds of sensitivities, and he delighted in their company. But to Lilik the question didn't exist. He was an Israeli, born in Jerusalem. He wasn't a Zionist, though, for it would never have occurred to him that he should proselytize another Jew about coming to Israel. Nevertheless, one warm sunny day when we sat on the rocks watching whales spout far out to sea, he told me he simply didn't understand why any Jew would want to live anywhere else permanently. A menorah wasn't a religious symbol to him but part of his normal life. Eventually, he took Louise back to Israel with him. Life at the Sur was never the same without him laughing and bursting at the seams with élan.

I don't mean to suggest that life at Big Sur was a romantic idyll in which we all sat around making brilliant conversation and drinking wine when we weren't making love. Sometimes it was like that, but frequently husbands and wives got into stupid quarrels, friends stopped talking over fancied insults, there was plenty of gossip and lots of worrying about making money. But the world at Big Sur was different in a fundamental way from that of Los Angeles. At Big Sur life, even the phony aspects of it, focused on personal creation as well as personal activities: writing, painting, sculpting, potting went together with eating, sleeping, drinking and fucking. In Los Angeles there was plenty of eating, sleeping, drinking, and lovemaking going on too, but not much creativeness.

Then, in 1951, a terrible personal crisis hit me, one that really shook me up badly: I got fired. Just like that, too. One day I was working, negotiating a contract, and the next day, when I got to the union office in Long Beach, the district director called me in and told me that Knight had fired me.

CHAPTER ELEVEN

FOR A CONFRONTATION with self, I can recommend getting fired. In fact, under certain circumstances, it provides such a confrontation with self that it's almost unbearable. It isn't only that suddenly you have to worry about where to get money; it's all the other things that go with it—you're no longer what you thought you were, you think people look at you strangely because they know, you don't know how to tell your friends, and suddenly you discover that all the invitations you got weren't really for you as you but were for you as the man from the oil workers' union.

And if you happen to get fired without warning, the way I did, it can really loosen the knots of self-confidence that hold you together. You have no time to build up the wall of defensive rationalizations that protect your ego—the boss doesn't like me, I don't really like this job, business is bad all over, and so on. It's just like getting a sudden kick in the balls from one of your best friends. Sitting in the union office in Long Beach, expecting to hear the district director make some routine request of me, and then hearing, but not really believing, what he was saying became a moment of terrible confrontation with myself: instantly, I descended from being the union president of my fantasies to becoming a thirty-three-year-old nothing.

It was a long, long, long thirty-mile drive home to Los Angeles. Ruth was just finishing her prelaw work and getting ready to enter law school. We had no savings. I had no prospects of another job. What was I to tell her? And all our friends? And everybody else who thought of me as "the union representative."

the big shot who flew back and forth to Washington and New York? That drive from Long Beach to Los Angeles is one that I never want to make again. I was utterly bewildered about what might have soured Knight on me. Though I never really found out, I heard rumors that another representative, who thought incorrectly that I was after his job, had enough influence with Knight to get me dumped. And I had been such a wise guy that I'd antagonized enough people to destroy my tiny personal base in the union.

Anyway, it was over, and I made up my mind that I'd never get in a position where my job was dependent upon one man. As always, Ruth was great in the clutch, denouncing not me but Knight, the son-of-a-bitch who had done such a thing to her husband.

Fortunately I wasn't out of work long. Soon I was recommended for a research job to work on a study of the aged that was being conducted at the University of California. And slowly independent unions, which were too small to afford full-time staffs, started asking me to represent them in contract negotiations or in arbitrations.

Although I didn't think so at the time, getting fired from the oil workers' union was the best thing that could have happened to me. Now I was free to act as I pleased politically. Far more importantly, however, the shock of getting fired forced me to shake off some of my fantasies about myself and accept some of the realities. I wasn't going to be president of the oil workers' union, and to some extent at least I wasn't going to escape being Jewish. I continued to joke about my Jewishness, but slowly a different way of coping with this element of myself was opening up for me.

Once, for example, I was negotiating a contract for a small union in San Diego and mentioned that I had driven down from Los Angeles instead of taking the train. The employer, who was a very nice old fellow, suggested that I might like to stay at a combination private beach club and hotel of which he was a director. I agreed, and he arranged for me to have an inexpensive room, not on the beach side.

It was all very pleasant when I checked in late that afternoon. The room was very nice and on a table next to the bed was some literature explaining the relationship between the hotel and the private membership. One rule leaped off the page into my eye, the one that explained the club was open to "white Christians of the highest social standing only." Now in truth I must confess I wasn't really horrified by this, since there are a hell of a lot of clubs in the United States with exactly the same restriction, but I did find it a little surprising that the management had been stupid enough to put its policy in writing.

The next morning I tucked the brochure in my pocket and set off for another day's negotiations, stopping only long enough at the hotel desk to ask in a very loud voice and my best Yiddish accent, "You got maybe here some mail for me? I vas expecting a wery, wery, important piece from mail." I waltzed out without waiting for an answer and took off for the company plant. The negotiations that morning were tough and we were getting no place until during a brief break in the argument I leaned across the table, saying to the employer, "You know, Walter, that's a nice hotel and club you're a director of, but it was the wrong place for me."

"What do you mean?" he laughed. "Just because you're a union representative? We've had other union officials there."

"It's not wrong for me because I'm a union representative," I answered, digging into my pocket for the brochure and sliding it across the table to him. "This is why it's not the place for me. I've got the wrong religion."

The table grew quiet. All the members of the union negotiating team looked curiously at me. The company team looked at their man, who slowly turned beet red as his eye hit the rule I had outlined. He stammered inarticulately, as if he'd been hit hard in the gut and couldn't get his breath. I said nothing more but began arguing heatedly for the union position. And he was so embarrassed that he gave up.

Doing such free-lance negotiating was pretty interesting, and I even made enough money in the next two years to enable us, when Ruth finished law school, to buy round-trip tickets to Europe and a car that was to be delivered in England. We took off after subletting our small house in Los Angeles along with Julius, the cat.

Europe was even greater than we had expected. Old friends who were living in England for a year took us in and introduced us to their friends. We visited Oxford and Cambridge and Scotland. In Paris new friends we'd made on the boat were waiting for us when we arrived armed with a personal guide letter to

Paris that Miller had written for us before we left. Faithfully we followed his directions on how to see the Paris he loved, and never once was his advice wrong. We drove slowly through France, Switzerland, and Italy, enjoying almost every day. But the place that had the most effect on us was Spain, and there we even became Jewish for a little while.

Not many liberals or ex-radicals were visiting Spain in 1953 —it was a country that was still being boycotted. We went there filled with fears about getting arrested by Franco's police, and we carefully hid all the books by Trotsky that I'd bought in England and had thrown carelessly into the back of the car. The fears turned out to be needless, for no one ever bothered us even though we talked openly of our own anti-Franco feelings with Spaniards who also expressed their attitudes freely. Fortunately I had studied Spanish before we set off on the trip, and we had an advantage in all our meetings with people. Not many Americans were traveling in Spain, living in cheap hotels, and eating in cheap restaurants as we had to do because we were getting very low in funds. This made us something of an oddity.

It was impossible to be neutral about Spain as we'd been about Switzerland, for instance. For me visiting Madrid, Guadalajara, Barcelona and Toledo was like opening up the wounds of the Spanish Civil War all over again. All along the highways markers celebrated the number of "Reds" killed by the nationalists in battles at those spots. Just reading the inscriptions on these markers was enough to depress us for hours. We discovered very quickly, too, that for Spaniards the wounds of the war had never even started to heal. The twelve years since the war were as nothing to them: they were still responding as if the war had ended just the day before.

One day, just at dusk, Ruth and I were walking on a deserted highway near our hotel when we saw coming up the road a woman, barefoot, with a little girl. The kid took one look at Ruth, who wasn't very well dressed but did have on shoes and stockings, and spit at her, screaming, *"Fascista!"* before running down the road as fast as she could. That experience was typical of the bitterness felt by so many Spaniards who talked to us with disgust of the aid that was then forthcoming to Franco from the United States. They would prefer remaining poor, they told us, rather than have the United States bolster Franco by giving him aid in exchange for the right to build bases in the country.

Neither Ruth nor I had ever seen such poverty as we encountered in Spain in 1953. Granada, in the south, was a nightmare to us because of a whole square filled with beggars, and we fled from Burgos in the north because we were pursued, literally pursued, in our car by a man on a bike trying to get us to stay at a hotel for which he was trying to solicit guests. And we hated ourselves for hating the beggars, especially after we discovered that the clichés about the proud Spaniards were really true. One noon soon after we arrived in the country we were sitting on a beach on the Costa Brava, eating a lunch of bread, cheese, wine, chocolate, and oranges when a man approached us from the highway. He was dressed miserably, with his toes protruding from the rags that were wound around his shoes and his elbows sticking out of the torn sweater he wore over a ragged shirt. In sign language he asked us for some food, and when I spoke to him in Spanish, offering him some money, he looked surprised but refused very courteously. Instead, he again asked for some food, pointing to where his wife was sitting, waiting for him on the road. We gave him all the food we had left and started walking slowly and in depressed silence back toward our car. We got into the car, neither of us speaking. As we drove past the man and his wife, we saw him tenderly putting a segment of the orange in her mouth. He saw us, stood up, and bowed.

And one afternoon in Toledo we were walking on the Rambla when in the crowds of people we came abreast a waiter from the cheap restaurant in which we had eaten. By coincidence, he was walking with the night clerk from the hotel in which we were staying and another man. The three of them greeted us very politely, and after a few minutes of further walking and talking, they invited us to join them in a bottle of wine. We accepted with alacrity, and they took us to a very poor working-class wine café. I remember that the bottle of wine we drank cost two and a half pesetas, the equivalent of a nickel. The five of us drank a couple of bottles while eating small, shriveled, bitter olives and talking continuously. The three men waited patiently while I translated what they were saying to Ruth. It had taken only a few minutes to discover that all three men had fought in the civil war on the loyalist side, and once I'd made my own political convictions clear, we all relaxed and began talking in earnest. A few hours later it was time for the fourth bottle of wine; when it appeared, I reached to pay for it, since the three men had each bought one of the previous bottles. But to my great embarrassment they got terribly angry and started to shout at me. Hastily I explained that in the United States it was the custom to take turns and they were mollified, but they still refused to let me buy a bottle as they explained to me that in Spain a guest was never permitted to purchase anything.

We had seen a few signs of Ruth's Jewish past in the Toledo area, for we had visited the city's old synagogue, now a museum. Ruth was very curious about the synagogue and wandered around in it as if she were asking herself how she, a descendant of the Jews who had once prayed in that room, would have fitted in before her ancestors were driven from the country. It was particularly striking because it was the first time I had ever seen her show that kind of personal interest in any synagogue.

A day or so later we left Toledo to drive on what turned out to be a terrible road to Madrid. Somewhere along the trip we stopped at a primitive gas station on the outskirts of a fairly large town and while the man was pumping the gas into the car by hand, we got out to stretch our legs. As we looked casually at our surroundings, Ruth called my attention to an old broken wall. High up on the wall were some letters in Hebrew, but although we could make them out clearly enough, we couldn't read them, for neither of us had learned the language.

I asked the gas-station man about the wall, but he knew nothing except that it had been up for hundreds of years. Then I asked him if any Jews had ever lived in the town, but he didn't know that either, although he did tell me no Jews lived there now nor had for as long as he could remember.

In Madrid we actually found some Jews by going to the synagogue on a Friday night. The Jews turned out to be German refugees rather than Spaniards, and the services were Orthodox, which meant that Ruth had to wait outside because the synagogue, a converted apartment, was too small to have a separate section for women. Fortunately the service was short.

Since our money was beginning to run very short, we drove from Madrid through northern Spain into France. Once again we visited our friends in Paris, and then returned to England, where we stayed with other friends.

While we were in England on our way home, I got involved in a typical controversy about America with Kingsley Martin, the editor of *The New Statesman*. Martin, like a good many other

Britons who were identified with the left, was convinced that the development of McCarthyism in the United States represented a serious trend toward fascism and that the country was becoming a police state. That pessimistic view of America was attacked by those who thought Martin was "soft" on the Communist issue, although they conceded he wasn't a Communist himself. To the American, British, and European ex-radicals, the British left seemed corrupted by many hangovers from the prewar People's Front period and the years of Allied cooperation with the Soviet Union.

I was right in the middle, between these two amorphous groups. Two of our good American friends in England were Irving Kristol and his wife, Gertrude Himmelfarb. Irving had been an editor of *Commentary* magazine, published by the American Jewish Committee, and had come to England to edit *Encounter,* a monthly magazine sponsored by the Congress for Cultural Freedom. The Congress had been organized after the war in an effort to fight the Communist influence among intellectuals by presenting them with an alternative group to which they could adhere. Although I was generally sympathetic to the Congress, I believed its anti-Communist emphasis had become obsessive. But despite my political differences with the Kristols, we remained good friends, and when we'd come to England, they had taken us in tow, opened their house to us, and introduced us to their friends in the British intellectual world, most of whom shared their viewpoint rather than mine.

My argument with Martin started when he insisted that no one in the United States would write for his magazine because they were afraid to have their names listed as contributing to it. He asked me how I had been able to get a passport, considering my radical past, and then went on to tell me that many American subscribers to *The New Statesman* insisted on receiving it in a plain wrapper because all the mail was watched and opened if it appeared to be politically suspect.

When I heard Martin describe America as if it were well on its way to becoming a concentration camp, I got furious and in response ended up defending the United States more than I really wanted to do. I tried to make the point with him that McCarthyism *was* an evil influence, that it *had* affected seriously and adversely the quality of American life, but that it was a disservice to exaggerate what was happening beyond the actual truth.

After a few more weeks in England, we realized we'd have to get back home soon, for our money was now dangerously low. Reluctantly we left, first shipping our little car, so that it would be waiting when we arrived and we could drive back to California. Our money finally ran out in Indianapolis, but fortunately we had friends there from whom we borrowed enough to get us home.

After the trip Ruth began studying for her bar examinations, and slowly, hesitantly, I began writing. The old-age study for which I'd been doing research had bogged down badly, and since I believed this to be partly my fault, I felt responsible for helping to complete it. Fortunately Phil Selznick generously offered to assist in getting the book written. It took quite a while, but finally Phil, another man who'd been working on the study, and I completed the manuscript.

While I was working on the book, I was still doing union work, for the most part representing the mechanics and flight engineers of a freight airlines. In addition to providing me with some income, this arrangement also gave me free, if slow, transportation across the country. Thus, even though I no longer had a credit card for the airlines such as the American Jewish Committee and the Oil Workers had given me, I was still flying to Chicago or Washington on union business. But now when I went to the airport, usually at night, I'd check in at the dispatcher's office in the hangar where the planes were loaded with all kinds of freight on wooden pallets. There were no seats for passengers on the freight planes, and I spent the long hours it took to fly across the country stretched out inside a sleeping bag on top of an air mattress on the bare floor of the plane or wedged in among the freight.

December, 1954, was a month of great excitement: John Cogley asked me to work on a report the Fund for the Republic had commissioned him to write on blacklisting in the entertainment industry; Max Ascoli urged me to write for *The Reporter* magazine; and Ruth passed her bar exams, making her eligible to practice law.

Cogley, who had been the editor of *The Commonweal,* a liberal Catholic weekly, had heard of me through a movie executive I knew and from Michael Harrington, a young, goodlooking radical who was on the staff of the Workers' Defense League, an organization that was part of the whole anti-Stalinist, radical, and socialist circle. I had met Harrington just before going to Spain, and we had liked each other immediately.

I was delighted to take on the assignment because of my strong feelings about the blacklist and because it was for the Fund for the Republic, the organization headed by Robert M. Hutchins, who had become a legend at the University of Chicago.

Although I didn't know Hutchins, I had worked with his assistant at the Fund, Hallock Hoffman, when Hallock had been on the staff of the American Friends Service Committee. Later Hallock told me that after the word spread about my being hired by Cogley, Hutchins had been visited by a group from Los Angeles who asked him to fire me because I was a redbaiter. According to Hallock, Hutchins looked surprised at the request and said something like, "What you're asking me to do is blacklist someone because of his politics from working on a study of blacklisting because of politics. Well, I won't do that, nor will I ask Cogley to do it."

Cogley, a short, stocky man who mumbled rather than talked, had assembled a very interesting crew for the blacklisting study. Harrington was his assistant and worked closely with him in New York and accompanied him when he came out to the West Coast. In California he had also hired a woman named Elizabeth Poe whom he thought better able than me to interview the blacklistees. He was right, too, for my reputation was very sour among those of that group who knew about me only as the man who had played a prominent role in dumping Bridges from the CIO and fighting the Communists inside the CIO.

In New York Cogley had put together another curious bunch to work on the way blacklisting had been handled in radio and TV. Many of them were liberal Catholics like himself or ex-Catholic intellectuals like Harrington. Those still in the Church shared one quality no matter how else they differed: they were engaged in a continuous effort to integrate their intellectual beliefs with their faith, to bring these two elements together. They were often cynical about much of the formal hierarchy of the Church and had battled at great personal cost against the blind support some elements of the Church had given McCarthy. But with the exception of a few, they had not rejected their faith itself. And I suppose one of the qualities I found most attractive about them was their willingness to face up to the conflicts they felt, even though they resolved them in ways I didn't understand.

Cogley himself was one of the most engaging as well as most intellectual of the lot, with a great capacity to laugh at himself. The depth and breadth of his knowledge surprised me continually, and I was greatly impressed with the deceptively simple quality of his writing. Like Harrington, he had come to New York and *The Commonweal* from the Catholic Worker movement, although at a much earlier date than Mike. John appeared to be terribly disorganized in the way he ran the blacklisting project, but somehow in the end it all fitted together.

Some of the experiences I had while actually gathering material for Cogley reinforced still further my view of how the whole issue of the Communists' role in America had been misunderstood.

I sat in the commissary of a movie studio eating lunch with a writer who had been an important part of the group of Hollywood liberals, and as we talked about the blacklist over our coffee, we saw Eddie Dmytryk, the director who had been one of the Hollywood Ten, stop at the counter to pay his check. Dmytryk had gone to jail with the others for contempt, but while in jail he had admitted to having been a Communist. Although he had broken with the party even before he had been subpoenaed, he'd gone to jail, he said, because he didn't want anyone to think his break with the party was caused by fear of imprisonment.

I knew Dmytryk casually from having interviewed him during the study, and when he caught my eye, I waved to him. He waved back, and the man with me made a kind of noncommittal chop with his hand, a motion that might or might not have been taken as a gesture of acknowledgment to Dmytryk. I looked at him curiously.

"What's with you and Dmytryk?"

"I hate him," he said.

"Who do you hate him?" I asked.

"Because he was one of my best friends, and when he got subpoenaed, I went to him and said, 'Eddie, are you a Communist? Tell me the truth because I'll defend your right to work in this industry even if you are a Communist.' He told me he wasn't a Communist, he swore on a stack of Bibles he wasn't a Communist, and I believed him. And even though I didn't like it, I defended his behavior at the hearings. Then, after he was in jail, he admitted he had been a Communist. I don't care so much about his having been a Communist, but he lied to me and I hate him for that."

You poor, innocent schlemiel, I thought to myself at the time. Eddie Dmytryk could have sworn to me on a million Bibles that he wasn't a Communist, and I still wouldn't have believed him. But then I had another thought: in his world, when someone you trust tells you something, you believe him even if he was a Communist; and in my world, I never believed anyone I thought to be a Communist. So I had to ask myself whose world was the better one, his or mine?

The distrust that naive writer still felt eight years later because he thought he had been lied to was only one of the evil legacies left to the country by the combination of the vicious role played by the Un-American Activities Committee and the political behavior of the Communists who defended themselves with silence rather than going to jail for taking open positions. The Communist party behavior during this period admirably suited the purposes of the Un-American Activities Committee, for it gave the Committee the opportunity to exploit the false issues it had raised without any debate over the real ones.

One night over dinner in a Hollywood restaurant Lee Cobb told me of how he held out until 1953 before he gave in under the pressure of unemployment and depression and finally testified at an executive hearing so that he could get back to work. Cobb was miserable at the role he had to play before the Committee, telling it nothing not already known in the most minute detail and giving no names that hadn't been given a dozen times before. And his misery was undoubtedly shared by dozens of other witnesses who became "friendly" only reluctantly, brought to that state by the lack of work—or, in the case of one director, by impotence as a result of blacklisting.

I know how strong the pressures were and I know how much these men wanted and needed to return to their careers. I also know how desperately some people tried to find other jobs but were so unsuccessful that finally, after a few years of unemployment, they were brought to their knees. I know all this and so I hesitate to judge them. But yet I do, and I find it hard to approve of what they did, just as I think all the Hollywood Communists should have done what a few people did do: say to the Committee, "Yes, I was a Communist [or am a Communist], and I became one because I thought that was the way to fight what was and is wrong in this country. I'll tell you anything you have a right to know about myself and my own activities, but I'll tell you nothing about others. If I know of any spies or espionage agents, I'll tell the FBI about them, but I won't discuss anyone in these hearings except myself, even if it means I must go to jail."

By June, 1955, I'd finished the research for Cogley. By then he and Harrington had become good friends of Ruth's and mine. Whenever they came to Los Angeles, the four of us spent as much time together as we could, and we introduced them to two of our close friends, Tom and Margaret Coffey. They, like Harrington, had left the Catholic Church, and we were always fascinated by the discussions that took place when they were together with Mike. As I listened to the three of them arguing heatedly about Catholic theology, I began to understand better the complicated involvement all of them had with the Church, and I was fascinated, too, to see that Cogley never participated in these debates. I always had the feeling that his commitment to the Church was so secure that he felt no need to defend it. But he kept asking me questions about how I felt toward Judaism; questions I couldn't really answer except to say that I was indifferent.

Occasionally while I was collecting material for Cogley, I went to New York for meetings with him and the other members of his staff. Toward the end of the time allotted for research, Cogley held a meeting at which all of us could report to Hutchins on our progress. It was a nervous meeting, for only a few of the staff members had ever met Hutchins, and nearly all of them were in awe of him.

I was, too, although I never would have admitted it or given any sign of it to him. But as he walked around the hotel suite where we were having the meeting, being introduced to everybody by John, I was struck by the fact that he looked even more distinguished than he had the one time I'd seen him, years before, walking across the University of Chicago campus. When John introduced me to him, Hutchins smiled and said, jokingly, "Oh, yes, I've heard of you. You're the famous redbaiter."

Only a short time before, by coincidence, my first article in *The Reporter* had been published, dealing with a decision of the California Supreme Court upholding the right of an employer to discharge a Communist solely on the basis of party membership. The article, titled "Should Communists Be Allowed To Eat?" attacked the court's decision, and after it appeared I spent hours just looking at my name in type. When people I knew called up to tell me they'd read it, I floated inside, even though I played it cool for them.

By the time I'd finished my work for Cogley, I was writing more often in *The Reporter*. Then Hutchins asked me to join the staff of the Fund as a consultant on West Coast activities. That summer the Fund's operations were expanding rapidly, and it was coming under an ever-increasing barrage from the McCarthy forces in America, spearheaded by Fulton Lewis, Jr., the rightwing radio commentator who was devoting nearly every one of his broadcasts to a denunciation of the Fund.

One of Lewis' targets was Adam Yarmolinsky, with whom I'd remained in contact ever since we'd met in the Army, and who was also working on a Fund project. Adam, who'd been a clerk to a Supreme Court Justice and had then gone into private practice, was commissioned by the Fund to make a study of the government's loyalty-security program. He, in turn, had asked lawyers all over the country, including Ruth, to help gather and analyze the data. After he'd finished the study, he, too, had become part of the Fund's permanent staff, operating out of Washington and New York. And so we saw each other even more frequently, for I began attending the hectic meetings of the Fund's board of directors, held every few months in New York.

I was always filled with a sense of wonder at my own presence at these meetings, for I could not accept the reality of participating in a discussion with Hutchins, Paul Hoffman, Chester Bowles, Harry Ashmore, Meyer Kestnbaum, Erwin Griswold, George Shuster, Elmo Roper, and other board members. The transition to this new phase of my life had been so sudden that I wasn't prepared for it, just as I wasn't prepared to be paid a salary for carrying out civil-liberties work I would gladly have done without pay.

One night, flying from Los Angeles to New York for a board meeting, the sense of unreality I felt almost overwhelmed me. The plane was a Constellation, a propeller-driven aircraft that

took about ten hours from coast to coast, and since I was scheduled to make a report to the board the next morning about a new
project we were considering, I had taken a berth. In those days,
the four berths in the sleeper planes still only cost about twenty
dollars above the regular fare.

When I got to the airport, I found that Paul Hoffman was
taking the same plane to the meeting and that he also had a
berth. We sat talking in the airport, and in a few minutes Chet
Huntley strolled in, on his way to New York that night to begin
his new career with NBC. He had another berth.

The plane took off, and we sat in the lounge, drinking and
talking about the fight for civil liberties while glancing out the
windows at the lights below. When I climbed into the soft berth
and thought of how I had hitchhiked and ridden freight trains
not very many years before, the dreamlike quality of this night
enveloped me so strongly that I had no way of separating fantasy from reality.

But the board meetings had a harsh tone of reality, for beginning in the fall of 1955, rightwing pressures on the Fund were
growing more and more intense. Some board members resigned
either because of the pressure or because they opposed Hutchins' view of how the attacks should be met. Board meetings became politely acrimonious as the debate went on among the directors.

Now the Fund found itself under attack by Henry Ford himself; he was anxious to dissociate the Ford Motor Company and
the Ford Foundation from any connection with our organization. While all this was happening, Hutchins was also under
increasing criticism from some former radicals who believed
he had no understanding of the Communist problem. The first
blast at Hutchins from this group focused on a bibliography of
materials about Communism published by the Fund. It was
charged that the bibliography was incomplete, that it had performed a service to the Communists by omitting important anti-
Communist material, and that an anti-anti-Communist attitude
had biased the work.

Whatever merits there were to the charges made against the
scholarship of the bibliography, the critics ignored the fact that
it had been authorized and prepared under the direction of a
distinguished law professor before Hutchins and Hoffman had
taken over the Fund's operations. Even had Hutchins wanted to

hold up its publication, he could not; and undoubtedly, had he done so, he would have been accused of suppressing the truth.

The harsh judgment made about Hutchins' naiveté by the "sophisticated" anti-Communist ex-radicals, especially those in the American Committee for Cultural Freedom group, was reinforced by a number of other incidents: when Hutchins authorized the hiring of a temporary public-relations man who had refused to answer questions of the House Un-American Activities Committee about his past membership in the Communist party; or when the Fund's board accepted a recommendation that it make an award to a Quaker meeting in Philadelphia which had refused to fire a librarian after she had declined to answer a similar inquiry.

They were disturbed also by what they believed to be the Fund's failure to distribute material on civil liberties written by some of them, while it did distribute books written by people they believed to be either "soft" or as naive as Hutchins.

The CCF's distrust of the Fund derived directly from its belief that the Fund failed to share the Committee's belief that "the greatest, though by no means the only, threat to cultural freedom today is from totalitarianism in general and the World Communist movement in particular." Their view of McCarthyism also grew from that belief. And the result was a position which began by saying that the rights of Americans were "gravely threatened by a new spirit of intolerance and suspicion" but moved from there to complain that the real danger of McCarthyism was that it indirectly strengthened the Communists, especially since, while the abuses of McCarthyism were "flagrant injustices," the influence of the Communist movement was "masked and insidious."

The strain between the Fund and the CCF group grew more and more exacerbated all during the fall of 1955, even though some of the people in it were working on a Fund-sponsored study of Communism in American life. Inevitably, too, the strain affected my own personal relationships with those members of the anti-Hutchins group who had been friends of mine for many years. I, too, was getting much more disturbed by the CCF's primary focus on the Communist issue to the virtual exclusion of all else. I was caught between conflicting loyalties.

William Gomberg, a member of the Committee for Cultural Freedom's executive committee, was a friend of Hutchins and genuinely disturbed by the bad feelings that had developed between the Fund and the CCF. Gomberg was a friend of mine, too, whom I had known from the days when I worked with the Garment Workers Union. We talked about the problem, and Gomberg arranged an informal unofficial meeting between Hutchins and myself, representing the Fund, and Diana Trilling, Sidney Hook, Paul Hays, Dan Bell, Norman Thomas, and Gomberg himself, to present the CCF viewpoint.

With some apprehension I went with Hutchins to the meeting, which took place the afternoon of December 1, 1956, in the lounge of the Columbia University Faculty Club. After the preliminary awkward chitchat, Hook got down to cases by vigorously attacking what he believed to be three incorrect positions held by Hutchins on the Communist question: a refusal to concede that some guilt could be attributed through association; a willingness to employ subversives in government posts; and the employment of Communists in institutions such as the university or the Fund itself.

Hutchins defended his view just as vigorously, pointing out that he had always opposed Communism as a system, but that he distinguished between that opposition and a blanket refusal to hire Communists. He pointed out that he believed it necessary to emphasize publicly the necessity for judging each case of a Communist individually because of the possibility, even though it might have been a very limited one, that an individual Communist might be worthy of employment.

After these two opening statements, everybody began participating in the discussion. Paul Hays, then teaching at Columbia Law School, argued that Hutchins had done the cause of civil liberties a disservice, because in a TV program which created a great deal of discussion Hutchins had defended the Fund's action in hiring an alleged Communist without making it clear that he might not hire him for some jobs. Norman Thomas brought up the question of the bibliography project, plus another one which seemed to bear the mark of naiveté on the Communist question; and it was only then that I entered the argument, pointing out that the attack on the Fund was for projects that had been started before Hutchins had taken over its administration.

Hook asked me what I meant by those remarks, and Danny Bell answered for me, saying to the group that what I had done was to place them on the defensive, the same position in which they had put Hutchins and the Fund. The debate soon shifted back to Hutchins, though; Diana Trilling argued, somewhat heatedly I thought, that Hutchins seemed to have an image of himself as the only embattled liberal and that he seemed to be under the misapprehension that there was something idealistic about the nature of the Communist party.

An hour or so later, the meeting broke up with a discussion between Hook and Hutchins on the nature of academic freedom. It had been much more amiable than I had expected. As Hutchins and I rode in a taxi back to the Fund office, he asked me why Diana Trilling could have thought that he had ever felt there was anything idealistic about the Communist movement.

"If I'd believed Communism was an idealistic movement, I might have joined the Communists, but I knew it wasn't," he said to me.

I tried to explain why the CCF people reacted so passionately about the Communists, but I don't think I was very successful, for Hutchins kept looking at me as if to say, "I never will understand your friends."

My own encounter with McCarthyism during this period was a painful example of the paranoia that afflicted the country during the 1950s and I discovered there was more truth in Kingsley Martin's view than I had believed: while I was working on the report for Cogley I discovered that I was a political Typhoid Mary and that contact with me had a damaging effect on others.

The first time I became aware that association with me had bad consequences was early in 1955, when a friend, the director of a university institute, came to me, puzzled and troubled, to ask for some advice. He'd been approached by the government about taking an important overseas assignment and had accepted the offer. After announcing his intention of taking a leave from the university and after making all the preparations for going overseas, his appointment was held up for security reasons.

I was one of those security reasons, he told me. He'd been informed that one of the things he had to do before being sent overseas was to satisfactorily explain his relationship to me.

"What should I tell them?" he asked me. "I don't even know what you're accused of being, so how can I explain our relationship?"

In fact, our relationship had been a very casual one, limited to poker games and occasional drinks at meetings we both attended. So I advised him to tell the government investigators that he knew nothing about my politics and very little more about me. But it didn't do any good; before he received his clearance, he died of a heart attack.

At about the same time a girl I knew almost as casually discovered that she had a similar problem because of me. She had been the roommate of a friend of mine in San Francisco and had then moved on to Washington. I saw her occasionally in Washington and gathered she was with the CIA, although she never once told me what she did there nor did I ever ask her.

Then she got an overseas assignment with the agency and came back to California to say good-bye to her parents. But by the time she returned to Washington to close up her apartment and leave, her clearance had been lifted. According to some mutual friends with whom she discussed the problem, her relationship to me, casual as it was, had been one of the reasons for the removal of her clearance.

By this time I was very disturbed by what was happening to others. My own life was unaffected by these security difficulties, for I hadn't applied for any government job, nor had I any intention of doing so. But now I was faced with the fact that my past history coupled with my current activities was having serious consequences for others.

The climax came when the army attempted to give a dishonorable discharge to Justin Grossman, a friend of mine who'd been drafted in 1955. His wife had been my secretary on the blacklisting report until Justin went into the army. Justin had been active in the Trotskyist and socialist youth movements both in Chicago and New York and had continued his activities while studying at UCLA. Although Jackie wasn't as politically oriented as he was, she, too, had been involved.

Justin had been in the army for about nine months when the attempt to give him a dishonorable discharge was made. The reasons for the discharge were that at the time he went into the army he'd listed his past memberships in socialist and Trotskyist groups; the intelligence reports on him gave the details of his activities; his wife had been a member of the same groups as he and he had listed me as a character reference on his army personal-history form.

Justin called me from Fort Ord, California, where he was stationed, to tell me what he was facing. "If you gave me as a character reference, they ought to kick you out for stupidity," I kidded him, but underneath the joking I was horrified. Fortunately, Francis Heisler, an old friend of mine and a new friend of Justin's, lived in Carmel, near Fort Ord. Heisler, a great civil-liberties lawyer, had known me in Minneapolis and had himself been very close to the anti-Stalinist radical movement. He took Justin's case and fought it out with the army.

Heisler was able to force the army to give out the details of the charge against Justin that involved me. It stated that Grossman had listed me as a character reference and then continued: "One Paul Leonard JACOBS admitted that he was a former member of the Young Communist League and the SWP (Social-ist Workers Party) in the late 1930s. He also subscribed to CP (Communist Party) and ISL (Independent Socialist League) publications. On 14 March 1953 Jacobs gave a lecture sponsored by the ISL at UCLA. The essence of the lecture was that stu-dents' rights have been infringed upon by the Federal Bureau of Investigation and the U. S. House Committee on Un-American Activities."

Heisler asked me if I would appear at the hearing to defend myself and Justin; naturally I agreed. The night before the hear-ing was to open on the morning of January 16, 1956, I flew to Monterey to meet with Heisler and Grossman. It was odd to see Justin in the same kind of uniform I'd worn ten years earlier, and we joked about it. But he was somewhat apprehensive about what he was facing and I was, too, for his sake. Heisler and I drove over to the base together, discussing the best strategy to follow in the trial. When I walked into the hearing room and saw the blank faces of the officers who were acting as judges, I thought for a moment of the three men who had played a similar role at the CIO trial of the ILWU. Only this time it was my ox that was being gored.

After I had finished answering Heisler's questions about my past and present political views and about my knowledge of Grossman's political views, the senior officer, a colonel, began querying me. As he looked down at a looseleaf book in front of him, I realized that we hadn't seen all the information compiled on me.

"Are you the same Paul Jacobs who is a member of the Board

of Directors of the Southern California branch of the American Civil Liberties Union?" he asked.

When I answered in the affirmative, he went on with, "Isn't that organization the one listed by the Tenney Committee as being a Communist front?"

I explained that the Tenney Committee had been only a state version of the House Un-American Activities Committee and that its reports had long since been discredited. As an example of the falsity of the Tenney Committee reports, I used the Committee's listing of Norman Thomas as a Communist, pointing out to the colonel that everybody knew Thomas to be a socialist.

He frowned at me. "Are you suggesting that a senator would issue a false report?"

I almost flared up, but I hung on, reminding myself that it was Grossman's future that was at stake here, not mine, and that it could only hurt him if I lost my temper with the colonel. Patiently I told him that Tenney had been a state senator and that he wasn't even that any longer since he'd been defeated some years earlier.

But I could see I had made no impression. To the colonel and his fellow officer, Grossman and I were Communists. That colonel's inability to distinguish between Communist spies and anti-Communist radicals was evident in the decision the officers made to give Grossman the dishonorable discharge. Luckily for Justin, Heisler was able to beat the case in court, and eventually Grossman received an honorable discharge.

The army's attempt to make me a reason for giving Grossman a dishonorable discharge had convinced me I had to find some way of changing the situation. For a while I considered filing a law suit against the government, but I was persuaded that such a legal action had no chance of success. Finally some friends prevailed on me to engage a Washington attorney, whom I had known for some time, to intercede with all the various government agencies on my behalf. Rather reluctantly I agreed to this course of action; I felt demeaned by the notion that I had to clear myself as the people in Hollywood had been forced to do. But I was constantly reminded that the pressure wasn't on me but on others who were innocent of anything except knowing me and that I had a responsibility to help them by removing any suspicion from myself.

Early in January, just at the time I was testifying at the army hearing, the attorney began collecting affidavits from such people as Norman Thomas; Murray Kempton, then writing a column for the New York *Post;* Clark Kerr, then Chancellor of the University of California at Berkeley; Gus Tyler of the International Ladies Garment Workers Union; and a host of others who knew my political beliefs.

Thomas's affidavit touched on one of the crucial issues in the whole loyalty-security tangle. He wrote that he had known me in the past as a socialist and Trotskyist who was an "active anti-Communist." Thomas went on to say, "In Hollywood, to my knowledge, he has been involved in a certain degree of controversy with some extreme right wing anti-Communists regarding the best methods of opposing Communism, but in no sense is he himself a Communist or a sympathizer with Communism."

That was the heart of the matter—for the judgmental standards the extreme right wing had imposed had become the standards for most of the country and for government agencies. Wherever the right wing had influence—in Hollywood, New York, or Washington—its adherents made certain that if someone weren't an anti-Communist in *their* way, that person was to be regarded with suspicion, even if it was someone like myself, whose anti-Communist credentials couldn't be challenged.

And the response of the ex-socialists, ex-Communists, and ex-Trotskyists who had become the left wing of the right wing was not to denounce the whole procedure but only to say that in a case like mine a mistake had been made. So it was that Victor Riesel, the labor columnist who had known me only as an anti-Stalinist fighter, wrote a column denouncing the army for using Grossman's relationship to me as one basis for its attempt to give him a dishonorable discharge. Riesel's attack on the army focused on the fact that the military didn't seem to understand what a great anti-Communist I'd been. He went on to say—incorrectly—that it was I who was responsible for getting the Mine, Mill and Smelter Workers expelled from the CIO, confusing it with longshoremen, and he criticized the army for still working with this union. Finally Riesel suggested to the army that "picking on Jacobs' friend is just the kind of thing the enemies of U.S. security want" and proposed that "the business of security" should be left to the professionals in the FBI or to people trained by the FBI. "A few more loyalty cases like this one and the whole vital policy of a security screening system will be discredited," he concluded.

The affidavit I submitted to the Washington attorney made my position on the political tightrope as explicit as I could. I wrote that "My public and private opposition to the Communist Party and to Bolshevism is well known. Equally well known is my opposition to many aspects of both the government's present security program and of certain Congressional investigating committees. . . ."

All during the early part of 1956 I was involved in working on loyalty-security questions for the Fund. I was writing more and more for *The Reporter,* too, including one article condemning the government for prosecuting Harry Bridges. I think I was obsessed with Bridges, as if a constant war were going on inside me, one side still reacting to the way I thought he'd followed all the twists and turns in the Communist line, and the other side filled with guilt for the way in which I had helped push him out of the CIO.

In the meantime Khrushchev had made his famous speech denouncing Stalin, and the entire Communist movement, which was pretty small by this time, was thrown into an uproar. Resignations and splits in the party took place on a scale unprecedented even when the Stalin-Hitler pact was announced. And every one of us who had attacked Stalin while he was alive couldn't help feeling some grim joy at being able now to say, "I told you so."

Then, in July, 1956, the Fund published Cogley's report on blacklisting. The report was denounced by everyone in TV, the movies, and advertising who had been involved in the blacklisting, and once again we were in the middle of a tremendous fight. And, sadly, Cogley had very few defenders. The climax of the attack on his report came when the House Un-American Activities Committee subpoenaed him to appear at a hearing in Washington.

Mike Harrington and I went with John to Washington, since we'd heard that he was going to be questioned about us and we thought we might want to demand the opportunity to testify ourselves. On the morning that John was scheduled to testify, the phone rang in the hotel room where Mike and I were sitting. John was out, taking a walk before going over to the hearing room.

The call was from Hutchins, and I answered it. I asked him

where he was calling from in case John wanted to call him back, and he gave me the name of a country club in Westchester.

"That's nice for you," I said sarcastically. "But you know my kind can't get in there." Hutchins made some wisecrack back and we chatted for a few moments about Jews not being admitted to Christian country clubs. Then, in a still almost bantering tone, Hutchins told me why he'd called.

"I don't know what John or you or Mike is going to tell the Committee, and I don't want to know. I just want all three of you to know that whatever position you take, all the money the Fund has left will back you up."

The hearing itself was pretty ugly. The Committee's counsel virtually accused Cogley of distorting the truth and biasing his report in favor of the Communists. One of the first questions he was asked concerned his hiring of me, Harrington, and Dr. Marie Jahoda of New York University, who had done some psychological research work for the project. The Committee counsel asked Cogley if he'd known that I had been a member of the Young Communist League, whether he also knew that Dr. Jahoda had been admitted to the United States only in 1945 and had a "connection with the socialist Democratic Party in Austria," and that Harrington was an active Socialist.

The hearing, which took six days, became a forum at which the people named by Cogley as being involved in blacklisting attacked him, me, and everyone else connected with the study. But in a few weeks all the newspaper publicity had died down, and we were back at our usual work, by this time veterans of such attacks.

The fall of 1956 was shocking to anyone's nervous system. The Hungarian revolt against the Communists, and the use of Soviet tanks to suppress the uprising, created great feelings of indignation. In Poland, too, the Communist society was in the process of a violent shake-up, while in the Middle East, Nasser's seizure of the Suez Canal had led to the invasion of Egypt by Britain, France, and Israel. One hardly knew where to turn, nor could anyone predict on one day what was going to happen the next.

My reaction to the Israeli role in the invasion of Egypt was indignation and horror. I was aghast at what seemed to be an utterly irresponsible act that might have created a very danger-

ous war situation, and I felt that the joint American-Soviet resolution in the UN condemning the attack was proper. My strong
reaction to the Israeli role was based at least in part on the way
in which the American Zionists seemed to expect all Jews to
defend automatically every action of Israel, including the invasion of Egypt. But since I had learned long ago not to argue
about such questions with Zionists, I had no one except the people in my own group of friends with whom to discuss these questions, and there was little point to that, since most of them felt
as I did.

One day during that same fall of 1956, while I was in Washington gathering material for a *Reporter* article on Jimmy Hoffa,
I ran into my old friend Greg Bardacke in the lobby of the May-
flower Hotel. Greg had been working for a number of years as
an American representative of the Histadrut, the Israeli trade
union that dominated much of Israeli life. With him was a slight,
wiry man whose ears jutted out from his head. After Greg and I
had finished noisily greeting each other, he introduced me to his
friend, whose name was Eppi Evron. He was an Israeli, about
my age, a Histadrut official, assigned as a liaison man in the
United States between his organization and its American supporters. Greg asked me to join them at lunch, and I agreed readily.

I liked Eppi from the moment we met. He seemed to me to be
straightforward and honest in his defense of Israel, not sentimental as were the American Zionists. As I listened to him speak,
I thought how surprised my father would have been that this
product of East European Jewry was now one of the people
running a country of Jews.

While Eppi was out of the room for a moment, Greg told me
that Eppi had been Ben-Gurion's private secretary and that he
was now a close associate of Pinchas Lavon, then head of the
Histadrut. It was a long lunch, and as we walked back into the
hotel lobby, we ran into Gus Tyler. He looked surprised when he
saw us, for he knew both Greg and Eppi.

"What are you two doing with Paul?" asked Gus.

"I'm going to make a Jew out of him," answered Eppi.

"No," said Gus. "You might make an Israeli out of him, but
you'll never make Paul into a Jew."

From then on I saw Eppi whenever I was in New York, where
he lived, and we argued spiritedly at every occasion. When the

two very long articles I wrote about Hoffa appeared in separate issues of *The Reporter,* he pretended to be angry with me because I had used a dinner Histadrut had given in Hoffa's honor as an example of how fund raising gives people status they could not get in other ways. But we never really got angry with each other, nor did he ever attempt to minimize the legitimate problems and faults of Israel nor fail to admit their existence. Instead, he tried only to explain the background of what had happened or justify what had been done on the basis of the Jewish experience during and after the Nazi attempt to wipe out the European Jews. I liked Eppi particularly because he made no hard sell for Israel. It was simply his country, and he could discuss its limitations and liabilities as honestly as I could those of the United States. I was struck, too, by how free he seemed of the conflicts I had about what being Jewish meant: whatever fantasies he had of himself, he must have been Jewish in all of them.

In 1957 the Fund had begun to change the direction of its work from dealing with civil-liberties problems to examining some of the basic institutions and issues in American life. Meetings were being held by a group of consultants which included men such as I. I. Rabi, the physicist; Reinhold Niebuhr, the Protestant theologian; John Courtney Murray, the Catholic scholar; Clark Kerr, by then president of the University of California; Scott Buchanan, the philosopher; Eugene Burdick; Henry Luce; A. A. Berle; and the staff of the Fund. The group eventually decided to begin studying the institutions of the society, and I was assigned to work with Kerr on a study of the trade unions.

During one consultants' session in New York, I was having dinner with Eppi and arguing with him, as usual, when he interrupted me.

"I'm tired of listening to you talk about things you don't know about. What about taking a trip to Israel at Histadrut expense so you can learn what the country is really like?"

I thought for only a moment before I agreed, and we decided to work out the details of the trip as quickly as possible. The chance came when early in 1958 it was announced that *The Reporter* was getting an award from a national journalism society for publishing an article I had written about the Atomic Energy Commission's exposure of people in Nevada and Utah to radiation without giving them proper protection or adequate warning. Just at that time Ruth and I had decided to move from Los Angeles to San Francisco. Some friends bought our house, we put our furniture in storage, went to New York for the award ceremony, and from there flew to Israel.

CHAPTER TWELVE

R UTH and I were pretty drunk when we walked up the ramp into the El Al plane one rainy night in May, 1958. The farewell party for us had gone on right up to the moment the plane's departure was announced. And while the people traveling in the tourist section of the Britannia prop-jet had pushed forward to get through the airport doors, we had time for another last-minute drink, since we knew our seats were reserved for us in the first-class section.

The airplane fascinated me. Not only was it an Israeli plane, itself an exotic thought, but it was the first time I'd been on one like it—no American airline was using the Britannia, the first large prop-jet aircraft ever built. When we'd settled down in our comfortable seats and the plane moved out to the runway for departure, I looked up and saw to my surprise that the seat belt and no smoking signs were in both English and Hebrew. Stupidly, until that moment and the one that immediately followed when the pilot began speaking through the public address system in Hebrew, I had not really understood that Hebrew was a language linked to such a specific reality as an airplane.

"How can you fly in Hebrew?" I asked Ruth. "Hebrew is for praying in Temple or for dipping your finger in wine during the Seder, but it's not for flying airplanes." It was, though, for in a few minutes the Britannia was roaring down the runway and was then airborne.

When we were aloft, the purser and the stewardess began putting plates on the trays in front of us. It was about ten thirty at night by then, and the last thing we wanted was another meal.

"Thank you," I said to the purser, "but we've already had our dinner. We'll settle for a drink."

He glared at me and answered, as if living out one of those schmaltzy El Al ads, "Look, a plate of chicken soup can't hurt you. So you'll eat it."

So we ate it. We ate all the way across the Atlantic and all the way across Europe. And we were still eating, I think, when the plane arrived the next night at Lydda airport outside Tel Aviv. I looked out the window as the plane came to a halt; on the concrete apron I could see a small group of people whom I assumed to be waiting for us. We collected our hand baggage, walked down the steps to the ground, and were greeted by two or three officials of the Histadrut, the organization that had brought us to Israel.

But as I talked with them of how wonderful the trip had been and walked toward the custom shed in the airport building, I kept looking around for Lilik, to whom I had cabled our arrival time. Just as I was about to give in to the disappointment I felt, I heard a familiar voice bellowing, "Paul! Ruthie! Paul! Ruthie!" I looked up and spotted him, up on the balcony of the airport building, waving at us frantically. And by the time we had been quickly ushered through the customs and passport-control offices, he was waiting to grab us in his huge hugging embrace.

When we finally all calmed down, we explained to the Histadrut officials that we'd like to spend a few days with our friends, the Schatzes, in Jerusalem before going off on the tour that they had arranged for us. They weren't very happy about the idea, but since we insisted and since Schatz was obviously a name of some prestige in Israel, they consented after Lilik promised faithfully to deliver us back to Tel Aviv in three days.

We set off for Jerusalem jammed into Lilik's open sports car, the only one of its kind in Israel. Lilik and Ruth sat in the front seats and I crammed myself into the rear along with all our bags.

"I can't believe it!" Lilik kept shouting excitedly as we drove to Jerusalem, twisting around in his seat to look at me or grabbing Ruth around the shoulders. "I can't believe it! You're really here! You're really here!"

The sky was blue-black on the road to Jerusalem, the stars were bright, and the moon was high enough to illuminate battered trucks alongside the highway. Ruth asked Lilik what they were.

"They're memorials," he said a little solemnly. "Those are the armored trucks that got shot up when they were coming along this road during the war with the Arabs. Those trucks kept the supply lines open to Jerusalem, and so after the war was over, they were left right where they'd been hit. All that's been done to them was to give them a coat of paint."

But Lilik couldn't remain solemn for more than a few minutes. Soon he was jabbering away at us about what he and Louise were doing, how many parties they'd arranged for us already, and asking us dozens of questions about Emil and Henry and Louise's sister, whom Henry had married after he and Lepska were divorced. Between questions he shouted, over the wind, the history of the places we were passing. An hour and a half later we started up past the deserted Arab village of stone huts on the long grade that led to Jerusalem. By the time we got into the city it was very late and very quiet. Lilik drove along the road down into the center of town to his sister's apartment, where we were going to stay, at the back of the art institute named after his father. There his sister was waiting for us, and in a few minutes his mother, Olga, one of the great old-timers of the country, came from her apartment next door to greet us.

For the next three days Lilik and Louise whirled us around Jerusalem. Later, when we got to Tel Aviv, we realized how lucky we had been to have gone to Jerusalem first; it is an ancient city of stone, a city that looks the way it should, reflecting honestly in its style and architecture its place in the Middle East, while Tel Aviv is just another ugly European city.

During those first three days we walked and drove all through Jerusalem with Lilik, a devoted guide whose love for the city of his birth showed in every proud gesture pointing out its wonders. But whenever he looked over at the other side of the walls or barbed wire or fortifications that separated Israeli Jerusalem from Jordanian Jerusalem, he seemed to wince; it was clear from what he said that he knew and missed all its streets and alleys.

Ruth and I were continually surprised by the different kinds and colors of people we saw on the streets of Jerusalem. "Are they Jewish, too?" we would ask Lilik naively, pointing to a very dark-skinned couple in robes, a man in a turban, or a woman in pantaloons and bare feet.

"Sure," he'd answer. "We've got all kinds of Jews here. Black ones and brown ones and yellow ones. Any color you want, but they're all Jews anyway."

Then, to make certain that we saw all the types of Jerusalem, including those he didn't like, Lilik took us to the Mea Shearim, the enclave of rigidly Orthodox Jews who live in Jerusalem today precisely the way their ancestors had lived hundreds of years ago. First we walked through the market place on the outskirts of the area. It was filled with exotic-looking people selling exotic goods from sidewalk stalls. The air was noisy as buyers and sellers argued shrilly with each other about the price of the beans, the coffee, the vegetables, the herbs, and the hundreds of other things being bought and sold.

From the market we moved into the streets of the Orthodox quarter, walking alongside the heavily bearded men with thick earlocks striding arrogantly down the narrow sidewalks. They wore huge round hats trimmed in fur, long coats with a fur facing, black shoes and stockings, and occasionally black knickers. Behind them walked their wives, faces down, dressed in the plainest of dresses with long sleeves, ugly cotton stockings, and heavy shoes. On their heads they had the *sheitels,* the wigs all Orthodox women must wear.

The little boys and big boys were exact duplicates of their elders except that their earlocks were wispy and they had no beards. Everyone seemed to look at us—hatless, in sport shirts, and laughing; we grew silent under their cold stares. We know you, they seemed to say, we recognize you for what you are—false Jews, who do not observe the Sabbath, who eat nonkosher food, who let your women expose their arms and legs, who use Hebrew, the sacred language, in daily conversation, and who never go to the synagogue.

Away from the chilling hostility of Mea Shearim, our spirits lifted, especially when we went to visit Lilik and Louise's friends, the writers and painters and sculptors of Jerusalem whom he had gathered to meet us. Then, it was as if we were back at Big Sur again, in the world we had loved so much.

Everyone in the group knew each other, and their rapid conversations flowed around and touched points in time and episodes with which they were all familiar. Except for the names and the places, the talk had a ring of familiarity, as if the people and events they were describing could have been just as easily in New York or Los Angeles as in Haifa or Jerusalem.

For our benefit the conversation was almost always in English. Someone pointed out to us that English was one of the legacies of the British Mandate for which the Jews were grateful. But when they talked with each other, they shifted rapidly from English to Hebrew to French and, in some cases, to Russian.

Except for Lilik, these Israelis were much more interested in politics and actively involved in political life than anybody at Big Sur had been. Most of them had fought in the underground struggles against the British and in the open battles with the Arabs. They knew all the differences between Stalinists and Trotskyists, they were worried about American foreign policy, and they were acutely aware of the tensions between America and the Soviet Union.

The extent to which they were familiar with what was happening outside their own country showed in an incident at the first party Lilik and Louise gave for us. One of their friends, a satirical writer, asked me if I was the Paul Jacobs who had written the article about fallout from the bomb testing in Nevada.

"Yes," I answered, somewhat surprised that he'd read it. "Why?"

"Hey, Lilik!" he shouted across the room to where Lilik was talking to Ruth. "Come here."

Lilik walked over and the writer said to him, "You see, I told you it must be the same fellow. He did write the article I told you about."

Bewildered, I looked at both of them as Lilik turned to me and, in an almost hurt tone, said, "Why didn't you tell me you were a writer? When you wrote that you and Ruthie were coming, I told everybody all about you and about how you were a union organizer. But Dahn said that a fellow named Paul Jacobs was a writer and I kept insisting that it must be another Paul Jacobs, for my friend Paul Jacobs was a union organizer. You never were a writer when I knew you at Big Sur."

"That's right, Lilik, I wasn't, but I am now. I'm the fellow who wrote the article."

These people began giving me a view of Israel I could not have gotten from any official source, in the country or from the violently pro-Zionist Jews in America. In fact, one of the most striking features of those first few days in Jerusalem with Lilik's friends was their often sour notion of themselves and their country. In great contrast, for example, to many American Jews with whom I'd gotten into violent arguments at dinner parties about the book *Exodus,* which was enormously popular in America then, I discovered that my view of the book as trash was shared by many of the intelligent Israelis. Back in California, if I described *Exodus* both as bad history and a bad novel, I was sure to get into a heated discussion with some nice middle-class Jews who got their kicks reading about how the tough Jews had kicked the shit out of the Arabs and the British. My theory was that these American Jews actually accepted the anti-Semitic idea that Jews were only capable of being businessmen and were too cowardly to fight for their rights if they were threatened. The great appeal of *Exodus* was that as the readers sat in their comfortable living rooms or around the swimming pool, they could identify with those Jews in the book who were so tough it took ten dirty Arabs to rape just one brave Jewish girl.

But the Israelis Lilik introduced us to in those first few days —the writers, painters, architects, designers—knew better. They had actually fought in the war against the Arabs, and their view of the Uris book was that, although it made good tourist propaganda, it had very little to do with the reality of their lives or the battles in which they'd fought.

Three long days and nights later Lilik, as he'd promised, drove us down to Tel Aviv. Except for the signs in Hebrew, the large number of bookstores, and an even larger number of cafés, Tel Aviv was undistinguishable from any other Mediterranean city. Its architecture is ugly, and it doesn't take advantage of its seafront. It has no green space, and it was obviously built without a plan. Yet there is no doubt that it is the real capital of the country. Larger than Jerusalem, it is the center of intellectual life and the headquarters for most of the country's important institutions, not the least of them being our sponsor, the Histadrut, the combination trade union, business organization, and social-welfare group that is uniquely Israeli.

Ruth and I spent our first night in Tel Aviv strolling along the boardwalk, gaping at the people. The variety of Jews on the boardwalk wasn't quite as exotic as we'd found in Jerusalem, but still the people who congregated at the southern end of the beach reminded us of the Mexicans in Tia Juana. And they seemed to behave like Mexicans, too, jamming the shooting galleries and cafés, dancing to loud jukeboxes or excitedly shouting at the progress their steel ball made down the labyrinthian ways of the pinball machines. These were the Oriental Jews. Just as Arab food, which is quite popular in Israel, is called Oriental food, so the phrase "Oriental Jew" is a euphemism used in Israel to describe the dark-skinned Jews who come from such Arab countries as Morocco, Algeria, Iraq, and Yemen.

That first night in Tel Aviv we went to bed early but went to sleep late, kept awake by the noise from the boardwalk cafés, for our hotel was right on the beach. Finally, though, the last orchestra quit playing, the last customer left, and the boardwalk quieted down. In the morning we ate our first hotel breakfast in Israel, usually the best meal one gets there. It includes herring, eggs, cheeses, vegetables, bread, butter, and coffee.

After we finished eating, we sat outside on the hotel veranda waiting for the car to come for us. It arrived soon, a limousine with two men in front. One of them, a man about my own age, jumped out and introduced himself in precise English as our guide for the next three weeks. We walked out to the car and met the driver, an older man, who also spoke English and was to be with us for the whole trip.

As we drove away from the hotel to the Histadrut headquarters, the guide, who told us he'd come from South Africa, started explaining the areas through which we were passing. Something he said, some phrase he used, caused a blip on my political radar to jog and I asked him, as casually as I could, what political group he had belonged to in South Africa.

"I was a Trotskyist there," he said, obviously surprised by the question. "Why do you ask?"

"Because I was a Trotskyist, too," I answered. "And something you said made me think that's what you probably had been."

So we two ex-Trotskyists fell on each other's political necks, and we began to get still another view of Israel, different again from that of Lilik's friends in Jerusalem.

For three weeks we traveled through Israel, in and out of Tel Aviv. We got to Jerusalem two or three times more as well, and Lilik and Louise met us once in Ein Hod on the Mediterranean, south of Haifa. Ein Hod was an old Arab village that had been converted into an artists' colony, and many of our new friends either lived there or spent week ends in the square stone houses they had rebuilt. And nights in Tel Aviv we made the Dizengoff Street scene, going from café to crowded café, talking continually and listening to the voices rise from the café seats in a babel of Hebrew, German, French, Russian, and English.

We drove to kibbutzim in the lovely green Galilee and to the new city of Beersheba, growing up on the site of the ancient one, where we saw the first camels we'd ever encountered outside a zoo. In Eilat we went out into the Red Sea in a glass-bottomed boat, and in Sodom we walked along under the oppressive cliffs while the operations of the salt works were explained to us. The red rocks of the Negev reminded us of New Mexico, and we gaped in awe at the copper mines that dated back to King Solomon.

Everywhere we went people talked continually. Sometimes it seemed to us that the whole country was one continual surge of voices that rose to a crescendo on Friday, stopped for a momentary breath on Saturday, the Shabbat, and then started in all over again on Saturday night. Gradually, too, out of the talk we heard in Hebrew, I began to separate out words and phrases, tones and emphases. I began to hear the language even though I couldn't understand the words, and I started being able to distinguish between the native liquid Hebrew of Lilik and the more harsh tones of those Israelis who were newer to the country.

Slowly I became aware of the power exerted in the country by the Histadrut. Whenever we arrived at a new place, our first stop was always the Histadrut headquarters, and it was always the Histadrut that sponsored the reception for us. If we went to see the mayor of a town, the local Histadrut chief accompanied us; if we went on a sightseeing trip, the local Histadrut secretary usually went along politely; and at a reception in Nazareth we were introduced to the Arab officials by the Histadrut man there.

As I grew more confident in my ability to make judgments about what we were seeing, the discussions with Israelis grew more animated and more detailed.

A disturbing undercurrent ran through the conversations whenever we began to talk about politics, and I began to sense that there were elements in Israel's internal life of which I'd never been aware. After only a few hours of sitting at a table in Fink's Bar in Jerusalem, eating goulash soup and drinking Israeli cognac, or drinking at the Café Cassit in Tel Aviv, it became obvious that the glossy picture of Israel presented by the Zionist fund raisers had very little to do with the Israel I heard discussed by the Israelis we were meeting now.

Listening to these Israelis, most of whom were former members of the Haganah and Palmach, the underground armed groups which had fought the British, I felt a curious kind of ambivalence. For two opposite reasons, I was glad that these internal strains, some of them evidently quite severe, existed. It proved that the Zionists were wrong in the picture they presented, thus satisfying my own anti-Zionism, but simultaneously I was glad to hear such open criticism of the government and Israeli life because it demonstrated a kind of internal vigor that was an unexpected and pleasant surprise.

The bitching that went on in Fink's or at the Cassit and at the parties in Lilik's house and in the homes of his friends was often generalized, directed at the failure of Israeli life to meet the expectations these people had for it; at the dependence of Israel upon American fund raising; at Ben-Gurion's seeming stranglehold on the life of the country; and, over and over, at the manner in which the Orthodox Jews were able to force their ways upon the country as a whole. Occasionally, too, we heard vague references to an incident that had occurred in 1954, when the Egyptians had broken up an alleged Israeli spy ring and executed two of the spies after a trial, imprisoning a dozen others. Once, when I was explaining that Ruth and I had been brought to Israel through the efforts of Eppi Evron, I caught an odd reaction to Eppi's name; when I pressed for an explanation, I was told that he, too, had been involved in the spy incident, along with Pinchas Lavon, head of the Histadrut, who was out of the country while we were there. Lavon had been defense minister when the "incident" had taken place.

I didn't understand yet that almost every Israeli outside of Lilik's immediate circle of friends and occasionally inside it had a double or triple history, had two or three past identities. Take Joel Palgi, for example. We had met Joel after we left Jerusalem and returned to Tel Aviv to begin our official tour of the country. He's a handsome man, now an Israeli ambassador, who speaks a very cultivated English and has a fine sense of humor. When we met him first in 1958, he was the head of operations for El Al, and we didn't know he'd been one of the Jews who had been parachuted behind the Nazi lines into Budapest, where he was imprisoned by the Nazis.

But hardly ever did we talk with anyone about being Jewish.

Primarily we were tourists in Israel: one night in an outdoor café at Tiberias we watched a group of young Israelis dance the cha-cha-cha and the mambo and joked with them about those native Israeli dances; another evening, in Beersheba, I got into a violent argument with an army officer, who told us the biggest error Israel had ever made was stopping the Suez war under the pressures of the United States.

"Next time we won't stop!" he shouted. "Next time we'll keep going the way we should have done."

We heard the other side of that argument, though, from Israelis who worried about the bad relations between Israel and the Arab countries and who blamed their own leaders as much as the Arabs for the hostilities. Initially politics in Israel fascinated me far more than the matter of its being a Jewish state. The political milieu in which we found ourselves was so familiar to me that it took only a few days before I was able to distinguish between the moderate labor socialism of the Mapai, the dominant political party, and the more orthodox Marxism of Mapam, a group which had split from Mapai. I found myself very much at home in Israel, not so much because it was a Jewish country but because it was a semisocialist Jewish one.

For Ruth the country's fascination seemed to have had more Jewish overtones, although she wasn't certain of their precise nature. And fortunately for both of us, what we saw and heard from Lilik's friends, combined with what our ex-Trotskyist guide showed and told us, gave us a far more rounded and more interesting notion of Israel than we could have gotten either as just official guests or as tourists. No matter where we went, when we finished a day's official touring, we could either visit someone whose name had been given us by Lilik or sit and argue with our guide in the context of our mutual political backgrounds.

Toward the very end of our stay in Israel we decided to get away from the official tour for a few days. On our own we went to a hotel on the sea north of Haifa, to swim, drink, eat, and relax on the beach without having to pay formal calls on anyone. Lilik and Louise drove there from Jerusalem, and the four of us did nothing for four days, Lilik and I lazily snorkeling through the warm sea, Ruth and Louise lazily sleeping on the warm beach.

Nights we went to Natanya, a nearby vacation town, where we sat in the cafés talking and drinking, occasionally getting up to dance in the back, where the orchestras were playing. Outside on the street Japanese lanterns waved in the warm Mediterranean breeze, lending an air of unreality to the little town. And on the last night, in Freddy's Bar, we sat and listened to Freddy play the piano and sing the café songs of Europe in French, in German, and in Hungarian. And when the people in the café began joining in the choruses, I was reminded suddenly of a night years before at the Selznick's in Santa Monica, when I'd seen two refugees, eminent scholars, begin weeping softly when a young Englishman had played and sung many of those same songs.

That was always a sad scene in Israel, the sight of the refugees who had come to Israel not so much from conviction but from necessity and were confronted, suddenly, perhaps through a song in a café, with the fact of their displacement. Wherever they lived, these refugees tried to create one tiny island to give them continuity with their past lives. Their bars, their cafés, their restaurants weren't like Fink's in Jerusalem or Cassit in Tel Aviv, which reflect the present in Israel. Instead, in Eilat, down at the Red Sea, we had been in a café run by a Hungarian couple who were trying to recapture Budapest in the hot desert, just as Freddy's, outside Natanya, was what a café might have been in Vienna or Paris.

A few days later, amid tearful farewells at the crowded airport we left Lilik, Louise, and all our new friends who had come to see us off and flew to Greece. There, thanks again to Miller's advice, we discovered something of the joy and bitterness of Greek life as we stayed on the little island of Hydra, then just becoming a center for bohemian tourists. We had a room in a hotel high up a whole series of steep steps, which we climbed, panting, two or three times a day.

One hot afternoon I was teasing Ruth as she lay on the other hotel bed, trying to nap, and in a little while she began to giggle.

"I guess you'll never grow up," she said. "We've been married twenty years and you're forty years old, but you're still not grown up."

"You're absolutely wrong," I responded instantly. "I'm not forty. I'm seventeen years old, I'm six foot one, and everybody calls me 'Curly.' "

"Okay, Curly, come on over here."

Later I began to think about what I had uttered so spontaneously. For the first time I had voiced a truth that I hadn't wanted to admit about myself before. And even though, at the time, I'd done it without any serious intent, the notion that I could think of myself as Curly began to trouble me. I joked about it for weeks, but beneath the joking I was working myself up to finding out what I could, by myself, about Curly and especially about whether he was Jewish.

Back in America we changed the pattern of our lives once again by moving from Los Angeles to San Francisco, a shift of only five hundred miles but a psychic one that covered an enormous distance. San Francisco represented our return to city life; by this time Los Angeles had become just one enormous suburb stretching for miles in every direction, without a central city.

More important was the fact that in San Francisco we were close to Berkeley, where Phil Selznick was now teaching. I'd been spending more and more time there with him and a few others, supervising the trade-union study for the Fund. And the more visits I made to Berkeley, the more I was attracted to the intellectual atmosphere of the community. The fact that San Francisco had always been a delightful city was another factor in our decision to move away from the freeways and smog of Los Angeles.

As always when we moved, it was more difficult for Ruth than for me. She had to give up the law practice she'd built up in Los Angeles and begin all over again in a new and strange community. But, as always, she did it.

Luckily we were able to begin life in San Francisco under fortunate auspices: we found a wonderful house to rent the day we arrived, our old friends were delighted to see us, and Ruth was offered space with a group of congenial lawyers, while I opened a small office for the trade-union study in Berkeley.

Simultaneously something else was happening to me: gradually, without even being aware of it, I had given up the role of the Jewish jokester. John Cogley called my attention to this change one day when he said to me, "You don't tell many Jewish jokes any more. It used to be that whenever we saw you, you always had a whole bunch of new jokes, but now we hardly hear any from you."

He was right, too. Somehow I had shifted roles. I'm sure all kinds of explanations accounted for my telling fewer jokes or using fewer Yiddish stories to illustrate a point as I'd done, sometimes even straining the point to bring in the stories. Perhaps I had become more secure in my relationship to other people and wanted a different kind of approval from them than I'd gotten in the past by telling jokes. I was beginning to think of myself as a writer rather than just a good talker, and I didn't need to project myself in quite the same way as I'd done in the past.

Inevitably, because we'd been to Israel, we began to take more of an interest in Israeli life. Still, Gus Tyler turned out to be right, for although the trip to Israel had fascinated me, it left unchanged how I felt about being a Jew. And my new interest never manifested itself in participation in Israel bond drives or Histadrut campaigns, and I still grew indignant whenever I read of some new fanaticism from either the Orthodox rabbis of Israel or the Israeli military establishment. But when I was in New York or Washington on one of my frequent trips, I spent a good deal of time talking with Shimshon Arad, who was in the New York consulate and is now Israeli Ambassador to Mexico, and Gershon Avner, now another Israeli ambassador.

With them it was possible to argue about America or Israel without fear that what I said would be construed as either anti-Semitism or anti-Israeli feeling. So argue we did, about such things as the Suez actions or an analysis of Histadrut which I wrote and distributed privately after returning from Israel.

As a result of our relationships with Eppi Evron, we met Pinchas Lavon and his wife, Lucy, when they came to San Francisco for the AFL–CIO convention in the late fall of 1959, Eppi brought them to our house for a short visit that stretched on for hours that day and took up all the next as well.

Lavon was a fascinating and strong personality, a shock to the nervous system, another one of those tough East European Jews at whom German Jews like my father sneered. He was a small man with gray hair, slightly protruding eyes, and tremoring hands, who smoked continuously while drinking great quantities of cognac, which seemed to have no effect upon him. He spoke English very well although with a marked European accent rather than the English one which younger Israelis like Arad and Avner had picked up from the British in Palestine.

Lavon's overriding interest was politics, and his knowledge of it was as broad as his analyses were brilliant. On the second day of his visit to us we took him and his wife sightseeing in San

Francisco, but while I pointed out the beauties of the city to him, he spoke only about politics. As we crossed the Golden Gate Bridge, I interrupted the flow of political talk to point out the wonders of the view. He stopped talking for a moment, just long enough to give a cursory glance out the car window, and went right back to attacking me for my misunderstanding of the Histadrut organization, which he headed.

A few minutes after he'd made a particularly cutting criticism of my views, my wife leaned forward from the back seat of the car and said, "Pinchas, how can you say such things to Paul? You're his guest!"

He turned around, surprised, to look at her. "What difference does that make in a political discussion? There's nothing personal in it. Paul knows I'm attacking him because I know he's wrong."

Lavon wasn't polite either in discussing American Jews, especially the Zionists who remained American Zionists, rather than emigrating to Israel. And he kept insisting that some day I, too, would move to Israel, the only place where he believed it possible for a Jew, especially a radical Jew, to lead an ordinary life. He shook his head in disbelief when I told him that in the United States Jews could also lead normal lives. We argued, more gently in this case, that even though America was vastly different from Europe in its view of the Jews, we were still not accepted totally and never would be.

"When will you come back to Israel again?" he asked when we said good-bye.

"I don't know. We miss our friends there and miss the country, but I don't know when we'll get back."

"Come and see us when you do. We'll argue some more."

But before we saw him again, I went to Germany, Poland, and the Soviet Union. And when I did see him again, he had become the central figure in a bitter fight with Ben-Gurion; a fight that nearly ripped Israel apart and that is still going on today.

I justified a trip to the Soviet Union on the basis of wanting to learn at first hand about Russian unions and their function in Soviet society. I had another, more important, motive, growing out of my background as a Trotskyist and a radical anti-Communist. For years I had hated the Communists and the Soviet Union with a hostility that reflected the bitterness I felt over the Stalinist betrayal of the Russian Revolution and of socialism. But now, under Krushchev, it appeared as if the Stalinist curse was being gradually lifted, and I wanted to see whether anything worthwhile was left of the socialism to which I had been so committed.

Once I'd made the decision to go, I began taking private Russian lessons every day, and by the time I left San Francisco I had a primitive speaking and reading ability. I had hoped to finance the trip by getting writing assignments, and I did get one from *Playboy,* of all magazines, which commissioned me to write an article I'd suggested on the social and political history of caviar. The article would have paid for the trip, but unfortunately what I wrote was too dull for the magazine, and I had to pay the travel cost myself. The trip to the Soviet Union was my first really long separation from Ruth, for although I had been traveling continually since we were married, I had never been away from her for more than a week or two at a time, and we'd always been able to talk by phone, something we obviously weren't going to be able to do on this trip. So, with mixed feelings of guilt, worry, and anticipation, I went to England in March, 1960.

Some of my friends there who were experts on the Soviet Union gave me an informal briefing at lunch one day about what to expect in Russia. And they also gave me some advice. "After a while you'll get bloody bored with listening to all the statistics they throw at you. Every time you ask a question, you're going to hear how much better it is in the Soviet Union, how much more concrete they have in their bridges, how many more students there are at the University of Moscow, how many new houses are being built. There's only one way to shut them up. Just look at them and say, 'Do you know that in China there are more children under the age of ten than the total population of the Soviet Union?' That'll quiet them down."

It did, too, I discovered later. I got one more bit of advice before I left from a member of the British Foreign Service who had served in Moscow for many years. He suggested that I have a business card printed with my name, title, and degree on it. "It doesn't matter what your degree is," he said, "because no one will ask, but you should have one." Dutifully I went to a printer and told him to make up a card that read "Paul Jacobs, H.S.G."

And I discovered that the Briton was right, for while everyone in the Soviet Union to whom I gave the card was very impressed, I never had to explain that the H.S.G. stood for "High School Graduate."

But first I went to Germany. I went there for two reasons: to see the little town where my father had been born and where my brother and I had been told we owned a house and to visit a young couple, friends of ours from New York, who were living in Frankfurt. I was determined not to carry into the country the strong feelings I had about the Nazis. The war was over, I kept saying to myself, and you can't hold all Germans responsible for what happened to the Jews. As we drove out of the airport where the couple had picked me up, a man ran from the sidewalk into the street and nearly got knocked down by our Mercedes convertible.

"Damn," said my friend. "I could have gotten you a Dubie as a welcoming present."

I was horrified. "What do you mean, a Dubie? You weren't serious about running him over, were you?"

"Only half serious," he answered. "He's a Dubie because that's what the GIs call Germans. I don't know why. No one seems to know where it started. Maybe it comes from *'du bist.'* Anyway, after you've been here a while you'll see why I was only half serious about running him down."

As we drove into Frankfurt, I became depressed very quickly by the ugliness of the city. Frankfurt had been leveled by bombing during the war, and when it was rebuilt the job was done without any grace. The squat buildings were just dumpy concrete blobs stuck down on the streets. And the people seemed just like the buildings—squat and ugly, without grace. Their clothes all looked gray: the streets seemed filled with women clomping along in heavy gray shoes, shapeless gray dresses, and ugly gray hats. And as I looked at them, I kept pushing away the thought of how natural they would have looked in the uniform of SS guards.

Frankfurt is a city of business, I realized as I looked at shop windows filled with merchandise, at the hundreds of camera shops and dime stores. And at the hotel all the conversations I heard all about me from the prosperous-looking Germans in the lobby dealt with *Geschäft,* with business. Another characteristic of the conversations hit my consciousness: everybody seemed rude to each other. It sounded as if everybody in the city was involved in one huge interminable argument. Inside the hotel the desk clerk was shouting over the phone at some subordinate and then smiling greasily at me when he'd finished the bawling out. Outside, grim and determined drivers were hurling their cars at each other, refusing to give way and cursing as they banged fenders, while policemen whistled at pedestrians. No one seemed willing to lubricate human contacts with courtesy or politeness except in dealing with foreigners.

That first night, when my friends and I went out to dinner and then to a few bars, I found myself getting very disturbed, for example, by the obvious contempt and hatred for the Germans displayed openly by the American soldiers who abounded in Frankfurt. Undoubtedly a great deal of this was simply the normal behavior of any group of soldiers toward a vanquished civilian population, but when I talked with the GIs, an added element of bitterness was clearly present. Most of the soldiers seemed convinced that the Germans with whom they had contact were only interested in squeezing as much out of the Americans as they could, and the GIs responded by contemptuously trying to do in the Dubies at every occasion.

The next day I drove in the rented Mercedes from Frankfurt to the village where my father, grandfather, and great grandfather had been born.

The place is so small it wasn't even on the road map we had in the car, but we found it finally by following signs. When we drove into the village, we stopped at the Gasthaus, the village inn, to ask about my family, but the couple who ran it were too young to remember anyone who lived there before the war.

After asking everybody on the street who might know about the village before the war, I was finally sent to an old man who lived along one of the back roads. I found his house and explained my mission to him, and he took me along to another house, where his father, a very old man, was living. To my great surprise, the father remembered the Jacobs family, although he couldn't distinguish between my father and my grandfather. But he told his son where the family home had been located, and we walked along a few streets to reach it. The original house had been torn down and another put up in its place, exactly like all the others in the village—narrow and gabled. While I stared at it, a boy of about fifteen came out, looked curiously at me, and picked up a spade and began shoveling cow manure from a pile in front of the house into a wheelbarrow.

That could be me or my brother when we were kids, I thought, if our family hadn't emigrated, and then I remembered that if it had been me or my brother, we would probably be dead now.

I walked back to the house where the old man was and thanked him for telling me where my family had lived. By this time he had become fully alert and asked me many questions about what had happened to the family. I answered as best I could, which wasn't very good, since he talked about people I'd never heard of before. Then I began to ask him about what had happened to those members of the family who had remained in Germany, and a terrible pall descended upon the conversation. Neither he nor the son knew anything, and in the awkward silence that ensued, I kept wondering what answer I might get if I asked these men what they had been doing during the Nazi period. But I knew they would say, as most Germans did, that they had known nothing and only worked in the post office. (From the number of people in Germany who claim to have worked only in the post office during the war, it must have been possible to deliver a letter, by hand, from one end of Germany to the other, in about an hour.)

Before I left the village, I stopped in at a combination drugstore and general store to buy a postcard to send to Cliff back in California. And as I drove out of the village, past the women with the kerchiefs on their heads, the heavy skirts, and shapeless blouses, I decided to tell Cliff that I had no interest whatsoever in pursuing our possible inheritance of the house, a feeling I knew he would share as soon as I described the village and the people to him.

It was raining the next day when I checked out of the hotel and took a cab to my friend's office in downtown Frankfurt so that we could drive out to the airport together. After I was in the cab with my bags, I told the driver in English where I wanted to go. In a few minutes we had come to the square where the office building was located, but instead of pulling up in front of the building itself, the driver stopped the cab at a bus-loading platform across the street from the building. I told him, again in English, that I wanted to go to the office building, and he answered rudely, in broken English, that he couldn't drive there because he would have to go around the square to make a turn so that he could get in front of the building. I had a vision of myself getting soaked by the rain, lugging two suitcases across three lanes of traffic, and at that I exploded and in a torrent of German started shouting at him to take me to the building entrance.

The instant I started screaming at him in German, he was transformed. It was almost as if he snapped to attention sitting in the front of the cab. He turned to me saying, *"Es tut mir leid, mein Herr, es tut mir leid, mein Herr"*—"I'm sorry, Sir, I'm sorry, Sir," and promptly drove me exactly where I wanted to go. But I felt dirty, sullied, for he had forced me to behave in exactly the way I hadn't wanted to; he had done what I asked only when I had shouted to him in just the way my brother shouted at me when we were pretending to be Germans to annoy my father.

After that little incident I could hardly control my impatience to leave Frankfurt, and it wasn't until we got into the Swiss plane on our way to Geneva that I began to relax.

Five days later, after enjoying the sights, sounds, and food of Geneva, I flew via Polish airlines to Warsaw. I left Geneva with mixed feelings of trepidation and anticipation: trepidation because I was going behind the Iron Curtain into a society run by the Communists who had been my enemies; anticipation because I had left in me still some feelings of commitment to the ideal of a socialist society. Before I'd left America everybody, including Ruth, had warned me not to argue about politics, and now in my worried fantasies I had visions of myself locked in a Polish or Russian prison, for I was convinced they would know of my Trotskyist past.

After a long flight—almost four hours—we arrived at the Warsaw airport. The customs inspection was perfunctory, and a man from Orbis, the official Polish travel agency, met me. We drove off through the suburbs to the city. Since it was quite dark, there was very little I could see except an extraordinary number of apartment houses along the way.

At the hotel I found a note waiting for me from a Polish teacher I'd met in Berkeley and with whom I'd grown quite friendly. I'd written him, giving my arrival date, and he'd left his phone number for me. I made an appointment to meet him the next day, then went downstairs and ate a good meal which included plenty of vodka. After dinner I took a walk through the darkened streets.

My first and overwhelming impression that night was of poverty. The contrast between the well-dressed Swiss and the well-fed Germans and the people I saw walking in the streets of Warsaw was very sharp. Most of the Poles were wearing shabby clothes; merchandise was very expensive, and salaries were low. The cheapest pair of shoes I saw was about ten dollars, and men's suits seemed to start at about fifty dollars.

I stared with open curiosity at the peasants in the streets: the women with babushkas on their heads, the men wearing caps and boots. They were a strange sight in front of the many new buildings going up everywhere in downtown Warsaw. That night the whole city looked to me like one huge excavation.

The next morning my Polish friend came to the hotel, greeted me warmly, and drove me through the city in his little car on a combined sightseeing and political tour. Slowly, as he showed me the city, we began to talk more freely about politics, a subject we'd generally avoided while he'd been in the United States. He was a member of the Polish Communist party, but his antagonistic attitude toward the Russians was characteristic of many Polish Communists.

We went first to the Palace of Culture, a huge, ugly building that looked like a tall wedding cake in the center of Warsaw. According to Jan, it had been built with Russian funds, by Russian workmen and according to Russian designs. As we walked inside, Jan said, "Do you know why you get the best view of Warsaw from the top of this building?"

"Because it's the highest in the city?"

"No. This building has the best view because when you're on top of it, you're in the only place in the city where you can't see it."

All through the city the contrast between the Russian and Polish styles was obvious and sharp. You could almost tell when an apartment house had been built just by its style: if it was heavy, massive, squat, and ugly, it was built while the Russians were still dominating the Polish Communists; if it was more graceful, a more airy design in interesting and gay colors, it had been built after the Hungarian revolt of 1956, when the Polish Communists, too, had asserted some measure of independence from the Russians.

We also went to a department store, where I watched people stand in line to buy food delicacies for Easter. Jan told me there was just enough food, but no abundance of it. Small TV sets were on sale in the store and small refrigerators, too, but both at unbelievably high prices.

Then we drove to the Old Town, a section of Warsaw that had been completely destroyed but was now completely rebuilt, just as it had been, only modernized. The houses were quite charming, with painted façades and walls decorated in colors and symbolic designs.

This successful recreation by the government of the Old Town was the first real shock to the image I'd held of a Soviet-dominated country such as Poland. I was unprepared to find the Polish Communist government putting beauty above utility and reconstructing the past rather than emphasizing the future.

I got another shock almost immediately when I noticed a very new and modern church in the Old Town section. It was constructed of brick and concrete, and the cross inside it was of twisted steel in a very modern design. When I asked about the church, Jan told me that it had been designed by one of the state architects and built with funds contributed half by the church members and half by the government. Jan explained to me that the church and the government had found it necessary to work out some kind of rapprochement, for although the Communist party controlled the government, the church still had great influence among the people, especially the older generation, which tended to be more reactionary. But even among the younger Poles, the church is evidently very important, either as one form of protest against the rigidity of life in Poland or because of religious commitment. (Indeed, a week after I left Poland, a bad riot broke out in the town of Nova Huta, where a large steel mill is located, when an attempt was made to use a site of a new church for a sports field. The people in the town simply marched out on the field and refused to move, even after troops were called out. Interestingly, too, Nova Huta is thought of as a model city, with clubs, theater groups, well-stocked libraries, and every other advantage the government and Communist party can offer.)

Late in the afternoon Jan left me for a few hours, and I took a long walk alone. I was struck by the extraordinary number of bookstores—hundreds of them, selling all kinds of books in every language. But there were some obvious limitations in the availability of political books; I saw no Koestler or Trotsky, although many other writers were available either in Polish or English. And some of the bookstores sold American newspapers and magazines.

Just as it was turning dusk, I went down into a basement that had been Gestapo headquarters in Warsaw. The Poles have preserved it just as it was, a museum of horror with all the torture instruments intact, with bullet holes and the pathetic scribblings of victims left on the walls. Gestapo posters announcing the execution of "140 Poles in retaliation for the death of 14 Germans" are hung in the corridors, to be stared at grimly by the visitors, including the children who are brought there to be reminded of what the Germans did during the occupation.

After I had spent an hour or so walking through that cellar of horror, I could better understand the bitterness so many Poles manifest toward the Germans. But I couldn't help thinking of how many Poles had either stood by or even helped while the Germans slaughtered the Polish Jews.

That night I went with Jan and his wife to a meeting at the "Crooked Circle Club." The club had taken over a house on a corner of a square in the Old Town. Downstairs was a café, but we walked upstairs to a large room jammed with people sitting in a square around a table. The room was a pleasant one with a beamed ceiling, chandeliers, and a complete absence of posters or photos of Communist officials. Eight people, the executive committee of the club, sat at the table together with a young film critic who opened the evening's discussion with a long analysis of a satirical film then showing in Warsaw. Jan pointed out the producer-director and the writer in the audience and told me they were friends of his. Most of the people in the audience seemed to know each other, and Jan told me they were all part of the "October" movement, named for the month in 1956 from which they dated their new freedom.

Even though I couldn't understand a word, the discussion was reminiscent to me of YPSL or Trotskyist meetings, at which everyone felt compelled to speak. A large number of women were also in the audience, although only a few of them participated in the discussion. The ages of the group varied from young students to an old patriarch with a snow-white beard who, Jan whispered, had been for many years a bulwark of the Polish co-op movement. There were writers, actors, economists, and university professors, but very few workers.

Jan estimated that about thirty per cent of the people in the room came from working-class families originally, with the rest drawn from the middle class and even a few from old aristocratic Polish families.

The discussion was as interminable as any in the United States. The director defended himself against a fairly strong attack by a prominent member of the party's writers' presidium who had been one of the leaders in pushing for a loosening of party control over the arts. Nevertheless, he objected to the film because in his view its satirical edge was not directed against anything specific. The director, obviously shaken by this attack, defended himself as a moral philosopher. Other people defended the film, too, including some who disagreed with the director. All of this I got in whispered translations from Jan, who finally took the floor himself, attacking both the party official and the director, who was Jan's close friend.

The discussion lasted three hours, and afterward Jan, his wife, and I went to a dismal restaurant to eat. We sat upstairs while downstairs an orchestra played and the audience sang such typical Polish songs as "It's a Long Long Way to Tipperary." The service wasn't very good, but the food was cheap. We drank vodka as Jan and I continued our discussion. He pointed out that at the meeting there had been no direct mention of politics. "But," he said, "whatever we talk about here, we are talking about politics."

After dinner we went to the director's house for coffee, wine, and more talk. He and his wife lived in one of the rebuilt houses of the Old Town, a charming house filled with books and paintings. The writer of the film joined us there, followed quickly by some of the actors, and all talked of the changes that had taken place since the Stalinist period in the Polish Communist movement. It might have been a conversation of my own friends at home: alive and stimulating, not at all what I had expected.

But everyone in the room was quite realistic about the limitations of their freedom. The writer and director described to me the difficulties they'd had getting their movie cleared by the censor. It had taken more than a year before permission had been received, and even then the film had been mangled considerably. Someone in the group argued, "The censor's really on our side most of the time. When the student satirical theater does a play, they go to the censor first and he says to them, 'Look, you just can't do it that way, so why don't you try changing it a little this way and then I think we can pass it.' "

The discussion nevertheless made it apparent that the satirical theater and the movies were only safety valves permitted by the state to blow off excess political energy without doing any serious harm to the party machine as a whole. I was told, for example, that immediately following the easing up of restriction after the 1956 events, avant-garde plays had been produced but this could be done no longer because the pressures were growing worse again, especially in the case of a playwright like Ionesco, who had written an anti-Rumanian article.

From that evening and others like it I got the feeling that life for the Polish intellectuals meant always walking on eggs. The eggs were hardboiled at the moment and fairly safe, but one never knows when they'll turn soft and crack if too much pressure is exerted on them. There are obvious limits to the area of possible discussion, points beyond which one cannot go, such as criticizing the fundamental premises of the party, but within those limits pretty free discussion is permitted, although not so much in writing or publishing. Nevertheless, the secret police seemed nowhere in evidence, and clearly no one seemed too inhibited in the lengthy discussions at the meetings or in the producer's home.

The next day was Saturday, the day before Easter, and by late afternoon, in front of every church, long, long lines of people were strung along the sidewalk, sometimes for two or three blocks, moving slowly into the church and then out of it to stroll along the streets, talking and window shopping. It looked to me as if everybody in Warsaw was in church, except for groups of young kids who flaunted their freedom from attending or caring.

The great crowds of people attending church was still a recent phenomenon in 1960, I was told late that night while sitting in the compartment of a train to Cracow, talking with an engineer. I was going to Cracow because Jan and his wife had left Warsaw for a few days of skiing and had suggested that I see the castle and cathedral there; my train friend was traveling with his little daughter to pay an annual Easter visit to his parents-in-law in Cracow.

The engineer was an interesting combination of drives, for while he wasn't a Communist, he accepted the party as a necessary instrument to remake Poland. And he saw no end to the dominant position the Communists held in Polish life, especially since the Soviet Union was on its eastern border.

"What choice we have?" he asked when we spoke of the United States and the Soviet Union while sitting in my compartment and drinking tea brought to us by the conductor. "I must work all the time to make money. So I no choice make. I take sleeper train not for me but for my daughter so she don't have to sit up. I could sit up but for her it's not good to sit up all night."

I could see why he thought so when we walked through the train into the coach sections. People were jammed uncomfortably on wooden benches and seats in cars that stank of sweat, food, and toilets. The peasants and soldiers in the coach sections looked at us incuriously, as if no connection existed between their lives and the existence of these two men, wearing suits and ties, sightseeing in the train.

The engineer told me, too, that Cracow was a very reactionary town which he only visited when he had to pay an annual call on his wife's parents. I thought of what he said as I sat in a car a few days later being driven through the peasant country from Cracow to Auschwitz. The idea of seeing Auschwitz had been suggested to me by Jan, but I'd rejected the notion until I'd gotten to Cracow. Then I suddenly decided to go. I would have liked to have driven by myself, but there was no way to rent a car without a driver.

Auschwitz has been left almost unchanged by the Poles from the day it was liberated. The same sign, *"Arbeit Macht Frei"*— "Work Liberates"—that the prisoners stumbled under into the camp still welcomes today's visitors. The underground gas chambers and the cremation ovens at Birkenau, a few miles from the main buildings of Auschwitz, have also been kept just as they were when the Germans left them. And although the railroad tracks that led to Birkenau were torn up by the Germans and the rails now lie twisted in their beds, the concrete siding still stands. On that siding the Jews and Poles were selected by the Nazis for either immediate death in the gas chamber or slow death in the camp itself. Right next to the platform are the gas chambers and ovens, their roofs blown up by the Nazis into great, broken chunks of concrete. And as I picked my way through the jagged boulders of concrete, I kept tripping over innocent-looking metal vents that protruded a foot above the ground. It was through these vents that Cyclon-B, the prussic acid gas, was introduced into the chambers below.

All of these details were explained to me by the guide who had been assigned to me in the camp office. He spoke German, as many Poles do, and he asked me almost immediately if I was Jewish. I told him I was, and he replied that not many Americans except Jews came to Auschwitz.

We started our tour of the camp at the railroad siding, and after he had taken me through the gas chambers and crematories, we walked toward a green pond set in the forest. While we were standing at the side of the pond, he poked around in the water and stirred the ashes and bits of bones that cover its whole bottom. The carts that hauled the bones and ashes from the ovens to the pond are still there, too, rusted to the tracks.

The guide was very quiet as we walked back toward the camp, nor did he say anything until I stopped to look at a huge pile of rusted knives, forks, and spoons on the ground outside the camp entrance.

"Those belonged to the prisoners. When they died or got taken to the ovens, the Nazis took away the knives and forks."

Inside the camp itself we started in the main men's barracks. The walls were lined with thousands of small photographs, for the Nazis had meticulously photographed many of their victims before execution. And every week end now the corridors are lined with Poles looking at the photos, hoping to find the picture of a missing relative. Some of the rooms in the barracks had been made into huge display cases, with glass walls going from one end of the room to the other. Behind the glass in one room was an enormous mound of human hair, shaved from the victims' heads to be sold by the Nazis. In another room the glass wall encased a great heap of gold and silver fillings wrenched from the teeth of the dead, while down the hall a mountain of shoes pressed up against the glass. One room had eyeglass frames piled up to the ceiling, and next to it was a hill of crutches and artificial limbs, all used by the prisoners until they took their last walk.

We next went into a special barracks which had a row of wooden chambers set along one wall. Each chamber was about five feet high, fifteen feet wide, and fifteen feet deep. One of the chambers had been cut out, like a model, so that inside I could see a small air vent on the back wall, leading to the outside. The vent had been light-proofed so that when the door was shut, it was completely black inside. I studied the chamber, thinking it had been used as a punishment cell, to keep a single prisoner in uncomfortable solitary confinement. But the guide explained to me that the Nazis had a different purpose for it: into the chamber they crammed as many women as they physically could jam into it, and then timed how long it took before the frightened, screaming creatures inside died, fighting each other to get near the air vent.

Outside, in the cold sunshine again, we walked past a wall covered with straw that stood between the barracks I'd been in and the one next to it. The straw had been put on the wall so that splinters wouldn't fly when bullets went through the bodies of the people who had been shot standing against it. Men had also been placed naked in front of the wall in the middle of winter, to freeze to death, while next to them other naked men were immersed in tubs filled with ice water, until they too died.

Reluctantly I walked over to the women's barracks, for by this time I was nearly numb. And when I got inside, one small detail made an even deeper impression on me than any of the ghastly sights I'd seen until then: the barracks were huge, with bunks placed on top of each other all the way up to the ceiling, and for all the hundreds of women crowded into each barracks, there was only one single water tap; one faucet, no more, to each barracks. (Two years later, in Tel Aviv during the Eichmann trial, I asked a woman friend who had been in Auschwitz about the single tap. She turned pale at the recollection. "That was how they made animals out of us. You couldn't get near it, and if you did, not enough water came out for washing yourself. Can you imagine how I smelled after only a week there without washing? Can you imagine how that barracks smelled with those hundreds of women in it who could never wash? No, you can't, no one can. But I tell you that's how they made animals out of us.")

In a deep depression I returned from Auschwitz to Cracow and from Cracow to Warsaw. There Jan took me to the place where the Warsaw Ghetto had stood. A monument is there now, put up by the Poles, and it was covered with wreaths. That night, visiting a professor and his professor wife, friends of

Jan's, I heard details about how they and some other Poles had tried, without much success, to save their Jewish colleagues from death in the ghetto.

They weren't melodramatic about what they'd done, but very matter of fact, although I knew from Jan and others that under the Nazis the couple had continually run great risks. They had smuggled Jews from the ghetto to their apartment and to the apartments of friends and they'd done this while they were conducting an underground university which was literally underground, since the classes met in the cellar of their apartment house.

"Under the Nazis, I ran an underground university, and when the Communists took over, I had to continue it because they wouldn't let me teach at the University either. The Communists didn't put me in jail, they just said, 'You can't teach any more.' Then after 1956, I went back to teaching, and so we dissolved the underground university.

"But now maybe we will have to begin it again soon. It's getting bad again. Between 1956 and 1959 I could write almost as I pleased, but now the censor would stop me if I wrote the kind of things I said then."

By the time I was ready to leave Poland, I was no longer frightened of being behind the Iron Curtain. But on the very long and tedious flight to Moscow, in an almost empty airplane, I got scared all over again.

I was convinced that the Russians knew who I was, knew of my Trotskyist past, and would be watching me every minute I was in the Soviet Union. (I was wrong on all three counts.) My initial trepidation about going to the Soviet Union in 1960 wasn't lightened very much by the surface easing of tensions that had taken place as a result of Khrushchev's 1959 visit to the United States, the prospect of the summit conference scheduled to be held in Paris while I was in the Soviet Union or Eisenhower's plan to tour the Soviet Union after the Paris conference.

Nevertheless, despite my uneasiness, I was excited at the prospect of seeing what had happened to the Revolution which had changed my whole way of life. I wanted to see for myself how much more political and personal freedom existed under Khrushchev than had existed during the horrible Stalinist period.

I spent a month in the Soviet Union with completely different circles of people, different from me and different from each other. Occasionally one of the circles would touch another or overlap as did the foreign journalists and foreign diplomats, but I found life in the Soviet Union far more compartmentalized than anyplace else I had ever been or have been since.

When I arrived in Moscow from Warsaw, the scene at the airport was sheer madness. The Moscow airport is enormous, seeming to stretch for miles and miles in every direction. The airstrip area was filled with hundreds and hundreds of Russian jets and propeller airplanes, while inside the airport itself people were milling around trying futilely to find out where their baggage could be collected or to get their passports back from the inspection office.

I, too, was caught up in this frantic eddying. I'd been told that someone from Intourist would come looking for me; Intourist is the official and only tourist agency, which makes all the arrangements for visitors' trips to the Soviet Union. I waited, and waited, and waited. No one appeared. Finally I saw an Intourist office, where a man seated by a phone was being harried by seven or eight other tourists who, like me, had arrived but had been met by no one. When I could get his attention, I showed him my papers, and he checked for my name on a long list without success.

At that point I got my first lesson in how to deal with the Soviet bureaucracy. The man's attitude was that, since he had no record of my expected arrival, he had no responsibility for me; and my attitude was that, since I'd made all the necessary arrangements, it was his responsibility to solve my problem. And so I waited in the office and repeated my demands as if I didn't understand his refusal to do anything for me. We talked in his broken English and my rudimentary Russian; and as the argument grew more heated, we both would break out excitedly into our own tongues, forgetting that the other couldn't really understand. After a couple of hours he got disgusted and made a series of phone calls that resulted in his getting a room for me at the Hotel Ukraina, which everyone in London and Warsaw had warned me was the worst place in Moscow to stay.

It was, too, and probably still is. But with all of its disadvantages, the Ukraina was a good place to begin a trip through the Soviet Union, for it represents an aspect of Russian life seen by the tourists. It's their headquarters, their home, and the center of their life while in the Soviet Union, a refuge from the outside world and a Soviet Grand Hotel movie inside.

In the lobby of the hotel I saw what Soviet life meant to foreign guests. Almost all the guests were foreigners, for it's rare to see Soviet citizens as guests in Soviet hotels, although often they will eat in the hotel restaurants. At a hotel such as the Ukraina, most of the foreign guests fall into one of four categories: members of official delegations, in the Soviet Union as guests of the government; members of tours, paying their own way but traveling together; private couples or families traveling with an interpreter-guide; and individuals, like myself, traveling alone.

Every morning the lobby of the Ukraina and the Intourist offices just off the lobby were crowded with Russian interpreter-guides, usually young men and women, busily talking to each other in rapid Russian. Then, as the elevators started slowly disgorging the foreign guests, the group would split up in a chorus of "Dosvidanya," good-bye, and individual guides would peel off to attach themselves to "their" guests, switching immediately into "Hello," "Guten Tag," "Bon jour," "¿Como esta Usted?" and every other language spoken in the world. It was an impressive sight—or, more accurately, sound.

The day might begin for the foreign guests with a visit to the Intourist office to pick up tickets for the ballet or check on arrangements for the flight to Leningrad or to exchange some more money, hard money—"valuta"—for rubles. This always took longer than anyone expected and often caused frayed tempers for everybody. The mail was always kept in the Intourist office, too, usually all jumbled together so that you had to sift through endless piles for one letter with your name on it, only to be told later that maybe your mail was over at the Intourist office in the Hotel National.

After that search was over, the tourists went outside to wait for a limousine assigned to them or, if they were in a group, for the sightseeing bus. In the evening they would return exhausted, wait an endless time for the elevator, go to their rooms, and try to get served in one of the hotel restaurants. This always took hours, unless you were part of an important delegation or were an important guest. In that case, a table was ready for you with a little flag of your country on it, bottles of vodka for the toasting, and a special corps of waiters and waitresses.

Inevitably, any tourist who couldn't speak Russian was almost completely dependent upon the Intourist guide and thus saw only a narrow part of Soviet life. It's even hard for someone who knows the language to make contact with normal life in its many aspects, but such contacts are almost impossible for a visitor who speaks no Russian.

About the only places where the non-Russian-speaking visitor could mingle easily with Soviet citizens were at public events like the ballet, the theater, or the circus. In Moscow tickets for the ballet and theater, even for tourists, were usually harder to get than for the circus, which is without doubt the greatest circus in the world. And as with the ballet and theater, going to the circus means stepping from drab Soviet reality into fairyland.

The first time I went to the circus was on my first night in Moscow, and I was accompanied by a correspondent for the London *Times* who was on his way to Communist China to write a series for his paper. The circus was a big one, but to my joy there was only one ring, not three, and the floor of the ring was changed for each act.

The acts were enchanting, exciting, thrilling, daring, and hilarious. I sat entranced or laughing so hard that a TV cameraman taking pictures of the spectators kept coming back to stand in front of me and film my reactions.

The greatest of all the acts was Popov, the clown. I have never seen his like. He uses no traditional clown mask or clown clothes, and his only concession to tradition is a cap and slightly theatrical clothes. But moments after he had come into the center of the stage, he had the entire huge audience tightly in his grip, and he never lost them for a moment. He was the butt of his own jokes and sight gags, and he spent a lot of his time in the ring working gently, with the children and teenagers. Then he started a monologue which I could barely follow because it was filled with slang and allusions, but it was obviously somewhat political and satirical in tone. And as I heard the audience roaring with laughter, I kept thinking how deprived they must have been of this gusto and bellylaugh humor during the grim Stalinist days.

The only person in the entire hall who didn't enjoy the circus was my English companion, who neither laughed, smiled, chuckled, grinned, or nodded once during the entire performance. Afterward, as we stood in front of the arena waiting for a policeman to hail a cab for us, I asked him whether he'd liked it. He said he hadn't, going on to explain that this was the first circus he'd ever seen, and he fully intended it to be the last one. Incidentally, the fact that a policeman was stopping cabs for us was another surprising bit of Soviet life, although I quickly became adjusted to seeing and even accepting the favored treatment all foreigners, except maybe the Chinese, got in the Soviet Union.

One night, for example, Priscilla Johnson, an American correspondent, and I went out to dinner in a restaurant she liked. When we got to the place, a crowd of fairly drunken Russians were pounding on its doors demanding to be admitted. Inside, the manager and a couple of waiters were shouting back that the restaurant was closed. But the moment they spotted us, clearly foreigners, the doors were opened, and we were motioned to enter. Amazingly, too, the crowd outside parted so that we could walk through them, and after we were inside they once again started shouting that they ought to be let in because they were Soviet citizens, an argument that seemed to have little weight with the manager.

Fortunately the Russian lessons I had taken in San Francisco gave me enough of an elementary grasp of the language that I could travel around Moscow alone, not afraid of getting lost or of not being understood if I wanted something to eat. Even more fortunately, I had introductions to a good many journalists and diplomats, so that I was able to see life in the Russian capital from their vantage point as well as that of the tourist. In the first few days I was in Moscow I used a guide as well, so that I could get some sense of the city. I was assigned a girl guide, and I suppose I must have been a great deal of trouble to her because I didn't want to see any of the things to which most visitors get taken.

I asked, for example, to be taken to an undertaker and to watch a driving test being given. I asked her to arrange for a library card at the Lenin Library in Moscow so that I could see the kinds of books and magazines available to the Russians. (And when we did go to the library, my card with the H.S.G. degree on it got me admitted to the professorial facilities, which were very good. In that library, the higher your academic rank, the more privileges are extended to you. The only trouble was that I couldn't get any of the books or magazines I wanted.)

To any request that was slightly offbeat her first reaction was to say that it couldn't be arranged. If I insisted, she would say she'd try to make the arrangements through Intourist, but somehow it never worked out. By that time I'd met enough people in

Moscow so that I could usually find out where I wanted to go, and I would go by myself or take her, protesting, with me. And just as my friends in England had told me, she talked only in statistics. At one point, when we were driving near what I knew from others to be the homes of the Soviet leaders, I asked her who lived in the houses with the fences around them and the big cars in the driveways.

"Just workers," she said.

"Ordinary workers?" I asked. "Workers in a factory?"

"No," she answered a little reluctantly. "More highly paid workers, maybe."

I was just about to tell her to knock it off, to quit lying and admit that the Soviet leaders lived in those houses—which, incidentally, weren't so very lavish—when I realized that it wouldn't do any good. So I shut up and listened, bored, to her explanation of how many people could fit into the grandstand in the sports stadium and how many students could be accommodated at the big, ugly Moscow University that I could see off in the distance.

The guide and I didn't talk politics very much, but one afternoon I was so obviously angry after a visit to the Lenin Museum that she asked me what was bothering me. And so I told her that I thought the museum was perpetrating a monstrous lie and a fraud; I told her that I wouldn't have cared if in all the photos and memorabilia of the Revolution and of Lenin's life they had put captions under the pictures of Trotsky, Zinoviev, Kamenev, Radek, Bukharin, and all the other leaders of the Revolution saying that these men had become traitors, but that to have a museum of the Revolution without showing their role was the falsification of history in its worst form.

She was terribly shocked both by my vehemence and by my obvious knowledge of Russian history. But the only effect of my outburst was to make her very cool from that day on, and it was with obvious relief that she ended her assignment to me.

The Soviet Union is considered a hardship post in the diplomatic service, and with good cause. But the hardships then weren't so much physical as psychological: the diplomat is effectively sealed off from direct contact with the people in the country, even assuming he speaks Russian, as many of the American, French, British, and Israeli diplomats did. I got my first taste of this isolation only a day or so after I arrived in Moscow. I had gone to the American Embassy, as instructed, to leave my name and the name of the hotel at which I was staying with one of the clerks. A few hours later I got a phone call from the embassy, for it turned out that one of the consuls had been checking through the list of new arrivals and had recognized my name from articles I had written in *The Reporter*.

He came and picked me up that evening, and we walked to his apartment. Alongside us in the street a police car drove slowly with two men in it, alternately letting us get ahead of them and then speeding up to where we were. The consul explained to me that the car followed him wherever he went, walking, in a cab, in an embassy car, or in his own automobile. The two cops made no attempt whatsoever to disguise their presence and even seemed to flaunt it. When we got to the diplomat's apartment house, a uniformed policeman stepped out of a sentry box, looked us over, recognized the consul, and saluted him as we walked inside. The consul explained to me that everyone in the house was either a foreign diplomat or a journalist, and that although the official reason given for the policeman's presence was that he was to protect the residents, his main function was to discourage visits by any Russians except on official business.

As a result of this sealing-off process, the diplomats become an incestuous colony, mostly seeing only each other or the journalists, who have a colony of their own which overlaps with that of the diplomats. If you went to a reception at the British Embassy, you would see the very same people you'd seen the week before at a French Embassy cocktail party or the night before at a farewell dinner for one of the reporters. The wives of the diplomats suffered from this isolation, too, for they were also very dependent upon each other, with all the disadvantages that entailed. It was like living in a very small town or being on an island with a very small population.

Of all the non-Communist foreigners in the Soviet Union, the Israelis have it worst. The Russians try to isolate them completely, to keep to an absolute minimum any contact they might make with the large Jewish population in the country.

It can't be done completely, of course, as I saw when I attended the celebration of Israel's Independence Day held in the embassy. Across the street from the embassy and down the block from it on both sides, large crowds gathered to stare as the diplomats drove up and left under the Israeli flag flapping from a pole on the building. But I had no way of knowing how many of these people were Jews, for none of them tried to pass through the large number of police standing around the entrance.

Inside, at the reception, the main topic of conversation was speculation on which Russian officials would attend; for until they showed up, no one knew exactly what status the Israelis had at the moment. Once the Russian group arrived, headed by a fairly high official, everybody relaxed and the talk grew more general. On the whole I was surprised by the intelligence and sophistication displayed by most of the diplomats I met in Moscow, and of all the groups I found the Israelis most impressive. It was obvious that the people they had sent there were among their best, and the man to whom I had an introduction was remarkable in his grasp of Russian politics and life.

The journalists were a pretty impressive lot, too, especially the Europeans. Some of them obviously hated their assignment and openly bitched about it all the time, generally for good reasons. A few, like Henry Shapiro of the United Press, had been in the Soviet Union for many, many years and had seen all the changes which had taken place. Shapiro was most kind to me and introduced me around at the combination cable and censorship office which was the journalists' unofficial headquarters. Since the censorship was still operating, all dispatches and radio broadcasts out of the Soviet Union had to go through that one office. Every day the journalists would write their stories, hand them across the counter to one of the girls, and then wait while she disappeared with them behind a door where the censors worked. But no one had ever seen the censors, or even knew whether they were men or women, old or young. After a time which could range from an hour to three days or even longer, the article would be returned, either passed or edited to suit the censor. There was no argument with the censor nor appeal from the decision, except perhaps in extraordinary cases. Phone calls and radio broadcasts were censored by being monitored so that they could be cut off if something was said which was objectionable from the Soviet viewpoint.

Of course it was possible to avoid the censorship by having whatever had been written smuggled out, either with an airplane pilot or by someone who was leaving the country. Sometimes this was done with newsreel film and very often with personal mail, but a regularly stationed correspondent or his organization couldn't do this, for once the article had appeared he could still be held responsible for it. Thus, the Russians were able to control very effectively the flow of information out of the country.

Some of the reporters were followed, too, as I discovered when I began spending some time with a BBC correspondent who was in Moscow with a newsreel cameraman to shoot some film in advance of the forthcoming Eisenhower visit. Wherever we went in their car, two detectives were close behind us, and since all three of us were staying at the Ukraina, we got to recognize the detectives very quickly as they waited for us in their car parked outside the hotel entrance.

Through English friends I had contact with a Briton, Ralph Parker, who had gone to the Soviet Union for the London *Times* during the war, become a Communist, and switched to the English *Daily Worker*. By the time I met him, he was no longer a correspondent for the *Worker* but still maintained close contacts with the Communists; and at a cocktail party in his very pleasant apartment I met a number of Communist journalists, including Wilfred Burchett, the Australian newspaperman who had first reported the alleged American use of germ warfare in the Korean war.

Once I got over my initial distaste for talking with him, I found Burchett an interesting type. When he picked me up in his car to take me on a visit to his apartment, I discovered that he lived well by any standards and very well by Russian standards. He, his wife, who was a Bulgarian Communist, and his children had an apartment high up in a house overlooking the river, and as we sat over drinks arguing about the nature of Soviet society, I noticed he had a servant as well. It was obvious that he had high status and lots of *protecktzia.*

I met other Communist journalists who lived much less affluently than Burchett, including a couple of Russians to whom I'd also been referred. But they were just bores, just parrots repeating whatever the party line was at the moment. I quickly gave them up for more interesting types like an East European married to a British girl, who showed me some very interesting abstract art, by young Russian painters, that he had in his apartment. But when I asked if I could see some of the painters, he refused, telling me that he didn't want to expose them, for which I couldn't blame him.

I talked with all the journalists I met, Communist and non-Communist, about the frustrations I was encountering in trying to interview the Russian trade-union leaders in Moscow. Every time I called or went to the offices of union leaders, the officials were out—out of the country, out of the city, or out of the office; and no one knew if and when they would return. I was assured by the correspondents that this refusal to see me was not an act of particular discrimination against me; they encountered it also.

I watched the May Day parade from the windows of Carl Mydans' rooms in the Hotel National, overlooking the entrance to Red Square. Mydans, who was photographing the parade for *Life,* was terribly busy, but around him swirled a big party. Quite a few journalists lived in the hotel, a very old and rather charming one, and they kept dropping in for a drink and some food and then leaving, to be replaced by a new batch of writers and diplomats. I kept looking down at the huge parade, comparing it with the May Day parades in which I'd marched in the United States and seeking for something with which I could identify in some small way. But the May Day parade in Moscow is no place for a radical socialist: it's a joyless and dreary march, broken only by occasional groups of amateur musicians who at least try to have some fun. The rest of it was like a combination of an American Legion Preparedness Day parade and a Kiwanis convention. And the worst part of the parade was that it was so characteristic of so much I was seeing in Soviet society: the values of nationalism, chauvinism, and conformity it glorified were the nonsocialist ones I detested in my own country, and what it deprecated was what I found to be most interesting and stimulating.

In the next days I continued my vain efforts to make contact with Soviet union leaders. Then, on May 5, when Khrushchev angrily announced that a U-2 plane had been shot down, I took off immediately for Tashkent, in Soviet Asia, the farthest place from Moscow the Intourist office would book for me.

The contrast between Moscow and Tashkent was amazing. Physically, Tashkent reminded me of southern California, for there was the same kind of vegetation and the same physical atmosphere. The people, too, were in marked contrast to the Great Russians who lived in the Moscow area, for in Tashkent they were dark-skinned and their faces had an Oriental cast. They were also a good deal friendlier, and once I had gotten over the initial awkwardness, their questions about the U-2 always sounded pained: "Why did you let the American generals do such a thing?" as if they assumed that I wouldn't have wanted to do such a thing.

I would answer that I didn't defend the flight of the U-2, but that the Soviet government was also engaged in espionage, as were all governments. This argument had little effect, for none of the ordinary Russians had ever heard of Colonel Rudolph Abel, or for that matter any other Soviet spy. It was then I realized the enormously wide gap that separates the Russians from the Americans, for it was a fact that the average Russians simply didn't know very much of what went on outside their country or even too much of what happened in it.

In Tashkent I became aware, too, of the internal divisions of Soviet life. In Soviet Asia the Great Russians behaved as if they were an occupation army, and the inhabitants regarded them in the same way.

In Tashkent I also went to the first synagogue I'd seen in the Soviet Union. The Intourist office in the hotel insisted that there was no synagogue in the city. But I knew that thousands of Jews lived in the area, and I assumed the existence of at least one public place of worship. After arguing vainly with the Intourist manager, who refused to give me a map of the city, I went outside the hotel and found a cab with an obviously Uzbek driver. I got in the cab and simply asked him to take me to the synagogue. He looked at me curiously and said he didn't know its exact location but would take me near it.

As we drove into the older part of the city, he kept studying my clothes. I was wearing a lightweight but dark-colored wash-and-wear traveling suit that rarely needed pressing. Finally, he fingered the material of the jacket and said to me, *"Russki?"*

"Nyet," I answered. *"Americanski."*

He nodded and put my hand on the harsh cloth of his jacket. *"Russki,"* he said, and then deliberately opened the window of his cab, leaned out, and spat loudly into the street. *"Russki!"*

The Uzbek dropped me off, and I walked along the ancient streets of Tashkent looking for a building that might be a synagogue. But I saw nothing that looked even remotely like one, and finally I asked an old man on the street where I might find it. He took me to it, and without him I would never have found it; it was just a little house down an alley behind several other buildings, unmarked in any way. It was closed, but as I stood peering in the window, a young girl appeared in the alley and, to my surprise, spoke to me in French. She told me that no one was in the building, but that if I came back the next day someone might be there.

The next morning I returned and found a man sitting on the porch, reading a book. We began to talk in a mixture of Russian, Yiddish, and German. He told me he was a Yiddish writer who had been moved to Tashkent from the vicinity of Kiev, and he explained to me that the synagogue was so small because the young Jews rarely came. We talked for quite a while, and just as I thought he was beginning to get some confidence in me, we were joined by a woman who lived next to the synagogue and her husband, both of them also Jewish. At that point the man stopped talking, and it became obvious to me that he was frightened of speaking in front of the two others.

I didn't blame him, either, for the woman especially was a fiery Communist who leveled her attacks equally upon the American imperialists responsible for the U-2, the West Germans who allowed former Nazis to hold high office, and the Israelis who offered false hopes to the Jews. It was hard for me to argue with her, since I had to agree with much of what she said about the Germans. I couldn't persuade her that Russians engaged in espionage, too, and she was so vehemently positive about the deplorable conditions existing in Israel that nothing I said shook her assertiveness.

I left as quickly as I could, since I knew that no more conversation was possible with the writer; but I returned again the same afternoon, hoping he'd be there. And he was, obviously hoping that I would return. We talked again for a little while, but he was so nervous that I decided to leave. Before I did I took his picture, and he asked me to tell a Yiddish cultural organization in America that he was still alive, not dead as they must have thought because he had not been able to publish anything in Yiddish for many years. I turned back once to see him, sitting on the porch of the synagogue, sadly watching me walk out the gate.

The next day I flew to Samarkand.

Samarkand was two cities: the ancient one with its mosques and market places, and the new one built since the Revolution. The old one was far more picturesque, but the new one was much cleaner. In Samarkand, too, I went looking for the synagogue, and this time I found it by the expedient of going to the old city and asking a stocky policewoman where it was located. She didn't know, but she stopped pedestrians to ask them. In a few minutes a young fellow came along who knew where it was, and she turned me over to him. We walked into the most crowded part of the old city to a building he found. An aged Jewish couple lived in the building as custodians, and he knocked on their door to bring them out. When they came, I realized they were from a group of Jews I had never seen before. They wore cloth wrapped around their heads, and neither the man nor his wife spoke either Russian or Yiddish. They were Bokharan Jews who spoke only Bokharan, an Asian dialect in which I couldn't hear a single familiar word. But they were very polite and showed me the synagogue, which looked like no synagogue I'd ever seen before, either, for the walls were festooned with long strips of paper.

Despite their politeness and that of a few more Jews who arrived to see me, the stranger, it was so frustrating not to be able to talk with them that I left very soon.

By this time, the U-2 incident had become a major crisis, for Khrushchev had baited his trap very well, and the American government stupidly fell into it by denying his assertions. The Russian newspapers were filled with stories about how the U-2 pilot had been captured alive and photos of him and his plane. I decided to return to Moscow and flew back in a plane so badly pressurized that my eardrums popped out and I lost almost all my hearing. In Moscow I went to the American Embassy to find a doctor, only to discover that he was on leave and his cases were being handled by the British Embassy physician. He examined me and told me there wasn't much that could be done for me except to wait and see if the eardrums would return to normal.

At the Israeli Embassy I asked the man I'd gotten to know through Eppi and Shimshon about the Yiddish writer I'd met in Tashkent. The Israeli told me that he had been thought dead for many years, and he was surprised to hear from me that he was alive. We talked in the Embassy garden, and when I asked him about the Yiddish organization in the United States which the man had asked me to contact, the Israeli said that it was probably not a very trustworthy group. He also told me that perhaps it wasn't a good idea for me to identify the man publicly or even privately, for it might endanger his life at some time in the future. We said good-bye then, for I knew I wasn't coming back to Moscow before leaving the country.

The sense of tension in Moscow was growing stronger, and it was obvious that Khrushchev's violent attacks upon Eisenhower had another purpose beyond the obvious one of expressing Russian indignation over the violation of its borders.

Yet individual Russians always seemed to distinguish between individual Americans and the "generals in the Pentagon" whom they held responsible for the U-2. At the Moscow airport, where I left at three A.M. for Stalingrad, I fell into a conversation with two Russian men as we sat in the restaurant drinking tea. They were very courteous with me and simultaneously very angry at the American imperialists.

Stalingrad was an ugly city, which seemed obsessed with its role in the fight against the Nazis, but I was able to make contact there with some union leaders. In Tashkent and Samarkand I had discovered that the way to get any action was to avoid the Intourist people and do what you wanted by yourself. In Tashkent I'd gotten inside a plant where women sat at machines stamping out what looked to be cafeteria trays, and I managed to stay in the plant for nearly ten minutes before the very flustered manager came roaring up to throw me out.

In Stalingrad, instead of asking Intourist for permission to visit the large tractor works, I told them I was going to the plant. And when I arrived at the plant, a delegation was waiting for me, consisting of the union president, the plant manager, and an interpreter. I talked to them a little in my bad Russian, which pleased them, before we used the interpreter for the more difficult questions and answers. We toured the plant, and I was struck by the fact that none of the workers seemed to know the union president.

After the plant tour was over, the president and I went over to the union offices with the interpreter. As we sat talking, I asked him, "How much would I get paid if I came to your factory and worked here?"

"What kind of work do you do?"

"Well, I'm a writer now," I answered. "But years ago I was a maintenance electrician and a union official, too, like you."

"Oh," he joked, "we need electricians badly. You could earn two hundred rubles a month."

"You'd have to give me more than that to get me here," I

bantered back. "I could earn that much in Moscow. Why should I come here, freeze in the winter and broil in the summer for the same amount I'd get in Moscow or Kiev or Leningrad?"

"Alright," he replied. "You could get an apartment in one of the houses the union owns, and we'd see to it that you get a good vacation down on the Black Sea. And if you're married, your wife could have a good job, too."

"Okay," I answered. "I'm going back to San Francisco and pack my things. But I want to tell you that one year after I return here, I'm going to run against you for president of the union. And I might win the first time because I'll be such a novelty. Even if I don't win the first time, though, I'll beat you the second or third time I try."

Up till then my conversation with the union president had been on a rather light note, and the interpreter had understood this, too. We'd been kidding each other, teasing a little, which isn't common with Russians, who don't really understand the kibitz as a form of communication. This union president was about my own age, a rather handsome dark stocky Russian. But the moment I said that I was coming back to run against him, he stopped joking. His face grew stern and angry.

"Listen," he rasped out as the interpreter translated, "you're welcome here as an electrician, but if you want to be president of the union, you join the party the way I did and work in the party the way I did."

Although I was somewhat dismayed that he reacted so violently to my feeble joke, I wasn't a bit surprised that he resented the idea of my running against him. After all, an American union president would have responded in exactly the same way to the suggestion. But suddenly the full impact of what the Russian had said hit me.

"If you want to be president of the union, you join the party the way I did and work in the party the way I did." That was the key phrase—to become a union leader, you rose through the party, not through the union. In Soviet society there is only one institution of real power, and that's the party. In the struggle for power nothing else matters. And the reason no one in the plant knew the union president was that he was an engineer put in by the party.

That night I went alone to see a musical play in the local theater, and in the very first scene I became uncomfortably aware of an anti-Semitic tone. The action was set in a busy market place. Into the market place came two peddlers, carrying their wares on trays slung from their shoulders. Both of them had huge hook noses—stage noses—and were hawking their goods in a very obnoxious way. As the play continued, I saw that it wasn't only the Jews who were being attacked, but also the Catholics, for in the next scene a priest was shown making love to a young girl who was trying to resist him.

In the intermission a man sitting next to me turned and asked me in Russian how I liked the play. Speaking very slowly, I told him I didn't. I said that I was an American journalist who spoke very bad Russian. He asked me if I understood German, and when I said I did, we began talking in German. He was very upset by my criticism of the play, and after it was over, he insisted that we take a walk while he explained that the play wasn't so much anti-Jewish as it was antireligious.

He was a teacher, he told me, originally from Yugoslavia, who had come to the Soviet Union because he didn't feel Tito was a strong enough Communist. We argued endlessly about Soviet politics and about Stalinism that night, and the next day he picked me up outside the hotel to take me to his new apartment. He was very proud of it because it had three rooms instead of the two in which he'd been living until then with his wife, two children, and mother-in-law. Once again, I realized how difficult it was to communicate with a committed Communist of his generation, and I kept wondering whether his son would be able to break through the ideological armor which encased the father.

In a day or so, I left Stalingrad on a river steamer that went down the Volga to Rostov. The three days and two nights on the ship were extraordinary, for in them were a few of the best moments in my life and of the very worst, the most exhilarating and the most depressing. I sat in my cabin and talked with a surgeon, who admitted to me that he was Jewish and admitted, too, that he would make no commitment of any kind to Judaism lest it hurt his career. I got happily drunk with the captain when he was off duty—or, more correctly, I got drunk and he stayed sober as he showed me all over the ship, including the below-decks section where the poor Russians had to travel. I was fascinated with the little villages and bigger towns where the ship tied up to load and unload cargo and discharge and pick up passengers

who seemed right out of a Tolstoy novel. The food was abomina-
ble, but the wine and beer were good. The Volga was quiet and
peaceful, and the ship rode it calmly. Best of all, the ship carried
a small group of young Russians, kids in their very early twenties or late teens, who had just graduated from engineering
school and were on their way to their first jobs.

Their leader, a handsome young man, spoke fluent German,
for his parents were Germans who had emigrated to the Soviet
Union after the Revolution, and so we talked for hours in German and Russian. They plied me with questions about the
United States and the world, and I asked them about their education, their home life, their aspirations. We stayed up all night.
They were warm and joyful, and as I sat listening to them singing, I felt that in this generation was the only hope for the future
of the Soviet Union. But the next day, a tough-looking Communist party official got on board and brought me back to his reality. He watched the students as they sat in the tiny dining room
talking to me, and then he warned them that they shouldn't
spend so much time with me. When they asked him why, he told
them that the United States was preparing to attack the Soviet
Union and that I was an enemy.

That night was one of the worst in my life. I spent it alone in
my cabin, not knowing what was really happening in the world
outside and badly frightened that perhaps a war was coming,
leaving me isolated thousands and thousands of miles away
from home. I had nightmares while I was awake, and after I
took a couple of sleeping pills, the nightmares continued, made
worse by the distorting effect of the drugs.

Then came a wonderful liberation. In the miserable morning,
when I went to get some breakfast, the students were waiting for
me and their young leader said, "We don't care what is happening with your country and ours. We know you want peace as
much as we do, and we don't care what *he* says. Today is our
last chance to be with you, and we want to spend as much time
as we can."

Late that afternoon we docked in Rostov. All of us cried
when we said good-bye to each other. Every one of them had
given me a little gift: a pocket chess set that was autographed, a
little doll one of the girls had carried for years, an ashtray someone had scratched his initials on, a book of pictures from Leningrad, and a tiny box. I had given them each something, too,

whatever I had to give: postcards of San Francisco, pencils and pens, a pair of colored socks, paperbound books. I have the pictures I took of them yet, and I think of them very often, always warmly.

From Rostov, which was ugly and depressing, I went to Odessa, which was much more interesting, for it's a port town and the harbor was filled with ships from all over the world. In Odessa I saw a gang of hooligans rush into a store and rob it while a policeman stood by, afraid to take any action. In Odessa, too, another policeman tried to stop me from taking pictures of a queue lined up on the sidewalk to buy some yard goods being sold from a kiosk outside a store. And one afternoon, on a side street, I heard two women speaking in Yiddish, but when I went up to them and started talking, they walked away from me as fast as they could, looking back, fearful that I would follow them.

My last stop in the Soviet Union was in Kiev, where I met two Russians at the opera the night I arrived. We spent the next seventy-two hours together, drinking, eating, walking, and talking. One was a writer, the other a teacher, and they had been friends during the war who were now having a reunion. I learned a great deal from them over bottles of wine and vodka and plates of caviar, for I still had lots of food coupons left which couldn't be exchanged. The morning I left for the airport, they were waiting for me, as usual, outside the hotel, and once again I exchanged gifts and genuinely tearful farewells with my two new friends.

The next day, in Vienna, I read that Ben-Gurion had announced the capture of Adolf Eichmann, whose name I recalled only very vaguely. I stayed in Vienna only a few days, avidly reading the newspapers and magazines I'd missed while in Russia and trying to catch up on what had happened in the world. I spent a week in London, where everybody was talking about the capture of Eichmann. Then I flew back to San Francisco and Ruth.

CHAPTER THIRTEEN

O N C E the initial tensions of return had ended, I picked up where I'd left off two months earlier in our life.

One new part of that life was that I joined a Jewish club, the San Francisco counterpart of the Harmonie Club in New York. While we'd still lived in Los Angeles, I had decided that I needed more exercise and had become a member of the Los Angeles Athletic Club. I'd gone to the club nearly every day to work out and swim. But the L.A. Athletic Club was a big, rather impersonal operation, where I'd had no contact with any other club members except those I knew by sight in the gym. I'd been told before I joined it that there was a kind of informal quota on how many Jews were admitted, but I had seen no evidence of this nor was the question of my religion raised either when I applied or after I'd been admitted.

But the Concordia Club in San Francisco was different. It was founded a hundred years ago by the wealthy German, Dutch, and French Jews of San Francisco who weren't allowed in the city's other clubs. Their children started using the club when they were kids and grew up into senior club membership, a tight group who all knew each other and about each other. Gradually over the years the club's membership had been enlarged to include not so rich Jews from not such old families and even a few non-Jews. Still no one in the club talked with a Yiddish accent.

My first contact with the club had come through a friend, Billy Coblentz, a lawyer active in civic affairs and in Democratic party politics. Billy had worked for the Fund for the Republic in its very early days, before Hutchins had taken it over, and had also been one of the attorneys who had worked with Yarmolinsky on the loyalty-security study. Billy and I had friends in common, and our own relationship had developed very rapidly soon after Ruth and I had moved to San Francisco.

Billy, whose family had been members before him, kept taking me to the club to play paddleball and then swim. After a few months I refused to go with him any longer. I began to feel uncomfortable using his locker and never being able to pay for a drink after we'd finished in the gym. Then Billy suggested I join the club so that we could keep on playing together, a notion I liked.

But I had doubts. I was troubled about the fact that the club was so dominantly Jewish even though it had a few non-Jewish members and one reason for its existence was the refusal of other clubs in San Francisco to admit Jews. Joining a Jewish club would be a positive act of accepting, even asserting, that I was Jewish and recognizing that I was different from other San Franciscans who liked sports. Then, too, I wasn't sure I would be comfortable with the other members or that they'd be comfortable with me. I knew that many of the Concordia Club members were Republicans, not likely to take kindly to someone with my political views.

But Billy kept insisting that other members of the club, including some of my friends, shared at least some of my views. On the plus side, too, were the club's great gym, pool, and other facilities, plus its convenient location, out of the downtown section of San Francisco and directly across the street from Ruth's office building. The building was a nice comfortable one, with a pleasant reading room, a bar, and a restaurant that served excellent food. And in all honesty, I think, membership in the club did have snob appeal for me.

I was determined not to join under any false pretenses. When Billy got me an application blank, I answered the question of what other organizations I belonged to by listing the National Association for the Advancement of Colored People, the Congress of Racial Equality, and the American Civil Liberties Union. And as I expected, there was some spirited discussion in the membership committee about my admission. But the fact that my sponsors were prominent and old members got me in without any real difficulty. Afterward I discovered that some members of the club were the San Francisco counterparts of Alfred Lowenthal, men who were committed to the tradition that they had to give of themselves to the community. And since I was in the club more for its athletic facilities than its social life, I had very little contact with those members who preferred to play cards or dominos in the upstairs game rooms rather than use the gym and the pool. All in all, being in the Concordia Club could hardly be described as making a Jewish commitment.

Naturally the capture of Eichmann and his forthcoming trial were the subject of much discussion at the club, as they were everywhere Ruth and I went, whether or not other Jews were present. The arguments about the kidnaping and trial raged continually, in Santa Barbara at meetings of the Fund staff, in Berkeley at faculty parties in the Selznick living room, and in New York at the literary cocktail quarrels I was beginning to attend.

By this time the Israeli government had given up its original pretense that the kidnapers were private citizens, acting on their own, and had virtually admitted that the action was one carried out under government orders. Thus, people's position toward the events could be predicted on the basis of their attitude toward Israel. The anti-Zionists were the bitterest in their condemnation of the kidnaping and trial, the pro-Zionists the strongest defenders of what had happened. My own reactions reflected my general uncertainty about Israel.

I was opposed to the idea of kidnaping political opponents from one country to another, including even Nazis. And I felt even more strongly that once Eichmann had been kidnaped, he ought not to have been tried in Israel but by some international court. Finally, I was convinced that if he was to be tried in Israel, it ought not to be by Israeli judges alone but by judges drawn also from other countries.

But all the arguments were futile and did nothing more than raise tempers at dinner parties. With my Israeli friends the discussions were much franker and far more honest. They conceded that the legal arguments weren't the important ones, no matter who was right. To them, the key issues were political ones: the kidnaping and trial were demonstrations to the world that in Israel, at least, the Nazi terror had not been forgotten, that Israel was the only state capable of acting on behalf of a crime committed against all Jews, and that the younger Israelis had to be shown one of the essential factors in the development of their country.

Gradually, I began feeling that I wanted to be in Israel when the trial took place, that it was something I had to see for myself. So I began looking around for some magazine or newspaper that might want me to cover the trial. At the same time, since I had determined not to return to Israel without being able to speak and read at least some Hebrew, I started taking Hebrew lessons for a few hours every day from private tutors, one an American girl who had lived in Israel on a kibbutz and the other an Israeli girl who was a student at San Francisco State College.

We were using as a textbook the fast Hebrew course taught in the Israeli ulpanim, the schools where new immigrants are taught Hebrew in six months or less; in a month or so the daily lessons began having a marked effect. I discovered very suddenly one day that I could read Hebrew words that weren't in the textbook: I was cooking dinner and reached up into the closet for a box of matzoh meal, which is very finely ground matzoh crumbs. I've used matzoh meal for years in cooking, and the box is very familiar to me. But that day when I reached up for it, I read it, read the Hebrew letters automatically without translating them into English—and they spelled out "Matzoh Meal."

I got the assignment I wanted from Alicia Patterson, the publisher of *Newsday,* a lively newspaper on Long Island. Alicia was a member of the Fund board of directors whom I'd come to know at board meetings. When I told her that I'd like to go to Israel to cover the trial for the paper, she agreed immediately, and we worked out arrangements for my taking another leave of absence from the Fund. The Israeli government announced a tentative trial date for early in 1961, and I started making plans for returning.

In the meantime, though, the Lavon affair broke in Israel, making front page news for days all over the world. The affair focused on a bitter dispute between Lavon and Ben-Gurion which reached back to 1954. Moshe Sharett had replaced Ben-Gurion as prime minister then, and Lavon had been minister of defense with Eppi, our friend, as his private secretary. During Lavon's tenure in the defense ministry, a whole group of Israeli spies had been captured by the Egyptian government and charged with plotting to bomb offices of the United States Information

Service in the hope that American-Egyptian relations would be strained because the United States would think the bombing had been done by Egyptians.

When the incident occurred, the Israeli government had denied all knowledge of the plot and had accused the Egyptian government of an anti-Semitic and anti-Israeli plot. Sharett, who had not known about the sabotage plot, made a speech denouncing the arrests and the subsequent trial of the Jews. Newspapers all over the world had joined in the protests, and when the alleged spies were found guilty, attempts had been made to intercede with Nasser to get a commutation of the death sentence which had been passed against two members of the group. But they were executed anyway, and the other members of the group, including one woman, were given long prison sentences.

After the capture of the Israeli group, a secret investigation had been held by the Israeli government to discover who had ordered the action and who was responsible for its failure. Lavon had denied giving the order, but the senior officer responsible for such activities claimed Lavon had given it. The results of the investigation were inconclusive, and Lavon resigned his post to become head of the Histadrut, the job he held when we met him. But he always protested privately that he had never given the order for the operation. Sharett had been replaced by Ben-Gurion, who came out of retirement at the kibbutz in the Negev where he'd been living. Very little more was heard of the incident publicly until 1960. Then an intelligence service officer, involved in a law suit, threatened to reveal details of what had happened, and the statement was made that Lavon's name had been forged to the papers which had been used as evidence that he had given the order.

Out of all this ugly mess had grown an even uglier one that threatened to do serious internal damage to Israeli life. On one side was Ben-Gurion, defending the armed forces of Israel against the notion that its officers were capable of forging papers, while against him was ranged Lavon, more insistent now that his name be cleared. An interminable series of committees investigated and reinvestigated, finally issuing a report that cleared Lavon. But Ben-Gurion refused to accept the report and demanded that a new committee be appointed to make the investigation.

The whole country split wide open, taking sides either with

Ben-Gurion or with Lavon. Many other issues underlay the fight, including the relative importance to be given to the armed forces; whether or not Ben-Gurion was an "indispensable" man, and what the relations were to be between the Histadrut and the state. Eventually Ben-Gurion forced Lavon out of his Histadrut post, and the battle between them grew even more bitter.

I was tremendously interested in the fight especially because of my acquaintance with Lavon and my friendship with Eppi, who was part of Lavon's group. I followed the affair as closely as possible from the distance and wrote an article about it for *Newsday* even before I left to cover the Eichmann trial in February, 1961.

I was more guilty, depressed and frightened when I left San Francisco than I would have admitted. I was depressed and guilty because even though Ruth and I had decided that she would meet me in Israel after the first few weeks of the trial, I was going to be away from her for a long time again. And it was going to be even longer than I had originally planned, for I was having a great deal of trouble with my ears as a result of the experience in the Russian jet and couldn't travel to Israel by plane. And I was frightened because I wasn't at all sure I could do the kind of writing about the trial that *Newsday* had a right to expect considering what the trip was costing them in my expenses and salary.

Because of my ears, I had to take a train across the country and then a ship from New York to Haifa. It was a very unpleasant journey, and the end of it was even more so: while I was still on the train from California, the Israeli government postponed the trial by a month. Thus, when I arrived in New York, I was faced with the prospect of either taking the train back home and repeating the trip in a few weeks or going on and spending the extra time in Israel, waiting. I opted for the latter since I couldn't face the prospect of two more long train rides across the country.

But I wasn't in a very joyous mood when I boarded the *S. S. Atlantic* on a gray, cold, and drizzly afternoon. The *Atlantic,* a two-class ship, was about one-third full, and it was obvious from the names on the passenger list that most of them were Jews on their way to Israel. There were tearful farewells on the decks, and kids ran around chasing each other at the top of their lungs while their parents tried vainly to quiet them down enough to take a photograph with Aunt Becky. But the ship itself was very comfortable-looking, and my cabin was very pleasant.

The voyage was fascinating. The seas were fairly calm the first night out, but by late afternoon of the next day they had become so rough that many of the passengers started disappearing. Luckily for me, I don't get seasick, and I wandered around the empty ship, foolishly proud of the fact that I wasn't in their condition, joking with the few others whose stomachs weren't susceptible either.

Finally, though, the seas grew calmer as we got out of the North Atlantic and headed south toward Gibraltar. The passengers began to emerge from below, wan and tired. They sorted themselves out roughly into a number of overlapping groups. First there were the Orthodox Jews, who ate specially prepared food from the kosher kitchen with which the *Atlantic* was equipped for its runs to Israel. There were some American Jews in this group, but most of them appeared to be Europeans or Israelis and many of them spoke no English but only Yiddish. They wore yarmulkas—skull caps—and two of them, heavily bearded rabbis, came to the table in their kapotes, the clothes worn by the very Orthodox Jews. These two men mingled very little with any of the other passengers, never appearing at the evening dances or parties. They spent most of their time talking in a usually deserted recreation room, where every morning and evening a whole group of the Orthodox met for their prayers.

Then there were the other passengers who, like me, didn't eat kosher food; most of these were also Jews. Lots of them were Zionists, going to Israel for a winter vacation, and to them everything in Israel was perfect although not perfect enough to make them live there. And because the ship stopped at Naples and Athens before going on to Haifa, it carried some non-Jewish passengers, who seemed politely bewildered by being surrounded by so many Jews.

Their bewilderment was particularly apparent one night in the lounge at a ship's party; the entertainment featured Jewish and Israeli songs and dances. For most of the non-Jews, especially those from the Midwest, it may very well have been the first exposure to Yiddish and Hebrew songs, and I felt a little sorry for them as they sat there, not understanding the words.

An Israeli girl was on board as part of the crew. She was a kind of hostess and social director who also acted as an interpreter for those passengers who spoke only Hebrew. After a few days at sea I asked her if she'd give me Hebrew lessons so I could continue studying the language. She agreed and for an hour or two every day we used the textbook I had brought with me. An Israeli doctor was on board, too, returning from a medical convention, and I found him an especially pleasant traveling companion. He was a Pole originally, and his Polish wife was a scientist. They had escaped from Poland to Sweden, and from there they had gone on to Israel.

Joe and I spent hours together, talking while we walked around the deck, played pingpong, dozed in deck chairs, or sat in the bar, drinking very late into the night. He had no illusions about Israel and was quite vociferous in telling me what he thought was wrong with his country. Yet his commitment to it was deep. I asked him if he'd been a Zionist as a boy, and he told me that his parents were prosperous business people who had brought him up as an anti-Zionist. But they had been wiped out by the Nazis after Poland had been invaded.

"Why didn't you stay in Sweden instead of going to Israel?" I asked one night as we sat in the bar. "Wouldn't the Swedes have let you?"

"Yes, I think we could have remained there and become citizens. And we liked it, too. The people were good to us and I enjoyed practicing medicine there, especially after I learned Swedish. But we decided to try Israel first before we made up our minds about settling anyplace."

"What persuaded you to stay in Israel?"

"It wasn't a nice reason," he said, but without showing any shame. "I was walking one night in Haifa, soon after we had arrived. I didn't like Haifa very much, I couldn't speak Hebrew yet and it was hard for me to talk with patients, although I was assigned to a clinic very quickly, maybe because I was a heart specialist. But, anyway, there I was walking down the street in Haifa and a policeman came walking up the street the other way. When he got to within a few feet of me, he said, in Hebrew, that he wanted to see my papers. I put my hand in my pocket to take out my wallet when I suddenly realized he wasn't talking to me, but to an Arab man walking right behind me. That was when I decided to stay in Israel. In Israel, the policemen don't ask the Jews for their papers, they ask the Arabs."

Joe looked at me. "You see, you're shocked. I told you it

wasn't a very nice reason, but it's hard for you to understand how I felt that night because you've never had to worry every time you saw a policeman. That's why I'll never leave Israel even though I'm sure we could live better in the United States or Sweden." He laughed as he lifted his drink and added, "And as you can see, I like to live well, and I wish I had a bigger car, even though I know how lucky I am to have even a little one."

One morning when Joe and I were playing pingpong in the recreation room on the upper deck, we saw the two Orthodox rabbis watching us. I motioned to them that they should join us in the game, but they turned away. For a few days more I tried teasing them into playing pingpong, always meeting with a silent, contemptuous rebuff. I talked about their attitude with Joe, who, like so many other Israelis, had difficulty reconciling his beliefs with those of the Orthodox Jews.

"Still, Joe," I said to him one day as we walked back down from the top deck, "if the future of Judaism depended on Jews like me, and maybe you, too, it would have stopped existing a long time ago. It's Orthodox Jewish bigots like those two, the ones I can't stand, who keep it alive more than I do."

Thirteen days after leaving New York the *Atlantic* arrived in the bay outside Haifa. By that time I'd been given the run of the bridge, and the captain was permitting me to spend all the time I wanted with him and the officers running the ship. The best time on the bridge was when the ship was coming into or sailing out of a port, for then the captain usually assumed personal command, along with a local pilot.

There was always a great scene on the bridge, a flurry of activity, as the captain arrived and took his place flanked by his executive officer. The watch officer stood at the engine telegraph, another mate was at the bow or stern, talking by phone to the bridge, the quartermaster was at the wheel, and a junior officer stood with a book in his hand, writing down the time and content of the commands. Sometimes it seemed like a comic opera to me with the pilot walking around telling the captain in an ordinary conversational tone something that always sounded like, "Hard a Leeboard" or "Stern the Focsle." Then the captain would shout, "Stern the Focsle!", the chief officer would echo, "Stern the Focsle!" and either the quartermaster or the watch officer would repeat, "Stern the Focsle!"

After the stern was focsled, it would all be repeated back

again up the line of command with everybody shouting at the top of their lungs, "Stern Focsled, Sir!" Sometimes, too, the junior officer had to simultaneously push the levers to the engine room and write down the time at which he'd executed the command. To me, it looked like the greatest featherbedding operation in the world, and I hugely enjoyed watching every single instant of the ritual.

When the Israeli pilot climbed aboard in Haifa, I was delighted to see that in great contrast to the uniformed officers, he was wearing a sport shirt, slacks, and a pair of sandals. He nodded very pleasantly to the officers, shook hands with the captain, introduced himself and very quietly took over.

An hour or so later he had brought the ship alongside the dock at Haifa, which was crowded with other ships tied up parallel to the dock. The captain was quite nervous about the proximity of one ship, whose bow was facing the *Atlantic*'s stern, and as the pilot kept giving orders that brought the *Atlantic* closer to the other ship, the captain started to get a little frantic.

"Have we got enough leeway?" he kept asking the pilot who, unperturbed, kept looking over the side of the ship toward the stern and ordering the ship to be moved backwards.

"Don't worry," said the pilot. "Plenty room."

"Are you sure? I'm going to check with my mate." The captain picked up the bridge phone and asked the mate in the stern how much room there was between the two ships. He listened and then turned to the pilot. "My mate says we're almost on top of her!"

"All right, if you're worried, I'll ask the wharf master," answered the pilot, sticking his head out over the bridge and hollering down to the dock. Moments later a man popped out of a little building on the dock and the pilot shouted down, "How much leeway in the stern?"

The wharf master craned his neck and then shouted back, "You got plenty room."

At this point, I thought the captain was going to explode. He rushed back to the phone and screamed into it, "How much leeway is there? Goddammit, how much is there?" He listened and then, with relief, turned to the pilot, saying, "It's okay, he was wrong before. There's still more than thirty feet between us."

"I told you not to worry," said the pilot with a grin. "Plenty room."

A few minutes later I left the bridge and went up on deck to watch the final moments of the ship's landing. On the wharf hundreds of people were jammed, waving up at their friends or relatives crowded along the rail. As I stood there, too, looking down at the crowd, an American woman whom I knew casually on the ship, started to cry. "Look," she said to me. "Look at that crane over there." I looked at the crane on the dock used for pulling cargo out of ships' holds. It seemed like a perfectly ordinary one to me.

"What's so special about the crane?" I asked.

"It has a Jewish star on it," she said. "It's a crane with a Jewish star."

I looked at her, amazed, almost ready to say, "So what?" but managed to keep silent, turning back to watch the last moments of the landing. In a couple of hours I had disembarked, had passed customs inspection, and was being driven in a Histadrut car to a joyful reunion with Eppi Evron.

A day later I went to Jerusalem to make sure all my press credentials were in order and to see Lilik and Louise. But since the trial had been postponed, I had a month to wait in Israel; I decided to travel around the country, getting material for such background stories as how the Israelis were responding to the trial and what attitudes about it could be found among Nazi refugees. I thought, too, I might be able to do an interview with Lavon, since his case was still very much in the news.

First, though, I made a phone call to my old comrade from the Trotskyist period, Fred Goldwater, the bitter anti-Zionist. Fred had been living in Jerusalem for a few years, and when he answered the phone by giving his phone number in Hebrew, I spoke to him in Hebrew, saying, *"Shalom, Ma Shlemcha?"*— "Hello, how are you?"

A little bewildered, knowing that my voice was vaguely familiar but uncertain about who was talking to him, Fred asked in Hebrew who it was and I answered, also in Hebrew, that it was me, his old *chaver,* Paul Jacobs.

"Paul Jacobs!" he burst out in English, "what are you doing here? And how come you talked to me in Hebrew? Paul Jacobs talking in Hebrew! That's the goddamnedest thing I ever heard of!"

"No more so than Fred Goldwater living in Israel with an Israeli wife and a couple of kids," I answered.

Half an hour later I was at Fred's house in a very old quarter of Jerusalem called Abu Tor, only a stone's throw from the Jordanian border. His small house had once been part of an Arab's estate that had been sold to some Jews. Fred's house was at the edge of the grounds, and a road ran alongside it up toward the border, where a group of old Arab stone houses were falling into disrepair.

When I arrived, Fred's two young stepsons were waiting outside the gates of the house, and the instant they saw my rented car come up the road, they started shouting to me in Hebrew, jumping up and down in excitement. By the time I had parked the car and gotten out, I was surrounded by a swarm of kids, all neighborhood friends, climbing all over the car. All they wanted, naturally, was a ride, and I promised to take them in the car after I had a chance to visit with Freddy and his Israeli wife, Etti.

It was Fred's talking Hebrew and his image of himself as an Israeli that I found the most incongruous and interesting aspect of his development. The changes in his personality were obviously related to the new relationship he had found with Etti and the children, but his speaking Hebrew as much as English and his use of "we" and "our" when we talked about Israel meant that he thought of himself as an Israeli.

Later, when we were alone, I pressed him about this, asking how he, the anti-Zionist, had become so identified with Israel that he was living a difficult kind of physical existence without complaint. But I couldn't get a really satisfactory answer from him, except that he found life in Israel less materialistic than it was in the United States and psychically rewarding enough to make him feel more at ease than in America. Bitter though he was about the pressure the rabbis exerted upon Israel's life, he was nevertheless resigned to it as the price he had to pay for remaining there. He could give only vague answers to my precise questions, perhaps because he wasn't very sure of what had motivated him to stay in the country. He was certainly no more "Jewish" than he had ever been; he paid no more attention than he ever had to rituals, holidays or religious beliefs. But it was obviously easier for him to be non-Jewish in that way in Israel than it had been at home in the United States.

After a few days I left Freddy, Etti, and the boys and spent the next three weeks exploring Israel and myself. I went alone to other places than the ones I'd been to with the Schatzes and the writers, sculptors, painters, and journalists I'd met through them.

One of the first people I went to see was Lavon. Lucy and he greeted me warmly in their Tel Aviv apartment where the phone rang so continuously that it was maddening, where men and women poured in and out in a steady stream, and where Lavon sat in the center of the swirling controversy, talking with newspaper reporters, getting reports from his supporters, and giving them advice in turn. He was still confident that he would win his fight with Ben-Gurion, and when we left the apartment to walk to the nearby café where he sat for an hour or so every day, everyone on the street turned to stare at us. It was like walking with a movie star, and in the café, as he sat drinking his cognac and coffee, his table was the focus of everyone's eyes.

Understandably, Lavon wouldn't discuss the affair with me except in the most general terms, nor would Eppi. They refused to talk about the "security mishap" that had been the central point in the investigation which led to the affair, but other friends, especially the writers and artists, had lots of gossip and stories to pass on to me as I sat with them in the cafés on Dizengoff Street. Indeed, sometimes it seemed to me that more gossip was known to more people in a shorter length of time in Israel than in any country in the world. Living in Israel reminded me of living on a street in the Bronx where everybody knew everybody else's business and talked about it all the time.

One bit of café gossip that I heard for the first time in Tel Aviv was about the existence of a mysterious group of Israeli secret agents, members of an organization called the Shin Bet. It was the Shin Bet, I was told, that had tried to blow up the United States Information Service buildings in Egypt, the Shin Bet that had captured Eichmann and flown him back to Israel, the Shin Bet that had captured the Russian spies working in Israel, and the Shin Bet that was also keeping a man named Mottke Kiddar in solitary confinement in the prison at Ramle, an old Arab town near the Tel Aviv airport.

Everybody's view of the Shin Bet differed. To some of my friends it seemed to be a sinister secret organization of great power, which they called "the dark apparatus." Others were convinced it was a necessary arm of the government, operating only in the best interests of the state. One fact did emerge, from all my friends' discussions and occasional heated arguments about the Shin Bet: if it was responsible for the capture and kidnaping of Eichmann, it had done a very good job of it. For the first time I heard what was purported to be the real story of how he had been brought to Israel from Argentina.

It had been obvious, I was told, that the only way to get Eichmann into Israel was by plane. But that wasn't simple, for he couldn't be taken on a commercial flight, and the Israeli airline didn't fly to Buenos Aires. So, in order to justify bringing an El Al plane to Buenos Aires, Argentina's Independence Day celebration was used as an excuse. Abba Eban, a high Israeli official, formerly Israeli Ambassador to the UN, was selected to be the representative. And, I was told with relish, for Eban isn't liked by many Israelis I know, the diplomat hadn't even known that he was being used as a decoy for the kidnaping operation.

"They picked Eban because no other Israeli official would have believed the government would send an airplane to Argentina just for him to attend a celebration."

But whether or not Eban knew the real purpose of the trip, very few other people outside the plane's crew did. An El Al official from New York flew down to Buenos Aires ahead of the plane's arrival in order to make certain its preparations for the turn-around return flight were quickly handled, since the plane was going to stay on the ground only long enough to get refueled and have Eichmann put aboard.

Naturally no Israeli official to whom I talked would verify this version of Eichmann's capture, but enough evidence piled up as the weeks went by to make it appear accurate to me. And the story was a good introduction to what I learned later about the efficiency of Israel's intelligence and espionage operations.

One night while I was in Tel Aviv, I went to hear Ben-Gurion address the concluding dinner of the annual convention of the Association of Canadians and Americans in Israel. The association's executive director at the time was Murray Greenfield, a former Long Islander who was married to a refugee from Czechoslovakia, and I had gotten to know them through neighbors of theirs, old friends of ours from Chicago, in Israel on a government mission. Ben-Gurion, whom I had never seen before, spoke in English with a Yiddish accent to the room filled with convention delegates, all of them living and working in Israel, plus a great many well-dressed American tourists.

But Ben-Gurion seemed not to understand that many of the official delegates were now Israeli citizens, for he kept referring to "your young president, Mr. Kennedy." At the table where I sat a member of the association kept whispering to his wife, in an undertone, "Doesn't he know my president is Ben-Zvi?" Ben-Gurion was fascinating to watch, for he was much smaller than I had thought he would be, his white hair flew out from his head in two wings, and his eyes flashed as he spoke with great vigor. But as he talked, he displayed the same kind of contempt for the "Levantine" Jews who had come to Israel from Africa and Asia as my father had shown for East European Jews like Ben-Gurion. He maintained that Russian Jewry had been the mother of the Jewish people since the nineteenth century, responsible for the creation of Israel, which he described as "the greatest creation in our history."

With wonder and some shock I listened to Ben-Gurion describe the African and Asian Jews who had emigrated to Israel after World War II as Jews "without moral or intellectual wealth." It was this lack of moral or intellectual wealth that troubled him so much, he went on, because "Israel is in grave danger of becoming a Levantine state."

He went on to point out that the Jews "are a unique people, endowed with intellectual and moral superiority." As one example of this superiority, he cited the fact that fifteen per cent of the Nobel Prize winners have been Jews. And when he began to talk about the American Jews, it seemed to me he displayed a great misunderstanding about the nature of American Jewish life.

"There is no assimilationist tendency among American Jews," insisted Ben-Gurion, but "Jews in America can only maintain their Jewishness by a strong, living link with Israel."

Then, as he concluded his speech, I found myself agreeing with him, for he did not hesitate to tell the audience, which included so many comfortable, well-off American Jews, that he "would like them not to be Zionists but in Zion." He added, in an obvious reference to the Israelis who remain in the United States, that "I prefer to have Americans in Israel rather than Israelis in America."

As he left the convention, I watched him go through the crowded tables and saw people reach out to shake his hand or hold up their children to see him. He was without doubt the center figure on the Israeli stage, the charismatic leader, the "Old Man." As he left with his wife, Paula, a strong character herself, tugging at his sleeve, I began to understand how difficult a task Lavon had taken on in fighting him.

At the convention I heard another man speak who interested me very much. His name was Michael Frischberg, and he spoke in Hebrew rather than in English, although I was told he had been an American. Frischberg lived and worked at Kibbutz Ein Dor, many of whose members were former Americans and members of the same Hashomer Hatzair group I had known in Rochester. After the meeting ended, I talked with him for a few minutes and asked him if I might come to the kibbutz and visit there for a week or so. He told me he'd talk with some of the other kibbutz officials and let me know when it would be convenient for me to come.

A few days later I called him and learned that I could come any time. I set off immediately for Ein Dor, which is up in the Galilee. To get there, I left the main highways with which I was fairly familiar, and used as many secondary roads as I could to get some sense of the country. As I drove across the mountains, through the lonely fields and gnarled olive groves, to Ein Dor, I began to get a better understanding and appreciation of what had been done in Israel by those ardent labor Zionists. I was out of the cities now, away from the conveniences and cosmopolitan atmosphere of Tel Aviv or the ancient verities of Jerusalem; here the countryside was rugged, here it took hard physical labor to survive.

It was drizzling when I got to Ein Dor and walked on the muddy paths to Frischberg's apartment. His wife was home, but Mike was still out in the fields, driving a tractor in one of the orchards. His apartment was small: a bedroom, living room, tiny kitchen, and toilet with a shower. There was no need for more than one bedroom, since the Frischberg children slept together with all the other kids from the kibbutz in a children's house, and there was no need for a big kitchen since the family ate almost all of its meals in the kibbutz dining room with the other kibbutz members.

In a little while Mike arrived, looking bigger in his work clothes than he'd seemed in Tel Aviv. He greeted me warmly and pulled off his muddy boots to relax for a few minutes in a chair before taking a shower. Then we sat and drank tea, and later he went off to the kibbutz office to find out where I could sleep while I stayed there. He took me to a room in a barracks where the unmarried young men and women lived, and showed me the community toilet facilities.

I stayed for a week at Kibbutz Ein Dor, half of whose members are former Americans. I talked with them for hours as we ate in the kibbutz dining room, in their small apartments over tea, or in the little espresso café they had set up in the community hall, but I could never bring myself to ask them whether what they had now in Israel was worth the years of struggle, or perhaps whether the struggle itself hadn't turned out to be more important than the achievements it brought.

Maybe that's enough, too, but I wondered whether at least some of them may not suffer periods of deep self-doubt about their migration to Israel. One man whom I got to know, a very nice fellow of my own age, teaches in the kibbutz school, and as we talked I kept speculating on what the differences would have been in his life if he had stayed in Detroit to teach in the school system there. Materially, he would have been better off in Detroit, with a home in the suburbs and a car; although the difference is no longer enormous between what he would possess as an American teacher and what he has now as an Israeli: many of the kibbutzim are fairly prosperous, and this man's present standard of living reflects their shift from the early precarious days of joyous socialist struggle, when everybody in the kibbutz shared only poverty. Today he lives in a rather small but adequate house, his children attend a good school, the family enjoys a community swimming pool and a movie theater, and eats decent food in the community dining room. The coffee house where we talked in the evenings served pastries that were delicious enough to have been served in the very best cafés of Europe. And with reason, too, for they had been prepared by the kibbutz baker, a refugee from Hungary, who had been a fancy pastrycook.

How is this reasonably prosperous kibbutz different from any predominantly Jewish suburb in the United States, I kept asking myself. Ein Dor is not on an Arab border, and so doesn't suffer the daily tension of war. Does the fact that it is physically located, not out on Long Island, but in the Galilee, in a Jewish state, fundamentally alter the character of its Jews? Couldn't I have had the same kind of reminiscent conversation about the good old days visiting friends in Baldwin, Long Island, or Van Nuys, California? And given the changes that have occurred in the nature of the kibbutzim, their moving away from the strict observances of socialist community life, are the children of my generous friends at Ein Dor going to grow up psychically healthier because they are Israeli Jews instead of American ones?

I thought about these questions as I sat in the little room I'd been given by the kibbutz and I realized that I was really asking questions about myself. I was trying to find out if Curly would have been better off had he joined the Hashomer Hatzair group in Rochester twenty-five years before and gone to Israel. Maybe then, however, Curly might not even have existed. But the only answer to such a question is "Yes, and if your grandmother had balls, she'd have been your grandfather."

The Eichmann trial was the subject of much conversation at the kibbutz, and Mike introduced me to some of the other kibbutz members from Europe who had escaped or survived the concentration camps. Most of the kibbutz members defended the Israeli action as being necessary and just, and from them I got an acute sense of the bitterness they felt toward Germans. One of them, a Hungarian, felt this so strongly that when a group of German students volunteered to spend the summer working on the kibbutz, he told the other kibbutz members he would resign if the offer was accepted. Mike told me the Hungarian had offered to work every Saturday, the day of rest, to make up for what the kibbutz would lose if the students didn't come.

"What did you do?" I asked Mike.

"We didn't bring in the German students and we didn't ask him to give up Shabbat, either."

From Ein Dor I went for a few days' visit at Ein Hashofet, another kibbutz of ex-Americans. It's far more political than Ein Dor and is associated with Mapam, the more orthodox Marxist party in Israel that once had close ties to the Soviet Union although in recent years those links have been broken or very much weakened. The Ein Hashofet kibbutz members seemed more doctrinaire in their politics than those at Ein Dor. But, except for one group, everyone treated me with the same courtesy and kindness I'd encountered at Ein Dor. The single exception was the young group, the young men and women in their late teens and early twenties, the sabras of whom Israel is so proud. They tended to be rude and refused to even speak with me except in Hebrew, even though most of them spoke English. I didn't mind talking Hebrew with them except that when it came to expressing intellectual abstractions or asking ideological questions, my Hebrew was very faulty.

In general, I found the younger generation of sabras a difficult group with which to establish any relationship, in great contrast to older ones like Eppi or Shimshon or my artist friends. The younger sabras behaved as if being born in Israel was a mark of special virtue on their part, rather than on the part of their parents, grandparents, or other ancestors. Still, in fairness to them, I had to agree that the behavior of many American and English Jews toward Israel was bad, a continual vulgar display of how generous the Jews outside of Israel were to their less fortunate brethren. And I did sympathize with the sabras who told me they'd rather do without one-third of the country's income than continue being dependent for that third upon American Jewry.

When sabras at Ein Hashofet talked with me about the Eichmann trial, their models for how the European Jews should have resisted the Nazis in the concentration camps were Israel's successful wars against the Arabs in 1948 and 1956. They understood little or nothing of the differences between their situation and that encountered by the European Jews. Even worse, they combined their arrogance with chauvinism and parochialism, as if nothing worthwhile existed outside the borders of Israel. In this group Israel was paying the price for its physical isolation in the Arab world. Israel is an island, surrounded by hostile lands instead of water but still suffering from the disabilities of all island people: a limited vision of the world.

Characteristically, too, one sabra, twenty-two years old, told me that he and all his friends were against the kind of trial Eichmann was being given. I reported what he said in one of the first articles I sent to *Newsday* from Jerusalem. "We think Eichmann should have been tried before some kind of people's court or tribunal and quickly executed if he was found guilty. But since they're going to have a trial, we want to know everything that happened. And if some of our own people, maybe even some of our leaders get hurt because of what they did, well, we'll be sorry about it but that's just too bad for them. It'll all have to come out now."

How easy it was for him and his friend to make judgments, I thought, because they never had to make decisions affecting the lives of others. It was not his age but rather the circumstances in which he'd been born that permitted him the luxury of saying that if some of his country's leaders "get hurt because of what they did, well, we'll be sorry about it but that's just too bad for them." Once before in Israel, during the 1956 trial of Rudolf Kastner, the country had been rocked by the revelations that some Jews, such as Kastner, had worked with the Nazis in what they claimed were attempts to save the lives of other Jews and what their enemies asserted had been acts of collaboration with the Nazis in order to save themselves and their families.

At the core of the sabras' view of the European Jews was their ignorance of the consequences to the Jews of life under the Nazis. The concentration camps made many of the Jews into animals, pitting themselves against each other in order to survive. The Jewish "kapo," the subordinate guard used by the Nazis to keep the prisoners in check, was even more hated than his Nazi boss, for he was even crueler toward the other Jews, to demonstrate to the Nazis that he deserved to live.

In the ghettos, too, the conditions under which the Jews were forced to live animalized them. A Jewish writer, killed inside the Warsaw Ghetto in 1942, wrote that "cruelty is revealed on every hand in the streets. One walks indifferently past scenes which elsewhere would have caused profound shock. One treads with the utmost indifference over corpses."

Until the trial of Kastner, there had not been much discussion of the different approaches ghetto Jews considered adequate toward the Nazis. A large group of these Jews, especially those who had been the community leaders before the Nazis took over, believed in cooperating with the Nazis in an attempt to stave off labor camps or death for as many Jews as possible. Many of them also opposed any actions of sabotage or resistance to the Nazis because they were afraid that in retribution the Nazis might kill the whole population. In addition, some Jews carried their political differences into the ghetto with them; even there could be found the hatred between the Communists and the Socialists, between the Zionists and the anti-Zionists. It took the realization that all the ghetto inhabitants were certain to be killed to bring about a united resistance to the Nazis.

Even outside the ghettos it was impossible for many Jews to understand that they were being torn from a way of life in which they had lived for hundreds of years and were being sent to their death. I sat one afternoon with a couple of young sabras at Ein Hashofet, trying to explain my own relatives to them, the refugees who had come from Germany to the United States but still were unable to accept what had happened to them. But how could these young Israelis, brought up in a tradition of a secret army and battles in the streets against the British and Arabs, possibly understand the stolid middle-class life of the German Jewish businessman or doctor? Faced with this ignorance, I felt some sympathy for the first time toward these Jews of whom I had always been so contemptuous because they were so frightened of the way I lived.

I learned something else about Israel from these sabras: they were open in their distrust of the non-Jewish world, a distrust that was shared but not admitted nearly as openly by very many older Israelis. "What shall I do with a million Jews?" Lord Moyne, the British Governor of Palestine had said when the pressures had mounted on him to admit the refugees from the Nazis, and a great many Israelis remembered the question. In the Kastner trial, the whole issue of the British refusal to open Palestine to the refugees had come up again, stirring up old memories and old hatreds. I began to sense that beneath the surface of Israeli life lay a deep suspicion of the Gentile world, as if all the ancient fears that the Jews felt had been deepened, not erased by the history of the country. To a great many Israelis there was little difference between a brutal pogromist at Kishnev in Russia and the polite Lord Moyne.

I went to see an Israeli writer, Matti Megged, who had visited us in San Francisco when he was touring the United States on a visit arranged by the State Department. Matti, whose political beliefs seemed close to mine, lived with his wife and two kids at a resident training school for kibbutz teachers not far from Haifa. When I arrived at the school at the edge of a lovely forest, I was again overwhelmed with a joyful greeting and again given a room for sleeping and writing. Since the school was in recess, I took my meals in the Meggeds' small apartment rather than in the school dining room, where they ate usually. Both Matti and his wife had been born in Israel, and they and their kids expressed the same willingness as had the sabras to do without material possessions if necessary rather than continue being dependent upon American Jews for their future survival.

Both Matti and his wife, an attractive blond woman who

spoke very little English, had been in the Palmach, the elite fighting corps of the Palestinian underground army that fought the British and Arabs. They knew all my other friends in Israel who'd fought along with them. Late one afternoon Matti and I were sitting on a sofa in their apartment while his wife was heating water for tea when I picked up a Hebrew book from a shelf. It was a book of photos celebrating the tenth anniversary of the Palmach. Matti and I looked at the pictures, laughing together at how fat this friend had gotten, how bald this other one was now, and how little his own wife had changed from the days she tore around the Negev in a truck. Then, in the background of one picture of a training group, I saw a few young men wearing kaffirs, the Arab headdress.

"Who are they?" I asked.

"Oh, they were the Arabized boys," was the answer. "They were the boys who spoke Arabic as well as they spoke Hebrew, who knew the Arabs as well as they knew the Jews, and who spent all their waking hours in training, learning to think as Arabs."

"What happened to them, after they finished their training?"

"They went into the Arab countries."

"Where are they now?" I inquired.

"I don't know," he replied. "I haven't seen very many of them since those days. Maybe they're still there."

"When were these pictures taken?"

"Oh, sometime around 1936 or 1937, I think," answered Matti. "Why?"

"Well, I was thinking that while over here Palestinian Jewish radicals were training soldiers for fighting the British and intelligence agents to work in Arab countries, at home American Jewish radicals like me were a hell of a lot more interested in training for the war in Spain. Funny, huh? I think I could have told you something about every war being fought in every country of the world during the thirties, but I never knew or cared what the hell you were doing over here."

Matti grinned at me and said, "That's your problem, not mine."

When I left the Meggeds and started driving back to Jerusalem, I stopped to visit friends at Ein Hod, the artists' colony south of Haifa, and spent a day or two in Tel Aviv at the government press office. The hundreds of international correspondents who were to cover the trial had started gathering, and the press offices in both Tel Aviv and Jerusalem were jammed. It was the first trip to Israel for a great many of them, and, understandably, they knew so very little about the country in any real sense that I found myself the expert among them as we sat drinking in the café of the "Journalists House" in Jerusalem, just in back of the press office building.

A day or two before the trial opened, Ruth arrived in Israel. The airport was jammed with Israelis waiting for their relatives and friends. If anything, it was even more crowded and noisy than usual. Passover was imminent, and many Jews come to Israel to spend that holiday with their families. On the sidewalk right outside the airport building was gathered a large group of bearded men wearing the black clothes that marked them as an Orthodox group. I asked who they were and was told that they were the followers of a famous rabbi. They had driven down from Jerusalem to welcome back the rabbi who had been on a trip to England and the United States.

When the plane arrived, I kept straining my eyes to see Ruth and finally saw her walk down the steps, the last person to leave the plane, looking cool and elegant in great contrast to most of the others who disembarked. She spotted me and waved happily, and I settled back to wait for her to get through the customs and passport controls. In about fifteen minutes, passengers started coming through the door of the airport; one of the first was the rabbi. A shout of joy went up from his disciples, who surrounded him, kissing his coat and seeking his blessing. Then they started dancing around him, singing at the top of their lungs, their beards flying. And as I watched, I realized that if I had been a witness to this same scene at an airport in the United States, I would have been embarrassed. Here I was not, for there were no Gentiles to witness behavior I would have thought of as unseemly.

Since the trial was due to begin in a day or so, Ruth and I had scarcely any time for a reunion. It was a time of tension, too. I was filled with anxiety about whether I could do my work properly; I had never before written under the pressures of deadlines, even such loose ones as *Newsday* permitted me.

The opening day of the Eichmann trial in the Beit Ha Am, the House of the People, in Jerusalem was a moment of high drama in modern history. The streets outside the newly completed building were crowded with people; police and soldiers were on the streets and on the roofs of the buildings to make sure that the security provisions against Eichmann's being assassinated were all observed.

The security precautions at the trial were so tight that every correspondent had been issued a pass with his photo on it and he had to show it to the guards at the gate to the building. Then, after passing that check, everyone, men and women alike, went through little buildings in the courtyard where a quick search was made to make certain no one brought any weapons into the courtroom. Next, every correspondent was issued a set of earphones attached to a small transistor through which he would be able to hear the simultaneous translations of the trial into English, French, and German.

As I took my seat inside the courtroom itself, an air of great tension manifested itself among the hundreds of correspondents who crowded the aisles and seats, talking to each other or taking notes of the scene. The courtroom was actually, as well as allegorically, a theater. On the stage beneath the Israeli seal on the wall were the seats for the judges. To the judges' right was the glass cage in which Eichmann would be during the trial, protected by bulletproof glass from the audience. The prosecution and defense attorneys sat in a row below the judges. The police were everywhere, making certain that all the correspondents were in their assigned seats, keeping a wary eye on everybody, and looking terribly British in their blue uniforms with white shirts and black ties.

Suddenly, without any warning, when everybody's back was turned, so to speak, Eichmann appeared in his glass cage, and while we all stared at him, he jumped to his feet. The judges had arrived. The trial began.

Much has been written about the Eichmann trial, and I have very little to add. The legal arguments about Israel's right to Eichmann had ended with the judges upholding the prosecution, as everyone knew they would, and the trial began in a surrealist atmosphere. A tape recorder on the stage was turned on, and excerpts were played from Eichmann's lengthy interrogation by his Israeli captors. The police officer who questioned Eichmann on the tapes was German, too, and so the entire conversation between them was in German.

Time functioned on a number of levels while the tapes were

playing. If you didn't understand German and merely listened to the tone of the conversation between the two men, you might have thought that they were sitting in armchairs having a casual conversation about the state of the world, the baseball season, and the last movie they had seen. All that was missing was an occasional laugh, a joke, a wisecrack. Eichmann in his cage, with a set of earphones, was also listening to his own voice and occasionally nodded in agreement with something he was saying on the tape.

In German, though, what he had to say had a quality that didn't come through in the flat English translation; in German, Eichmann's voice rose and fell, it modulated, paused and occasionally took on a reminiscent tone. When he described one trip in a car he made to an extermination camp, he said, "I still remember to the right of the road there was an ordinary house." Then he went on to tell the Israeli policemen how surprised he had been that the officer driving with him in the car to the camp "did not have his tunic on and his sleeves were rolled up. He had a very common voice, maybe he drank."

It took a moment or two before you realized that what Eichmann was describing was an assignment not to buy millions of paper clips but to arrange the killing of millions of people. Yet to him there seemed no difference between the assignments, despite his occasional protestations of how horrified he'd been.

In a week or ten days the trial settled down into a routine of its own. Eichmann had managed to convert the atmosphere of his prisoner's booth into that of an office to which he came to work every morning, promptly at eight fifty. And for the rest of the day he would sit in the booth, surrounded by papers and files, as if it were a glass-enclosed office cubicle and he the chief clerk in, perhaps, the premium division of an insurance company. The office illusion was heightened by the fact that Eichmann never once glanced at the audience in the courtroom: for him they did not exist. Only the judges and the witnesses had any reality to the prisoner, not the spectators. Looking at him was like looking through a one-way mirror at someone who doesn't know he's being observed.

Downstairs, in the press room, the daily routine of writing and broadcasting was quickly established. Soon the reporters grew to know and leave each other alone at the varying times during which they each had to file their stories. Outside the courtroom the Israelis settled back into the daily routine of their lives in a shorter time than I thought possible. The trial became simply another story in the paper, and the daily broadcast about it drew no more attention than other newscasts. Soon the correspondents began leaving, for it was obvious that the trial was going to go on for months.

A few weeks after the trial started another sensation hit the country: Israel Beer, a trusted military advisor of Ben-Gurion, was arrested on charges that for many years he had been a Russian spy.

"How can one small country with just two million people cause such a tumult?" I asked Lavon one Sunday when Ruth and I had driven down to Tel Aviv to visit with our friends. Lavon laughed and answered, "What you forget, Paul, is that it's not just two million people, it's two million Jews."

In Tel Aviv and Jerusalem I was now hearing more and more stories about Mottke Kiddar, the man allegedly being held in solitary confinement in the Ramle prison. Many of my friends had known Mottke quite well and obviously relished telling me about him, sometimes so vividly I found it difficult to sort out truth from fantasy.

Mottke was a sabra, born when Israel was still Palestine. But either his father or mother, or perhaps both, had deserted him when he was still a child, and he grew up a very strange boy. As a youth he was so fascinated by guns that he became an avid and skilled hunter. Soon he got interested in hunting larger and larger game, including men. My friends told me all kinds of stories about how Mottke would go down to Beersheba, then still a wild kind of frontier town, and deliberately pick a fight with a "Negev cowboy," one of the tough young men working in the desert. Mottke would taunt the cowboy until he pulled a gun, after which Mottke would swarm over him so quickly that in an instant the cowboy would be pinned to the ground, with his own gun pointed at his head by a wildly laughing Mottke.

During the war against the Arabs, Mottke's hunting and killing skills were used in the service of the state, and he became a kind of minor hero. But afterward, when an uneasy truce prevailed, Mottke turned to other modes of earning a living. Stories began to float around Israel of how Mottke had robbed a bank at Afula, a city in Galilee, and killed a man on a Mediterranean beach near Hadera. Mottke disappeared from the country for a time, returned, and was mysteriously arrested just before the kidnaping of Eichmann.

Wild rumors about Mottke circulated among those who supposedly were on the inside of what is happening in Israel. Some of the stories connected him with the Lavon affair. Late at night, when Ruth and I sat in Fink's bar in Jerusalem eating goulash soup and listening to the complaints of the Israelis who had turned sour on their country, inevitably the case of Mottke would come up as an example of how lousy the country had become since the end of the war with the Arabs and how little protection the citizen had from the Shin Bet. But when I began asking government officials questions about Mottke, I got two kinds of responses: either an embarrassed silence or genuine bewilderment.

Then one afternoon in the press room at the trial, a government official I knew slightly came up to me.

"Paul, you've been asking about Mottke Kiddar, haven't you? Are you planning to write something about him?"

"Yes," I answered, "I have been asking and I might write about him if I get any answers."

"I want to ask you, as a Jew yourself, not to write about Kiddar," he said.

"Of all the arguments you could have used with me," I answered angrily as I walked away from him, "you picked the very worst one."

The next day I had a visit from another official whom I knew somewhat better.

"Paul," he said, "in the United States you must have people in government services who are fools, huh?"

"Yes, indeed," I answered. "I even know some of them. Why?"

"Because we too have fools working for us, like the man who talked to you yesterday. When he asked you not to write about Mottke because you're Jewish, he was talking like an idiot. No responsible person in our government would ever make that kind of request. As a matter of fact, some of us in the government hope you will write about Mottke, so we can find out what happened to him. The only thing I ask you, as a friend, is that whatever you write, you write with rachmonis." ("Rachmonis" is the Hebrew word for "pity.")

Later, before we left Israel to return home, I asked Lavon

whether Mottke had any connection with the Affair. He said
"No." And I couldn't answer him when he and Eppi asked me
why I, an American, was so interested in what had happened to
Mottke and how the Israeli intelligence service operated. I didn't
know why, then, myself.

After we left Israel, I began to forget Mottke. I was hung up
badly on an article I was writing about the trial, a summing up
of all my impressions. On the way home we visited friends from
San Francisco who were living in Greece on a Fulbright and
drove with them for a week, stopping at seaside fishing villages
for swimming, eating, and overnight stays. But the damned article was always on my mind.

I was still trying to write it in Vienna the day we went to the
American Express office to make arrangements for taking the
train to Paris. As we walked out of the office, a man came up to
us on the street and started talking to me in Yiddish. Very surprised, I asked him in German what he wanted. He was a Jewish
beggar, he told me, showing me a card in his wallet, a kind of
certification by the Jewish community of Vienna of his status.
As we walked down the street, he told me a story so full of woe
and agony that quickly I gave him some money.

Then, very curiously, I asked him why he had spoken to me in
Yiddish. "Because you are a Jew," he said.

"How did you know I was a Jew?" I asked him.

He looked at me pityingly, as if such a stupid question hardly
deserved an answer. "Any Jew can tell another Jew," he said.
"And besides you look like a Jew."

His answer shook me up so much that I finished the article
before we left Vienna. In it I discussed the Israeli suspicion of
the Gentile world and Israeli belief in the Gentile responsibility
for the Nazi slaughter of the Jews. I tried to explain some of the
parochialism and chauvinism of Israeli life. I attacked both the
uncritical support given by so many American Jews to everything Israeli and the equally uncritical attacks made on the
country by a smaller number of American Jews. I attempted to
discuss my own feelings of guilt for ignoring the agonies of European Jews during the thirties and instead identifying much more
closely with the loyalists of the Spanish Civil War. The article
ended with my writing that before the trial I had always believed
"I was an American who was also, incidentally, Jewish. Now I
have started to wonder if the American Gentile world has always

regarded me as a Jew who is also, incidentally, an American."

In London one night, two weeks later, I was discussing what I had written with some friends of ours. Suddenly, one woman in the group, the wife of a Labour party M.P. and a good socialist herself, slapped down her knife and fork and burst out that she didn't honestly know whether Jews could or should expect to be defended by Gentiles from anti-Semitic onslaughts if the Christians had to risk their own lives or those of their children in order to protect Jews. Everyone at the dinner table except she and I was embarrassed by her frankness in admitting what many Christians must feel. They tried shifting the conversation to some neutral subject, but she persisted, pointing out that the trial had now raised such questions and for the first time she felt free to discuss them honestly.

A few nights later, back in the United States, at a dinner party discussion about the trial in a Washington home, I got involved in an ugly and bitter argument with Felix Frankfurter, who believed that what I was saying about the trial was far too critical of Israel. He also attacked me harshly for what he believed to be my failure to understand the nature of the Jewish response to the Eichmann trial. It was an unpleasant evening, for I felt unable to defend myself. Instead, because I knew he was sick and bitter and because the room was filled with embarrassed people who were his old friends, I sat quietly while he scolded and excoriated me. And although some of the charges he made against me were without any basis, there was enough truth in what he said to make me wince.

After the article appeared, first in *Newsday,* then in *The New Leader* and *Midstream,* the reactions to it, whether delivered personally or by mail, struck me as being far more interesting than the essay itself. Some of the responses were easily predictable. There were those Jews who wrote that I was really an anti-Semite, more who attacked me as anti-Zionist, some who thought I had now converted to Zionism, and a very few who addressed me as a new Messiah—junior grade. But it was the Gentile reaction that really fascinated me, especially that from my friends.

"Never once have I thought of you as a Jew," Justice William O. Douglas wrote me. "Brandeis, Cardozo, Ben Cohen . . . Frankfurter . . . all of these are not Jews to me but Americans. A person who thinks of you as a Jew is not an American."

What Bill Douglas said to reassure me was repeated by other

good friends: ". . . the dichotomy you suggest is essentially false," was the way Willard Wirtz put it. "Any association of feelings about religion and citizenship would be characteristic of an extreme of bigotry which wouldn't bother you anyway. Even those who talk about anything they're prejudiced about as being un-American aren't really thinking usually in those terms—anymore than 'SOB' reflects a biological analysis." Or, as Hale Champion, California State Finance Director, described it: "You have damned little to do with Jewish identity. Momentary identification through the Eichmann trial may involve you briefly, but it is clear to me, at least, that you are not concerned so much about six million Jews as you are about six million people who were Jews. . . . All this makes the last paragraph the product of an overstimulated writer at work. I don't know quite what the American Gentile world is, but I don't think there is much profit in putting the question of its way of regarding you as you have. To anti-Semites, Jews are Jews, first, last and always, and Americans only by virtue of unfortunate Constitutional and legal provisions. To most of the rest of the community, at least in my experience, Americans are only incidentally Jews or Gentiles or whatever."

But I didn't really believe all this nice talk from my friends.

CHAPTER FOURTEEN

A FEW MONTHS later I was back in Israel again, this time with a group from the Center for the Study of Democratic Institutions. We had been invited to Athens to hold a seminar on issues of world government which was going to be attended by scholars and political leaders from Europe and England. And since we were going to be so close to Israel, I made arrangements with Shimshon Arad, who was still in the New York Consulate of Israel, for the group to fly from Athens to Israel at the conclusion of the seminar for a ten-day visit as guests of the government.

The trip to Athens had a looney quality about it. We flew to Greece in a chartered flight from Chicago with a group of wealthy Chicagoans who were also going to attend the seminar. John Cogley, Stanley Sheinbaum, who is an economist on the Center staff, and I sat together, getting very drunk very quickly on the champagne that was opened the instant we got up in the air and never stopped flowing until we arrived in Paris, where we stopped to refuel. In Athens, where we arrived in the hot afternoon, we were met by government officials, photographers, speeches, sticky cakes, and more liquor.

Since we had one day to ourselves before the seminar opened, Cogley, Sheinbaum, and I rented a car and drove off with Dennis and Grace Healey, my friends from London whom Hutchins had invited to speak at the seminar. It was a fine, lovely day, with Stanley driving us expertly over the bad Greek roads, with coffee and beer at lots of cafés, continuous giggling from Grace, and belly laughs from Dennis. The day after the seminar started,

I flew over to Israel to make all the final arrangements for our tour. A week later I was at the Lydda airport with a group of Israeli officials to meet the others as they came in from Athens.

It was a very odd group to travel around with in Israel. From the Center, it included Bob Hutchins and his wife, Vesta; Scott and Miriam Buchanan, who had been in Israel before; Hallock and Gene Hoffman; Harry Ashmore; Walter Millis; John Cogley; Stanley Sheinbaum; and myself. A few non-Center couples had been invited too.

The week in Israel was a hectic, enthusiastic, and almost arduous one because we were moving all the time. We traveled on a bus provided for us by the government, and we were accompanied by Gideon Saguy, a tall Israeli diplomat, who had been stationed in the United States for a good many years. The bus covered the whole country from the north to the south, stopping for sightseeing and visits with Israelis. The President gave a small reception for us, and the faculty of the Hebrew University gave a luncheon in our honor. In Nazareth the government had made arrangements for us to talk with the Catholic bishop, George Hakim, who told us that he thought the Arabs had been treated unfairly in the land program. We saw the huge Lachish planned urban-rural settlement, and we stood close to the Syrian border at a kibbutz where only the week before there had been bitter fighting between kibbutz members and Syrian soldiers. And that night I watched the usually dignified Hutchins munching on raw onions in a kibbutz dining room while talking animatedly with some of the kibbutz members.

Cogley, Sheinbaum, and I were together almost all the time. John had been in Israel before, but it was Stanley's first visit. The three of us tried to sneak off occasionally from the official itinerary to spend time with my Israeli friends. One day, as we were walking down the street in Jerusalem, coming from a visit with Olga Schatz, Lilik's mother, John turned to me and said, very quietly, "Are you going to live in Israel?"

"Why do you ask me that?"

"Because you seem so much at home here, or maybe you don't know how much at home you seem," he answered.

I laughed a little shakily. "I don't know whether I'm going to come live here, but I don't think so. And if I seem at home here, it's because I have so many friends that in a way I do feel it's part of my life."

By the time our successful tour of Israel was over, I had almost forgotten John's question. And at home, involved again in my work for the Center, it receded into the background of my consciousness, especially since I was involved in some serious controversies about unions.

I had been writing increasingly critical articles and papers about unions, focusing especially on union democracy and the way in which unions were lagging in admitting Negroes to membership. The articles I'd written attacking the leadership of the machinists' union for expelling some dissident members and the bartenders' union for not admitting Negroes had created a great deal of bitterness toward me, and as a result a good deal of strain had developed in some of my personal relationships with friends who were still union officials.

More and more they began linking me with Herbert Hill, the labor secretary of the NAACP, who was engaged in a fierce controversy with the official union leadership about what the NAACP considered the very slow rate of Negro integration into the unions. It was all a Trotskyist plot to undermine the unions, some of them said. The climax of my own difficulties came when *Harper's* magazine published an article I had written severely criticizing David Dubinsky's leadership of the ILGWU.

The article attacked Dubinsky on several fronts: that he had refused to deal with a group of his own organizers who had formed a union of their own and that this refusal reflected the kind of autocratic paternalism by which he ran the entire union. As one example of this autocratic paternalism I cited the fact that the union contributed heavily to Jewish causes, far out of proportion to the size of their present Jewish membership. In addition, I tried to make the case that the union and Dubinsky usually justified its behavior by claiming that it was still a quasi-socialist organization; while in fact it had made the same kind of accommodation to the employers that any other union had done.

When I wrote the article, I knew in advance that I was very likely to be attacked for it, but I was a little unprepared for the violent storm that broke over it. Employers wrote letters to *Harper's* denouncing me, the union press was in a state of high dudgeon, and the ILGWU, understandably, was in a fury. The most bitter attack by far centered on the Jewish question in the article. To the ILGWU and its supporters, that became the primary issue.

The *Jewish Daily Forward,* a Yiddish paper published in New York, ran a long, vitriolic story about the *Harper's* article, defending the ILGWU and Dubinsky against "all the poisons that the enemies of the INTL [the *Forward's* abbreviation of the union's full name] and Pres. Dubinsky have spewed forth lately." The *Forward* reporter discussed the article with Dubinsky and quoted him as saying that to recognize a union of its organizers, as I felt was proper, would be "a violation of the ethical principles of the INTL and a degrading of the traditions of the union."

But it was on the Jewish question that the *Forward* really let loose, in a polemical style that is unfortunately disappearing. In my article I had mentioned the fact that Dubinsky has a heavy Yiddish accent. He has; and I felt it was a valid bit of descriptive material, as valid as if I'd said he has a heavy southern accent. Of this, the *Forward* said: "[Jacobs] pokes fun at Dubinsky's Jewish accent;" the paper changed the word "Yiddish" I had used to "Jewish." And toward the end of the *Forward* story its reporter wrote that Jacobs "is probably chagrined at the fact that the INTL generously supports the Jewish Labor Committee and that Dubinsky is the treasurer of the JLC. It is a shame that it had to be a Jewish young man that spreads such stuff and suppresses the fact that the JLC helps a group that lost six million people, slaughtered by the German Nazi beasts."

When the *Forward* takes off on you, you know it.

At a more serious level Gus Tyler, the union's assistant president who had once told Eppi that I might be made into an Israeli but never into a Jew, accused me of being mathematically inaccurate in my analysis of the funds contributed by the ILGWU to Jewish causes. Tyler wrote me that the article had reinforced the caricature of the Jew as a greedy money-grubber who taxes all kinds of people to send money to Jews. And Shlomo Katz, editor of *Midstream,* a Jewish magazine which had reprinted my article on the Eichmann trial, wrote me in the same vein, stressing the fact that what I had written would only inflame Negro anti-Semitism in America.

In fact, I did get a letter which thanked me for having exposed the fact that the ILGWU "was rotten and that it was run by a bunch of those Jews who want to grab everything for themselves." The letter went on to say, "If it wasn't for people like you those Jews might get even more power and keep on doing the things they have been doing. Well, we are going to stop them or try darn hard: me and my friends and people like you who keep us informed and give us the fuels for the fire."

Another gem forwarded to me from the magazine complained that my article did not adequately "convey the powerhouse of Jewish propaganda contributed directly or funded by the ILGWU." That letter went on, "In addition, the lowering of ethical standards; the vulgarity and promiscuity engendered; all are reasons why the public should exercise a selective boycott of the garment industry until decency is restored. Another objective would be to secure a greater participation by the Christians who finance this form of enterprise."

Interestingly, though, my Israeli friends who read the article and disagreed with me about it never raised the kind of issues that had been brought up by Tyler, Katz, or the *Forward*.

The row stirred up inside the unions by the article went on all through 1963, and I still hear occasional repercussions three years after its publication. A good many people were and still are critical of me for having written it, even though they agree with the validity of what I said about the ILGWU and Dubinsky. To them, it is wrong to publish such an article, *even if it is true,* because the consequences may be to create anti-Semitism or deepen the anti-Semitism that already exists.

I reject this argument, although I know it is a serious one which requires careful deliberation, and I can conceive of certain circumstances in which it might have a great deal of weight. But when one of my friends in the unions tells me that I shouldn't criticize a union official because unions are under attack by the forces of reaction, I think he's wrong. When a Negro leader complains because someone has published statistics about Negro crime which seem to bear out white stereotypes of Negroes, I also defend the publication of the statistics if they are accurate ones. It is not the statistics that are at fault, but the social situation which creates them.

"Don't act like a kike," my parents used to tell me. "Don't make rishis," the plant owner in New York said; and a critical article about Dubinsky becomes, to the *Jewish Daily Forward,* an attack upon the "six million people slaughtered by the German Nazi beasts."

Not only Jews raise such issues. "Don't publish this," a young girl once told me early in 1964 after she had finished typing a long piece I was writing then about the Shin Bet.

"Why not?" I asked her.

"Because I think it would be bad for Israel," she said, "and there's enough anti-Semitism in the world already."

The article wasn't published, but not for her reasons. It was a bad article, confused, unsure, and chaotic.

For reasons that I didn't understand at the time, I had again become obsessed with the stories I'd heard in Israel about Mottke and the Shin Bet. When I returned home after the Center staff's tour in 1961, I began reading everything I could find about the intelligence services and asking questions of anyone who might have any knowledge.

I found out that in the undeclared guerilla war between the Palestinian Jews and the Arabs and British during the mandate the Haganah was helped immeasurably by the SHAI, a very loose intelligence organization of Jewish policemen, clerks, and every other kind of government official who nominally worked for the British but whose real committment was to the Zionist movement. The SHAI head wrote a book about its operations in which he said, "The loyalty of the government employees, i.e., the policemen or the clerks to their government posts were secondary when they witnessed things which they believed were detrimental to the Jewish population, the revelation of which would be useful for the purposes of Jewish defense."

Thus, if the British police got information on illegal Haganah weapon dumps, as they frequently did, the SHAI members inside the police force were almost always able to warn the Haganah in advance, so that the arms could be removed and hidden elsewhere. In a very short time the British discovered that practically every move they made was known in advance by the Haganah; sometimes so far in advance that British officers and men were informed of their orders only after the Haganah staff had read them, reproduced them, and distributed them to whoever was involved.

Typical, too, was the case of a SHAI member arrested for smuggling arms. Shortly after his incarceration another SHAI member wandered the streets pretending to be drunk, was arrested by a Jewish police officer acting under orders from Haganah, and was hauled up before another officer, who was also a member of the Haganah. The "drunk" was then sent to jail for forty-eight hours, more than enough time to make contact with the first man and tell him how to defend himself in court.

The outbreak of World War II brought about a temporary alliance between the British and the Zionists. Indeed, the British army even set up a training camp at a kibbutz to train Palestinian intelligence agents for work behind both the Arab and the German lines in the event that Rommel's drive on North Africa succeeded. And while some Palestinian Jews operated radio transmitters inside Syria, others acted as advance scouts for the British in a famous foray into Syria. (Ironically, Moshe Dayan, who later became one of Israel's most famous generals and who participated very actively in the daring raid, had been arrested by the British a few years earlier for participating in secret military training.) In the European war, too, Palestinian Jews played an important underground role behind the Nazi lines, made parachute jumps into Nazi-occupied countries, and fought in many campaigns. Even in far-off America a Palestinian Jew was a key figure in training American cryptographers.

The end of World War II inevitably intensified the conspiratorial aspects of Zionist activity. The British refused to open Palestine to the European refugees, and splits took place within the Jewish political organizations over the correct policy to be pursued. The two terrorist groups, the Irgun and the Stern Gang, began carrying out violent anti-British actions opposed by the Haganah. Each of the three groups had their own agents inside the others, and they all attempted to place agents within the British administration. In Europe the massive illegal immigration started, staffed by Palestinian Jews masquerading as Greeks, Italians, Frenchmen, and any other nationality whose passports they could forge. The success of that operation, of the tiny tramp ships that loaded refugees from obscure Italian ports in the dark of the night, that tunneled out from under barbed-wire fences in British internment camps on Cyprus, and that landed desperate Jews on the shores of Palestine depended very much on the "Shoo-Shoo Boys," the intelligence agents who worked day and night, spurred by the urgency of their tasks.

Nasser and many others in the present generation of Arab leaders learned to respect the Israeli skills in organizing their resources. In the truce negotiations which ended the 1948 war between Israel and the Arab countries, Nasser, then an aide-de-camp to a Sudanese general, sat for hours on a stone parapet talking with his Israeli counterpart, Yerucham Cohen, who was

ADC to General Yigal Allen.

"The subject Gamal Abdel Nasser invariably discussed with me whenever we met," according to Cohen, "was our struggle against the British, the way we organized our secret resistance movement against them, and the way we succeeded in mobilizing world public opinion on our side against them."

When I asked knowledgeable people in this country about current Israeli espionage operations, I heard similar reports. Allen Dulles, then head of the CIA, was reported to have described the Israeli intelligence and espionage operations as among the best in the world, and one intelligence officer to whom I talked in Washington told me, "They are extremely efficient, although we know less about them than we do about any other such operation in the world, including the Russians. And we worry more just because we don't know."

But the most disturbing analysis I heard, one that shook me up so much I finally got a clue to my own obsession, came over a drink in the bar of the Concordia Club in San Francisco. A man I knew who had been a high official in the Eisenhower Administration had come to San Francisco on business, and we'd met for a drink at the club. I started talking to him about the Israeli intelligence service.

"The Israelis are the greatest realists I ever encountered in any government," he told me. "They aren't afraid of coming to a decision and following through on it. Their reactions are quick and crisp. The Israelis learned the very hard way what it takes to create a state and keep it operating under the worst kind of pressure. They've trained some of the best diplomats in the world, and so their intelligence service is one of the best, too. But remember, after all, they're helped considerably because Israel isn't so much a country as it is a headquarters."

When I heard that last statement, sitting late one afternoon in a quiet bar of a Jewish club in San Francisco, I winced, for it sounded like an echo of the *Protocols of Zion,* the forged document that is the anti-Semite's Bible. And yet I knew that the man talking to me has many Israeli friends, and always showed great sympathy for Israel while he was in government service.

Yet he suggested that some Israeli operations are assisted by Jews in other countries. And I knew that, at least to some extent, his charge was true. During the war against the Arabs, for example, American Jews had helped get arms into Israel illegally;

and I knew that had I been in Europe during the period when the Palestinian Jews were smuggling refugees, I might have helped them steal trucks and ammunition.

But there's an important difference between Americans helping refugees get into Palestine in 1946 because they have no place else to go and being part of a "headquarters" for another sovereign state. So I rejected his explanation, especially since never once had my close friends, Eppi or Shimshon, or any other Israeli either, ever asked me or anyone else I knew a single question that could not be answered without the slightest hesitation on the part of any American, Jew or not. They had always been as overly circumspect in discussing American problems with me as they'd been freely critical about Israel.

But his remark opened a door slightly for me and gave me a glimpse of why I was so involved in trying to find out all the details about the Israeli intelligence operations. As I thought about what he had said, slowly I began to understand that I was really asking questions about myself all the time, questions such as whether the people who accused me of attacking Dubinsky in order to solve my own problems about being a Jew were correct in making that charge. Why had I felt more at ease talking to an Israeli diplomat in the Soviet Union than to an American one when I wanted to discuss the condition of the Russian Jews? What would I tell an Israeli diplomat about Jews that I wouldn't tell a French one, say, or a Japanese?

I don't want to suggest that during all this period I was doing nothing but worrying about Israeli spies and American Jews. I wasn't. I was still attending meetings at the Center in Santa Barbara, still writing articles for magazines, publishing a book about unions, collecting material for a new book on unemployment, making trips to the Philippines and Hawaii as an evaluator for the Peace Corps, making speeches, getting drunk with Ruth at parties, visiting friends, cooking, eating, playing paddleball every day I could, living every way I could, and trying to write this book. But the book made me think Jewish some of the time. One Sunday I went to the Reform Temple in San Francisco, where I sat in on a Sunday school class a fellow member of the Concordia Club was teaching, and then addressed the confirmation class. Nothing had changed in the temples, I discovered, since I had been a pupil nearly forty years ago. The kids still squirmed in their seats, still paid little or no attention to their teacher, still got the same kind of nominal Jewish education I had received, and still were as bored with my speaking to them as I would have been when I was their age.

I kept up with Israeli events through reading the weekly edition of the Jerusalem *Post* or through Israelis who came to visit in San Francisco. These contacts increased even more when Gideon Saguy, who had been our escort during the Center's tour of Israel, was made Israeli consul in San Francisco and arrived there with his wife.

Suddenly in 1963 the Israeli intelligence service was back in the spotlight again for two more operations: finding an Israeli boy who had been kidnaped from his nonreligious parents by his ultra-Orthodox grandparents and eventually smuggled into New York City; and attempting by a variety of methods to dissuade German scientists from working on the development of Nasser's rocket and missile program.

The Israeli press had for many months reflected the split that had developed in the country over the case of the kidnaped boy, Yossele Schumacher. "Where's Yossele?" was a fighting slogan of the non-Orthodox Jews who were resisting what they thought was the increasing domination of Israeli life by the Orthodox rabbinate. There was no question that Yossele's grandfather had kidnaped him; the only question was where he had been taken. But neither the grandfather nor anyone else connected with his ultra-Orthodox group would give the answer, even though they were jailed for their refusal. Finally, when it appeared that the issue of Yossele might have very serious internal political effects by upsetting the coalition of parties that governed the country, the intelligence services were put on the case. In a matter of days Yossele was found in an apartment house in Brooklyn, turned over to the American immigration authorities, and taken back to Israel to his parents.

The activities of the Israeli intelligence operations directed against the German scientists were of a far different nature than hunting down a little kidnaped boy. Israel was accused of having sent parcel-post bombs to the Germans which had exploded and maimed members of their staff; it was rumored that Israeli agents had kidnaped a German scientist and were holding him as a prisoner in Vienna; and it was believed that the Israelis may have been responsible for an airplane crash in which the wife of another German scientist was killed.

All these rumors came out when in the spring of 1963 the police in Basle, Switzerland, arrested two men who were sitting at a table in a restaurant talking with a girl. One of the men was an Austrian doctor and the other an Israeli official. The girl was the daughter of a German scientist, and the Swiss police accused the two men of threatening the life of her father if she didn't dissuade him from working for the Arabs. Their evidence lay in a recording made by a tape recorder fastened beneath the restaurant table, a Swiss waiter, actually a detective, who overheard part of the conversation, and a revolver found in the Israeli's overcoat.

When this incident was reported, I talked with Dan Mich, the editor of *Look,* and persuaded him to give me an assignment writing an article about the Shin Bet. This meant I would have to visit Israel, Egypt, and England. But as a spy hunter I turned out to be a dud, for in Israel I didn't really discover anything that wasn't known about the intelligence service. However, I did find out what had happened to Mottke, and a high Israeli official did give me a view of the world, especially the Middle Eastern world, which was very frightening. In Egypt, too, I found out very little about espionage operations, but a good deal about politics.

The bare facts I discovered about Israeli intelligence and espionage operations were simple enough. It's done under the direction of the Central Institute for Intelligence and Security, not the Shin Bet, as is popularly believed. The Institute, headed by General Meir Amit and located in a secret headquarters in Tel Aviv, is directly responsible to the Prime Minister. Amit is a sabra in his middle forties who grew up and was educated on a kibbutz.

As Institute chief, Amit, a quiet, thoughtful, very introspective man, has a wide range of heavy responsibilities. First of all, the Institute is directly responsible for gathering what is described as "positive intelligence" outside of Israel. "Positive intelligence" is a nice way of saying espionage and of describing the very dangerous activities of the Israelis who have been living in Arab countries, some of them for thirty years. It is because these agents pass successfully as Arabs that Israeli officials knew in a matter of hours that in 1960 the Russian ambassador to Egypt had falsely warned Nasser of an impending Israeli attack. Such agents are also able to supply the UN with the names and villages of Arab border raiders only hours after they have made a foray. And if these spies are captured, they are almost certain to be executed, as was Eliahu Cohn, whom the Syrians hung, publicly, in May, 1965. Cohn had entered Syria in 1962 and masqueraded so successfully as a rich Arab emigrant that it was reported he had been taken on tours of military installations along Israel's border. The Israel government tried desperately but unsuccessfully to save Cohn's life, offering to exchange captured Syrian spies, materiel or money for him, all to no avail.

The tracking down and kidnaping of Adolf Eichmann and the unending chase for other ex-Nazis is also the direct responsibility of the Central Institute. When the Israeli agent argued in a Swiss restaurant with the daughter of a German scientist, he was under the orders of the Central Institute. And if it is true, as is widely believed in Europe, that the Israelis have kidnaped another German scientist and are holding him in Vienna, then the job was done under Central Institute orders. Military instructions given to Jews in other countries is another responsibility of the Central Institute.

And that's not all the Central Institute does. Its staff operates a special school to which all the other Israeli intelligence arms send their agents for instructions in the latest espionage techniques. Finally, Amit is the chairman of the committee which coordinates the work of those other agencies, arranging for the frequent exchanges of staff that take place among them and for the intricately worked-out arrangements whereby each arm contributes personnel and specialized skills to the carrying out of such major operations as the kidnaping of Eichmann.

Next in importance to the Central Institute is the Shin Bet, whose area of operations is generally inside Israel. The Shin Bet, whose name is nothing more than the Hebrew initials of its full name, is often credited by Israelis and the world press with exploits that are in fact the work of the Institute or of other agencies. Formally the work of the Shin Bet is restricted to counterintelligence and antiterrorist activity inside Israel. It was Shin Bet agents who discovered in 1961 that Israel Beer was a Russian spy.

The collection of specifically military information is carried on by military intelligence personnel. And the Foreign Office has its own intelligence and research operations. So does the Israeli police force, which is a national one. But while each of these five agencies has its own specific area of responsibility, they are all under the over-all guidance of the Central Institute.

The Israeli secret agents are underpaid and overworked. Some of them are former American Jews who went to Israel to fight in the 1948 war against the Arabs; some of them are European Jews who survived the ghastly experience of Hitler concentration camps. And the older ones are the committed Zionists, the men and women who came to Palestine for philosophic and social motives.

Agents have been recruited also from the ranks of Haganah, the illegal Jewish army of Palestine; from the membership of Jewish terrorist groups like the Stern Gang and the Irgun; and from the newer wave of immigrants from Europe and the Arab countries who came to Israel after World War II. Ironically, one of the great strengths of the Israeli espionage operation, and one reason why it is so very efficient, is that the persecution of the Jews has provided Israel with a population once native to many other countries of the world.

There are also a few non-Jews among the agents, who are willing to take on dangerous, lonely, and thankless tasks because of a strong belief in Israel's mission coupled with a sense of guilt about what Jews have suffered from the Christian world. Very few professional adventurers can be found among these agents, both Jews and Gentiles.

But Mottke Kiddar was one of the few adventurers, and I did find out, in Israel, what Kiddar had done and what happened to him. Kiddar was hired by the Military Intelligence Service to do a job in South America. But as might have been anticipated from his history, he doublecrossed his bosses, first stealing large sums of money from his South American cover, and then brutally murdering him. Kiddar repeatedly stabbed the other agent with a penknife, evidently taking a psychopathic delight in watching the man's slow and agonizing death.

Because Kiddar had forged papers, he was ultimately forced to return to Israel, where he tried unsuccessfully to cover up the murder and theft with a phony story. It was then that he was secretly jailed and kept in solitary confinement while security agents began a long and difficult investigation in South America. Witnesses against Kiddar were brought quietly into Israel, and he *was* given a trial, albeit a secret one, for the murder. The trial was held by a different branch of the intelligence service, lest the group that hired him also judge him.

"Kiddar defended himself at the proceeding," I was told by someone who had been present, "and did a brilliant job. But there was no doubt of his guilt, and he was convicted and sentenced to life imprisonment." Mottke had no connection with the Lavon affair or with the heavy concentration of Israel's espionage and intelligence operations in the Middle East.

Since 1954 at least fifty alleged spies for Israel, some of them not Israelis, have been caught and convicted in Egypt. Actually, the total number, kept tightly secret by both sides, is unknown. Of the fifty known spies, thirteen were executed and the remainder given prison sentences ranging from fairly short terms to life imprisonment at hard labor. And in Syria, where a far more ferocious attitude toward Israel exists, *almost* any Israeli, spy or not, is *almost* certain to receive the harshest treatment. In 1964, when eighteen captured Syrians were exchanged for eleven Israelis, only the three Israelis who had been picked up a few months before, in Lake Tiberias, were in reasonably good physical condition. The remaining eight, most of whom had been in Syrian prisons for a long time, were all broken hulks, fit only for mental hospitals, because of the torture they had undergone. According to the Israelis, they were kept in cells with dogs, hung by their feet for hours at a time, rolled around inside automobile tires, and given repeated electric shocks on their genitals.

In Israel thirty members of Egyptian sabotage and intelligence units were discovered and shot dead in border ambushes and skirmishes by Israeli forces during the single year of 1963. In all, claim the Israelis, thirteen hundred cases of infiltration were recorded during 1963, and a hundred and fifty cases of property destruction by enemy agents inside Israel. But no figures are available on the total number of Arab spies caught by the Israelis.

In late 1963 I discussed Israeli espionage in the Arab countries with Shimon Peres, then still Israel's Deputy Director of Defense. "We believe that the Arabs mean it when they say Israel will be destroyed, and so we view our intelligence as an early warning system, a human radarscope, to tell us what is happening in the Arab world," he said to me as we talked and drank lemonade in his sparsely furnished office inside the complex of the defense-department buildings near the heart of Tel Aviv.

"Most other countries having major difficulties with each

other go through a period of deterioration in relationships before actual hostilities break out. But in the Arab-Israeli relationships we are long past the deterioration stage, and since we are such a small country, surrounded by Arabs, any sudden attack could endanger us in a few hours. We must be prepared at all times because we fear what the Arabs might do to us if they attack. They wouldn't just occupy the country, they would annihilate us, wipe us out!"

The ancient Jewish dread of the pogrom, never far below the surface in Israel, was manifest to me in his voice that afternoon despite the quiet tenor of our conversation. His eyes grew colder and colder as he talked to me about the possibility of Israeli's annihilation by the Arabs. For a moment or two he seemed very far away and then, as if wrenching himself back from some awful sight, he said to me in a chilling voice, "We Jews in Israel will *not* be slaughtered in pogroms the way that many Jews were for hundreds of years. We will die fighting, and if necessary we will take our enemies with us to death."

No matter how much I deplore such sentiments, I know that his viewpoint developed from the hatred which has grown between Israel and the Arab countries, a hatred which has made Israelis and Arabs commit enormous amounts of their slender resources to military measures, including espionage. I wasn't shocked by the statement that Israeli Jews would resist annihilation by their enemies, but the questions about the relationship between Israel and Jews in other countries that had troubled me during the Eichmann trial came up again immediately. I asked him whether the Israeli security services are prepared to act on behalf of Jews who are threatened any place in the world.

"Israel *does* consider it its duty to help Jews who are physically menaced anyplace in the world. It is not a problem of formalities: we will certainly help Jews of any country in self-defense if their lives are endangered."

Israel's position is based partially on a conviction that no other country, including the United States, would act vigorously or quickly enough to stop such persecution, and it creates a terrible dilemma both for Israel and for the Jews outside Israel. In the conflict between France and the Algerian nationalists, for example, many of the Algerian Jews, who were part of and identified themselves with the urban communities of European Algerians, became part of the active opposition to the Algerian nationalists in the FLN. Ultimately, too, some of them were drawn into the secret OAS groups which supported the rebel French generals and colonels. And the Jews' position vis-à-vis the Moslem nationalists was made even more untenable by the rumors circulating at the time that Israeli forces were helping to train the OAS.

Now, in fact, there seems to be no evidence whatever for the assertion that Israelis did help train OAS groups, but considering the position stated to me that afternoon in Tel Aviv, it's easy to understand why such rumors would develop. Later, Peres made the Israeli position explicit when he said, "Israel is not the continuation of the way that Jews lived before the State was created, but a new reality based on Jewish self-defense."

"Jewish self-defense" means nothing to me, for as a radical and a union organizer, I was as prepared to defend myself before the state of Israel existed as I am today. But—and it is a big but—even if I weren't, I live in America, where despite the continued existence of anti-Semitism in social and business life, I am protected by law against physical persecution and not likely to need training in "self-defense."

I have no need of secret help in military training from Israeli agents. But what of the Jews in some South American countries where the governments are not friendly to the Jews? Who, except Israelis, will help them if they are menaced? So even while as an American I rejected the implications of what I was told about Israel's training Jews for "self-defense," I was worried because I thought that perhaps the Israeli official was correct in his assessment of other countries.

The quiet discussion of Israel's mission on behalf of Jews in other parts of the world also brought me closer to the core of my difficulty in accepting Israel's claim that it had a unique right to kidnap and try Eichmann because it was the only Jewish state in the world. Now the outlines of my obsession were beginning to emerge more clearly.

A few days later I was in Cairo, where the obsession took on shape. I had no difficulty in getting into Egypt, even though the Egyptians knew I had come from Israel. Normally, if you go to Israel before going to Egypt, you must ask the Israeli passport control people not to stamp their entrance and exit permits in your passport but on a separate sheet. And in some Arab countries Jews are not allowed at all. But after I got the assignment from *Look,* I had contacted an Egyptian diplomat I knew in San Francisco. He was most helpful, even telling me that I didn't need to answer the question of my religion on the visa application. But I insisted that since the question was asked I ought to answer it, and I wrote "Jewish" on the blank.

The only real physical problem I had in Cairo was more uncomfortable than serious: my bag got lost someplace between Tel Aviv and Athens, where I had gone to change for a flight to Cairo. For the first few days after I arrived in Cairo, I tried asking the Arab airline on which I'd traveled to find my bag, without success. Then I realized that asking an Arab airline to find a bag lost on a flight out of Tel Aviv was about as foolish as asking Dubinsky to sponsor me for honorary membership in the ILGWU. So I went to the Greek airline and explained my situation to them; they got the bag for me just before the clothes I was wearing fell off.

In Cairo the elevator boy in one of the buildings I visited spent his time between up and down trips reading a textbook on electricity, and one afternoon I saw two Arab men chase another Arab away from a couple of tourists whom he was trying to hustle into buying something he was selling. I even saw a policeman arrest another fellow who was selling dirty postcards on the street. In Cairo, at least, it seemed that Nasser's attempts to change the old ways were having some effects.

But it was also clear that it will take a long time before Egypt is a modern, industrialized society. Technology is still not as natural a part of Arab life as it is to Western society or in Israel. A government official took me to a steel mill outside of Cairo which obviously wasn't producing much steel despite the official's assertions to the contrary. And the bureaucratic disorganization found in all newly developing societies was sharply apparent in every government office I visited.

Out of it all I nevertheless got a sense that a new national identity for the Egyptian was being created. Unfortunately an important component of that identity is hatred of Israel. Once the polite superficialities were out of the way and Egyptian officials started talking honestly with me, hatred of Israel almost burst out of them.

"We will never accept Israel as a neighbor, never," one high Egyptian official told me, his voice choking with anger. "We will never coexist with them. Israel is the door through which imperialism and colonialism try to return to the Middle East! They are the cat's-paws of the imperialists, and when the Israelis joined in with the French and British in attacking us during the Sinai campaign in 1956, it proved we were right in what we thought of them."

He went on to tell me about the injustices done by the Israelis to the Arabs. "What *they* have done to the Arab refugees is worse than what the Nazi did to the Jew. And to right the wrong of their stealing Arab land, our land, from us, we will wait twenty-five, fifty, a hundred, a hundred and fifty years if necessary, but we will do something to get it back! They are a small country and we are growing, so we can wait. Even though Arabs may fight Arabs as we are doing in Yemen, that is a different kind of fight. We are all Arabs, even if we fight among each other. They are not. This is our world, an Arab world, and *they* don't belong here!"

Even more frightening than what I heard from officials was an ordinary conversation I had with a young Egyptian woman who worked for an American I met in Cairo. She was modern, well-educated, well-dressed, and very pleasant. One day I asked her where I might find a restaurant that served good Arabic food.

"What kind of food do you want?"

"Well, I'd like to eat some hummus." (Hummus is a thick paste made from chick peas, ground sesame, oil, garlic, lemon juice, and herbs. It's served all over Israel in what are described as "Oriental" restaurants, but which in fact serve Middle Eastern food.)

"Where did you learn to eat hummus?" she asked me.

"In Israel," I said. "Everybody eats hummus in Israel."

Her black eyes started to flash with anger. "I wish you hadn't told me that," she almost shouted. "I love hummus and now I will never be able to eat it again!"

I thought she was joking, but she was in deadly earnest. As she talked on, telling me of her hatred of Israel, knowing that I was Jewish, I realized the awful gap that separates the Israelis from the Arabs, a gap which no one in either country seems to know how to close, even those who want most to do so.

Before I left Egypt, an official in the Ministry of Information gave me three pamphlets. One is titled "Eichmann, the Face in Israel's Mirror," and its theme is stated in an alleged quote of Eichmann that "If I had been a Jew, I would have been a fanatical Zionist." The second is on the Lavon affair, and it suggests that behind the fight between Lavon and Ben-Gurion is a struggle between those groups in Israel like Lavon's "which retains a sense of human solidarity," and those who, like Ben-Gurion's supporters, advocate "Hebrew racialism."

The tone of the third pamphlet, "Ben-Gurion and the Jews of the World," is the most bitter, savage, and revealing. According to it, what Ben-Gurion seeks "is a new influx of Jews to carry the frontiers forward, to conquer new areas with raw materials, so that a viable Israel may at last bestride the trade-routes of the world. Such an Israel cannot be created by sewing-circles and holidays in Israel by blue-rinsed Jewesses from Dallas and Detroit. What Ben-Gurion wants is an influx of young, trained, active Jews from America: vigorous imperialists to ginger up a society which has begun to lose its earlier dynamism."

The pamphlet cites Ben-Gurion's fear of Israel's becoming a "Levantine state" as showing his "desire to import American storm-troopers; and it also shows his contempt for the area in which he has chosen to build his Israel. For Levant only means the country where the Mediterranean sun rises: the east." And the Arab publication claims also that when Ben-Gurion told the 1960 Zionist Congress that American Jews were in a state of sin if they remained in the United States instead of coming to Israel, he demonstrated "his total contempt for 'dollar-Zionists'—that is American Jews who enjoy the American way of life while paying their tax-free Danegeld to help other Jews colonise Palestine."

What disturbs me about these pamphlets isn't so much their specific contents as the hysterical tone in which they are written. After all, the Arabs aren't the only ones to deny the validity of Ben-Gurion's statements that Jews living outside of Israel are in a state of sin: the American Jewish Committee let him know that they were pretty damn unhappy, too, about this description of their membership. And it is true that Ben-Gurion's references to the "Levantine" are derogatory ones, just as the description I heard him give of the African and Asian Jews showed his feelings of superiority to them. But when the Egyptians talk about the "blue-rinsed Jewesses from Dallas and Detroit," they reveal their true subsurface feelings about all Jews, not just Zionists.

Disheartened and despondent, I came away from the Middle East convinced that too many Israelis still hold to the old notion that the Arab world is made up of rich effendi who exploit the poor and force them into becoming beggars, pimps, and thieves incapable of fighting a war, while too many Arabs still believe in the image of an Israel dominated completely by a war-seeking Ben-Gurion backed up by an army of toughs and bullies, supported by vast millions in funds from American Jews.

Although traces of the truth can be found in both these views, such an Israeli picture of the Arab and such an Arab conception of the Israeli are basically inaccurate. Unfortunately the total lack of communication between the Israelis and Arabs means that each sees the other through a distorting haze of their own fears.

When I returned from this trip, I tried to write the story of the Israeli espionage operation for *Look*. But what I wrote was unsatisfactory. No matter how hard I tried, I couldn't bring myself to be completely honest about what I had learned. As a result, what came out of the typewriter was pinched and thin. *Look,* which had paid for my trip, got nothing out of this venture except my eternal goodwill for its editorial decency in accepting my failure. But I discovered something important from my inability to write the article.

First, I learned that one reason I had been so determined to find out about the Shin Bet was that I wanted to find faults in Israel. Israel threatens me. It threatens me because I do feel at home there and I don't want to. I am as split in my feelings about the country as it is split about itself.

I grow livid with rage, for example, when I read in an Israeli paper that the Orthodox Jews have prevented a Christian Science minister from renting a hotel room for a meeting: that's the kind of bigotry I loathe and fight in the United States. Yet, paradoxically, those fanatics may perhaps be right. What sets Israel apart is that it's a Jewish state. How is it possible, then, to separate synagogue and state as we do? What would be Jewish about Israel then? The fact that everybody speaks Hebrew isn't enough; the official language of Ghana is English, but that doesn't make the Ghanians British.

Is there a cultural tradition in Israel distinctive enough to give it character as a state? I don't think so. A great many traditions mingle in Israel, but, understandably, the dominant one is that of the East European Jewish socialists who created the state. But that tradition is no more peculiarly Jewish than that brought to

Israel by the "Levantine" Jews about whom Ben-Gurion worries. And I don't find that the tradition of the ancient military heroes like Bar Kochba, who are glorified in Israel, so attractive: I am as depressed by the sight of a huge tank with a Jewish star painted on it as I am by the tank with the Soviet star or the one with the American flag.

The great paradox of Israel is that if it's going to be a Jewish state, it may need the synagogue, need the Orthodox synagogue, not the discreet Reform or Conservative ones. If the survival of Judaism for five thousand years had depended on Reform Jews, it would have died out a long time ago; it takes fanatics to keep something alive throughout decades of persecution.

But, at the same time, thousands of Orthodox Jews would be dead now if it hadn't been for the tough antireligious labor Zionists who ran the refugee operations; and today it's the arrogant, chauvinistic young sabras who stand between the Orthodox Jews and their Arab enemies. In Israel the Orthodox Jews and the irreligious Jews are locked in an unwilling embrace from which neither can escape.

That embrace frightens me, for if I were caught in it, I would be crushed. And that's one reason Jews like me don't emigrate to Israel; not, as many Israelis think, because we are unwilling to give up the material benefits of life here. After all, one can find very attractive material benefits in Israel: I have been in some elegant homes in the Carmel hills of Haifa; an increasing number of Israelis now own their own cars; the golf course at Cesea-rea is a pretty sporty one; and there are plenty of nightclubs in Jaffa where you can run up a whopping bill. But if that's all Israel is about, if all it offers is a miniature version of what can be found in the United States, done in Hebrew instead of English, there's no reason to go.

Obviously it offers more than that, for otherwise I wouldn't be so split about it. What's attractive about Israel is that it is struggling to evolve a sense of ethical values around which a decent society can be built, values which are somehow related to being Jewish. Very unwillingly, too, I must admit that in Israel it's possible to become actively involved in doing something about social problems without having to worry about whether what you say or do is going to reinforce anti-Semitism.

But that's a foolish worry: there will be anti-Semitism in the United States no matter how I or any other Jew behaves. In the summer of 1964, when President Johnson's antipoverty bill was coming up for Congressional approval, a Southern congressman walked up to an administration lobbyist in the House Office Building and said to him, "If you want our votes, you'll have to get rid of that little kike."

The "little kike" was Adam Yarmolinsky, who had been slated to be Deputy Director in the antipoverty program. A few days later Yarmolinsky was sacrificed in exchange for the votes, and the congressman could report to his constituents that he had succeeded in getting rid of "the little kike." Adam and I have disagreed violently on foreign policy: he is as strong a supporter of American policy there as I am an opponent of it. But to the Southern congressman, I'm sure both of us are "little kikes."

In that sense, Jews are more free in Israel than in America, where many Jews still have the same fear of antagonizing the Gentiles that was such a strong element in my father's view of the world. The worried headshaking at the Concordia Club because a large number of students with Jewish names were actively involved in the crisis at the University of California is characteristic of the deep Jewish uncertainty felt by many Jews who think that they are still only on a temporary leave of absence from a pogrom.

But I won't stop urging resistance to the U.S. policy in Vietnam and the Dominican Republic because of that fear, nor do I think Jewish students should behave more circumspectly because they are Jewish. Now, however, I do understand better why some Jews look at me reproachfully, just as my father did, after they've read in the morning paper about a speech I made the day before.

It has taken me a longer time than it should have to discover the answer to "Is Curly Jewish?" He is now, even though he may not have been when I created him. At forty-seven, then, I'm a Jewish radical of a rather peculiar kind, and Curly, who is still only seventeen, is Jewish, too. Why is Curly only seventeen and six foot one? I don't know, but perhaps now that I've discovered his religion, I can learn some other things about him, too.

Abel, Rudolph I., 271
ACLU. *See* American Civil Liberties Union
ADL. *See* Anti-Defamation League
AFL-CIO, 141; convention of 1959, 246. *See also* American Federation of Labor; Congress of Industrial Organizations
A.F. of L. *See* American Federation of Labor
AJC. *See* American Jewish Committee
Allen, Yigal, 316
American Civil Liberties Union (ACLU), 152, 195-6, 227, 280
American Committee for Cultural Freedom, 222-4
American Council for Judaism, 140, 141, 160
American Federation of Labor (A.F. of L.), 113, 135
American Friends of the Middle East, 141
American Friends Service Committee, 216
American Jewish Committee (AJC), 214, 215, 327; Los Angeles chapter, 160ff; National Labor Service, 143-4, 159; New York chapter, 139, 140-58
American Jewish Congress, 140, 141
American League Against War and Fascism. *See* American League for Peace and Democracy

American League for Peace and Democracy, 101
American Legion, 168, 197, 199, 202; Preparedness Day, 270
American Veterans Committee (AVC), 152, 154
American Zionist Council, 140, 142
Amit, Meir, 319-20
Anti-Defamation League (ADL), 100, 140
Anti-Negro prejudice, 18, 144-5, 156; in unions, 311. *See also* National Association for the Advancement of Colored People; Congress of Racial Equality
Anti-Semitism, 5, 18, 38, 82, 83, 140ff, 164-5, 194, 210, 283, 307-308, 313, 329-30; in California, 161ff, 172, 179; in employment, 100; in Minneapolis, 55-6; in San Francisco, 280; in Soviet Union, 165, 276; in unions, 123, 125, 127, 129, 144. *See also* Arab-Jewish War; American Jewish Committee; Hitler, Adolf; Nazis
Anti-War Club, 90
Arab-Jewish War, 83, 162-3, 230-1, 234ff, 283, 297, 315ff. *See also* Nasser, Gamal Abdal
Arad, Shimshon, 246, 309, 317
Armed Services Education Division, 129
Army Air Force, 128
Art Institute (Jerusalem), 205
Ascoli, Max, 215

Ashmore, Harry, 220, 310
Association of Canadians and Americans in Israel, 292
Association of Catholic Trade Unionists, 152
Association of Motion Picture Producers, 197
Auschwitz (Nazi concentration camp), 258-9
AVC. *See* American Veterans Committee
Aware, 202
AZC. *See* American Zionist Council

Bardacke, Greg, 73, 231
Bardacke, Teddy, 73-6, 167
Beer, Israel, 304, 320
Bell, Dan, 223
Ben-Gurion, David, 163, 231, 242, 278, 283-4, 291, 292-4, 304, 327-329; replaced by Sharett, 282
Berle, A. A., 232
Bernadotte, Count, 163
Blount, Walter, 155
B'nai B'rith, 140-1
Bolsheviks, 30, 229; Minneapolis, 48, 52. *See also* Communists; Lenin, Vladimir Ilyich; Marxists; Socialists
Bowles, Chester, 220
Brewer, Roy, 199-200
Bridges, Harry, 101, 165, 187, 188, 189-91, 216, 229; cross-examines Stone, 190-2
Brooklyn College, 22
Buchanan, Miriam (Mrs. Scott), 310
Buchanan, Scott, 232, 310
Bukharin, Nikolai I., 266
Burdick, Eugene, 232

California, University of, 209, 228, 330
California at Los Angeles, University of (UCLA), 225, 226
California Supreme Court, 220
Calisher, Hortense, 148

Catholic Worker movement, 152ff, 217
CCF. *See* American Committee for Cultural Freedom
CCNY. *See* College of the City of New York
Center for the Study of Democratic Institutions, 309-11
Central Institute for Intelligence and Security, 319-20
Champion, Hale, 308
Chanukah, recent significance of, 9
Chapayev, 35
Chicago, University of, 216, 219
CIO. *See* Congress of Industrial Organizations
Civil rights movement, 46. *See also* Anti-Negro prejudice; Congress of Racial Equality; National Association for the Advancement of Colored People
Cobb, Lee J., 218
Coblentz, Billy, 279-80
Coffey, Margaret, 219
Coffey, Tom, 219
Cogley, John, 215, 216-17, 219, 220, 224, 229-30, 245, 309-11. *See also* Hollywood, blacklisting in
Cohen, Ben, 307, 316
Cohn, Eliahu, 320
College of the City of New York (CCNY), 10, 16, 18ff, 22ff, 89, 90; The Alcoves, 18, 47
Columbia University, 80, 141; Faculty Club, 223
Coming Struggle for Power, The, 19
Commentary, 214
Commonweal, The, 215-16, 217
Communist League of America, 21-22
Communists, 11, 19, 21, 30-2, 34ff, 54ff, 68-9, 75, 81, 82, 83, 91, 101-2, 108-9, 111, 130-1, 149, 151ff, 176, 184ff, 214-15, 217ff; American Communist approval of Stalin-Hitler pact, 100-1; proposal to abolish American party, 152; American Protestant in-

Communists (*continued*)
volvement with, 70ff; anti-Communism of 1950's, 55; assassination of Trotsky, 52, 108; and Communist International, 46; demand jailing of Trotskyists, 112; denounce Al Levy, 130; in Eastern European countries, 164; Hollywood purge of, 196ff, 215ff; Hungarian revolt against, 230, 254; and Khrushchev's speech denouncing Stalin, 229; opposed by labor unions, 113, 151-2, 184ff; and People's Front, 53, 101, 165, 195, 196, 214; in Soviet Union today, 252ff; Spanish agents, 81; under Stalin, *see* Stalin, Joseph V,; street-corner meetings, 86ff. *See also* Stalinists

Concordia Club (San Francisco), 279-81, 316, 317, 330

Congress for Cultural Freedom, 214

Congress of Industrial Organizations (CIO), 113, 115, 135, 139, 151-2, 175-7, 184ff, 216, 228; Constitution of, 189. *See also* AFL-CIO

Congress of Racial Equality (CORE), 156, 280

Coughlin, Father Charles, 87, 89

Counsellor, The, 135

Counterattack, 202

Daily Worker, 34, 269

Day, Dorothy, 152

Dayan, Moshe, 315

Deputy Run, battle of, 42

Deutsch, Babette, 134

Dewey, John, 134

Dewey, Thomas E., 164

Dmytryk, Edward, 217-18

Dobbs, Farrell, 42

Douglas, William O., 307

Dubinsky, David, 112, 124, 325; criticized by Jacobs, 311-13, 317; denunciation of Thomas, 113. *See* also International Ladies Garment Workers Union

Dulles, Allen, 316

Dunne, Ray, 47, 48, 50, 52, 53, 60

Eban, Abba, 292

Eichmann, Adolf, 260, 326-7; capture of, 278, 281, 291-2, 320, 324; trial of (1961), 284, 296-297, 301-6, 307, 308, 312, 323-4

Eisenhower, Dwight D., 261

Eisenstein, Sergei M., 35

Emergency Relief Administration, 18

Encounter, 214   . .

Engels, Friedrich, 29

EPIC movement, 165

Evron, Eppi, 231, 246, 282, 289, 291, 297, 312, 317

Exodus, 239

Farm Holiday organization, 55-6, 124

Farmer, James, 156

Fascists, 54, 81, 87; growth in Europe of, 46; German, 55, 82-84, 111; Italian, 18, 19, 47, 55, 128; Spanish, 38, 41, 54, 55, 81, 97. *See also* Hitler, Adolf; Nazis; Stalinists

FBI. *See* Federal Bureau of Investigation

Federal Bureau of Investigation (FBI), 110-11, 193, 219, 226, 228

Federation of Jewish Charities, 171, 174

Field, B. J., 79, 93, 96, 103

Fieldites. *See* League for a Revolutionary Workers Party

Ford, Henry II, 221

Franco, Francisco, 55, 108, 211. *See also* Spanish Civil War

Frankfurter, Felix, 307

Freedom Now movement, 157

Frischberg, Michael, 294, 296

Fuchs, Klaus, 193

Fuller, Ann (Mrs. Edmund), 148, 156

Fuller, Edmund, 148, 158

Fund for the Republic, 215-16, 220ff, 245, 279-80, 281-2

Gardner, Herbert, 25
Garland, Judy, 197
General Petroleum Corporation, 175, 177
German-American Bund, 87. *See also* Nazis
Gingold, David, 135
Gold, Ben, 101
Gold, Harry, 193
Goldberg, Arthur, 141, 188
Goldwater, Fred, 86, 92, 95, 102, 105, 289-90
Gomberg, William, 222-3
Gompers, Samuel, 141
Gousenko, Igor, 193
Granger, Lester, 145
Green, William, 135
Greenfield, Murray, 292
Greenglass, David, 193
Griswold, Erwin, 220
Grossman, Justin, 225-6

Hakim, George, 310
Harmonie Club (New York City), 26, 28, 142, 279
Harper's, 311-12
Harrington, Michael, 216, 217, 219, 229-30
Hashomer Hatzair, 68, 69, 294, 296
Haynes, Alfred, 114
Hays, Paul, 223
Healey, Dennis, 309
Healey, Grace (Mrs. Dennis), 309
Hecht, Ben, 163
Heisler, Francis, 226, 227
Hill, Herbert, 311
Himmelfarb, Gertrude, 214
Hiss, Alger, 164, 194
Hitler, Adolf, 18, 55, 81-2, 83, 135; march into Poland, 133, 286, 298ff; and Stalin-Hitler pact, 100-2, 111, 130, 229. *See also* Fascism; Nazis
Hoffa, Jimmy, 231-2

Hoffman, Gene, 310
Hoffman, Hallock, 216, 310
Hoffman, Paul, 220-1
Hollywood: blacklisting in, 215ff; purge of Communists in, 196ff
Hook, Sidney, 223
Hoover, Herbert C., 17
Hoover, J. Edgar, 152
House Committee on Un-American Activities, 17, 162, 167, 196ff, 218, 222, 226, 227ff. *See also* McCarthy, Joseph R.
Houser, George, 156
Hudson, Roy, 190
Huntley, Chet, 221
Hutchins, Robert M., 216, 219, 220, 221-4, 229-30, 280, 310. *See also* Fund for the Republic
Hutchins, Vesta (Mrs. Robert M.), 310

IATSE. *See* International Alliance of Theatrical Stage Employees
ILGWU. *See* International Ladies Garment Workers Union
Independent Socialist League (ISL), 226
International Alliance of Theatrical Stage Employees (IATSE), 199
International Ladies Garment Workers Union (ILGWU), 109, 110, 112-27; *passim*, 311-13, 325; anti-Stalinist feelings, 113. *See also* Dubinsky, David
Into the Night Life, 205
ISL. *See* Independent Socialist League
Israel, 234-44, 284ff, 309-10, 315ff. *See also* Arab-Jewish War

Jacobs, Cliff (brother of Paul), 84-5, 95, 127, 136, 251
Jacobs, Paul: with American Jewish Committee, 140-57, 159ff; apprentice in Trotskyist movement, 23; in Army, 129ff; asked to testify at Smith Act Minne-

Jacobs, Paul (*continued*)
apolis trials, 110; and blacklisting in entertainment industry, 215ff, 229; and California oil strikes, 175ff; changes name to Paul Jackson, 20, 29; in Chicago, 96-102, 122ff; collects affidavits concerning political beliefs, 228-9; at College of the City of New York, 16, 18ff, 22ff, 47; and Communism, opposition to, 32, 68, 129-30, 149, 151ff, 162ff, 176ff, 184ff, 195, 216, 229, 248; criticizes Dubinsky, 311-13, 317; and Defense Bonds, refusal to buy, 112-13; and depression, effect of, 12, 17ff, 61ff; in Ducannon, Penna., 115-17; fired by O. A. Knight, 207-9; at Fort Wayne, Ind., 131-136, 138-9; in free-lance union negotiating, 209ff; and Fund for the Republic, 220ff; in Germany, 249-52; at Grandview-on-Hudson (Nyack, N. Y.), 147-8, 155-156, 157-8, 161; in Greece, 244-245; and Grossman trial, 226-7; in Harrisburg, Penna., 121; on hitchhiking, 61-2; with International Ladies Garment Workers Union, 110, 112-27 *passim,* 134; in Israel, 234-44, 284ff, 309-10; and Judaism, rejection of, 15-16, 20; with L. & M. Kahn and Co., 23ff, 41, 42, 51, 107, 142; in League for a Revolutionary Workers Party, 79-80, 84, 90-3, 96, 98, 112; in Los Angeles, 159-233 *passim;* in Louisville, Ky., 93; married to Ruth Rosenfield, 95; meets Henry Miller, 202; in Minneapolis, Minn., 42ff, 51-2, 110; in Moscow, 261-72; and Nazis, hatred of, 83-4, 111; becomes Ohlerite, 33-4, 96; in Poland, 252-61; and race relations, 140ff; and relief benefits, efforts to obtain, 91, 96; resigns from League for a Revolutionary

Workers Party, 107-10; in Rochester, N. Y., 65-73; as salesman in New York City, 77-85 *passim;* and sit-ins, 156-7; in Soviet Union, 247-9, 252-78 *passim;* in Spain, 211-13; in Spartacus Youth League, 21ff, 33, 38, 39; in Stalingrad, 274-6; in Syracuse, N. Y., 73-6, 102; at Townsend Harris High School, 10-16, 147; at University of Minnesota, 41ff; writes about Eichmann trial (1961), 284, 297, 301-6, 307, 312; and Young Communist League, 16, 17ff, 21, 22, 35, 46, 226; with Young People's Socialist League, 65ff, 84, 89-90; as youth organizer in St. Paul, Minn., 57-60
Jacobs, Ruth Rosenfield (Mrs. Paul), 90-5, 102ff, 114, 122, 124, 127, 137, 146ff, 156-7, 180, 183, 205, 210ff, 234ff, 244-5, 281, 301, 304-5, 317; in Chicago, 96-102; goes to law school, 171, 208, 210, 215; married to Paul Jacobs, 95
Jahoda, Marie, 230
Jean Christophe, 20
Jerusalem Art Institute, 205
Jerusalem *Post,* 318
Jewish Centers Association, 167
Jewish Community Council: Community Relations Council, 160-162, 167, 169, 180; Fort Wayne, Ind., 138; Los Angeles, Calif., 160ff
Jewish Daily Forward, 312-13
Jewish Labor Committee (JLC), 140, 141, 144, 168, 312
Jewish People's Fraternal Order (Los Angeles, Calif.), 161, 167, 168, 170
Jews: African, 293; Arab-Jewish War, 230-1, 234ff, 283, 297, 315ff; Asian, 293; Conservative, 329; Eastern European, 10, 246; and emigration to Palestine, 68, 156, 293; and fear of Christian culture, 15; German, 5, 9, 10,

Jews (*continued*)
12, 15, 25-6, 28, 81-4, 142, 144, 159, 165, 246; immigrants, 113; in Israel today, 234ff, 284ff, 309ff, 315ff; and Jewish organizations, 159ff; middle-class, 82, 145, 159-60, 172; in Montreal suburb, 81; Orthodox, 68, 143, 168, 213, 237, 246, 287, 328-9; Reform, 5, 8, 9, 15, 59, 317, 329; in Rochester, N. Y., 67-8; and socialists, 68-9; Spanish, 213; in unions, 124-5; upper-class, 83; working-class, 82-3, 173; Yiddish-speaking, 10, 11, 76, 205

JLC. *See* Jewish Labor Committee
Johnson, Lyndon B., 330
Johnson, Priscilla, 265
JPFO. *See* Jewish People's Fraternal Order
Justice, U.S. Department of, 191

Kahn, Walter, Jr., 25, 27, 28, 36, 73, 107
Kahn, Walter, Sr., 24-5, 26
Kamenev, Lev B., 266
Kassalow, Everett, 189
Kastner, Rudolf, 298-9
Katz, Shlomo, 312, 313
Kempton, Murray, 228
Kennedy, John F., 293
Kerr, Clark, 228, 232
Kestnbaum, Meyer, 220
Khrushchev, Nikita S., 32, 54, 261, 273; denounces Stalin, 229
Kiddar, Mottke, 291, 304, 306, 314, 319, 321-2; arrest of, 305, 321
Knight, O. A., 175-6, 179, 192, 207, 209
Kristol, Irving, 214

LaGuardia, Fiorello H., 11
Lavon, Lucy (Mrs. Pinchas), 246, 291
Lavon, Pinchas, 246-7, 282-4, 291, 294, 304-6, 327

Lawson, John Howard, 197
League for a Revolutionary Workers Party, 79-80, 84, 90-3, 96, 98, 107, 110, 112
Lenin, Vladimir Ilyich, 29, 31, 34, 40, 45, 50, 75, 266
Leonard, Dick, 186-7
Levy, Al, 114, 118-19, 120, 121-2, 134-5; denounced by Communists, 130
Lewis, Fulton, Jr., 220
Lewis, John L., 130
Liebnecht, Karl, 29
Life, 270
Lloyd, Georgia, 135, 136
Times, The (London), 264, 269
Look, 319, 325, 328
Los Angeles Athletic Club, 279
Lowenthal, Alfred, 23-6, 27, 28, 32, 40, 41, 42, 48
LRWP. *See* League for a Revolutionary Workers Party
Luce, Henry, 232
Luxemburg, Rosa, 29

McCarthy, Joseph R., 192-3, 195, 217, 220
McCarthyism, 214, 222, 224
March, Fredric, 197, 200
March of Time, 49
Martin, Kingsley, 213-14, 224
Marx, Karl, 29, 31, 34, 45, 50, 75. *See also* Marxists
Marxists, 22, 28, 29, 34, 38, 40, 80, 112, 127, 128, 243
Meckler, Zane, 168-9
Megged, Matti, 299-300
Merchants of Death, 19
Meyers, Donna, 59
Meyers, Paula, 59
Mich, Dan, 319
Midstream, 307, 312
Miller, Henry, 202-7, 211, 244
Miller, Walter, 310
Mills, C. Wright, 71
Mine, Mill and Smelter Workers, 228
Minnesota, University of, 41ff

Moscow purge trials, 53, 54, 75, 130, 134
Moscow University, 266
Mount Sinai Hospital (New York City), 26
Moyne, Lord, 299
Murder, Inc., 109
Murray, John Courtney, 232
Murray, Philip, 135, 152, 184, 185, 187, 191
Mussolini, Benito, 55. *See also* Fascists, Italian
Muste, A. J., 65, 155, 156
Mydans, Carl, 270

NAACP. *See* National Association for the Advancement of Colored People
Nasser, Gamal Abdal, 230, 283, 315-16; rocket and missile program, 318
National Association for the Advancement of Colored People (NAACP), 149, 154, 156, 280, 311
National Labor Service, 143-4, 159
National Maritime Union, 190
National Student League, 54
National Youth Administration, 47-8
Nazis, 29, 38, 83, 87, 111, 128, 165, 232, 242, 249, 251, 259-260, 261, 272, 281, 297, 306, 312, 313, 315; march into Poland, 133, 286, 298ff; rise to power, 11. *See also* Eichmann, Adolf; Hitler, Adolf
Nazi-Soviet mutual aid pact. *See* Stalin-Hitler pact
New Deal, 18, 72, 164-5. *See also* Roosevelt, Franklin D.
New Statesman, The, 213
New Theatre League, 35
New York *Post,* 163, 228
New York *Sun,* 10, 21
New York University, 230
Newsday, 282, 284, 297, 301, 307
Niebuhr, Reinhold, 232

Nitgedaiget (Communist camp), 35
Nobel Prize, 293
NYA. *See* National Youth Administration

OAS. *See* Organization of American States
Ohio State University, 20, 21, 41
Oil Workers International Union, 175, 195
100,000,000 Guinea Pigs, 19
Organization of American States (OAS), 324
Orwell, George, 81

Patterson, Alicia, 282
Peace Corps, U.S., 317
Peres, Shimon, 322, 324
Pilot, 190
Playboy, 248
Poe, Elizabeth, 216
Potemkin, 35
Progressive party of California, 165ff, 184, 185
Protocols of Zion, 316

Quill, Mike, 189

Rabi, I. I., 232
Rachlin, Carl, 153
Radek, Karl, 266
RAND Corporation, 195
Reed, John, 20
Reporter, The, 215, 220, 229, 231-232, 267
Reuther, Walter, 113, 184, 186, 187
Revolutionary Workers League, 34
Riesel, Victor, 228
Rochester, University of, 66, 67, 69
Rolland, Romain, 20
Roosevelt, Franklin D., 17, 101, 111, 165

Roper, Elmo, 220
Rosenberg, Ethel, 193-4
Rosenberg, Julius, 193-4
Rosenfield, Ruth. *See* Jacobs, Ruth Rosenfield
Russian Revolution, 31, 34, 54, 108, 266, 277; Stalinist betrayal of, 248
Rustin, Bayard, 156-7

Saguy, Gideon, 310, 318
San Francisco State College, 282
Sayre, Nevin, 155, 156
Schachtman, Max, 33-4, 37
Schatz, Lilik, 202, 204-5, 235-44 *passim,* 289
Schatz, Louise (Mrs. Lilik), 236, 243, 289
Schatz, Olga, 310
Schumacher, Yossele, 318
Scott, Sherman, 131-2, 148
Selznick, Gertrude (Mrs. Philip), 195, 281
Selznick, Meg, 195
Selznick, Philip, 194-5, 215, 245, 281
SHAI (Jewish intelligence organization), 314
Shapiro, Henry, 268
Sharett, Moshe, 163; replaces Ben-Gurion, 282-3
Sheinbaum, Stanley, 309-10
Shin Bet. *See* Kiddar, Mottke
Shuster, George, 220
Siff, Hilda, 143
Sigman, David, 143
Sinatra, Frank, 197
Sinclair, Upton, 165
Smith Act: and trial of Minneapolis Trotskyists, 110-11
Socialist Workers Party (SWP), 226
Socialists, 11, 20, 21, 22, 21, 44, 54, 55, 65, 82, 98, 100, 111, 127, 130, 216; Jewish, 68; in Rochester, N. Y., 66; and Trotskyists, absorption of, 49, 66; and Yiddish Socialist homes, 11, 20; youth movements, 225.

See also Engels, Friedrich; Lenin, Vladimir Ilyich; Marxists; Trotskyists
Soviet Union, 31, 32, 130, 149, 164, 193, 317; anti-Semitism in, 165; Jacobs' visit to, 247-9, 252-78 *passim*. *See also* Communists; Stalin, Joseph V.; Trotskyists
Spanish Civil War, 29, 44, 46, 53, 54, 81, 97, 211, 306
Spartacus Youth League, 21ff, 33, 38, 39
Stalin, Joseph V., 32, 53, 54, 75, 108, 135; death of, 72; denounced by Khrushchev, 229. *See also* Stalinists
Stalin-Hitler pact, 100-2, 111, 130, 229
Stalinists, 18, 30, 33, 35, 37, 54, 55, 68, 71, 87, 96, 108-9, 164, 203, 216, 226, 238, 264; betrayal of Russian Revolution, 248; disputes with Trotskyites, 53, 55, 130, 134; opposed by International Ladies Garment Workers Union, 113
Standard, William L., 190
Standard Oil Company of California, 175-6
Stone, M. Hedley, 190-2
Strachey, John, 19
Stulberg, Louis, 109
Super Market Merchandising, 106
SWP. *See* Socialist Workers Party
SYL. *See* Spartacus Youth League

Teamsters Union, 60. *See also* Dunne, Ray
Ten Days That Shook the World, 20-1
Tenney Committee, 227
Thomas, Norman, 21, 223, 227, 228; denounced by Dubinsky, 113
Townsend Harris High School (New York City), 10-16, 31, 147; abolished, 11
Transport Workers Union, 189

Trilling, Diana, 223, 224
Trotsky, Leon, 29, 34, 40, 45, 134, 211, 266; assassination of, 52, 108; theory of a permanent revolution, 98
Trotskyists, 18, 20-2, 30, 54, 71, 75, 79, 91, 101, 108ff, 127, 130, 170, 185, 238, 255; disputes with Stalinists, 53, 55, 130, 134; dissolve into Socialist party, 49, 66; Minneapolis, 42ff, 51, 110-111, and Smith Act trials, 110-111; youth movements, 57-60, 222. *See also* Jacobs, Paul; Marxists; Socialists; Spartacus Youth League
Truman, Harry S, 152, 165
Tyler, Gus, 228, 246, 312, 313

UCLA. *See* University of California at Los Angeles
Un-American Activities Committee. *See* House Committee on Un-American Activities
Union Oil Company of California, 175-6
United Electrical Workers, 135
United Nations, 163-4, 319
United Office and Professional Workers of America, 149, 150-1, 153-4
United States Information Service, 282-3, 291
University of California, 209, 228, 330
University of California at Los Angeles (UCLA), 225, 226
University of Chicago, 216, 219
University of Minnesota, 41ff
University of Rochester, 66, 67, 69
UOPWA. *See* United Office and Professional Workers of America
U-2 plane incident, 270-1, 272, 273-4

Wallace, Henry, 152, 164, 165-6, 184
Walter, Stephen, 28, 36
Wheeler, William, 201-2
White, Emile, 202-4, 206
White, Walter, Jr., 145
Wirin, Al, 196
Wirtz, Willard, 308
Workers Defense League, 149, 216
Workmen's Circle, 69
Works Progress Administration (WPA), 18, 48, 97
Worthy, Bill, 156-7
WPA. *See* Works Progress Administration

Yale Law School (Yale University), 134
Yarmolinsky, Adam, 134, 220, 280, 330
Yarmolinsky, Avram, 134
YCL. *See* Young Communist League
Young Communist League (YCL), 14, 16, 17ff, 22, 35, 46, 53, 74, 226, 230; Midwest unit, 170
Young People's Socialist League, 49, 84, 89, 90, 255; Rochester, N. Y., branch, 65ff; Syracuse, N. Y., branch, 73ff
Young Women's Christian Association (YWCA), 149
YPSL. *See* Young People's Socialist League
YWCA. *See* Young Women's Christian Association

Zinoviev, Grigori E., 266
Zionist Congress (1960), 327
Zionists, 56, 83, 86, 140, 142, 156, 161, 162-3, 168, 205, 207, 231, 238, 247, 281, 286, 290, 293, 298, 307, 315, 321, 327; labor, 67-8, 159, 329. *See also* American Jewish Committee; Jews

PAUL JACOBS

Born in New York City in 1918, Paul Jacobs attended, very briefly, City College of New York and the University of Minnesota. He first became active in the union movement as an organizer, and later served as an international union representative, co-publisher of a labor paper, and a labor consultant. He is on the staff of the Fund for the Republic's Center for the Study of Democratic Institutions and is associated with the University of California at Berkeley. He is the author of *The State of the Unions* (1963), co-author with Frank Pinner and Philip Selznick of *Old Age and Political Behavior* (1959), and co-editor with Michael Harrington of *Labor in a Free Society* (1959), a collection of essays. Mr. Jacobs lives in San Francisco, California.